Tom Mann,
1856–1941

Tom Mann, 1856–1941

The Challenges of Labour

CHUSHICHI TSUZUKI

CLARENDON PRESS · OXFORD
1991

Oxford University Press, Walton Street, Oxford OX2 6DP
Oxford New York Toronto
Delhi Bombay Calcutta Madras Karachi
Petaling Jaya Singapore Hong Kong Tokyo
Nairobi Dar es Salaam Cape Town
Melbourne Auckland
and associated companies in
Berlin Ibadan

Oxford is a trade mark of Oxford University Press

Published in the United States
by Oxford University Press, New York

British Library Cataloguing in Publication Data
(data available)

Library of Congress Cataloging in Publication Data
Tsuzuki, Chūshichi.
Tom Mann, 1856–1941 : the challenges of labour / Chushichi
Tsuzuki.
Includes bibliographical references and index.
1. Mann, Tom, 1856–1941. 2. Labor leaders—Great Britain—
Biography. 3. Socialists—Great Britain—Biography. I. Title.
HD8393.M3T78 1991
331.8′092—dc20 [B] 90-26015
ISBN 0-19-820217-2

Typeset by Downdell Ltd, Oxford
Printed and bound in
Great Britain by Bookcraft Ltd,
Midsomer Norton, Bath

Preface

THIS is an attempt to write the life of Tom Mann, 'the world's Missioner for Labour' as his friend Ben Tillett once called him. He was truly an international as well as a national figure in his day when British labour made some of its most spectacular bids to reform society and shape the country and the world according to its own ideas. A special emphasis is placed on the London Dock Strike of 1889, which was the starting-point for Tom's career as the champion of labour. He embodied the solidarity of the working classes in this strike and in many a challenge labour was to make in the subsequent decades to the increasingly sophisticated system of exploitation under world capitalism.

The great strike itself represented a revolt of the lowest strata of the workers who had been forced to bear the heaviest burden of the structural and cyclical changes of the British economy in the heyday of liberal capitalism. It was conducted by a collective leadership in which Tom Mann along with Ben Tillett and John Burns occupied an honourable position. This collective leadership continued for some time after the strike, and the comradeship bred among the men of 1889 survived the differences and rivalries that accompanied the later development of the movement. Indeed, the common experiences of the Dock Strike and its aftermath drew them and their friends together, and there emerged a coterie or rather a band of warriors, fighting with different weapons in a war of classes, for which the term 'circle' may be too precise. What Tom Mann and his friends formed among themselves was an amorphous group held together with shared experiences. Their mutual relationships, however, were enlivened by the sense of dedication to a common cause, and it is in this sense that the term 'circle' is used in this book.

Tom Mann deserves special treatment, mainly because he alone among the leaders of the strike remained in the vanguard of the working-class movement throughout, and consequently the vicissitudes of his agitational work, for which he became somewhat notorious, indicate the changing fortunes of socialism and class struggle in Britain for over half a century before the Second World War. He is also to be remembered as the one who sought consistently to promote international contacts between, and a sense of unity among, the workers in the stormy years of world history when national antagonisms and ideological conflicts made such an attempt so difficult and often futile. It is for this reason that the book will concentrate on the life and struggles of Tom Mann, though it will also place him in a wider context through a discussion of Tom's 'circle', Tillett and Burns among others.

This study would not have been possible without generous help and encouragement from many people and institutions. I owe a great deal to Dona Torr's pioneering works on Tom Mann, and in the process of retracing the sources that had provided the basis of her studies, I was assisted by some of those who edited her works, notably Christopher Hill and Edward Thompson. Edmund and Ruth Frow very kindly allowed me to make free use of their remarkable collection of books, periodicals, and manuscripts on British labour. Professor John Saville and Dr Joyce Ballamy generously helped me with their expertise on my subject. Dr Ken Coates very generously supplied me with valuable information on Tom Mann from the materials for the book on the Transport Workers he and Tony Topham had been preparing. I am greatly indebted to my friend Alan Drabble of Armthorpe, who gave me valuable opportunities to gain an insight into British working-class life and ethos. I was very fortunate indeed to be able to have an interview with Mr Tom Mann, Jun., at his house at Hythe some time before his terminal illness. Mr Charles Mann, his brother, who looked very much like his father, kindly invited me to come and chat with him over the local cider and to stay overnight to see the papers still left at his house near Taunton. It was a blow to me, indeed, to learn that he had passed away shortly before the completion of this book, for I had felt he should be the man who would take the greatest interest and delight (as I hoped) in my account of his father. His son Robin and his daughter Marian, who also helped me when I visited their father, made generous arrangements for illustrations for the book from the photos of their grandfather now left for them.

In the course of my study I was favoured with valuable advice from a number of friends: Dr Henry Pelling, Professor James Joll, Professor Sidney Pollard, Professor Andrew Gamble, Professor Royden Harrison, Mr John Halstead, Professor Christopher Heywood, Mr Graham Healey, Mr Steve Ludlam, Mr Patrick Renshaw, Mr Andrew Whitehead, Ms Betty Reid, Ms Yvonne Kapp, Dr Angela Raspin, Mr R. A. Storey, Professor

Takao Matsumura, Professor Takashi Mitani, Professor Yui-
chiro Nakagawa, Mr Takashi Koseki, and many others. I am
also indebted to the staff of the following libraries for their
co-operation: British Library, British Library of Political and
Economic Science, Coventry City Library, Warwick University Library, Nuffield College Library, Cambridge University
Library, Sheffield University Library, Liverpool University
Library, Bodleian Library, National Museum of Labour History,
and Hitotsubashi University Library. I started my research on
Tom Mann when I was at St Antony's College, Oxford, as a
Nissan Visiting Fellow. Towards the end of my work I spent
a year again in England as a Jerwood Fellow at the University
of Sheffield. The Rockefeller Foundation gave me a heavenly
opportunity to write part of my book at its magnificent villa at
Bellagio, Italy. I make grateful acknowledgement of their most
generous help. The Hitotsubashi Academy kindly allowed me to
reprint part of my article on 'John Burns and the Great War'
published in the *Hitotsubashi Journal of Social Studies*, 21: 1
(1989). The readers for the Oxford University Press who took
the trouble to go through the book helped me with their most
useful comments. Lastly but not least I am very grateful to Dr
Anthony Morris, history editor of the Press, whose patience
and timely advice sustained me and did much to improve my
book.

Hiroo, Tokyo   CHUSHICHI TSUZUKI

Contents

List of Plates

Plates 1, 4, and 5 and the photograph used for the dust jacket are from the Tom Mann collection now deposited at the Coventry City Library and are reproduced by courtesy of its director.

Plate 2 is from the family photo collection that once belonged to Tom Mann's sons and is reproduced by kind permission of Marian and Robin, Tom's grandchildren.

Plate 3 is from the photo collection at the National Museum of Labour History, Manchester, and is reproduced by courtesy of its director.

Plate 6 is reproduced by courtesy of Professor Richard Hyman of Warwick University.

List of Abbreviations

AEU	Amalgamated Engineering Union
AFL	American Federation of Labor
ASE	Amalgamated Society of Engineers
BL Add. MSS, JBP	British Library, Additional Manuscripts, John Burns Papers
BLPES	British Library of Political and Economic Science
BSP	British Socialist Party
CGT	Confédération Général du Travail
CI	Communist International
CWS	Co-operative Wholesale Society
DTP	Dona Torr Papers, Communist Party Library, London
ETU	Electrical Trades Union
IFTU	International Federation of Trade Unions
ILP	Independent Labour Party
IMP	Ian Mackay Papers, Modern Records Centre, University of Warwick
ISEL	Industrial Syndicalist Education League
ITWF	International Transport Workers' Federation
ITWFA	International Transport Workers' Federation Archives, Modern Records Centre, University of Warwick
IWW	Industrial Workers of the World
LCC	London County Council
LEA	Labour Electoral Association
LGB	Local Government Board
LRC	Labour Representation Committee
LUL	Liverpool University Library
MFGB	Miners' Federation of Great Britain
MM	Minority Movement
NEP	New Economic Policy
NMM	National Minority Movement
NTWF	National Transport Workers' Federation
NUDL	National Union of Dock Labourers
NUWM	National Unemployed Workers' Movement
OMS	Organization for the Maintenance of Supplies
PLA	Port of London Authority
RILU	Red International of Labour Unions
SDF	Social Democratic Federation
SDP	Social Democratic Party
SSWC	Shop Stewards' and Workers' Committee
SWMF	South Wales Miners' Federation
TCP	Twentieth Century Press

TGWU	Transport and General Workers' Union
TMP	Tom Mann Papers, Coventry City Library
TUC	Trades Union Congress
VSP	Victorian Socialist Party (Melbourne)

Introduction

IT would not be wide of the mark to say that in retrospect the years 1889–1926 formed a special, heroic period for labour in British history, for in spite of occasional set-backs labour as a whole made a steady advance on the road to a brave new world in which trade-unionists would ensure a full citizenship for working men and might even achieve a hegemony of labour. A century of industrial revolution, while turning Britain, the first industrial nation, into the commercial and financial centre of the world, had produced powerful trade unions such as those of the Engineers and the Miners. These giant organizations of labour enjoyed the fruits of industrial and commercial prosperity and remained content with their cosy position once described by Friedrich Engels as 'the tail of the great Liberal Party'. This comfortable picture was soon seriously disturbed by the Great Depression which marked the beginning of the relative decline of the British economy and which also formed the background to the rise of socialism as well as of the onset of protectionism and imperialism. The emergence in 1889 or thereabouts of fighting, class-conscious unionism, often called New Unionism, was an offshoot in some sense of the 'socialist revival' of the 1880s, and it provoked the employers' counter-offensive which took the form of setting up their own associations or federations to fight the unions (especially in shipping and engineering) with organized black-legging on the one hand and legal actions on the other. A period of class confrontation ensued (with the Dockers in the forefront), and solidarity became a virtue on both sides. At the same time technological innovation impressed on the workers, especially in the older trades, the need for greater solidarity, solidarity between the skilled and the unskilled, as old skills became obsolete and new skills and semi-skills emerged. In due course a movement sprang up for yet greater solidarity in the form of amalgamation and federation of the existing unions. It is not surprising that Tom Mann, the strong-minded skilled engineer who became the leader of the Dockers and who was deeply involved in confrontation tactics, should become the most consistent champion of labour's solidarity.

Some of his colleagues in the leadership of the London Dock Strike of 1889 shared his aspirations, though they naturally adopted different strategies and laboured in different fields of action. His 'circle' included Ben Tillett, himself the leader of the dockers before Tom Mann, who proved to be Tom's only lifelong friend, John Burns, a lone wolf, whose colossal vanity failed to mask his proletarian origins and class identity even after he had become a Liberal Cabinet minister and who remained somehow linked with Tom through their dedication to the same cause, and J. Havelock Wilson, the Seamen's leader, who shared Tom's devotion to industrial action but whose later excesses in patriotism and class collaboration alienated him from Tom.

This period of confrontation came to an end with the collapse of the industrial Triple Alliance of the Transport Workers, the Miners, and the Railwaymen, which had no real opportunity to test its strength, and with the failure of the General Strike of 1926 led by the TUC. Like many other militant trade-unionists Tom refused to submit to the apparent defeat of labour. His syndicalism, itself a strategy for solidarity, had been characterized by its emphasis on international dimensions, and he had been welcomed into the fold of international communism. Probably we should count Harry Pollitt, the Communist leader, among the members of Tom's circle, but the circle had almost disintegrated by the time he arrived.

Burns had deserted Tom years before. Though he longed to return to the forefront of the battle at times of labour unrest, he disappeared completely from the public scene after August 1914. Tom's close relationship with Wilson became untenable when patriotism divided itself between the rabid and the rational. Tillett's position as the Dockers' leader was coming to an end, and his new career as a parliamentarian was not outstanding and apparently not to Tom's taste.

Tom, however, valued friendship and comradeship as precious treasures in human life, as can be seen from some of his letters to Ben Tillett. (His somewhat tangled marital relationship can also be explained in similar terms.) Indeed, Tom's life and work could not adequately be appreciated without bringing his close associates fully into the picture.

Jack Gill, at one time editor of the Transport and General Workers' *Record*, once called Mann, Tillett, and Burns 'the trio that set London alight in '89!'[1] On the fiftieth anniversary of

---

[1] J. Gill to B. Tillett, 24 Nov. 1939, IMP.

the London Dock Strike, they were described as 'the three men who nearly overthrew our society and constitution', an over-statement perhaps influenced by the more recent memories of 1926.[2] After the strike Tom became president of the Dockers' Union, and distinguished himself as a member of the Royal Commission on Labour, itself a Government response to the strike. He was known as the dedicated preacher for the Labour Church and the devoted secretary of the Independent Labour Party in its early days. He was the founder and initiator of a succession of working-class organizations: the International Transport Workers' Federation, the Workers' Union, the Victorian Socialist Party (Melbourne), and the Industrial Syndicalist Education League. He was the inspiring organizer of the locked-out miners at Broken Hill, New South Wales, and the able leader of the Liverpool Dock Strike of 1911. He was welcomed by a host of workers in the countries he visited, which included South Africa and China. He was always on the side of the rank and file of the trade-union movement, and of the unemployed. He started several trade-union and socialist papers at various times of his long and versatile career. He suffered imprisonment three times at home and three times abroad. Yet at eighty he was described as 'a calm, very digni-fied old gentleman. His hair, though snowy white, is still thick on top, and his moustache curls fiercely as ever. He doesn't look a day over 60'.[3]

'For me Tom Mann remains always young, the Peter Pan of the Socialist movement, to whom life is a series of adventures, and who resolutely refuses to grow up', wrote W. Stephen Sanders, former secretary of the Fabian Society.[4] Yet the remarkable thing about Tom is that he was respected by many as a man of principle, despite the apparent inconsistency of his association with the changing facets of the working-class move-ment. He was said to have 'possessed a tidal intellect', recalled J. R. Clynes, deputy leader of the Labour Party for many years: 'Though Mann was everything by turns, and nothing long, no one could charge him with lack of principle.' 'He was impatient, restless', added Clynes, 'and new aspects of old aspirations attracted him so that he was always with the newest movement. A robust orator, he had small patience for administrative work or for the constructive service of negotiation.'[5] Indeed, his racy

2 F. W. Hirst to J. Burns, 14 Aug. 1939, BL Add. MS 46204, JBP.
3 *Evening News* (9 Apr. 1936).
4 W. Stephen Sanders, *Early Socialist Days* (London, 1927), 53.
5 J. R. Clynes, *Memoirs 1924–1937* (London, 1937), 264.

eloquence often concealed his ability for practical work as a party secretary or as a strike leader, which was by no means meagre.

A more sympathetic picture of his life has been provided by Raymond Postgate in a radio broadcast: 'What Tom Mann had been, that he was to the end of his life. He dedicated himself to the working class. That isn't just a phrase, it is a plain statement of fact.' That fact will constitute the bulk of this book. Postgate goes on to portray Mann's attractive personality.

He was an unexpected figure for a 'firebrand' as they call him. He was plump, short, very neatly dressed, with waxed moustaches and rather prominent eyes, and carefully brushed hair. He walked as if he were on springs. He came into the room, light brisk and energetic, and ready to take charge of everything, like a floorwalker in a department store where things were going wrong. And when he went into the trade union movement the variety stage lost one of the greatest comic actors of the century.

Postgate elucidates some of the Chaplin-like qualities Tom displayed on the platform of the Albert Hall.

He dramatised everything. He could inspire the deadest, most unsuccessful, rain-drenched meeting. He could handle 10,000 people as capably as 200. . . . It [the Albert Hall] takes some thousands of people and for most of them the men on the platform must be midgets, and their voices are mere piping. I have heard Tom Mann hold that whole packed hall enraptured with a piece of silent miming. He was a syndicalist you know, and despised Parliament; that night he was giving a sketch of an ambitious M.P. trying to catch the Speaker's eye. He put his feet up on the table. He half started to speak, and then slumped back disappointed. He bristled his moustache. He waggled his eyebrows. He twiddled his thumbs, boredly. Then he twisted his hands in fury, listening to the other imaginery wind-bag who had got in front of him. It was monstrously cruel and unfair; an impersonation of baffled self-importance. But the whole hall shook with laughter, and [he] had hardly spoken a word.[6]

'He was a great orator, perhaps the greatest of this century, comparable to Henry Hunt', recalled Edmund Frow who had heard Tom speak some time in the 1930s: 'he slaps the man on his back, and hugs the woman and kisses her to show his comradeship with the people he associated with. He inspires his audience to such an extent as no other speaker has done before or since.'[7]

---

[6] R. Postgate, 'Cloth Cap and Red Flag', *Listener* (8 July 1948). I owe this to Mr Edmund Frow.

[7] An interview with Mr Edmund Frow, 7 Jan. 1987.

He was not simply a great orator. Behind his eloquence and his comic pantomime lay a deep-rooted conviction that the working class was capable of abolishing poverty and securing its freedom and opportunities for culture through the destruction of the capitalist system, possibly by direct action of the trade unions. He sought to work out a strategy for such a revolutionary change, and was always interested in ideas that would explain the usefulness of a particular strategy in ushering in a co-operative commonwealth.

Unlike some of his close friends who gave free reign to a sort of working-class anti-intellectualism, Tom was always fascinated by ideas. At an early stage of his life he rebuffed the lure of the doctrine of predestination with the aid of Mrs Annie Besant and other secularist orators, and it was by way of Henry George and his panacea of single tax that Tom came across Marx's ideas of class struggle and its decisive role in history. But did he remain a Marxist? Did he become an evolutionary socialist? Was he not a libertarian at heart? Had he really reconciled his syndicalist convictions with the Comintern theses when he became a communist? These are some of the questions that will be examined in the following account of Tom's life and work. Devoid of formal education, he aspired to be an educator for himself and for the working class at large. In fact, he was an educator all his life, and a public lecturer almost by profession. We now turn to the beginning of his career in order to see how some of his fine qualities and life-long convictions began to be formed in the humble setting of a working-class family in the industrial Midlands of the mid-Victorian era.

1. From a Colliery Boy to an Engineer

The Birth of an Agitator

RAPID industrial changes throughout the nineteenth century
and the ups and downs of trades and occupations affected
many working-class families and often uprooted the child from
the course of life to which his forebears had been accustomed.
Child labour, still prevalent in many industries, obviously
worked in the interests of the manufacturers, and was sometimes valued even by parents for its contribution to family
income. Although the bright and ambitious child became independent at quite an early age, moved out of the family circle,
and came into contact with new ideas and vistas, the rudiments
of education, not readily available until 1870, were won only by
a strong will and rare application.

Tom Mann's lifetime spans the years in which Coventry, his
native town, transformed itself from the weaving and watch-
making centre in the Midlands to a modern industrial city
based on the production of bicycles and motor vehicles. When
he was born, the old industrial basis of the town was already
on the decline, and its workforce endured great hardship for
years before the rise of the new industries. More than eighty
years later, his death coincided with the destruction of the city
in the Second World War, although the northern suburb where
he was born and the small house where he spent his childhood
survived the devastation wrought by that war. These still
retain something of the uncouthness of his childhood to
this day.

Thomas Mann, soon to be known as Tom Mann, was born on
15 April 1856 at Bell Green, Foleshill, Coventry. Foleshill,
Mann later recalled,

is a large parish with a number of villages and hamlets, primarily
agricultural, but near to the Colliery which was known as the Victorian
Colliery, was what was known as the Stop, on the Oxford Canal. This
meant the place where the Locks were & gangings of cargoes &c took
place here which resulted in a number of activities, including boat
building & so a big village developed. . . . I do not know how long the

Colliery had been working prior to my being there but not less than 25 years probably more.[1]

Coventry, he further explained,

was industrially a watch making and silk weaving city, & spread over to a number of villages in Foleshill, especially to Longford, Foxford, & Bell Green. The men wove in many instances, had looms & wove ribbons for the Coventry firms, in other cases they used Bar Looms, these were much larger & the power was that of a boy turning the wheel that drove the loom, in the other case the woman gave the power by treadles.[2]

Tom's father Thomas Mann was a bookkeeper at the Victoria Colliery: his job was to weigh the tubs and pay the butty, the subcontractor, and boss down the pit, according to the tons of coal raised by his men. Tom's grandfather William Mann was a cordwainer and was known as the village fiddler. 'Without one or other of the only two tunes he knew no local junket could begin.'[3] He died in 1863 at the age of eighty-two. His son Thomas married Mary Ann Grant, a domestic servant from Elgin, Scotland. Ann's father Duncan Grant came from Glen Morriston near Inverness and was proud of the clan and the tartan. Thomas and his young wife had four children: Frances Ann, George, William, and Thomas. William died in infancy, and Frances, or Fanny as she was known, took her father's job at the colliery office when he was not available.

In November 1858 when Tom was two and a half years old, his mother died at the age of thirty-seven. Five years later, his father married her sister Harriet Grant, though marriage with a deceased wife's sister remained illegal until 1907. Indeed, jumping over the broomstick was as valid for marriage among the working class as any legal sanction. The presence of an aunt as their stepmother so many years after their mother's death apparently did not affect the children in any adverse way. By Harriet, Tom's father had five more children: Charles, Hugh, Alfred, William, and Laura.

George was apprenticed to a butcher in Coventry. Tom attended a school for three years from the age of six to nine: for two years he went to the 'Old Church' Day School and then for one year to the Little Heath School which was connected with a Congregational church, both at Foleshill. At nine he was considered old enough to start work on the colliery farm 'doing

---

[1] T. Mann to Dona Torr, n.d., DTP.

[2] T. Mann to Dona Torr, 1 Apr. 1937, DTP.

[3] Dona Torr, *Tom Mann and his Times* (London, 1956), 22.

odd jobs in the fields, bird-scaring, leading the horse at the plough, stone-picking, harvesting, and so on' for one year. Beyond his house which stood at the end of a lane, as it does now, the fields spread out as far as the canal. At ten he was sent down the pit, and helped to make and keep in order the air-courses (small roads to convey the air to the coal faces worked in the mines). 'These air courses were only three feet high and wide', he wrote in his memoirs,

and my work was to take away the 'mullock', coal, or dirt that the man would require taken from him as he worked away at 'heading' a new road, or repairing an existing one. For this removal there were boxes known down the mine as 'dans', about two feet six inches long and eighteen inches wide and of a similar depth, with an iron ring strongly fixed at each end. I had to draw the box along, not on rails; it was built sledge-like, and each boy had a belt and chain. A piece of stout material was fitted on the boy around the waist. To this there was a chain attached, and the boy would hook the chain to the box, and crawling on all fours, the chain between his legs, would drag the box along and take it to the 'gob' where it would be emptied. Donkey work it certainly was. The boys were stripped to the waist, and as there were only candles enough for one each, and these could not be carried, but had to be fixed at the end of the stages, the boy had to crawl on hands and toes dragging his load along in worse than Egyptian darkness.[4]

For the first two years in the mines Tom attended the air-course men, who, as skilled men, worked only eight hours, though without a break. Then working on the bank, his hours were from 6 a.m. to 6 p.m. with a dinner-break. The memories of the inhuman length of his working day in the mines stuck in his mind, supplying a source of inspiration for his later struggles on behalf of his fellow workmen. A fire that broke out spontaneously in the mines, however, proved so serious that the colliery was closed down altogether in 1870. Tom's family migrated to Birmingham. There his father, having obtained a job as timekeeper at the tool-making firm of Thomas Chatwin, managed to get Tom apprenticed as a turner in the same firm from October of the same year.

Tom's father, a stout man weighing eighteen stone, was a fine violin player, and Tom himself began to play the violin. His stepmother, a good-natured, hard-working woman, ran a small butcher's shop to keep the crowded household going. Tom's life at his Birmingham home in a dark lane among the congested area was, according to Dona Torr to whom he gave accounts of his childhood when she saw him on many occasions towards

[4] T. Mann, *Tom Mann's Memoirs* (1923; London, 1967), 4–5.

the end of his life, 'not unhappy or "uncomfortable"'.[5] Although the 1870 Education Act came too late to be of any help to Tom, he attended Sunday school regularly, and also became 'a regular church-goer' at St Thomas's, Holloway Head.[6]

Birmingham, once the stronghold of 'moral-force' Chartism, was still dominated by the small workshops engaged in the manufacture of a great variety of hardware. They were the breeding ground for reformist radicalism, though modern industry which was to produce more overt class antagonism was already in the making. In the course of the seven years Tom spent as an apprentice at Chatwin's, a small-scale engineering firm, there emerged new powerful industrial combines such as the great Nettlefold and Chamberlain machine screw factory. These were the years when the prosperity enjoyed at the time of the Franco-Prussian War was followed by the onset of the Great Depression.

At the early stage of his apprenticeship Tom derived benefit from the victory won by the Engineers in their Nine-Hour Strike. The strike had begun in Sunderland in the spring of 1871 and had been conducted by the Newcastle Nine Hour League led by John Burnett of the local Amalgamated Society of Engineers (ASE) involving both society and non-society men. Tom had been working sixty hours a week and overtime, starting at six in the morning and frequently leaving at eight in the evening. He knew nothing about trade-unionism; indeed had no clear idea about the 'Society men'. He never saw the *Beehive*, the trade-union paper, though he heard it casually mentioned. The young men like him were not induced to join the society nor even informed of what was going on. Apparently Birmingham played comparatively little part in the struggle, though Mann became aware of some kind of activity among the men in the summer of 1871. At last he learned that the men were negotiating with the firm about the nine-hour day. When all the proposals on the issue had been endorsed at a meeting of the men employed in the firm, 'the first meeting of the kind I had ever attended' he confessed, negotiations continued till the firm granted the men's conditions. 'How truly pleased I was I need not trouble to add, and how thoroughly all enjoyed the dinner held to celebrate the event required no further comment!'[7]

The reduction of working hours to nine a day and the virtual abolition of overtime had a lasting impact on Tom's life and ideas. The free time now gained in the evening was almost

[5] Torr, *Tom Mann and his Times*, 41.   [6] Mann, *Memoirs*, 4.   [7] Ibid. 5.

entirely devoted, for the remaining five years of his apprenticeship, to education which combined science and religion, a great
theme of his day. The Science and Art Department of the Board
of Trade, South Kensington, which had been set up following the
Great Exhibition of 1851, had been promoting classes of general
and technical education so as to keep Britain's industrial
supremacy intact. Tom attended the Severn Street Institute to
study machine construction and design under E. Shorthouse, a
devoted teacher and Quaker. Tom was an Anglican, but he
attended a Bible class run by another Quaker, Edmund Laundy,
one evening a week and learned a good deal about correct
speaking and clear writing. He was persuaded, in due course,
to take a class himself at his Sunday school. Almost every
Sunday evening, accompanied by his friend Edmund Thurston,
a saddle-tree-maker's apprentice, Tom recalled, 'I attended a
church or religious service of some kind, and became familiar
with all varieties, not only of forms of worship and doctrine,
but also of preachers and their styles'.[8]

He frequented the Birmingham public library to satisfy his
thirst for knowledge, but his reading was still unsystematic and
perhaps even superficial. He enjoyed public speeches at the
town hall where he was much impressed by the oratory of John
Bright and the reformist zeal of Joseph Chamberlain. Tom
admired Joseph Arch, an agricultural labourer from Warwickshire, who succeeded in organizing the farm labourers at about
this time. It was, however, the secularism advocated by the
iconoclast Charles Bradlaugh, Bradlaugh's formidable partner
Mrs Annie Besant (whose speech 'transfixed' the young Tom),
and G. J. Holyoake the former Owenite that formed the bulk of
his political education in Birmingham. In fact, free thought
developed partly as a form of workers' protest against the
class hegemony of the day which was supported, or so it appeared, by the established Church. Tom also became a devotee
of the temperance movement which was often the first stage of
the evolution of the self-respecting worker in his effort to
uplift himself and his fellows, and to reform society at large.
As a fife player in the temperance band Tom took an active
part in excursions. For three years from 1876 to 1878 he was a
complete vegetarian, living on bread and fruit, believing that
proper use of the land should have beneficial effects on the
standard of life of the workers. William Hoyle, a prolific writer
on temperance, contended in his writings that if temperance
habits prevailed, the hours of labour would not be more than

---

[8] Ibid. 6; Torr, *Tom Mann and his Times*, 41.

four per day, an argument which had a profound influence on Mann. Although he worked hard in the temperance movement 'as an adjunct to church work', the realization grew that he 'ought to try and change [the vicious] environment by social activities'.[9] In October 1877, having completed his apprenticeship, Tom left Birmingham for London to try his lot as a skilled workman in the most advanced sections of the engineering trade.

Trade was slack: a spell of unemployment was Tom's first experience in London. Rather than remain inactive, he took a job as warehouse clerk at Swan & Edgar's, Piccadilly Circus. For a qualified skilled engineer this temporarily involved a severe loss of status; but Tom was eventually prepared to accept an even humbler job as a porter for a tailor in Hampstead Road. Attempts at 'the salvation of the soul', the main theme of his Birmingham days, and 'food reform' apparently kept him going. For a while he became a Sunday-school-teacher at St Stephen's, Westminster, and came to know Joseph Slade, a japanner of Kentish Town, enthusiastic Swedenborgian, and a good violinist like Tom himself. He also befriended Ellen Edwards, a Suffolk country girl two years his senior, whose father was described as a 'gentleman', but who worked at a nearby draper's shop. On 2 October 1879 Ellen and Tom were married at the New Christian church of the Swedenborgians, Argyle Square, with Joseph Slade as one of the witnesses. Ellen later told her daughters that her wedding-day 'was typical of her married life, as the weather that day included sunshine, rain, hail and storm!'[10] The Swedenborgian doctrine of 'uses'— to do good, to render service to one's fellows—sustained Tom, and the newly wedded couple started life in lodgings above a baker's shop at 38 Seymour Street, St Pancras, where their eldest daughter Rosalind was born. Before the end of the year Tom was able to find a better job at an engineering shop in Marylebone. His tasks included work on the escape gear and fire-extinguishing apparatus at the new Empire Theatre, Leicester Square, and helping to fix grates to Lord Salisbury's house in Arlington Street.

In 1880 Tom had moved to Cubitt's engineering works in Gray's Inn Road, where he worked as a turner on a chuck lathe. From there he moved to the Westinghouse Company, Canal Road, King's Cross, which produced automatic brakes: the machinery used was mostly from America: 'the atmosphere

---

[9] Mann, *Memoirs*, 8–10; Torr, *Tom Mann and his Times*, 55, 57.
[10] Emmeline Mann to Dona Torr, 27 May 1946, DTP.

of the works was that of America, and it suited me well'.[11] Here he joined the Marylebone branch of the ASE and participated for the first time in a strike, against the introduction of piece-work. All the ASE men left work, and Tom returned to Cubitt's. His workmate on the next lathe at Cubitt's was a Scotsman named Jeffries whose love for Shakespeare impressed Tom: 'from that time I was never lonely so long as a volume of Shake-speare was available'. After Cubitt's he went to the firm of Peter Brotherhood, the inventor of the torpedo engine, at Comp-ton Street, Clerkenwell, where he turned forty sets of pistons for the same number of engines ordered by the admiralty. 'No talk here of social problems', Tom recalled, 'but every man was in the ASE and seemed to me to possess ability of the highest grade. Nothing could prove insurmountable to them as mech-anics'.[12] They were the veritable aristocracy of labour, proud and confident. Then he went to work at Thorneycroft's, the torpedo-boat builders at Chiswick, where he came to know several enthusiastic co-operators. It was during this period in 1881 that he read Henry George's *Progress and Poverty* and found an effective antidote to Malthus's theory of population which had attracted and vexed him for some time past.

Although he had read *The Fruits of Philosophy*, an American work on birth-control, reissued by Bradlaugh and Mrs Besant in defiance of prosecution, he did not put its teachings into practice. All this time he was living in Chelsea, where three more daughters were born: Emmeline, Gertrude, and Effie. Emmeline, reporting what her mother had told her, wrote: 'Mother . . . used to take him watercress in the lunch hour! She says he was full of fun always. By the way, he was back from America when I was born, but away over there all the time I was on the way.'[13]

While working at Thorneycroft's in Chiswick in 1882 he made his first trip to Paris for a week, not with Ellen who was busy looking after the little Rosalind, but with his friend Joseph Slade. In May of the next year we find him in New York by himself, carrying his toolbox. He worked there for four months, starting the second day after his arrival in the engineering department of Harvermeyer & Elder's Sugar Refinery, Brooklyn. It was the day of celebration, in which he participated, for the opening of the Brooklyn Bridge. The engineers or machinists in the United States were still working ten hours a day. Only one

---

[11] Mann, *Memoirs*, 12.　　　　　　　　　　　　　　　　　　[12] Ibid. 18.
[13] T. Mann to Dona Torr, 26 May 1937; Emmeline Mann to Dona Torr, 24 May 1946, DTP.

workman whom he met had any knowledge of Henry George. He was a Scotsman and an ASE member, staying at Tom's lodgings, Lafayette Hall, Delancey Street, who died of a weak chest shortly afterwards. No service was held, and no speech made. An abrupt, unceremonious end of a man like himself—'it seemed to me awfully callous', he recalled.[14]

In the autumn of 1883 he returned to London and at once started working for his old firm Thorneycroft's in Chiswick. He was, however, absorbed with the self-imposed task of educating himself and his fellow workers, and accepted the presidency of the Shakespeare Mutual Improvement Society when it was formed among his workmates. It organized evening lectures at the Devonshire Club and Institute in Chiswick High Road: subjects covered not only Shakespeare, their primary interest, but also electricity, chemistry, biology, and the history of London, and Tom himself gave two lectures, one on 'Progress and Poverty' and another on 'Astronomy'.[15] He read Carlyle, Ruskin, and J. S. Mill. Thorold Rogers's *Six Centuries of Work and Wages*, published in 1884, in which the author proclaimed that the hours of labour were only eight a day in medieval England, became one of the main intellectual sources which were to direct his course of action in the years to come.

By the early 1880s Tom had managed to set himself up as a skilled workman in the advanced sectors of the engineering industry, cherishing an intense desire for self-improvement as an artisan and a cultivated citizen. Such a laudable aim as the pursuit of one's amelioration and even perfection was shared by many other working-class men of his day who later distinguished themselves in the trade-union movement, but his 'not uncomfortable' childhood, no doubt due largely to his family circumstances, was unique as it owed a great deal to his practical mind and sense of balance as well as to his constant search for new ideas. His hard, unremitting labour at a tender age evoked his indomitable, independent soul, and his experience of poverty and insecurity as a skilled worker at a time of depression gave him food for thought, and led him to a small group of socialists who had already begun their agitation. Yet he was singularly devoid of bitterness and enmity and free from self-righteousness and arrogance. His natural humility and his whole-hearted devotion to a cause made Tom Mann the agitator so much more attractive in his mature years.

[14] Mann, *Memoirs*, 22.   [15] Ibid. 19.

2. Social Democracy

New Hopes and Disenchantment

THE twenty years of the so-called 'Great Depression' from the mid-1870s to the mid-1890s may have been a period of steady increase in real wages for the workers except for those affected by the recurring slumps, which caused a high level of unemployment, and also for the labourers in agriculture, which was depressed throughout. Yet the sufferings of those exceptions must have been very great. Indeed, these were the years when investigations were made to prove the shocking fact that a large percentage of the people, especially those engaged in irregular work, were living below the poverty line. Above all it was a period of business depression, of the 'absence of profit or its meagreness'.[1] Signs of the relative decline of Britain in the world economy became visible, with every strong nation-state striving to industrialize with high tariffs and with challenges, both commercial and military, posed especially by Germany and the United States.[2] The critical situation for a free-trade Britain provoked new ideas and remedies for the evils supposedly responsible for the difficulties.

Social democracy, one of these ideas, emerged early in the 1880s and attracted attention not so much for its remote connection with Chartism as for its revolutionary propaganda linked with continental Marxism. British social democracy, however, was an eclectic system of ideas which would appeal to a Tory democrat as well as to a Radical artisan. It was the time when the great Liberal Party was foundering on the rocks of the Irish question, and no adequate remedies seemed to come from the established quarters to meet the exposed and threatened position of Britain. The Democratic Federation that had been started in 1881 by H. M. Hyndman, a Tory democrat studying Marx, soon shed its middle-class Radical supporters and began to attract politically advanced working men, many in the secularist movement. Henry George's spirited book

[1] Royal Commission on Depression, Third Report, 1886, quoted in Helen Merrell Lynd, *England in the Eighteen-Eighties* (new imp., London, 1968), 46.

[2] Andrew Gamble, *Britain in Decline* (London, 1981), 53.

Progress and Poverty, itself a powerful attack on land monopoly in America, and George's sensational tour in England in 1884 brought Tom Mann as well as George Bernard Shaw to the brink of accepting a more revolutionary doctrine—Marxism. Land nationalization (if not George's gospel of single land tax) was in the air. A Fellowship of New Life, the prototype of the Fabian Society, came into existence to suit the taste of those intellectuals who were at once more idealistic and more cautious. William Morris, the poet and designer, was rendering yeoman's service in making socialism appear more creative and attractive in terms of human values. Tom Mann, then a member of the Hammersmith branch of the ASE, began advocating a shorter working day, and submitted a resolution in favour of an eight-hour day at a branch meeting; the local 'aristocracy of labour' voted against it by 70 or 80 to 5.[3] Yet the socialist challenge developed with greater force, and the workers were increasingly found in the forefront of the attack in spite of Hyndman's frock-coat and silk hat, in which attire he invariably appeared before his audience.

It was at this moment (towards the end of 1884) that the Social Democratic Federation or SDF (formerly the Democratic Federation) split into two groups. Morris and his friends, who resented Hyndman's autocracy as much as his Anglo-Saxon biases, now parted company with him and formed their own body, the Socialist League, with less emphasis on parliamentary politics. The three prominent working-class members of the SDF executive, John Burns, Harry Quelch, and Jack Williams, however, remained with Hyndman. Special efforts were made to keep their newspaper *Justice* going, and to open new branches after the split which had caused a considerable decline in their strength. It was John Burns, an engineer like Tom Mann and a socialist before him, who took the initiative in launching the Battersea branch of the SDF which was set up in May 1885. Tom Mann and John Ward, the hero of the Sudanese war and later Colonel John Ward, MP, were two of the earliest members of the Battersea SDF.

John Burns was a Londoner of Scottish origin.[4] At some time in the 1850s the Burns family drifted from Edinburgh (originally

[3] T. Mann, *Tom Mann's Memoirs* (1923; London, 1967), 22–3.

[4] For the life of John Burns, see Arthur Page Grubb, *From Candle Factory to British Cabinet: The Life Story of the Right Hon. John Burns* (London, 1908); Joseph Burgess, *John Burns: The Rise and Progress of a Right Honourable* (Glasgow, 1911); G. D. H. Cole, *John Burns* (Fabian Biographical Series, 14;

from Ayr) to London and settled in Wandsworth Road, South Lambeth, where John was born on 20 October 1858 as the sixteenth child and the second son. With so many children to look after (though some of them had died in Scotland), his mother worked as a washerwoman to assist her husband who was an engineer. Poverty tore John away from school at an early age. At ten he became a page-boy at Hampstead; at twelve he started work at Price's Candle Factory at Battersea Road. He somehow completed a period of apprenticeship at an engineering shop by 1879 and joined the West London branch of the ASE. An ambitious but cautious young man, he had saved a hundred pounds by the end of his two-year employment as a foreman engineer in the service of the Niger Company at Akassa on the Niger delta of the West African coast. On his return he married Martha Charlotte Gale ('Pattie'), the daughter of a Battersea shipwright. He soon identified himself with the advance guard of the working-class movement (as it awoke gradually from the lethargy that had fallen upon it following the reform agitation of the 1860s and the union legislation of the early 1870s), he frequented most of the workmen's clubs in London and was one of the founders of the Metropolitan Radical Federation. In due course he became a regular contributor to *Justice* where he wrote: 'The tussle between capital and labour must be transferred from the workshop to the House of Commons, or rather a National Convention, through the ballot box'.[5]

Meanwhile Tom Mann, who had been discharged from Thorneycroft's on 4 July 1884, his 'Independence Day', after some vain attempts obtained work in an engine shop connected with Tilbury Docks, which were then under construction. He lodged in Grays, Essex, and went home at weekends. Then he found a more congenial job at Brotherhood's, his old employer, who had opened a new factory at Belvedere Road, Lambeth, and his family now moved from Chiswick to Battersea to be near his workplace. Thus Tom joined the Battersea branch of the SDF when it was formed by John Burns, and 'did his share of the rough and tumble work of those days. His energy and enthusiasm were unbounded', wrote H. W. Lee, later secretary of the SDF.[6] Mann's speeches delivered at Battersea Park

London, 1943); William Kent, *John Burns: Labour's Lost Leader* (London, 1950); Kenneth D. Brown, *John Burns* (London, 1977). The John Burns Papers in the British Library still remain unexplored for the details of his life and work.

[5] *Justice* (19 July 1884).

[6] H. W. Lee and E. Archbold, *Social-Democracy in Britain* (London, 1935), 99.

began to be reported in *Justice*. He also addressed a 'good meeting' in Hyde Park, and helped the branch 'distribute *Justice* among the shops in the neighbourhood'.[7] Mrs Mann, Ellen, 'was not unsympathetic, and went so far as to sell "Justice" . . . although it was agony for her to be so conspicuous', wrote her daughter Emmeline: 'what worried her—not unnaturally—was the knowledge that he was risking losing his job through his activities, which of course happened time after time'.[8] Mann and Burns the branch secretary co-operated in public meetings at the park. After one of these meetings six quires of *Justice* and eighteen copies of *Socialist Catechism* were sold; over a hundred members seem to have attended a general meeting of the branch.[9] A period of close collaboration between Mann and Burns now began.

At the general election of 1885, Burns stood as a Social Democratic and Labour candidate in the Western Division of Nottingham. Tom Mann became treasurer of his election funds, and as his wife feared, was sacked from Brotherhood's. Burns's candidature, which was misrepresented as an attempt to split the Liberal vote, incurred the wrath of the radical working men, and the polling day ended in a mêlée: he polled 598 votes out of the total of 11,004. Obviously, Burns did not draw much encouragement from what had happened at Nottingham. Moreover, the 'Tory Gold' scandal over the two SDF candidates in London, Jack Williams in Hampstead and John Fielding in Kennington, winning 27 and 32 votes respectively, was disclosed after the elections, their campaigns having been financed by money transmitted to the party funds from Maltman Barry, formerly Marx's 'errand boy', now a Tory agent, through his friend H. H. Champion, a former artillery officer and an executive member of the SDF. Although Burns did not draw on these monies, his discomfiture must have been very great. Thirteen leading members of the SDF with Tom Mann now prominent among them, though excluding Burns and Williams, issued a statement declaring it to be 'a matter of the most perfect indifference whether the money expense to spread our doctrine in aristocratic Hampstead and genteel Kennington came from Radical, Tory or from neutral sources'.[10] As Henry Snell, Burns's election organizer, noted, the incident 'shocked London Radicalism, to which Tory money was abomination'.[11]

[7] *Justice* (19 July 1884).
[8] Emmeline Mann to Dona Torr, 27 May 1946, DTP.
[9] *Justice* (18 July 1885).   [10] Ibid. (12 Dec. 1885).
[11] Lord Snell, *Men, Movements, and Myself* (1936; London, 1938), 64.

Burns's hopes for Social Democratic politics, his dreams about himself defending the cause of Labour in the House of Commons were shattered for some time to come.

At a time when the Great Depression was trailing on and another deep trough was accompanied by a steep increase in the number of the unemployed, the SDF felt it opportune to intensify its agitation on behalf of the unemployed. Its rivals in this field were the 'Fair Traders', the precursors of the Tariff Reform movement, and they were led by Lemon, Kelly, and Peters. Lemon, known as Captain Lemon, was president of a 'bogus' trade union called the British Seamen's Society, and the other two were each associated with some riverside trade in East London; and they were the people who were soon to cause trouble when Tillett tried to organize riverside workers in the Docklands. The Fair Traders, after an unsuccessful interview with Lord Salisbury, decided to hold a demonstration at Trafalgar Square on 8 February 1886. The SDF executive sought to steal their thunder. The occasion was marked by a series of dramatic events: clever manœuvring on the part of the SDF leaders who addressed the assembled crowd from the railings on the north side of the square, a procession to Hyde Park led by Burns waving a red flag, the stone-throwing at club windows on the way, and the looting of the West End shops by the inevitable thugs. The immediate sequence of these 'West End riots' was the arrest and trial of Burns, Champion, Hyndman, and Williams, the four main SDF speakers in the square, on a charge of seditious conspiracy.

Tom Mann, too, played a leading role in the unemployed agitation of the SDF, presiding over a great demonstration held shortly after the riots in Hyde Park, at which all the defendants, free on bail, spoke.[12] The trial was held in April at the Old Bailey. Burns defended himself in a speech which attracted wide attention when published in a pamphlet *The Man with the Red Flag*. He pleaded 'Not Guilty', and objected to being saddled with the 'bread and lead' phrases or with the 'powder and shot' interjections made by other men in the crowd whom he tried to control. He did not conceal his suspicions about 'Peters, Kelly, Kenny, Lemon' who were 'regarded as arrant impostors by the workmen of London', and said he did all he could to avoid a conflict between the unemployed workmen and 'the dupes of these bogus representatives'. Then he came to the main point, asking: 'Is it revolution to demand that the workers should be allowed to live like men? Was it sedition for a man

[12] *Justice* (27 Feb. 1886).

to ask his brothers to combine?' He may have used strong language, but the occasion demanded it.

Riot it was not, it was nothing more nor less than honest poverty knocking at the door of selfish luxury and comfort, poverty demanding that in the future every man should have the wealth created by his own labour. That meeting of February 8th called the attention of the people of Great Britain to this fact—that below the upper and middle strata of society there were millions of people leading hard, degraded lives.

And he emphasized that the Social Democrats who advocated necessary changes were 'the . . . true "guardians of law and order"'. It was a cleverly contrived speech, and contributed to an acquittal of the defendants.[13]

In the meantime, a new problem arose which, though one of the SDF's palliatives from the beginning, was to rock the boat of a small band of socialists in a very serious way—the renewed emphasis on an eight-hour day. The First of May Eight Hour Strike in America, which was accompanied by a 'police outrage' in Chicago,[14] added fuel to the flame of the debate on the subject. Tom Mann took the problem in hand, and advocated an eight-hour bill as 'a palliative', though he apparently favoured trade-union action for the measure.[15]

Tom started his campaign among his workmates. After his dismissal from Brotherhood's in the autumn of 1885, he managed to obtain a job at the Peckham works of the manufacturers of air compressors for the Whitehead torpedo; there he urged the need for a reduction of hours of work on the ground of remarkable improvements in their machinery. Ruskin's *Fors Clavigera* and Carlyle's 'Conditions of England Question' supplied ammunition for his arguments. Towards the end of 1885 he gave an address on 'The Eight Hour Working Day' at a Fabian meeting.[16] No doubt his new agitation imposed considerable sacrifice on his young family. All this time he lodged near the firm and returned home to Battersea only at weekends.

In June 1886 Mann's first pamphlet, *What a Compulsory Eight Hour Working Day Means to the Workers*, came out from the Modern Press which was run by H. H. Champion who had set up as a socialist publisher. Mann had by now definitely parted with the reformist Radical ideas of 'the Malthusians, the Teetotalers, the Financial Reformers, and well-intended

---

[13] J. Burns, *Man with the Red Flag* (London, 1886), *passim*.
[14] James Blackwell, 'American Notes', *Justice* (29 May 1886).
[15] *Justice* (15 May 1886).   [16] Mann, *Memoirs*, 38.

Radicals'. Their panaceas all proved a failure, because they did not understand the 'Iron Law' of wages which said: 'So much as will keep life in you *and no more* shall go to you, O ye workers, so long as the profit system remains.' Yet even under this relentless law of wages an eight-hour day would secure remuneration and leisure that would help the advancement of learning among the workers and enable them to criticize the present system more effectively. He took exception to middle-class views that the workers would become contented if conditions of life were made easier for them; such views were 'the opinions of these theory-loving, poverty-accentuating block-heads'.[17] More leisure should mean better opportunity and greater desire for knowledge. His view later attracted attention as an argument against the mechanical 'theory of increasing misery',[18] but it was, rather, the view of the working-class élite advocating class self-help, and was a reflection of Mann's firm belief in the boundless future possibilities of industrial struggle. He called for an aggressive union policy, and made a special appeal to trade-unionists: 'How long, *how long*, will you be content with the present half-hearted policy of your Unions?'[19] This was indeed a clarion call for what was soon to be known as 'New Unionism'.

Tom Mann's pleading, especially for trade-union action for an eight-hour bill, gained little support within the SDF. When he sought to advocate it at the Battersea branch of the SDF, John Burns, in spite of his earlier favourable views on the subject, was opposed to it even as a palliative, since he believed —after the West End riots—that the capitalist system was on its last legs—so they would not need to compromise. John Ward fully supported Burns's revolutionary stance.[20] In view of the general hostility of the branch to his idea, Tom, with a group of like-minded members, decided to form an Eight Hour League based on the Battersea Progressive League that he had earlier brought into existence. His fellow workers at the Peckham works apparently helped him. As secretary of the London centre of the Eight Hour League Tom now appealed to the workers in London and the provinces to form branches of the league by selling the league ticket (one penny each) and to

[17] Id., *What a Compulsory Eight Hour Working Day Means to the Workers* (London, 1886), 5–8.

[18] Dona Torr, *Tom Mann and his Times* (London, 1956), 213.

[19] Mann, *Compulsory Eight Hour Working Day*, 11.

[20] 'The two ultra-revolutionaries made history, one as a Liberal Cabinet Minister and the other as commanding officer of troops to crush the first Socialist revolution': Torr, *Tom Mann and his Times*, 212.

organize meetings for lectures and discussions on the subject throughout the country so as to force the Government 'to legislate as we demand'—'and if they did not, then we should be prepared with an alternative'.[21]

Meanwhile, in the pages of *Justice* an attack was launched against Mann's eight-hour agitation by A. P. Hazell and others, who maintained that the measure would only strengthen the labour aristocracy in the trade unions. To this Mann retorted by saying that he saw no sign of an immediate outbreak of a revolution ('I do not believe the Revolution can take place for eight or ten years') and that it should be possible even before a revolution to protect and strengthen the workers by giving them necessary leisure 'to deliberate, to agitate and to organise'. He said that the reason why he set up the Eight Hour League as a separate organization was that it was 'an inexpensive organisation acting rather as a number of committees'; thus each branch of the SDF could set up its own eight-hour committee which would act as canvasser at an election for an eight-hour bill; similarly 'all workmen's clubs—Liberal, Radical, Tory, & Socialist' could co-operate.[22] Mann was perhaps one of the earliest advocates of the tactics of 'United Front from Below'. The league organized several branches in London, a few in other towns, and its ardent supporters regularly met at a coffee-house in the Westminster Bridge Road.[23] A conference of London trade-unionists held at Bricklayers' Hall, Southwark Bridge Road, gave him an overwhelming support on this matter.[24]

Mann's agitation for an eight-hour day, however, did not prevent him playing an active role in the SDF. He was prominent as a speaker on the Lord Mayor's Day in November 1886, in a sort of guerrilla demonstration at Trafalgar Square held in defiance of a police ban. Unfortunately this led to the loss of his job at Peckham; so he spent the rest of the year in Birmingham where his relatives lived, and formed a branch of the SDF there. He published an optimistic report on 'The Cause in Birmingham' in *Justice*.[25] Returning to London early in 1887, he obtained brief employment at Allen's in Lambeth, but otherwise his job search remained unsuccessful.

It was under these circumstances that Tom was increasingly drawn into a new campaign Champion had launched in order to

---

[21] *Justice* (30 Oct. 1886).   [22] Ibid. (26 Feb. 1887).
[23] Torr, *Tom Mann and his Times*, 214–15; *Labour Leader* (5 May 1894).
[24] Mann, *Memoirs*, 44.   [25] *Justice* (11 Dec. 1886).

build up a Labour Party which would cut across the sectarian-
ism of the existing small socialist bodies like the SDF or the
Socialist League. Joseph Burgess suggests that it was Maltman
Barry who advised Champion to 'drop the Socialists and hitch
on to the Trade Union movement'.[26] At the Hull TUC in
September 1886 the idea of Labour representation was hotly
discussed, and a Labour Electoral Committee was launched.
Barry, who attended the congress as a Labour journalist, urged
Champion to join it. Unlike Burns, Champion became disillusioned with the revolutionary 'tactics' of the SDF after the
West End riots and began to make a direct appeal to the
'labour interest'. As Henry Pelling pointed out, 'he saw himself
as the Parnell of the Labour movement',[27] but this was exactly
what Barry had been advocating for him.[28] In 1887 the Labour
Electoral Committee developed into the Labour Electoral
Association (LEA), and Champion organized its Metropolitan
section. Tom Mann became a willing recruit, for his eight-hour
day was an essential part of the 'Labour Question' (Champion's
programme for labour welfare), and Champion's attempts to
intervene in parliamentary by-elections were what Mann himself had advocated for his eight-hour agitation.

Champion's effort culminated in the Mid-Lanark by-election
in the spring of 1888, in which Keir Hardie, an independent
labour candidate, was assisted by Champion with funds and
speakers including Tom Mann. Champion sought to make the
Metropolitan section of the LEA the nucleus of the National
Labour Party, and Tom Mann helped him in his new venture,
though he had reservations about Champion's quarrelsome
nature. Being less doctrinaire than most of his colleagues and
more intensely committed to the broad unity of the working
class, he was perhaps less disturbed by Champion's latent
Tory socialism or of the implications of his connection with
Maltman Barry. With the fresh rift in the SDF over Champion's
new move, the vigour and attractiveness of revived socialism in
the 1880s were to be marred by petty squabbles and personality
clashes.

In this sterile atmosphere of intolerance it was Burns as well
as Champion who became disillusioned by the SDF leadership.
The occasion was provided by the dramatic clash with the
police in Trafalgar Square on 13 November 1887, 'Bloody
Sunday' as it was soon to be called. The demonstration on that

[26] Burgess, *Burns*, 94.
[27] Henry Pelling, 'H. H. Champion', *Cambridge Journal*, 6: 4 (Jan. 1953), 226.
[28] *Justice* (17 Oct. 1885).

day, however, was not planned by the SDF but by the Metropolitan Radical Federation as a protest against the arrest of William O'Brien, the Irish Nationalist MP, and the part played in the fray by the SDF, apart from John Burns, who was arrested along with Cunninghame Graham MP in the square, was not very prominent. Burns's speech delivered at his trial at the Old Bailey in January is perhaps worth quoting, if only for the reason that it impressed Tom Mann very much, as we shall see presently.

In his speech Burns placed a special emphasis on unemployed agitation: 'These men, the unemployed', he said, 'taught the politicians the very elements of government: how to organise society during the transitional period from the present competitive system where the policeman is absolutely necessary, to the co-operative system where the teacher will take his place'.[29] He and his friends demanded of the Government that it should start useful relief work through the local authorities, build artisans' dwellings, reduce the hours of work in government employment to eight a day, and introduce a compulsory eight-hour bill for the employees of railway, tramway, and omnibus companies. As for the police, he blamed the police commissioner who sought to 'militarise what should be a civic force'. 'The causes that make them sell their physical ability are the same that drive men into the army, that crowd our streets with prostitutes, that fill the street with gangs of unemployed workmen: want of work, or work at remunerative wages.' 'I am anxious to preserve for the people their open air town halls and forums', he declared, 'I don't want the poor to adopt in England ... the continental method of removing grievances.' This was why he had decided to take risks by challenging 'the illegal conduct of the police in closing the Square'. 'If riot there was, [it] was caused by the police attacking people before we reached the Square.' He said a few words on socialism and concluded by saying that 'the "State" ... is a unity of citizens co-operating.... Its political expression would be a convention of labour delegates, elected by universal adult suffrage'.[30] Burns felt that his speech had 'created favourable impression'.[31]

Burns and Graham were found guilty not of riot but of unlawful assault and were sent to Pentonville Prison for six weeks. The SDF, however, refused to make a martyr of Burns and went so far as to attack the Law and Liberty League set up

[29] J. Burns, *Trafalgar Square: Speech for Defence* (London, 1888), 6.
[30] Ibid. 7–15.   [31] J. Burns, Diary, 18 Jan. 1888, BL Add. MS 46310, JBP.

for 'the arrested comrades' as 'another middle-class affair'. On the other hand, Hyndman who had warned against a premature uprising was no longer able to restrain Quelch from advocating 'the Gospel of Force'.[32] Burns's disillusionment with the SDF began with Bloody Sunday and its aftermath. He had himself indulged in the free use of revolutionary rhetoric, but he sobered down when he saw his own bragging image reflected in the sectarian announcement by the SDF extremists of their revolutionary intentions.

Nevertheless, Burns worked hard for several SDF branches, especially for the Battersea branch, but his position within the SDF council became increasingly vulnerable, as the party leadership sought to reassert itself with a new drive for more centralized administration coupled with new assertions of doctrinal rigidity. He visited Champion and had a 'long chat with him about Labour Party'. He felt very depressed about the immediate future of the movement: 'Am convinced that we have dissipated nearly all our energy in the wrong direction and upon the wrong men', he noted in his diary.[33] He had come round to Tom Mann's view on the need for change in the organization. At the annual conference of the SDF held in August 1888 he launched an attack on the leadership, criticizing various reports which, he said, were 'depressing and discouraging from everyway they looked at it'.[34] He helped to defeat 'the centralisers' in their attempt to create 'a central Executive'. 'The S.D.F. as a national body representative of the workers must be remodelled not to say merged in other bodies ere it does practical work', he commented.[35] He again met Champion who was 'jubilant about Congress', the Bradford TUC at which Keir Hardie spoke on labour representation as well as on an eight-hour bill. Burns, unlike Tom Mann, however, was cautious about his new ally: 'Champion is a splendid friend but the most dangerous foe for any man to have, gentlemanly withal'.[36] He certainly distrusted Hyndman more. The Battersea branch refused to endorse the charges against Champion made by Hyndman and his followers at a special council meeting. 'From tonight', he wrote in his diary, 'dates the public downfall of a man who has never lost an opportunity of showing his jealousy, proving his cowardice and proclaiming himself a skunk.'[37]

[32] *Justice* (10 and 31 Dec. 1887).
[33] Burns, Diary, 9 and 10 May 1888, BL Add. MS 46310, JBP.
[34] *Justice* (11 Aug. 1888).
[35] Burns, Diary, 6 Aug. 1888, BL Add. MS 46310, JBP.
[36] Ibid., 9 Sept. 1888, BL Add. MS 46310, JBP.
[37] Ibid., 26 Oct. 1888, BL Add. MS 46310, JBP.

All this time Tom Mann was in Newcastle as an SDF organizer actively engaged in opening up new branches in the area. He had been sacked from several jobs, having gained notoriety as a socialist agitator, and had gladly accepted the offer to go North as a paid organizer when it was made.

The struggle of the Northumberland coalminers, enfranchised in 1884, but now on strike over a wage-cut, had attracted considerable attention from the socialists both of the SDF and of the Socialist League. E. R. Pease, soon to become secretary of the Fabian Society, was then in Newcastle and helped the campaign. The North of England Socialist Federation, a local socialist body, decided to join the SDF in April 1887. Apparently there was a new ferment of socialism in the North. 'This consideration', wrote H. W. Lee, secretary of the SDF,

led to the desire to have an organiser permanently in Newcastle for propaganda in the coalfields. Tom Mann agreed to undertake this heavy task. The hard work was certain—the payment equally uncertain. I am not sure whether the 'screw' that Tom Mann was promised was 30s. or 40s. a week . . . the head office [of the SDF] . . . agreeing to make up whatever balance was needed after collections had been taken. Tom Mann went to Newcastle with his wife and family. He threw himself into the work with his customary fire and vigour.[38]

Tom Mann arrived in Newcastle in May. 'The miners of Northumberland and Durham are rapidly becoming Social-Democrats', he reported in June: 'No less satisfactory is the spirit shown by the engineers in Newcastle.'[39] Soon there were ten branches of the SDF in existence in these two counties.[40] He made a trip to the Clyde accompanied by a Glasgow engineer 'for the sake of seeing the actual condition of the yards' and found that 'out of a total of 50 stocks only 20 of them [had] boats on'. He spoke at several meetings and took part in the SDF's 'anti-Jubilee demonstration' held on the Glasgow Green.[41] Back in Newcastle he addressed the members of the ASE on 'The Decline of Trade Unions' and debated with a conservative opponent on 'The Abolition of the Standing Army and the Establishment of a National Citizen Force, & People to decide on Peace or War'.[42] He also reported on the engineers' strike at Bolton which took place in the summer of the same year. Strike-breakers were brought in, clashes with the police took place, and a detachment of the 10th Hussars arrived from

---

[38] Lee and Archbold, *Social-Democracy*, 123.
[39] *Justice* (5 June 1887).　　　　　[40] Ibid. (16 July 1887).
[41] Ibid. (18 and 25 June 1887).　　　[42] Ibid. (23 July, 20 Aug. 1887).

Manchester. Tom and his friends spoke to 'those of our own class dressed in the Government trappings'. 'It also afforded me', he went on,

an excellent opportunity for pointing out how our own fellows are driven into the army because they cannot work; that while in the army they are used at the bidding of the capitalists to trample down their fellows; but that in a very short time they find themselves in the ranks of the unemployed,

a theme that would remain with him all through his long career as a labour agitator.[43]

'It was a stiff time, a hard time, but I enjoyed it', Tom Mann recalled of his Newcastle days: 'I fairly revelled in preaching the principles, speaking at every conceivable time and place, filling the Cathedral with unemployed, worrying the Town Council, Board of Guardians, &c., &c.'.[44] One such demonstration was colourfully reported in the *Newcastle Weekly Chronicle*. On Sunday 6 November a number of people, 'respectably clad and otherwise', assembled near the Sandhill and opposite to the gates of St Nicholas's Cathedral. A few men wore red ribbons round their hats and in their buttonholes.

Presently Mr. Tom Mann, the organising secretary of the local branch of the Social Democratic Federation, similarly adorned, came upon the scene, bearing a small red flag. This he proceeded to wave in the air as a signal to those interested in the morning's demonstration to follow him. The signal was instantly obeyed, and all haste was made to the 2½-ton crane on the Quayside. . . . The crowd behaved in a most orderly and good-humoured manner all the way to St. Nicholas Church, which was reached in good time. . . . [After the service] the crowd started for the Quayside. . . . There seemed to be a kind of rush to reach the 60-ton crane. When the crane had been safely reached, Mr. Mann addressed the huge concourse of people who had assembled.

In the afternoon an open-air meeting was held in the Bigg Market, at which Tom Mann moved a resolution 'reminding the local authorities that there are now 5,000 men out of employment, and asking the Corporation to find employment for as many of them as possible, which was seconded and unanimously carried'.[45] One of the demands made on behalf of the unemployed was carried out by the corporation—the planting

---

[43] Ibid. (9 July 1887).
[44] T. Mann, 'How I Became a Socialist', in *How I Became a Socialist: A Series of Biographical Sketches* (London, c.1894), 81.
[45] *Newcastle Weekly Chronicle* (12 Nov. 1887).

of trees around the town moor which became a valuable asset to the city many years later.

Tom Mann remained in Northumberland and Durham all through 1887 and often visited mining towns and villages, but as he recalled, the existence of the two Miners' Associations for the pits on the north and south sides of the river, contributed to the final defeat of the Northumberland men in spite of the encouragement and contributions from the Durham Miners on the south side who did not join the strike. Similarly those SDF branches in the area that had been founded in the heat of the strike, did not last. H. W. Lee recalled:

Ashington, which began with 150 members, dwindled to a stalwart few and finally fell through ... Consequently the income from district subscriptions and collections fell off. ... Bit by bit some of his [Tom's] books went to a second-hand book seller at "rock-bottom prices", then other articles, with the exchange of a decent dining table for a common kitchen one for the sake of a few shillings needed for food.[46]

Not only books but also his favourite violin and a telescope had to go to obtain necessities. Apparently Mrs Mann did all she could to make ends meet, though she must have often been driven to the brink of despair.

On New Year's Eve Mann wrote a long letter to Burns who was awaiting the trial for 'Bloody Sunday':

You will perhaps be surprised to hear I have started work at the North Eastern Marine Engineering Co., Wallsend. Various reasons impelled me to this. First, my screw was not coming in regularly, second the outdoor agitation shows such poor results that my enthusiasm has cooled down a little, third, I wanted to show some fellows hereabouts in the organisation and out of it, that now an amalgamation of the two bodies has taken place, and therefore a likelihood of expenses being covered, I was prepared to drop out and leave the thing to take its course, fourth, it's some satisfaction to myself to turn out early and tackle the ordinary routine of workshop life, fifth, I also want to see the inside of some of these big Tyneside Firms. Criticism will be all the easier with more intimate knowledge, sixth and last, I want to be able to say to some who visit Queen Victoria Street [*where the SDF Central Office was then located*], be d—d to you & the job. Of these the *third* one is the real reason, tho' the first one hastened the decision.

By amalgamation he obviously meant the drive among the local socialists, especially in the North-East, for amalgamation between the SDF and the Socialist League. 'I am writing a pamphlet', he added: 'I did intend it to be on industries under

---

[46] Lee and Archbold, *Social-Democracy*, 123.

Socialism', but it did not come to much. 'E. R. Pease I like very much, he is working with us now heartily. Miss V. Roche sent the children a picture book for X-mas.' And he wished John Burns 'a right good New Year'.[47] Everything went well with his job for about four days, but when pay-day came, he was sacked. A similar experience was repeated the following week at Clarke Chapman's on the south side of the river. He and his family were then living at 42 North View, Heaton, Newcastle, where they experienced some of their worst privations.

From the same address Mann wrote another letter to Burns who had just been released from Pentonville Prison. 'Wife and I are very glad to know you have not suffered materially in health.' He went on to describe his search for a job in Sheffield and in Manchester:

Trade is pretty brisk in Manchester but some 300 Society men are out, so I returned home & on Saturday I started at an out door job on a boat on the Tyne, a 4 or 5 days job[,] expect to finish tomorrow but I am on the look out for another which I may get. The wages here are 30/-, Manchester 30/- to 34/-, Sheffield 34/- . . . . I feel somewhat tired of the propaganda work & should like to be quiet for while. . . . The awkward thing is that I have been banging away at others for not doing more that for myself to do less looks inconsistent.[48]

From Newcastle another letter from Mann came to Burns:

Thank you for the Battersea & Old Bailey Speeches, the latter is an exceedingly good one. I should say it will be the best propaganda pamphlet we have had for a long time, its vigour, terseness & comprehensiveness impress me as being your best production yet. Mrs. M[ann] whom I read it to quite agrees with this. . . . I suppose you are now working all right, hope so anyway. I'm not, cant get it. I have 4 starts, averaging 3 days each. I haven't tried Armstrongs, as I used to go pretty frequently to their gates to speak but I think I shall try on. There is no money coming in locally or from London, so matters are rather flat.

He asked Burns about socialist politics in London.

Champion doesn't seem to be working in harmony with any group apart from the Labour Electoral Association. Will that affair develop do you think? . . . Do you think the S.D.F. as an organisation will ever develop to considerable proportions[?] I confess it looks horribly slow work. I cant see much headway that's been made the last eighteen months, as an organisation, while in this district since the Amalgamation things are duller than when there was some amount of rivalry. . . . *Justice* will not

[47] T. Mann to J. Burns, 31 Dec. 1887, BL Add. MS 46285, JBP.
[48] T. Mann to J. Burns, 22 Feb. 1888, BL Add. MS 46285, JBP.

sell, no matter how skilfully it's handled the first week, it's not puffed, it's not asked for. The *Link* [of Mrs Besant] doesn't seem to be much better, what do you think?[49]

His personal circumstances were desperate enough, and he almost despaired of the movement as well.

As we have seen, a strike of engineers in Bolton had occasioned Tom's visit to that town. Early in 1888 the Bolton SDF asked him to take up his residence there to assist the movement in Lancashire. So he and his family moved to Bolton where they started a tobacco and newsagent shop to eke out a precarious living. 'I found scope for effective propaganda. I usually spoke from the Bolton Town Hall steps twice a week; and I regularly visited Bury, Rochdale, Blackburn, and Darwen', wrote Mann in his *Memoirs*.[50] A more intimate account of his life and work in Lancashire can be gleaned again from his letters to John Burns. In June 1888 shortly after his removal he was writing from his Bolton address, 96 Deansgate:

I like Bolton well, so does the wife. It is much easier worked than some towns I have tried. . . . I was in Manchester yesterday, but there is no Branch there worth speaking about except to condemn it. Watts seems to think it desirable to work with a few young bundle handkerchief men who really don't care a dim for Socialism or any other ism except what may tickle them for a wee while. I am determined not to work with such rifraff. I'll see the whole thing in blazes rather than be a mere street corner cheap Jack & entertaining a few insignificant nothings. . . . Nationally I have lost hope as regards S.D.F. tho' I am sanguine concerning one or two districts. The Hazel Blackburn Hyndman policy will not do for me, let those who like it go for it.[51]

In July Tom wrote another letter to Burns:

I had hoped that Hyndman was changing for the better. I much regret that differences should have been accentuated instead of blended. . . . Hyndman wrote me about a month ago, a friendly sort of letter, the first (I think) since I left London. He complained of the Council being composed of delegates. . . . I can't feel enthusiastic about the matter. . . . Bolton Branch is steadily growing after losing three fourths of its members. Yesterday one of the Councillors . . . joined. . . . The Bolton men are about to start a workshop.[52]

Then in the autumn Tom Mann had a moment's respite, as he was sent by the Bolton ASE to attend the International Trades

[49] T. Mann to J. Burns, 16 March 1888, BL Add. MS 46285, JBP.
[50] Mann, *Memoirs*, 49.
[51] T. Mann to J. Burns, 25 June 1888, BL Add. MS 46285, JBP.
[52] Ibid.

Union Congress held in London in November. An entry in Burns's diary for 5 November read:

went [to] work, left at 5, hurried home. Just reading a letter from Tom Mann when in he rushed in his usual buoyant style. Elected by Bolton Engineers' 1100 for the district on I.T.U. Congress. After tea and pleasant talk we proceeded to Westminster Palace Hotel, to official reception of Foreign delegates, Shipton in the chair. . . . Drinks were freely handed round (too freely) with cigars, food etc. Songs were sung. Foreigners very temperate indeed. Mann and I never accepted anything in the way of Refreshment!

On the following morning Burns, accompanied by Mann, proceeded to the Café Moreau to hold a preliminary meeting with foreign socialist delegates. 'At Congress we had a very difficult task to defeat Shipton and others who wanted the Congress smashed up. Large number of Socialists present. Battersea well represented.'[53] George Shipton, the veteran secretary of the London Trades Council, was elected the permanent English chairman by 61 votes against 48 for Burns. A French resolution in favour of 'a distinct class party' for the workers was passed by 48 to 31: 30 out of the 31 were English votes, as they voted against it by 30 to 12.[54] Burns found 'English delegates determined to put off the voting on 8 hours'. 'Fenwick M.P. [the Miners' leader] very angry because I wanted, and asked him to hold his hand up for 8 hours. How they did howl when I told them Trade Unions on their present lines were played out.'[55] Mann in his *Memoirs* wrote that he was responsible for a resolution for the unemployed but no decisions of vital importance were made.[56]

The co-operative workshop started by some members of the Bolton SDF and apparently supported by Tom at its beginning, however, was to become a major source of dissensions within the branch which caused Tom Mann's undoing as an SDF organizer. His next letter addressed to John Burns was written shortly after Christmas 1888, by which time he had been asked to resign from the SDF council. He dwelt on the circumstances of the trouble:

The tobacco shop I was in was intended to be a source of remuneration to me which along with 25/- a week guaranteed by the Lancashire Branches was to be my income. . . . The first 3 months I was there the

[53] Burns, Diary, 5 and 6 Nov. 1888, BL Add. MS 46310, JBP.
[54] *Justice* (17 Nov. 1888).
[55] Burns, Diary, 10 Nov. 1888, BL Add. MS 46310, JBP.
[56] Mann, *Memoirs*, 51.

membership of Bolton Branch rose from 50 to 170, then troubles began by a section of the Branch headed by one Matt Phair deciding to start a Socialist workshop, called by them the Co-op Commonwealth. This proved to be a very great hindrance to the progress of the branch & in a short time partly owing to a less vigorous propaganda, resulting from the members devoting time to what they thought was the practical side of Socialism. The membership soon began to decrease, considerable dissensions arose in the branch & at nearly every meeting quarrels took place. I took no part in them but turned my attention more to other Branches & did my best [to] develop Blackburn & Darwen Branches. . . . Being asked in October to go to Northwich for the Labour Party I at once consented, subject to agreeing with the Committee of Bolton, & made several visits there. . . . All this time I was living up to the 25/- a week & the shop was not paying its way . . . & when the first quarter rent was due I had to get 2 £5 loans & commenced to pay them back by weekly instalments & I was still doing this when the next became due ditto the next & of course had to borrow as I continued to spend the 25/- on the Family. When the colder weather set in the 25/- was not forthcoming, only a part of it & we were put to great straits. . . . The dissensions previously alluded to developing caused a proportionate falling off of sales [of *Justice*] & for several weeks running I had the bother of the paper, & considerable monthly loss also, ultimately I told the committee definitely that they must take charge of the paper so that they would realise the necessity of either purchasing it or ordering less. This has been used on the Council as a sign of my animosity to the S.D.F.

Indeed, Tom's sin against the SDF was of a serious, sacrilegious nature, because he went to Stockton-on-Tees to assist the National Labour Electoral Association, Champion's Labour Party, and when asked, supplied copies of Champion's weekly *Labour Elector*. 'This is the great offence of which I have been guilty', he went on;

The Darwen Secretary, a young energetic fellow with the best intentions I suppose became incensed that any other paper than *Justice* should be read, & wrote to Bridge saying I had weaned some of their members &c. The one result of my being in Lancashire is that for the first time in my life I now owe a monthly debt of £15, which I am trying to pay at 2/6 a week but stand a real risk of having my goods seized. This then is what I have gained monetarily, though as for gaining a little experience it may be worth it.[57]

In fact, Tom had been assisting Champion in his intervention in the 'labour interest' in a series of by-elections. He was sent by Champion, as we have seen, to help Keir Hardie at the Mid-Lanark by-election in April 1888. After this, he and Keir Hardie

[57] T. Mann to J. Burns, n.d., BL Add. MS 46310, JBP.

were seen carrying out Champion's instructions, speaking in the name of the Labour Party, in support of a Liberal candidate, at a by-election in the Ayr burghs in June. In December they were assisting 'a fair employer of labour' pledged to an eight-hour day, at the Maidstone by-election.[58] Tom's visits to Northwich, Cheshire, mentioned in his letter to Burns, are of special interest, for he secured a job under the assumed name of 'John Miller' at Brunner's chemical works there, and with his findings as a general labourer not only defeated the threatened legal proceedings by the company against Champion's paper that had publicized the wretched working conditions in the works but helped the men obtain an eight-hour day.[59] Tom's work for *Labour Elector* and for the Shop Hours Regulation Committee, another creation of Champion's, allowed him to return to London early in 1889.

In 1889 William Stephen Sanders, later secretary of the Fabian Society, was a lad of eighteen, a newcomer to the Battersea SDF. According to him, the Battersea SDF, like any of the thirty or so other SDF branches in those days, was composed on the one hand of the respectable, skilled artisans and on the other of the general labourers usually connected with the building trade. The unskilled labourers and skilled workers in seasonal trades were often 'bitter and suspicious' and generally in angry revolt against the system of society that refused them a decent living. The better-situated mechanics—working-class élite—joined and led the movement more from 'impartial' or fellow-feeling,[60] though they, too, began to suffer from the introduction of advanced machinery. Now in Battersea, John Burns, the better-placed mechanic, though often victimized like Mann for his socialist views, established himself as a popular hero among radical working men after the Bloody Sunday of November 1887, which was indeed a fight for free speech. 'His power as a popular orator was then at its zenith', recalled Sanders, and the first opportunity for his rise to power came when the first London County Council election was held in January 1889. Sanders undertook to organize his election campaign. Although Burns stood as a Social Democrat, his appeal went beyond the SDF and reached the heart of the radical workers. His speeches 'quickened the latent sense of citizenship' of his hearers, and he won the seat with the handsome vote of 3,071. His supporters, both socialist and Radical,

---

[58] *Labour Elector* (1 Apr. 1893).   [59] Mann, *Memoirs*, 56–7.
[60] W. Stephen Sanders, *Early Socialist Days* (London, 1927), 17–18.

were now organized into the Battersea Labour League with a programme to 'promote the interests of labour' by 'securing direct labour representation in parliament, the county council, the School Board, the Board of Guardians, the vestry and other administrative bodies', by the diffusion of knowledge through lecture halls and club rooms and by promoting unified action among all the sections of the workers.[61] In short, they were urged to educate and agitate for political action.

Recovery of trade had encouraged the revival of trade-union activities, and its first notable result was the successful strike of the matchgirls employed at Bryant and May, Bow, assisted by Mrs Besant and Herbert Burrows of the SDF. Tom Mann, after his return from Bolton to London, kept in close touch with John Burns. 'I have a clear recollection', wrote Mann in his memoirs, 'of being with Mr. John Burns one day when we met Mr. Will Thorne, and other workmen of his', telling, in short, how disappointed they were with Sydney Buxton, then MP for Poplar, who in an interview took a pessimistic view of the prospect of an eight-hour bill. 'As the result of the conversation with John Burns and myself, the group of gasworkers saw the necessity of our contention that they must first organize industrially, and then put in the claims direct to the Gas Companies.'[62] It was during the agitation for the Gasworkers that Tom Mann first met Ben Tillett who was also helping them. The negotiations following on the organization of the men resulted in the Metropolitan Gas Companies granting their demands: an eight-hour day, twelve shifts a fortnight, and a sixpence per shift increase in wages.

Meanwhile, animosity to Champion in the SDF had become so bitter that he was expelled in November 1888 for the official reason of his continued association with the 'notorious Tory agent' Maltman Barry. Mann's and Burns's connections with the SDF were also soon to lapse. The incident had further repercussions. In the negotiations for the starting of the Second International, Mann and Burns were drawn to the Marxist camp who were opposed to the French Possibilists or reformist socialists led by Paul Brousse, the former anarchist and 'a dedicated international anti-Marxist',[63] and to their English

[61] Sanders, *Early Socialist Days*, 24, 67–8; G. H. Knott, *Mr. John Burns M.P.* (London, 1901), 55–6; Chris Wrigley, 'Liberals and the Desire for Working-Class Representatives in Battersea', in Kenneth D. Brown (ed.), *Essays in Anti-Labour History* (London, 1974), 132.   [62] Mann, *Memoirs*, 58–9.

[63] David Stafford, *From Anarchism to Reformism: A Study of the Political Activities of Paul Brousse* (London, 1971), 247.

allies Hyndman and the SDF. Eleanor Marx, in her attempt to gain trade-union support for the Marxist congress, invited Mann and Burns to her house to see Eduard Bernstein who was engaged in a polemic against the Possibilists.[64] In Paris the two founding congresses, Marxist and Possibilist, were held simultaneously in July 1889 for the new international which fully manifested the doctrinal and organizational differences that had divided the First International. Although Burns was sent to Paris to attend the Possibilist congress as a delegate from the ASE, he proposed the fusion of it with the Marxist congress. When a violent attack was made by Saverio Merlino, the Italian anarchist, on all labour legislation, Burns

in sledge-hammer style advised him to tell the Gas Stokers of London to work 12 or 14 instead of the Eight they now work. Reduction of hours was of great importance. Unskilled workers were especially in need of it. . . . Legislation often helped those who were too poor to combine and win it for themselves.[65]

When Burns returned home, the revolt of the unskilled workers began to spread like wildfire. The poorest workers, too, were learning how to combine. Tom Mann now threw in his lot with the revolt of the lowest strata of society, the dock labourers in East London.

[64] Chushichi Tsuzuki, *Life of Eleanor Marx* (Oxford, 1967), 190, 192.
[65] J. Burns, 'Paris International Congress', *Labour Elector* (3 Aug. 1889).

3. The London Dock Strike

The Revolt of the Dockers

A RAPID growth of trade in eighteenth-century London had led
to the construction and expansion of the docks to relieve the
pressure on the river. The West India Dock which opened to
Limehouse Reach was built in 1802, the London Dock nearer the
City in 1805, the East India Dock down the river at Blackwall in
1806, and St Katherine's Dock upstream near the Tower in
1828, all on the north side. The south side too saw developments at Rotherhithe which were later to be consolidated as
the Surrey Commercial Docks, catering for bulky goods like
corn and timber. The age of sail was to give way to that of
steam, and the effects of tide and wind were superseded by
mechanical appliances and quick turnover. Two rival companies had emerged after the amalgamation of various docks
north of the river. They competed by building modern facilities
further down, the great Victoria and Albert Docks for the
London and St Katherine's Company in 1855 and 1880 respectively and the huge Tilbury Docks for the East and West India
Company in 1886. The ruinous competition between the two
had been aggravated by the opening of another modern dock at
Millwall. The advent of Free Trade permitting the wharfs to
handle previously dutiable goods further intensified competition as the lighters carried cargoes from abroad from the docks
to the wharfs. The days of great profits with extensive charters
and privileges for the docks were coming to an end. The port,
over-docked and over-wharfed, was decaying. Thus towards
the end of 1888 the two most powerful dock companies on the
north side set up a joint committee to meet the crisis which had
taken the form of a collapse of dock rates and which led to the
great revolt of the waterside workers.

The revolt was led by men of extraordinary calibre. Joseph
Havelock Wilson, who had organized seamen and firemen on
the North–East coast and the Bristol Channel in 1887, and who
was also involved in the London Dock Strike of 1889, wrote of
his colleagues:

I remember my first talk with my friends Ben Tillett and Tom Mann.
They were not very impressed with me because I was a provincial man,

but, nevertheless, they were very kind with me. ... The strongest character at that time amongst the London men was Tom Mann. The man I thought who could hold the audience most was John Burns. He appeared to me to dominate every meeting. On the other hand no one was more popular than Ben Tillett. He was called 'Little Ben'.[1]

'Little Ben', Benjamin Tillett, who was to set up a union worthy of its name among the dockers, had come to London after a period of resistance to all little tyrants in his youthful days. He was born on 11 September 1860 at Easton, a suburb of Bristol. His father Benjamin Tillett was then working as a railway labourer. His mother, who came 'of gentle Irish stock', died when Ben was just over one year old. His father, now working as a polisher at a comb factory nearby, married a woman whom the young Ben disliked. Sunday school, to which he was sent, was a nightmare. His attempts to hide as a stowaway on board a ship at the Bristol Broad Quay failed. He was assisted in an escapade by gypsies, from whom he learned that he should fight for his life. He joined Old Joe Baker's Circus, wandered about the Black Country and then went on a long journey to Stratford where one of his sisters snatched him away, brought him to her home, and sent him to the national school in the town. But in due course his 'gypo laws' got the upper hand over school discipline; he knocked his teacher unconscious and was expelled from the school.

He returned to the life of roving and fighting and his little odyssey of adventures went on till 1873 when at the age of thirteen he joined the Navy at Bristol. And it was the Navy that provided his apprenticeship. Unusually puny as he was, he nevertheless excelled in racing over the cross-trees. But his excessive passion for all the tricks and arts high up the mast caused a serious hernia which put an end to his life in the Navy. He later joined the merchant marines and returned to the sea. After several transatlantic voyages he tried his luck in East London, and sought to join the Stevedores' Union, but was not accepted. He presented himself at the 'cage', so called because of strong iron bars made to protect the 'caller on' from the men who 'ravening for food fought like madmen for the ticket, a veritable talisman of life'.[2] He spent some years on and off at sea, and finally found a job at the Monument Quay Warehouse at London Bridge most agreeable. More or less secure in his work on the docklands, on 2 April 1882 Ben Tillett, 'cooper', married Jane Tomkins sister of his brother-in-law. Ben, like Tom Mann, was anxious to improve himself,

---

[1] J. Havelock Wilson, *My Stormy Voyage through Life*, i (London, 1925), 16.

[2] B. Tillett, *Brief History of the Dockers' Union* (London, 1910), 12.

though under more adverse conditions. He worked hard, saved money to buy books, and attended lectures given at the Bow and Bromley Institute. 'I . . . had bent my head and aching body to the task [of reading] after the work had meant scores of tons on my back, carrying up and down flights of stairs,' he recalled; 'Nay I had meant to be a barrister, but I was to hold a bigger brief; I was to be one among others to hold the brief for humanity in a fight which has gone on all these years, in all trades, and in all countries of the world.'[3] This is to anticipate, but there is no doubt that Tillett had found his life's mission.

Jack Gill, later defending Ben Tillett against the current sneer that he was living off the reputation he had made in 1889, stated that 'if Ben did nothing else but organise the mass of brutalised humanity that fought like beasts at the docks for jobs in 1887, he achieved a social miracle. . . . And our little Ben, no speaker then, and suffering from a stammer in his speech, set out to organise them! What a task he set himself!'[4] 'A social miracle' it truly was. How it took place, how the people looked at it, how the leaders themselves saw its development and their roles in it, how the historians interpreted all this for posterity, in short an analysis of the origins and main features of the London Dock Strike, is the theme of what remains of this and the following chapter.

Tillett has not been treated kindly by historians. John Lovell, in his most scholarly account of the dockers and stevedores, wrote that he was 'highly emotional, over sensitive to criticism, and lacking in application', and 'no administrator'. Jonathan Schneer blamed Tillett for 'inconsistency' and 'ambiguities'.[5] Yet his devoted work as a trade-union organizer in the two years preceding the strike of 1889 was to say the least, extraordinary and even titanic, and would explain the secret of the 'social miracle'.

His trade-union career began at a meeting held early in July 1887 in the Oak Tavern, off Hackney Road, where the tea-workers met and discussed the ways and means to resist the wage reduction imposed by the East and West India Dock Company upon the workers at the Cutler Street Warehouse. Tillett represented his workmates at the Monument Warehouse as he already had some knowledge of trade-union organization.

    [3] Tillett, *Brief History*, 10–11.
    [4] J. Gill to Ian Mackay, 19 Jan. 1951, IMP.
    [5] John Lovell, *Stevedores and Dockers* (London, 1969), 95; Jonathan Schneer, *Ben Tillett: Portrait of a Labour Leader* (London, 1982), 7.

When working at boot-making he had learned something of it from Charles Freak, London secretary of the National Union of Boot and Shoe Operatives. His giant Irish friend Flemming now hoisted the little Ben on to a table and bade him speak. 'My stammering lips, tripping me the more rapidly I spoke, urged the necessity of organizing, suggesting the method'.[6] So the Tea Coopers' and General Labourers' Association was launched with Ben as its secretary on a wage of £2 a week.

His address delivered at a meeting for his union held at St Mary's School, Whitechapel on 27 July 1887, soon came out as a pamphlet, *A Dock Labourer's Bitter Cry*. In contrast with the more famous *Bitter Cry of Outcast London* (1883) by the Revd Andrew Mearns, who appealed for Christian 'operations' against poverty and degradation, Tillett's *Bitter Cry* contained his principal ideas on trade-unionism. His aim was to set up a general union in the docklands—'to gather the whole of the men employed in dock and wharf labour, to band [them] together in union'. His union would strive for 'a fair day's pay . . . guaranteed for a fair day's work', regulation of the hours of labour, and reform of the current system of contract and sub-contract, that would lead to 'a system of greater regularity and better pay'—in short, decasualization. He would rely solely on 'legitimate combination'—'we want a bloodless victory; no strike, no violence. . . . We want our position so adjusted that by arbitration we shall prevent conflict with our employers'. Tillett set to the hard work of union-building. George Howell, the veteran trade-unionist who assisted Tillett in registering his union, later wrote:

In his original conception of forming the Union, Mr. Tillett had no notion of founding a new Trade Unionism. He merely wished to go on the old lines, but not to embark upon provident benefits, as the wages of the men would not permit of a contribution sufficient to run the risk. The contributions were fixed at twopence a week.[7]

His union was a poor man's union above all. The work of organization was slow; there were several obstacles in the way of growth. Beatrice Potter, who as a rent-collector made an investigation of the conditions of labour in East London, declared in her article 'The Dock Life of East London', published in October 1887 in *Nineteenth Century*, that there was no trade union among dock or waterside workers. Her Fabian approach was already evident in her attempt to 'determine the exact line between the preventable and inevitable in the evil of East-end

---

6 B. Tillett, *Memories and Reflections* (London, 1931), 97.
7 George Howell, *Trade Unionism: New and Old* (1891; London, 1907), 153.

life'. She believed that a man's character would degenerate by living in the Docklands. 'His mind and body have become by a slow process of deterioration adapted to the low form of life which he is condemned to live. . . . In truth, the occasional employment of this class of labour by the docks, waterside, and other East-end industries is a gigantic system of outdoor relief.' The stern reality of life drew them together, and 'as a class they are quixotically generous. . . . Socially they have their own attractiveness; economically they are worthless, and morally worse than worthless, for they drag others who live among them down to their own level.' She found that 13 per cent of the population of Tower Hamlets did not enjoy a decent standard of living, while 22 per cent were on the poverty line.[8] Tillett criticized her article as having been written 'from the office standpoint'.[9] In November 1887 Beatrice attended a meeting of dock labourers in Canning Town opened by Tillett, whom she described as 'a light-haired little man with the face of a religious enthusiast', 'honest, undoubtedly, but ignorant and unwise'. She did not like his 'ranting' against 'white slavery' and his denunciation of the system of subcontract and irregular hours.[10] 'Humanitarians' like Miss Potter soon came round to support him, though 'somewhat condescendingly' as Tillett added.[11]

The worst enemies he met, however, were within, for trade-unionism on the Thames waterfront was generally distrusted because of the shady, dubious activities of bogus labour organizations that were formed to provide gangs of thugs. Thus Tillett's union, when formed, became 'immediately suspect'.[12] Even John Burns, when approached by Tillett, was not helpful: 'I urged John Burns, at the offices of the S.D.F., to give a hand. His reply was terse and unprintable.'[13] Burns's encounter at the time of the West End riots with Lemon, Kelly, and Peters, the leaders of such waterside organizations as worked for the Fair Traders, would account for his initial hostility to Tillett. In fact, as late as May 1888, the *Star*, the Radical newspaper edited by T. P. O'Connor, compared Tillett's union to the 'Dock and Riverside Labourers' Society', one of the spurious unions run by 'Lord Salisbury's "dear Kelly"' Thomas Kelly. 'They attacked each other. They looked upon each other with as

[8] Beatrice Potter, 'Dock Life of East London', *Nineteenth Century*, 22: 128 (Oct. 1887), 479, 494–6.   [9] Tillett, *Brief History*, 13.
[10] Beatrice Webb, *Diary of Beatrice Webb*, ed. Norman and Jeanne MacKenzie, i (London, 1982), 224.   [11] Tillett, *Memories*, 109.
[12] Lovell, *Stevedores and Dockers*, 98.   [13] Tillett, *Brief History*, 15.

much jealousy as a couple of rival old clo' men in the same alley, "you're a fraud", cries one in effect. "You're another", is the retort.'[14]

From Tillett's diary for the year 1888 it is possible to obtain glimpses of his devoted hard work. A council was set up, rules were adopted, and it was decided to register the society as a trade union. 'Received note from George Howell M.P. about rules, offered to assist.'[15] 'Out early 6 p.m., Canning Town, round Albert & Victoria Docks, gave bills away round each . . . came home & then proceeded by appointment to meeting of men of Butler's Wharf, same very satisfactory. Home & meeting at Poplar, 4 new members. Out till late & very tired. Rules came down from Registrar.'[16] The initial enthusiasm soon lapsed into indifference and inertia. Branches lay low: 'Poplar, poor attendance, work very slack. . . . Canning Town, very poor meeting.'[17] In April when he made up accounts, he 'found only 2/- in hand'.[18] Yet he continued his organization work doggedly. '[Gave] lecture, Sold few copies of "Bitter Cry" & made two members, spoke about 1 hour & a half.' 'Early meeting, Spoke for 3 quarters of an hour to rather fair gathering, was very hoarse, & tired. Sold 4 pamphlets & had animated conversation with a stevedore about Society & its work.'[19] In May things looked up as the waterfront became busy, but he was 'very sorry to see sad falling off in contributions. Only 12/2 left after deducting expenses'.[20] In June Mrs Besant came, and Tillett was 'very much impressed by her speech'.[21]

The *Star's* 'scurrilous attack' continued. George Howell recalled how the sorry accounts of his union, which the secretary so manfully published, were laid hold of by his opponents and sent to the *Star* which censured him several times. So Howell himself 'went to the *Star* . . . and begged that they would not strive to strangle this young, feeble, and struggling but *bona-fide* Union'.[22] It was in the midst of his organization work that his father died on 17 July in Bristol at the age of sixty-seven. On 20 July he went home and the following day 'buried father very unsatisfactorily "safe in the arms of Jesus"'.[23] He visited his own mother's 'home and birth place' and 'stood on old stone'.[24] The diary was again crowded with

14 *Star* (24 May 1888).
16 Ibid., 26 Jan. 1888.
18 Ibid., 28 Apr. 1888.
20 Ibid., 26 May 1888.
22 Howell, *Trade Unionism*, 152–3.
23 Tillett, Diary, 21 July 1888, IMP.

15 B. Tillett, Diary, 12 Jan. 1888, IMP.
17 Ibid., 8 and 9 Mar. 1888.
19 Ibid., 29 Apr. 1888.
21 Ibid., 27 June 1888.

24 Ibid., 23 July 1888.

union affairs. 'Another large number joined'; 'meeting very enthusiastic. 9 joined.'[25] In August there was a dispute among the stevedores which led him to see Tom McCarthy, secretary of the Amalgamated Society of Stevedores, a London Irishman from Limehouse—'little Tom—with the big heart and the head of a giant' as he called him[26]—who became a staunch supporter of Tillett. A great rally was held at Tower Hill on 30 August. 'Band punctual, Police in plenty, very satisfied with arrangements. Band in good order, Inspector very snappy . . . Great enthusiasm, speech complimented by all.'[27] A few days later he was writing letters to the stevedores and those who had assisted him, and sending copies of a resolution passed at the meeting to Lord Salisbury, the Prime Minister; C. T. Ritchie, president of the Local Government Board; Sydney Buxton, the local MP; Earl Dunraven, the Irish peer; the Earl of Aberdeen; and others.[28] His union was now growing fast. 'Dock visited. Poplar very enthusiastic—passed with three cheers a vote of thanks to me. Animated meeting. Many joined.'[29]

We shall follow the further development of Tillett's union because it will give a foretaste of what was soon to come. His organization was now extended to Tilbury Docks where the men were receiving 4*d.* an hour, a penny less than in the older docks, and the work averaged three hours a day throughout the year. A strike began in October among the men, and Tillett's union was tested for the first time and, contrary to his original designs, in its fighting capacity. After all, a poor man's union had to be a fighting union. About 400 men were out at Tilbury, demanding an increase of 1*d.* an hour. 'Stevedores cheered effort', and Herbert Burrows of the SDF came and 'urged all present to help the workers'.[30] This time the *Star* stood on his side, and described his union as 'a protective union for dock and general labourers' which had acquired a certain strength and influence, having a membership of 23,000 (somewhat inflated!), and about £130 to its credit.[31] Tillett kept watch over the picketing, especially along the river. 'Up early,' on the 24th, 'Men about 200 coming over by boat. Induced them to come out with [the] rest of Strikers. Got up a winch stand by the pier. Whole marched together to place of meeting. A great many of them very enthusiastic over events.'[32]

[25] Tillett, Diary, 24 July, 5 Aug. 1888.
[26] Tillett, *Brief History*, 14; id., *Memories*, 114.
[27] Id., Diary, 30 Aug. 1888, IMP.   [28] Ibid., 3 Sept. 1888.
[29] Ibid., 6 Sept. 1888.   [30] Ibid., 23 Oct. 1888.
[31] *Star* (24 and 25 Oct. 1888).   [32] Tillett, Diary, 24 Oct. 1888, IMP.

The *Star* reported cases of public sympathy, though still on a modest scale: Miss Grace Hawthorne at the Princess Theatre gave 'a ticket benefit for the aid of the Tilbury dock men on strike'; and two local tradesmen supplied a dinner of bread and cheese for 200 men.[33] Samuel Montague, the local MP who contributed £5 to the strike fund, accompanied Tillett in a meeting with Colonel Du Plat Taylor, manager of the East and West India Company, who boasted that he could get men to work for 2d. and 3d. an hour.[34] A *Star* reporter interviewed several dockers on strike. A former boiler-maker who had earned 2s. a week in the dock said: 'How do we live? We manage to scrape through somehow. It is nothing unusual to be without food for a whole day. Some of them who get to work live in lodging-houses in Gravesend, and others live in empty houses on the marshes. . . . Many of us live principally on potatoes from the farmers' fields.' This, added the reporter, was the kind of theft which, Cardinal Manning would say, was no crime. The strikers complained that the preference men receiving 5d. an hour were those who curried favour with the foremen. They ('all those spoken to') had served apprenticeships to various trades. They deplored that their places as the striking dockers were being filled by boys and women.[35] Tillett stuck to his guns. Meetings were held at Gravesend, processions organized, and 'shop-to-shop' collections were made.[36] 'Battle renewed' on the 29th: 'Picked out Deputation, went with them to London. . . . Would not see Dock Company on account of their refusing to give publicity to the interview. Du Plat chagrined.'[37]

The men's suffering was great. Many of them had been sleeping on the marshes in the open air. Owing to the incessant rain they were compelled to rent two houses, the cost being borne by the union.[38] On 1 November Tillett asked the men's opinion about continuing the strike: 'unanimous determination to resist to the end'.[39] A week later the 'men still determined in their fight. Will not submit to wrong doing'.[40] The SDF, especially members of the Limehouse branch, and its active campaigner H. W. Hobart of the London Society of Compositors, came and assisted Tillett at Gravesend.[41] Apparently socialism did not provide enough ammunition for the men to stay in the battle. 'Funds not coming in very fast. Men wanting

---

[33] *Star* (30 Oct. 1888).   [34] Ibid. (26 Oct. 1888).   [35] Ibid.
[36] Tillett, Diary, 27 Oct. 1888, IMP.   [37] Ibid., 29 Oct. 1888.
[38] *Star* (30 Oct. 1888).   [39] Tillett, Diary, 1 Nov. 1888, IMP.
[40] Ibid., 8 Nov. 1888.   [41] *Justice* (27 Oct., 17 and 24 Nov. 1888).

food', wrote Tillett. A week later on 19 November, 'Men gave in [and Tillett] declared "Strike closed" '.[42]

On the following day, 20 November 1888, Tillett, the general of the defeated army, gave testimony at a session of the Select Committee of the House of Lords on Sweating Industries with Lord Kenry (the Earl of Dunraven) in the chair. To enlighten the august members of the committee he explained what the 'plus' system was, how the contract and subcontract system worked, and dwelled on irregularities of work, the impact of mechanization, and the harsh competition for a job in the docklands. He suggested that 'the contract should be given to the men direct, and that they should work on the co-operative principle'. From his personal experiences he testified that dock labour had been a profession before, but now two-thirds of the men working at the docks and wharfs were not dock labourers by trade. Some of those in the rope-making and engineering industries were driven to the docks by the machinery introduced in their own trades. Those in tailoring, shoemaking, and baking were ousted from their trades by 'the foreigners' and came to the docks, and he reckoned himself among them, having worked as a boot-maker, 'as a laster in London at Markie's in Finsbury' before. He pointed out that the recent tendency was to allow only the 'Royals' (preference men) to partake in the 'plus' or saving which was effected by the foreman hiring as few hands as possible and making those employed work as hard as possible by speeding up the work, the foreman usually retaining four shares of the surplus to himself. Each docker should have his fair share of the 'plus', and for this to be possible the union should be properly consulted.[43] Many other problems were touched upon, such as payment during mealtimes, the difference in time between mustering of the men and actual commencement of the work, employment of boys ('a lot employed at the Tilbury Dock'), and the speeding up of operations on mail boats where men sometimes worked twenty-two consecutive hours, whereas the 'right hours would be a fair day's work', that is to say two calls of four hours each.[44]

As for the life of the dockers, he stated:

The majority of the dock labourers are forced to live in either one or two rooms. I should say that about 70 per cent. of them are married

[42] Tillett, Diary, 13 and 19 Nov. 1888, IMP.

[43] *British Parliamentary Papers*, Select Committee on the Sweating System, 1888 (Industrial Relations, 14; Shannon, 1970), 111, 120–5, 173.

[44] Ibid. 130–3.

men; the others are frequently to be found in what we call 'doss-houses'; they pay there for a bed at the rate of twopence or threepence a night. But the reason of their being able to live at all is that there is some kind of communism among them, for they help each other and it is the practice among them to pay for each other's beds or 'dosses' when the man has not had a turn of work. But the majority of the labourers live in back rooms, the more respectable would be the 'Royals', or permanent hands working at the docks.

The ordinary dockers would require contributions from wives who did 'washing, matchmaking, charring, all kinds of rough work'.[45] What a contrast this picture presents to the one depicted by Beatrice Potter who said: 'Jack having secured a ticket [for work] by savage fight, sells it to the needier Tom for twopence, and goes off with the coppers to drink or to gamble'![46]

In his testimony Tillett complained of 'the indifference of the skilled organizations throughout the land to our wants'. Indeed, the Tilbury strike was a lone fight. 'We have been in existence now 18 months; during that time there has not been a representative from the Trades Council that has ever come and helped us.' He was sure that given the same power as the stevedores enjoyed, the dockers' work would be regulated by his society, and there would be a better chance of a fair adjustment of wages.[47]

Tillett appeared again as a witness on 22 November and stated that after the Tilbury strike, members of his union had been victimized. He now touched upon the cause of the failure of the strike: in spite of the effective picketing by the union which prevented the company obtaining men from London, 'they have scoured the district round, and got the whole of the farm labourers'. Furthermore, the strike was paralysed by the 'system of intimidation' by the police. The remedies he suggested included municipalization of the docks, restriction of foreigners coming to England to take jobs, and some 'land law' that would encourage peasant proprietorship and thereby keep men on the soil.[48] Several members of the Select Committee, including the chairman, sought to elicit a protectionist testimony from him, especially on the question of food supply, but he refused to be drawn.[49]

---

[45] Ibid. 135.   [46] Potter, 'Dock Life', 495.

[47] *British Parliamentary Papers*, Select Committee on the Sweating System, 1888, pp. 136, 147.   [48] Ibid. 190, 193–4.

[49] Ibid. 205; *Star* (23 Nov. 1888).

Although the strike was lost, it was a good fight, and he was able to plead the cause of trade-unionism among the unskilled dock labourers before the Select Committee. He concluded his diary for this eventful year 1888 with a new hope and determination: '31 December Monday. Cold worse than ever. Went to Chapel. Old year out. Like to live the New Year a more useful life than last, hope to go straight & true, & no swerving from right & truth.' Exposure and overwork in the cold and damp during the Tilbury strike, however, produced an attack of congestion of his lungs which compelled Tillett to stay at Bournemouth for a while to recuperate. He had been in touch with Cardinal Manning since he had sent him pamphlets on the dock labourers earlier in 1888.[50] Now almost 'sick to death of life and of the movement', he wrote to the Cardinal for advice, and received a reply containing 'so subtle a castigation that it stung me to effort and faith again': his Eminence urged him to be a strong man who would not 'want a crown without carrying a cross'.[51]

When he recovered, however, his union had almost melted away: its membership dwindled, according to Howell, from about 800 to 300.[52] He now set to work again, speaking at dock-gates, and assisted Will Thorne in drafting the rules of his union, the Gasworkers and General Labourers' Union, whose membership soon reached 3,000. In June Thorne was elected general secretary of his union, having defeated Tillett by 2,296 to 69 in a ballot. Why did Tillett challenge Thorne's obvious leadership? The rapid growth of the Gasworkers' Union which had over sixty branches, forty-four in London by July, led many dockers to wish to join it. Many gasworkers worked in the docks in summer. The two general unions were almost interchangeable for many of their members. His own union still suffered from the effects of the defeat of the previous year. His challenge may have been derived from his desire to see one big union for all the workers on the waterside, but it foretold demarcation disputes among the general unions, which even led to contradictory accounts of the origins of the London Dock Strike of 1889. These we shall examine in the remaining part of this chapter.

Hubert Llewellyn Smith (later Beveridge's permanent secretary) and Vaughan Nash (later private secretary to Asquith), the two men from Toynbee Hall who helped the dockers' strike

[50] Cardinal Manning to B. Tillett, 3 Mar. 1888, IMP.
[51] Tillett, *Brief History*, 15.   [52] Howell, *Trade Unionism*, 153.

committee with relief work in the summer of 1889, frankly admitted in their joint history of the strike that it 'took the world by surprise' and its beginning was 'wrapped in obscurity', while the leaders of the strike found themselves in disagreement as to its origins.[53] Dr Lovell, the author of the best modern account, has written that its immediate origins were 'of a somewhat confused and controversial nature'.[54] Moreover, a statement made by H. H. Champion, one of the strike leaders, to the effect that socialists were welcomed in the strike 'not because of their Socialism, but in spite of it',[55] has encouraged an underestimation of the roles played by the SDF members in preparing the ground for the awakening of the unskilled workers in East London.[56] Even accepting the valuable contributions made by Social Democrats such as Burrows and Hobart, difficulties still arise, because the main participants in the strike took divergent views of the role played by Tillett in organizing the dockers, which we have examined in some detail.

Will Thorne and John Burns sought to belittle Tillett's Tea Operatives' Union: Thorne was obviously hurt by Tillett's opposition to his candidature for general secretaryship of the Gasworkers' Union, while Tillett and Tom Mann chose to ignore an attempt made by W. Harris with the support of Thorne and Burns to organize the dockers in Canning Town, Thorne's stronghold, obviously an instance of a demarcation dispute. In July 1889 W. Harris, Thorne's personal friend, a tugman, and a member of the Canning Town SDF, announced in *Justice* his intention to form a new dockers' union, 'the Amalgamated Society of Dock Company's Servants'.[57] 'Why such a step should have been necessary, with Tillett's union already in existence, is not really clear', wrote Lovell.[58] It was apparently a Social Democratic affair, but prominent SDF leaders were in Paris attending the inaugural congress of the Second International. By the time the founding meeting of Harris's union was held on 4 August in Canning Town, it had fallen under the patronage of Champion's *Labour Elector*. John

---

[53] H. Llewellyn Smith and Vaughan Nash, *Story of the Dockers' Strike* (London, 1889), 28–9.   [54] Lovell, *Stevedores and Dockers*, 100.

[55] H. H. Champion, *Great Dock Strike in London* (London, 1890), 10.

[56] A critical review of such an underestimate by Dona Torr can be seen in Victor Rabinovitch, 'British Marxist Socialism and Trade Unionism: The Attitudes, Experiences and Activities of the Social-Democratic Federation 1884–1901', Ph.D. thesis (Sussex, 1977).

[57] *Justice* (20 July 1889).   [58] Lovell, *Stevedores and Dockers*, 99.

Burns, who had returned from Paris, came and addressed the crowd at this meeting on the advantage of unionism, declaring that 'in point of numbers, the Dock Labourers are more than double the Gas Stokers'.[59] Meanwhile, discontent was simmering among the dockers at the South-West India Dock at Poplar, Tillett's stronghold, over the division of the plus or bonus money on a cargo unloaded from the *Lady Armstrong*. On the morning of Monday 12 August Thorne, having received a telegram from Harris, arrived at the dock-gates to attend a meeting which was chaired by Tom McCarthy of the Stevedores' Union. 'I backed up Tom's appeal to them to form a union and then refuse to go to work,' wrote Thorne; 'Finally the proposition was put to a vote of the meeting, and every man voted to stay out. That was the beginning of the great dock strike of 1889.'[60] This is really a one-sided, misleading account, for it would give the impression that Harris's union started the strike.

John Burns, in an article written shortly after the end of the strike, bluntly stated that the Gasworkers' victory 'induced the strike of the dockers'. Harris appealed to Burns to help him to form 'a permanent dock hands' trade union'. 'I consented', wrote Burns,

and held a meeting of two thousand men, at which many members were enrolled. These were men who had refused to join the old dockers' union, which from one cause and another, had ceased to be worth its name. But the formation of the new union forced the old one into an activity which it had not theretofore displayed; and of this unwonted activity the immediate outcome was the strike in the South Dock on August 13th.[61]

This 'unwonted activity' obviously concerned Tillett's union. Thus Burns grudgingly did justice to Tillett without naming him, but he had ignored the gallant fight of Tillett's union in the previous year. Perhaps the initial, mistaken distrust of it and of its founder still remained with him.

Perhaps Tom Mann, free from Thorne's egotism and Burns's prejudices, provides a fairer testimony. Mann's account of the origins of the strike was published nearly half a century later in an article in the *Labour Monthly*. Naturally matters secondary and inconsequential were blurred over. Tillett's union, wrote Mann, sought to extend its operations, but not many responded at first. The stevedores, the lightermen, and the mechanic sections of the dry-dock workers (in short the skilled

[59] *Labour Elector* (10 Aug. 1889).
[60] Will Thorne, *My Life's Battle* (London, 1925), 84.
[61] J. Burns, 'Great Strike', *New Review* (Oct. 1889), 416.

workers in the Docklands) had been organized, but these were only a minority. The mass of workers were strangers to trade unions, but

the need for action was in the air, and Ben and his most immediate Union colleagues were watching and taking part in developments. Ben had helped in the agitation for the Gas Workers' improved conditions and had determined to get something done for the mass of Dockers, when the men at the South West India Dock, Poplar, showed that they had been preparing for action. They were getting a wage of five pence an hour, and 'plus'. . . . A sailing vessel named the *Lady Armstrong* was in the dock and the men who discharged kept careful tally on their account, as to time and tonnage, and were expecting at least a penny per hour plus, but the local dock superintendent refused to admit their claim and the men refused to accept the bare time rate. Investigation on the part of the office resulted in an additional halfpenny being offered but the men declined to take less than a penny 'plus'. The local superintendent said he would not deal with the matter further, the men must go to the Dock House in the City. No redress being obtained, and the help of the Union asked for and given, Ben Tillett took the matter in hand. As he knew where he could find me in the City, about midday on August 14 I received a wire from Ben asking me to meet him at South West India Dock. I was informed of the necessary details on arrival and the men were assembled for a meeting in the Dock premises. From that time till it was over five weeks after I gave no attention to previous jobs; the rest is a twice-told story.[62]

Tom Mann did not even mention the name of Harris. Apparently Harris's attempt to form a union was only an episode irrelevant to the development of the drama or something Mann did not approve of—an early case of rival unionism.

Now Tillett, in an article written evidently as an answer to Burns's allegations, declared himself to have been 'the originator and organiser of the late strike'.[63] 'A fortnight before the great strike', he said, 'I sent a letter to the dock officials, setting forth the claims of the men, and asking for some mild reforms. A formal acknowledgement was the only result of my application.' Tillett had been holding regular Sunday morning meetings at the East India Dock gate, and on Sunday 4 August he spoke on the recent developments of the working-class movement. On the following Sunday, 11 August, there was a much larger attendance at his meeting, a reflection of the simmering dispute over the 'plus' in discharging the *Lady*

---

[62] T. Mann, 'Dock Strike of 1889 and After', *Labour Monthly*, 20: 9 (Sept. 1938), 548–51.

[63] B. Tillett, 'Dockers' Story', *English Illustrated Magazine*, 3: 74 (Nov. 1889), 97–101.

Armstrong in the dock. 'On the following day [12 August], after discussion among themselves, a deputation came to me with a request that I would place the men's demands as drawn up by themselves before the dock officials, and ask that an answer should be given on the next day.' The time was short, but he remembered that he had written to the management a fortnight before asking for reform without receiving a satisfactory reply. 'The men were determined, and it was with difficulty that I prevailed upon them, when no answer was received to their satisfaction in the time stated, to continue to work for the remainder of the day [i.e. 13 August].'[64]

Tillett was more frank when years later he wrote in his memoirs that 'I could hardly believe my ears' when on the night of 12 August two members of his union, Marshall and Fitzpatrick, came to him with a demand that his union should declare a strike at the South-West India Dock: 'months of heartbreaking effort and organization amongst the poverty-stricken and dispirited dock workers had not encouraged me to expect any such manifestation'.[65] With the secretary of the struggling union, now called the Tea Operatives' and General Workers' Union, placed in the centre of the conflict, on Wednesday 14 August 'a general strike [sic] was agreed upon, and after a meeting of the South Dock workers a procession was formed and a visit paid to the gates of the other docks. The enthusiastic shouts of the men soon acted as a call to arms to those working within', wrote Tillett.[66]

Tillett ignored Harris's union altogether in his accounts and memoirs. It so happened that on the third day of the strike, when a meeting was held in the evening at the school in Hack Road, Tidal Basin, to decide the course to be taken by the men employed at the Victoria and Albert Docks where the men had already been paid 6d. an hour, Tillett the main speaker referred to Harris's union as 'composed of the dock companies' officials'. A man stood up in the audience and challenged the speaker, calling him 'a liar!', and a row ensued until the man was ruled out of order.[67] Harris's union had originally been intended for the permanent men, and Tillett's and ordinary dockers' antipathy to the 'Royals' or the preferred permanent men was apparently deep-seated and widely shared.

Tillett in his *Brief History of the Dockers' Union: Commemorating the 1889 Dockers' Strike* (1910), which gives a day-to-day account of the strike, emphasized the continued existence of

[64] Tillett, 'Dockers' Story', 101.   [65] Tillett, Memories, 119.
[66] Id., 'Dockers' Story', 101.   [67] Star (17 Aug. 1889).

his union since its beginning in July 1887. Although its membership was decimated by the defeat of the Tilbury strike in
November 1888 and both it and Tillett were overshadowed by
the remarkable success of the Gasworkers in the following
spring, the Tea Operatives' Union which was soon to become
the Dockers' Union was not in such a moribund state as John
Burns sought to imply. 'Little' Ben now undertook the leadership of the great army that began a bold assault on the dock
companies that controlled the greatest port in the world.

4. The London Dock Strike

'The "Tanner" or A General Strike'

THE riverside labour force in East London suffered chronic unemployment. A great many of them were casual labourers, whose somewhat irregular life has been emphasized and even romanticized by the historians of the strike Smith and Nash. They were 'the drift of all classes', for 'the failures in every branch of life, professional, commercial, and industrial filter down through the various strata of labour until they reach the lowest layer of all'; many a story was told of a '"casual" Lord' or 'a black prince who had exchanged the air of the Falkland Islands [!] for that of the Isle of Dogs' or a former doctor who kept a silk hat and a black coat at a tavern.[1] They were the objects of public curiosity and sympathy, and of slumming and charitable assistance. But the dock labourer was 'a man radically different from the creature of whilom popular imagination', wrote Burns: '"The forlorn hope of the army of labour" he always was; but neither degraded nor a loafer. . . . The coals we blew upon were working-men; oppressed, beaten down; but working-men still, who had it in them to struggle, and to fight, for their daily bread.'[2] Between the lines of description by Tillett of the East London casuals such as 'we . . . are among the "Lazaruses" that starve upon the crumbs from the rich man's table', we can read his determination to help them regain 'the dignity of their manhood'.[3]

These casuals, however, constituted 'a broad fringe' of the labour force on the waterfront.[4] As we have seen, Tom Mann pointed out that there were skilled workers and specialists connected with port work. The stevedores, engaged in the relatively skilled work of loading for the export trade, well organized and better paid, formed a 'higher class' on the waterfront.[5] The lightermen and watermen were entrenched in

---

[1] H. Llewellyn Smith and Vaughan Nash, *Story of the Dockers' Strike* (London, 1889), 24–5.   [2] J. Burns in *New Review* (Oct. 1889), 414.

[3] B. Tillett, *Dock Labourer's Bitter Cry* (London, 1887), 20.

[4] John Lovell, *Stevedores and Dockers* (London, 1969).

[5] Smith and Nash, *Dockers' Strike*, 23.

a close corporation nearly two centuries old and held a strategic position in a labour dispute on the waterfront. The seamen and firemen with a two-year-old union of their own were also to play a vital part in the coming struggle. There were other cases of specialization: timber porters and corn porters at the Surrey and Millwall Docks, whose arduous work required a strong physique and considerable skill, were mostly country-born and regularly employed, forming a class apart.

An interpretation of the strike would depend largely upon an attitude to and an understanding of the dock workers, whether to view them as the object of charity and public sympathy, or to regard them as the workers who would try to regain their self-respect by themselves by means of a concerted action to control the conditions of work. It was the Webbs who emphasized the former view, while introducing a new definition of the strike, applied, first of all, to the matchgirls' victory which they regarded as epoch-making: 'Hitherto success had been in almost exact proportion to the workers' strength. It was a new experience for the weak to succeed because of their weakness by means of the intervention of the public.'[6] Indeed, the role of public sympathy had a strong influence on the conduct of the strike as well as on the interpretation of its character.

We now return to the beginning of the strike to find out what really happened. It was on the night of 12 August that Tillett formulated the men's demands in writing: four hours' call as a minimum, an increase in wages to 6d. an hour and 8d. overtime, abolition of the 'plus' system, and alteration of the existing contract system. The letter dated 13 August was addressed to the deputy-superintendent of the West India Dock and was delivered on the morning of that day, probably by Tillett himself who went to the South Docks and 'parleyed with the management'.[7] The letter requested a reply before the noon of the same day, which was an impossible condition, and Tillett knew it. The management complained that the strike which practically commenced on the afternoon of 13 August was a 'carefully prearranged' surprise attack.[8] Tillett, however, advised the men to work till the evening of that day so as to give more time for the management to reply, and at a meeting of his

[6] Sidney Webb and Beatrice Webb, History of Trade Unionism (new edn., London, 1920), 402.
[7] B. Tillett, Brief History of the Dockers' Union (London, 1910), 17.
[8] H. J. Morgan, secretary of the London and India Docks Joint Committee, to the editor of The Times, published in The Times (23 Aug. 1889).

union held in the evening of 13 August, it was unanimously decided, as there had been no reply by then from the company, not to return to work until their demands were met.[9] The ultimatum expired on the noon of 13 August, but the strike was officially decided upon on that evening.

'On Wednesday, August 14, we began our big movement, little dreaming the portentous results or meaning of the fight now begun', recalled Tillett.[10] He at once sent a telegram to Tom Mann, asking him to share the burden of strike organization. He remembered that Mann had spoken at Deptford Green with 'virility and force': 'He oozed the energy of being'.[11] About 400 men were out on the first day at the South Dock alone, of which 200 were members of Tillett's union.[12] The strikers led by Tillett sought to persuade the workers at the East India Dock to come out, and returned to West India Dock gates to hold a meeting, which was addressed by Tom McCarthy and Tom Mann who had hurried to the scene of battle. *The Times* put the number of the dockers on strike on the following day, 15 August, at about 2,500 and described their demonstrations as 'orderly'.[13]

On Friday 16 August nearly 10,000 men were out on strike. It was on this day that the first procession of the strikers—about 2,000 strong—marched along Commercial Road to the City, and to Dock House, the headquarters of the London and India Dock Joint Committee, in Leadenhall Street. On arrival at the destination a deputation of six headed by Tillett were given an interview with C. M. Norman, the chairman of the joint committee, and some other directors, in the course of which it transpired that the company would promise nothing unless the men had returned to work. On behalf of the delegation John Burns, now making his first appearance as a leader of the strike, announced the results of the interview to the men who assembled outside the London Dock. Burns had many excellent qualities for such a role. He combined the fame of the 'hero' of Trafalgar Square with a newly acquired reputation as a member of the London County Council. Added to this he had the prestige of being a member of the executive council of the ASE, probably the largest trade union in the world. His career already symbolized the transformation of wild rebellion into orderly progress. He appealed splendidly to the masses. His voice was stentorian, and his speech commanded attention by

[9] *Labour Elector* (17 Aug. 1889).   [10] Tillett, *Brief History*, 19.
[11] Ibid. 16.   [12] *Labour Elector* (17 Aug. 1889).
[13] *The Times* (16 Aug. 1889).

virtue also of its picturesque idioms. 'He was our best show-man', admitted Tillett: 'He wove wonderful happenings out of inventions; the pressmen listened and were astounded at the wonderful things to be.'[14]

This first procession to the City was enlivened by the parti-cipation of a number of stevedores carrying the banners of their unions: they had turned out, protesting against the importation of 'blacklegs' into the South Dock. The councils of the two stevedores' unions, Amalgamated and United, met on Saturday (17 August) at the Blue Post in the West India Dock Road to discuss the matter. Tillett pleaded with them, and the victory inside of the war party led by Tom McCarthy was welcomed by the dockers and stevedores outside 'amid a scene of wild enthusiasm and a display of coloured fires'.[15] Their manifesto issued on the 18th stated their reason for action: 'We feel it our duty to support our poorer brethren'.[16] On Monday 19th about 1,800 stevedores came out and joined the labourers on strike.[17] With their experience in organization and administration, the stevedores provided 'the backbone of the strike'.[18]

The same Monday saw a vast extension of the strike: the men at the Victoria and Albert Docks came out, and the London and St Katherine Docks were effectively picketed by John Burns. Tillett took the early train to Tilbury in company with Harry Orbel, president of his union, who was to lead the difficult strike at Tilbury with tact and determination. By Tuesday 20th the strike had extended to all the docks. The following day the Lightermen met at the York Minster in Philpot Street and decided to cease work 'until the dock companies concede the just demands of the men'; they added some demands of their own for a reduction of their long hours of labour.[19] On Thursday 22nd the Seamen, too, decided to join in the strike, 'to help the Stevedores'.[20] The Surrey Commercial men also came out. By the middle of the week 'from Tilbury to Upper Thames Street', wrote Tillett, 'all that means ships and quays is idle, as from Gravesend to Blackfriars Bridge the human bees . . . are in revolt'.[21]

[14] Tillett, *Brief History*, 25; see also *The Times* (17 Aug. 1889), and Smith and Nash, *Dockers' Strike*, 37.

[15] Smith and Nash, *Dockers' Strike*, 40; Lovell, *Stevedores and Dockers*, 104.

[16] First Manifesto of the Two Stevedores' Unions, 18 Aug. 1889, in Smith and Nash, *Dockers' Strike*, 175.   [17] *The Times* (20 Aug. 1889).

[18] H. H. Champion, *Great Dock Strike in London* (London, 1890), 16.

[19] Smith and Nash, *Dockers' Strike*, 66.

[20] *The Times* (23 Aug. 1889).   [21] Tillett, *Brief History*, 21.

The two stevedores' unions at once set up a strike committee at the Wade's Arms in Jeremiah Street, Poplar, with James Toomey of the Amalgamated, 'a big and lusty man' as Tillett recalled, as its chairman. 'The stevedores' council is rapidly assuming the position of a sort of Parliament in this huge strike of riverside men', reported the *Star*.[22] Tillett's union for its part set up a committee at its headquarters at Wroot's Coffee-House nearby. They had only 7s. 6d. to start with in their exchequer for fighting purposes and a few pounds in arrears,[23] but the proceeds of collections began to come in. On the 20th a finance committee was set up to organize relief work, with Burns as secretary and Mann treasurer. It was, however, only after the amalgamation towards the end of the week of the two committees and the setting up of the United Strike Council at the Wade's Arms that any effective relief was worked out.[24] Wroot's, nevertheless, remained the picketing headquarters and pay-office throughout the strike. There Tom Mann performed 'what is demanded of a strike field marshal', planting himself in the doorway with his foot raised against the wall and allowing each one of a crowd of 4,000 men to creep under his leg to get a ticket: 'Hour after hour went by, while Tom Mann, stripped to the waist, stuck to his post, forcing the men down as they came up to him, chaffing, persuading, remonstrating, whenever the swaying mass of dockers got out of control, until at last the street was cleared.'[25]

On 30 August *The Times* reported that some 80,000 of the poorest men in London were out and in spite of the help they received 'the sight is one of the most pitiable upon which the human eye could rest'.[26] In order to keep the idle men occupied, and to sustain their morale, a daily procession was instigated. It took on such a huge dimension that the one on the 21st 'circled right around the triangle formed by Leadenhall-street, Gracechurch-street, and Fenchurch-street': the heart of the City was encircled by the starving men.[27] The procession also had an air of festivity. The one on the 23rd, one of the largest in the strike, wound its way from Tower Hill to the City. 'There were eight brass bands and many drum and fife bands, and a large number of flags and banners', reported *The Times*;

There was also a large addition of allegorical groups in wagons, representing the coal heavers, the ship scrapers, the hydraulic men,

[22] *Star* (22 Aug. 1889).   [23] Tillett, *Brief History*, 20.
[24] Smith and Nash, *Dockers' Strike*, 63.   [25] Ibid. 94–5.
[26] *The Times* (30 Aug. 1889).   [27] *Star* (22 Aug. 1889).

and the lightermen, who brought some boats, all fully manned. Represented in the procession, too, were the dockers' children, thin and ill-clad, contrasted with sweaters' children, well fed, plump, and well dressed. Then there were illustrations of the sweaters' well supplied dinners, contrasted with the bones, offal, and garbage which were representing as forming the dockers' dinners. The procession, which marched eight abreast and numbered over 70,000, after a long walk through the City, returned to the West India Docks.[28]

The police were friendly to the marchers from the start. John Burns boasted that 'the soldiers of the City are on our side'.[29] On reaching the City boundary the Metropolitan Police handed them over to the City police to the tune of 'Auld Lang Syne'.[30] The procession usually was headed by a small van 'in which John Burns's [white] straw hat, becoming well-known now as a sort of fiery cross of labour movements in London, waved to the men the direction they should take'.[31] This straw hat was said to have been suggested by the police because they wanted to know 'where to find the champion of law and order'.[32] Indeed, Burns would say to the assembled crowd on Tower Hill before the departure: 'Now lads, are you going to be as patient as you have been? ("Yes"). As orderly as you have been? (Shouts of "Yes"). Are you going to be your own police? ("Yes") Then now march off five deep past the dock companies' offices, and keep on the left hand side of the street.'[33]

The dockers' strike secured public support, the *Star* emphasized, 'because they show praiseworthy self-control. They have a good cause, and they have not marred it by excess'.[34] One night Burns appeared at the *Star* office. Stroking a bag he carried, he said: 'I collected in this bag alone £250 this morning.' 'This', he went on,

is the most democratic strike that ever I have seen. It has no leaders; it was not promoted from without, it is spontaneous, and it governs itself. ... The men are acting splendidly! Would you believe ... that not a single man throughout all the time of strain has come with a request for a half pint of beer?[35]

'The real, live part of the fight was in the picket line', wrote Tillett.[36] As the strike spread fast in the Docklands, the companies placarded the whole district with posters offering permanent employment to 1,000 men at £1 a week. The news

28 *The Times* (24 Aug. 1889).   29 *Star* (27 Aug. 1889).
30 Smith and Nash, *Dockers' Strike*, 35.   31 *Star* (19 Aug. 1889).
32 Smith and Nash, *Dockers' Strike*, 117.
33 *The Times* (28 Aug. 1889).   34 *Star* (22 Aug. 1889).
35 Ibid. (27 Aug. 1889).   36 Tillett, *Brief History*, 25.

that the companies had secured men from Liverpool caused great excitement; many of them employed at the East India Dock were persuaded by the pickets to come out.[37] When the Dundee Shipping Company brought in 70 men from the Scottish port, the pickets prevailed on 66 of them to come out. These men, however, demanded strike pay, or else desired to be sent home: there was a strong opinion among the strikers that they must have known the situation, and 'deserved to be made to walk back, or they could go to Poplar Workhouse'.[38] Tom Mann was given the task of paying special attention to picketing and organization on the south side of the river where the men worked mostly by the piece and found the 'Tanner' unattractive.[39] In spite of some such troubles and difficulties, the organization of picketing worked well. Guards were relieved every twelve hours, and inspectors were appointed to ensure vigilance. Pickets were out in boats and on railways. It was estimated that altogether several thousand blacklegs had passed into the docks during the strike but a great majority of them were soon induced to come out. The police wisely kept themselves in the background as far as possible, and this reduced the conflict to a minimum.[40]

The true nature of the strike came to the surface in the last week of August. On the 28th a conference was held all day at the Dock House as a result of the intervention by the wharfingers led by Henry Lafone of Butler's Wharf, and granary owners, who had been hoping for a compromise in the dispute. Burns, Tillett, and Mann were invited, and the men's demands were further clarified. It became known late in the evening that the conference was suspended over the issue of a penny increase in wages.[41] In fact, the management had been shrewd enough to perceive the crucial importance of the other demands, especially abolition of the contract and subcontract system, which would affect the current method of control of work: this they astutely accepted in principle, obtaining the reluctant consent of the delegates for a postponement of its implementation until a later date.   Thus the real issues of decasualization and control of work were relegated to the background, and the epic struggle of the dockers was presented as a fight for 6d., the dockers' 'tanner'. Moreover, the directors hoped that their uncompromising attitude on this

[37] *The Times* (22, 23, 24 Aug. 1889).   [38] Ibid. (27 Aug. 1889).

[39] Smith and Nash, *Dockers' Strike*, 131.

[40] Ibid. 106, 115.   [41] *The Times* (29 Aug. 1889).

one issue would soon bring about tangible results: exhaustion of the men and collapse of their morale.

As the conference was somewhat confused, so were the reports in the newspapers. 'Victory Near', read a headline in the *Star*.[42] Apparently labour was partly resumed. 'There were more loaded and unloaded vans passing to and fro in the broad thoroughfares. . . . More life, too, was visible on the river', reported *The Times*.[43] Engels, in a letter to his friend connected with the strike committee, most likely Eleanor Marx, wrote: 'I envy you your work in the Dock Strike. It is the moment of the greatest promise we have had for years and I am proud and glad to have lived to see it. If Marx had lived to witness this!'[44]

The strike committee, however, was not so sanguine as the *Star* or Engels would appear to have been. Indeed, the strike was bound to collapse, if work was seriously resumed without a satisfactory agreement. Moreover, the number of men on strike increased faster than the size of the strike fund, so much so that the strike committee had to issue a manifesto on the 26th, criticizing 'the rash action' taken by unorganized workmen not directly connected with the docks of coming out on strike.[45] On the 29th the minute-book of the strike committee for the first time revealed that funds were running short and it was decided to post up a notice telling the men that no further relief was available that day.[46] The directors' strategy appeared almost to have succeeded. Hunger began to gnaw into the hearts of the men. The crush at the committee-rooms for relief tickets was 'fearful': 'many had to go empty away. But the last words of Messrs. Mann and Tillett, "Be patient with your wives and children, men", and "You, women, be brave", were not without their desired effect', read a report in *The Times*.[47]

The impatience and anxieties of the strike leaders soon found clear expressions in their speeches. Burns's speeches became more forceful and threatening. He accentuated his attack on the dock directors, 'financial Jack the Rippers' as he called them, with such remarks as 'Upon what compulsion, Shylock?'[48] Tom McCarthy, who presided over the demonstration in Hyde Park on Sunday 25th, informed the audience of the new moves among the Gasworkers who were considering

[42] *Star* (29 Aug. 1889).   [43] *The Times* (18 Aug. 1889).
[44] *Labour Elector* (31 Aug. 1889).
[45] Smith and Nash, *Dockers' Strike*, 177.   [46] Ibid. 74.
[47] *The Times* (29 Aug. 1889).   [48] Ibid. (26 Aug. 1889).

a sympathetic strike to 'put London into darkness unless the demands of the dockers were granted'.[49] On the following day the Gasworkers' officials denied the rumour that they had already been out on strike, and at a meeting at the dock-gates Will Thorne explained that his union could not advise a strike of its members partly because seven days' notice was required. Instead the Gasworkers decided to contribute £50 for the relief of the strikers.[50] On the 28th Burns declared in a speech that he had been 'too polite with the dock directors' and that if the whole of London came out he would still 'march at the head'.[51] On the following day Tom Mann addressed the strikers at a meeting held at the Custom House, telling them the men 'might be called on to take more definite and decided action in more ways than one'. Havelock Wilson, too, delivered 'a speech of considerable vehemence' in which he said, he 'did not discourage the idea of a general strike' and emphasized 'the notion of a struggle of capital and labour'.[52] If shipping were to be diverted from London to other ports, his union would block every port in the United Kingdom.[53]

Indeed, Tom Mann was 'very kind' to Wilson, and came to have a special liking for him as a dogged fighter in industrial disputes. The seamen, whom Wilson had organized into a national union, had been engaged in sporadic strikes for a wage increase on many ports earlier in the year when prosperity returned to the shipping trade. Moreover, sailors and dock workers were closely tied to each other by the nature of their work: when sailors struck, dockers found themselves out of a job and vice versa.[54] The Seamen now gave full support to the London dockers on strike. Their representatives visited every ship on the Thames and persuaded them not to undertake the dockers' or stevedores' work. These efforts were so successful that the American crews on three American cattle boats not only refused an offer of 2s. 6d. an hour to do the stevedores' work but left the ship and joined the strikers' procession.[55] Wilson, who admitted he was 'a provincial man', was emerging as a national figure by identifying himself with the cause of the London dockers now in open revolt.

Born in Sunderland in 1858 as the son of a foreman draper,

[49] *The Times*; *Star* (26 Aug. 1889).   [50] *Labour Elector* (31 Aug. 1889).
[51] *The Times* (29 Aug. 1889).   [52] Ibid. (30 Aug. 1889).
[53] *Star* (26 Aug. 1889).
[54] H. A. Clegg, Alan Fox, and A. F. Thompson, *History of British Trade Unionism since 1889*, i (Oxford, 1964), 56–8.
[55] Ann Stafford, *Match to Fire the Thames* (London, 1961), 118.

Wilson, like Tillett, went to sea at an early age. Apprenticed to a shipowner, he served as a seaman in various capacities. After his marriage, he came ashore permanently in deference to the wishes of his wife whose father had been drowned at sea. He owned a temperance hotel at Sunderland, which served as the meeting-place of his union.[56] Tom in his memoirs described Wilson as 'a straightforward, honourable, and loyal comrade': 'he was always at his post early in the day, tackling the most difficult tasks with the utmost readiness'.[57] Wilson obviously fully supported Tom when the latter suggested a general strike for the London dockers, and this will explain much of the reason why Tom held Wilson in high esteem in spite of his difference with him in other matters related to labour and politics.

Apparently from about 25 August the idea of a sympathetic or general strike had been mooted among the strike leaders partly for fear of a quick collapse of the strike and partly from the desire to threaten and compel the management to accept the men's terms at once. These deliberations came to a head when on the evening of Thursday 29 August the strike committee met and formally discussed the idea of a general strike. Tom Mann proposed its adoption. The debate that followed was 'so excited . . . that the minutes were forgotten'.[58] Mann, Champion and a certain Smith, most likely G. Smith of the United Stevedores, were asked to form a subcommittee to draft an appeal to the trades in London to cease work in twenty-four hours. 'Wiser counsels prevailed', wrote Champion, and Monday was substituted for Friday as the day for the general strike.[59] The 'No-Work Manifesto', as it was called, read in part:

Our studied moderation has been mistaken by our ungenerous opponents for lack of courage and want of resources. We are therefore compelled to take a step which we are fully aware may be followed by the gravest consequences. We now solemnly appeal to the workers of London of all grades and of every calling to refuse to go to work on Monday next unless the directors have before 12 noon on Saturday, 31st of August, officially informed this committee that the moderate demands of the dock labourers have been fully and frankly conceded.

[56] J. McConville and John Saville, 'Joseph Havelock Wilson', in *Dictionary of Labour Biography*, iv (London, 1977), 200–8.
[57] T. Mann, *Tom Mann's Memoirs* (1923; London, 1967), 207.
[58] Smith and Nash, *Dockers' Strike*, 75.
[59] Champion, *Great Dock Strike*, 18–19.

A restatement of the men's demands was followed by forty-six signatures including all the representatives of the stevedores' unions, the Sailors' and Firemen's Union, and some of the most important East London trades.[60] It was expected that in the Sailors' and Firemen's Union alone, 60,000 men would be involved, and the strike leaders appointed picketing parties to wait on each of the large firms. 'Local committees are being appointed, and firm promises received', wrote the *Star*. Its headline unmistakably stated the issue of the strike: 'The "Tanner"—or a General Strike'.[61] The tanner had become the symbol of public sympathy for the dockers, and the headline could be rephrased as public sympathy or direct action which would invite public outcry.

In fact, the manifesto was 'almost universally condemned', wrote Champion.[62] *The Times* denounced it as 'a deliberate attack upon the social organisation of the metropolis'. The more sympathetic *Star* hoped that it would not be put into effect.[63] Smith and Nash later called it 'a counsel of despair'.[64] *Justice* denounced it as 'the most treacherous manifesto' produced by the 'middle-class political tricksters', implying that Champion among others was responsible for it. In fact, Champion the former military officer had been very active on the strike committee, frequently inspecting 'the innumerable pickets engaged night and day' in their difficult task.[65] Engels the military strategist, however, regarded the manifesto as 'a very foolish resolution', because this was 'playing *va banque*, staking £1000 to win possible £10' and 'casting away wilfully all the sympathies of the shop-keepers and even of the great mass of the bourgeoisie who all hated the dock monopolists'— in short 'a declaration of despair'.[66]

Everyone, from Engels to the *Star* and *The Times*, expected that the men would win only with the help of public opinion and public support, with the bourgeoisie in sympathetic neutrality.

[60] *The Times* (31 Aug. 1889); Smith and Nash, *Dockers' Strike*, 178.

[61] *Star* (30 Aug. 1889); *The Times* (31 Aug. 1889). The role of public opinion in the London Dock Strike was rightly appreciated by Ken Coates and Tony Topham in their joint work *New Unionism: the Case for Workers' Control* (Harmondsworth, 1974), 25, in which the Dockers' victory was described as 'the first social victory of the emerging mass media'.

[62] Champion, *Great Dock Strike*, 18.

[63] *The Times* (31 Aug. 1889); *Star* (31 Aug. 1889).

[64] Smith and Nash, *Dockers' Strike*, 124.

[65] *Justice* (7 Sept. 1889); Champion, *Great Dock Strike*, 24.

[66] F. Engels to Laura Lafargue, 1 Sept. 1889, in Friedrich Engels, *Engels-Lafargue Correspondance* (Paris, 1956), ii. 316–17.

Moreover, as Champion wrote, 'those who were on the spot and were acquainted with the strength and the weakness of the Dockers' position' thought otherwise. Given the financial position, the barometer of public sympathy, as it stood on the 29th, it was obvious that the strike could not go on much longer and the directors would win. On the other hand, people like Tom Mann and Havelock Wilson had a faith in direct industrial action to compel the reluctant employers to come to terms. But they took realistic views of the situation. Apparently the manifesto was intended in its first stages to provide pressure single-handedly on the management. Thus the dock directors were given three days of grace instead of twenty-four hours as originally planned.

What took place in these three days decided the course of the strike. First of all, it became clear that the organized trades 'were not going to show such self-sacrifice as had been exhibited by the Stevedores' and Sailors' Unions', wrote Champion, 'though they were prepared, if the manifesto was withdrawn, to make very heavy levies upon their members' to help the dockers.[67] A Boilermakers' deputation called the manifesto 'a very wrong action to take', while promising financial help on the understanding that it be withdrawn.[68] This weighed more heavily with the strike leaders at Wade's Arms than the moral support of Cunninghame Graham, who outside the West India Dock shouted hoarsely: 'Revolution was not made with rose-water. ... I call on you to paralyze all industry in every trade in the metropolis.'[69] Even so, the promised help from the trades was not certain, for the name of the Boilermakers did not appear on the list of the contributors among the British unions, and their contribution remained modest as a whole.[70]

There were other developments on that day, Friday 30th. Cardinal Manning, who had family connections with one or other of the dock companies, began to intercede with the Dock House, pointing out to them 'the growing gravity of the crisis'. Another portentous event was the arrival of the news that the Wharf Labourers' Union and the Federated Seamen's Union, Brisbane, had sent £150 and £100 respectively to help the

[67] Champion, *Great Dock Strike*, 19.
[68] Smith and Nash, *Dockers' Strike*, 124.
[69] *The Times* (2 Sept. 1889).
[70] Strike Committee, London Dock Strike of 1889, *Great Dock Labourers' Strike 1889: Manifesto and Statement of Accounts: An Epitomized History* (London, 1889), 12–15.

London dockers on strike.[71] They could expect even more from that source.

The dock companies received the manifesto 'with equanimity',[72] and persisted in their rigid attitude, while the wharfingers and shippers renewed their effort for a settlement on Saturday morning. That afternoon, Burns and Tillett went to the Dock House, and after a three-hour meeting the joint committee of the dock companies announced that they were not prepared to accept proposals submitted. Later at night Tillett told *The Times* reporter:

Negotiations have been curtly refused by the dock companies. . . . The so-called concessions of the dock companies are not concessions at all. . . . Now the directors want to introduce a system of piecework which is task work, and that means the substitution of sweating task for contract work. . . . They are carrying out in a callous manner their threat to starve us. . . . We are only pledged to the ultimatum we have issued, to which we adhere.[73]

During the whole of Saturday the No-Work Manifesto was the subject of anxious talks in the East End as well as in the City. Tillett now felt that he had not been properly consulted in drafting the controversial document. Apparently he was not consistent in this. At a meeting of the strike committee on that night he secured Tom Mann as a seconder for a more conciliatory policy. In the small hours of Sunday morning 1 September, the No-Work Manifesto was formally withdrawn by issuing a countermanding manifesto inviting the workers of London to 'supply us with the sinews of war'.

On that day Tom Mann spoke from a wagon in Hyde Park:

He carefully explained the position of the dock labourers and the reasons which had induced the strike committee to withdraw their manifesto. He said that this course had been taken because by letter and by word of mouth various trade unions promised funds if it was withdrawn. 'We wanted', he protested, 'to show that we were acting rationally'.[74]

It was Tom Mann, the realist, who with Tillett cancelled the planned general strike. Smith and Nash cynically remarked: 'Tom Mann might at least congratulate himself on the success of his strategy in arresting the attention of the [other] unions. . . . The moral support of the public had been the mainstay of the strike so far, and was not to be trifled with for the sake of a

---

[71] *The Times* (31 Aug. 1889).   [72] Ibid. (2 Sept. 1889).   [73] Ibid.
[74] Ibid.

few trades union pounds.'[75] In effect, 'trades union pounds' amounted to a little over one third of the public sympathy expressed in money terms. Yet public sympathy obviously was not enough to win the war. Meanwhile, industrial action was curbed and restrained.

The prospect at the beginning of September, however, was not so dismal as it might appear from the tactical retreat, or even the blunder, as it might seem to many, of the strike leadership. The final breach between some of the wharfingers and the dock companies which took place at the time seemed to justify the withdrawal of the No-Work Manifesto and the adoption of the new tactic of boycotting special employers. On 4 September the strike committee concluded an agreement with Lafone of Butler's Wharf who had accepted the men's terms. In the small hours of the following morning work was resumed at Butler's Wharf: 'without any delay, a steamer laden with fresh currants from Greece was brought up for the purpose of being unloaded'.[76] By 9 September altogether twenty-two wharfs had accepted the men's terms. The tactic of 'splitting the enemy ranks', as Tom Mann called it, doubly benefited the strike committee which was now relieved of feeding so many mouths, while strike funds were increased by the contributions of the men now working at certain wharfs. The ship-owners, too, were pushed to the verge of 'revolt against the dock companies'.[77] The Lafone arrangement, however, caused some trouble to the specialized men on the south side of the river where the conditions of work were different from the north; it was probably at this stage that Tom Mann was sent there to assist the South Side Central Strike Committee at Sayes Court to co-ordinate diverse demands of deal porters, lumpers, corn porters, and others, and worked for their acceptance by the wharfingers and the granary owners.[78]

Coupled with the disarray thus created on the employers' front, the unprecedented support of the working classes and others in Australia finally turned the scale. It was a generous race: two Australian banks competed with each other for the privilege of sending remittances without charges. Victoria alone sent nearly £20,000 and the total Australian contribution amounted to over £30,000, almost three times as large as the amount raised by domestic public sympathy.[79]

[75] Smith and Nash, *Dockers' Strike*, 124.   [76] *The Times* (6 Sept. 1889).
[77] Ibid. (3, 6, 10 Sept. 1889).   [78] *Star* (11 Sept. 1889).
[79] Smith and Nash, *Dockers' Strike*, 120, 127.

The intervention of the Lord Mayor began. On returning from his tour in Scotland, Alderman Whitehead invited Cardinal Manning, the Bishop of London, Sir John Lubbock (president of the London Chamber of Commerce), Sir Andrew Lusk (acting mayor while Whitehead was away), and Sydney Buxton to confer with him at the Mansion House. The object was to bring about a settlement of the strike by allowing the dock directors to beat a retreat with as much dignity as possible. After some more attempts at delaying the inevitable on the part of the employers, especially about the date of enforcing the new agreement about to be adopted, and with Cardinal Manning tenaciously persisting in his role as a mediator even when the men's representatives were accused of 'breach of faith' in the course of the tortuous negotiations, the men's demands were substantially accepted on 14 September to be implemented from 1 November.

On Monday 9 September, when the end was still uncertain, John Burns made 'one of his finest speeches'. He appealed to the men to stand together till the end. 'This, lads, is the Lucknow of Labour . . . and I myself, looking to the horizon, can see a silver gleam—not of bayonets to be imbrued in a brother's blood, but the gleam of the full round orb of the docker's tanner.'[80] All men were to return to work the following Monday, 16 September. The day before, the last procession marched to the sound of the 'Marseillaise' and 'Rule Britannia' from the East and West India Docks via the Mansion House to Hyde Park where Tillett spoke on the value of a union to the men and the imperative need to keep the pledge. Burns delivered his last oration in which he touched on socialism, one of the few occasions he did so. 'I, as a Socialist, say that you must not let the rich have all that makes life tolerable' and urged the men to seize every opportunity to educate themselves. 'For the rest', commented *The Times*'s correspondent, 'he was in a moral mood, and the sternest Puritan living would have found nothing to reprehend, but rather much to praise.'[81] A new leaf was turned in his record as an agitator, and in fact in the pages of working-class history.

The port of London was reopened on 16 September. Tillett's Tea Operatives' and General Labourers' Union changed its name to the Dock, Wharf, Riverside, and General Labourers' Union of Great Britain and Ireland (usually referred to as the Dockers' Union). Its membership rose to 30,000 by the end of November. Tillett remained secretary, Mann became president,

[80] Smith and Nash, *Dockers' Strike*, 147.   [81] *The Times* (16 Sept. 1889).

and Burns one of its auditors. The strike council, before its dissolution, published a manifesto and a statement of accounts. It emphasized that the strike had been an industrial action, 'conducted to the end without any socialistic political leadership, religious or sectional elements being allowed in the fight'. As we have seen, this was hardly correct. It also expressed 'our high esteem' to the Australian people, the Trades' Hall, Melbourne, the *Melbourne Age*, and their London representatives for their support. It thanked the English public and press, the Commissioners of the Police, and especially Miss Margaret Harkness the authoress, who was the first to ask for the help of His Eminence Cardinal Manning—who, together with Sir James Whitehead and Sydney Buxton, gave great assistance to the men. The expenditure on the strike amounted to £41,307 of which the sum of £21,396, just over one half, was spent on food tickets, which were the major form of relief. Payments to various trade unions involved in the strike for support of their members totalled £12,260: the largest share, £4,606, went to the Amalgamated Seamen and Firemen's Union and there was £2,338 for Tillett's Dockers' Union. Another conspicuous item in expenditure was £1,251 for 'Pickets and Banner Bearers'. Income totalled £46,499 of which the largest item was 'Remittance from the Colonies: £30,423'. Compared to this, contributions from British trades were rather modest, headed by £670 from the ASE, followed by £301 from the London Society of Compositors, £213 from the Co-operative Wholesale Society, and £104 from the Amalgamated Society of Railway Servants. The balance stood at £5,202.[82] Cardinal Manning took pains to remind Burns of the pledges he had given when he received a cheque from the Lord Mayor and wrote:

any remaining balance ought not to be scattered by distribution, because among so great a number no effectual help could be given by small sums. But that it ought to be held in hand for the permanent advantage of the Dock Labourers by strengthening their Union Benefit Society, or some such general & permanent distribution.[83]

True to the Cardinal's advice, Burns became an exemplary auditor for the Dockers' Union.

Burns was right when he said that the London Dock Strike had been 'spontaneous' and 'democratic', but he was on doubtful ground when he added that it had 'no leaders'. It was in fact

---

[82] Strike Committee, *Great Dock Labourers' Strike 1889: Manifesto*, passim.
[83] Cardinal Manning to J. Burns, 28 Nov. 1889, BL Add. MS 46286, JBP.

due largely to the leaders' tact and patience in dealing with the men as well as the employers that the strike ended in a victory for the workers. Burns's contention may have been a concession on his part, because there had been persistent rumours of a split in the leadership between Tillett and Burns. *The Times* noticed 'some considerable difference of opinion' between the two, 'one point in particular being as to who really was the head of the strikers'.[84] Tom Mann, for his part, was free from any such egotism, and kept himself busy with the task of bringing the south-side dockers into harmonious relationships with the strike leadership on the north side.

Champion pointed out four factors that had contributed to the success of the strike: five weeks of uninterrupted dry and fine weather, rare in London in summer; the return of industrial prosperity; effective picketing; and 'fair play' by the police.[85] The most obvious effect of the strike, according to Smith and Nash, was decasualization. Organization and regularization of dock labour now began. This process, by securing increasingly regular work to the 'fitter' section of the labourers, would squeeze out 'the lower-class casuals', the residuum. This, they said in truly Fabian fashion, would help separate the treatment of 'social disease' from the essentially different problem of dealing with the claims of labour.[86] It was on the strength of their argument that the apparently Social Darwinist aspect of the effects of the Dock Strike has attracted considerable attention. Not only the new, positive attitude of the middle class towards trade-unionism but also the role of trade unions among the unskilled workers has been treated as conducive to decasualization by separating the fit from the unfit.[87] This is the view which, Tillett would say, was an elaboration of 'the office standpoint'. The fact is that decasualization did not take place to such an extent and in such a way as the working-class leaders, even the middle-class sympathizers for that matter, desired. Tillett, as we have seen, advocated regularization of dock work in his testimony to the Lords' Select Committee, and again in 1891 he complained of 'the irregularity of employment' on the waterside in evidence given before the Royal Commission on Labour. In spite of the abolition of the contract system after 1889, the same casual labour continued, 'only that those responsible for it are not the sub-contractors, but the respect-

---

[84] *The Times* (2 Sept. 1889).   [85] Champion, *Great Dock Strike*, 23–5.
[86] Smith and Nash, *Dockers' Strike*, 164–5.
[87] Gareth Stedman Jones, *Outcast London* (London, 1971), 317.

able dock company, the honourable shipowner'.[88] Tom Mann, on the other hand, welcomed the abolition of the contract system in the docks mainly because it seemed to guarantee an increase in the jobs available.[89] What Tillett and Mann were after was 'an absolute popular control of the dock', as Tillett stated in his evidence,[90] and the municipalization of the docks that they advocated was a step in that direction. To this problem we shall return later.

As recession set in in the winter of 1890–1, the company-led process of decasualization came to be 'regarded by many port workers as a system of slavery'.[91] It is fair to conclude that the dockers' victory in 1889 'did not open the route to decasualization'.[92] But the recent emphasis on the attractiveness of casual labour, 'a traditional, almost pre-industrial rhythm of work and leisure',[93] shows the reverse side of the coin described by Beatrice Potter. What Beatrice had condemned is now adulated and idealized. It is an idealization of 'pre-industrial' culture which was in fact born of hard labour and privation under industrialism, communal sharing of hardship, and a little luxury, such as the one night's bed offered to a friend described by Tillett.

In 1889 the dockers obtained their 'tanner', but the greater aim of their struggle—control of their work, decasualization under their own control—was not attained. Not only was it not obtained, but it also led to the beginning of modern class warfare on a gigantic scale. In fact, public sympathy shown during the strike soon gave way to class antagonism. The use of 'free labour' aggravated class conflict and confrontation. London Dockland after 1889 did not become a paradise for Social Darwinist reformers nor an idyllic enclave of pre-industrial culture. The Webbs once compared the work of the SDF in the 1880s to that of the Owenites in their role as fomenters of a larger movement. In a similar vein it is possible to compare the Dock Strike and the revolt of the unskilled workers to the mobilization of the masses in Chartism. In fact, the veteran Chartist George Julian Harney was so impressed by the dimensions of the 1889 strike that he went out of his way to

---

[88] British Parliamentary Papers, Royal Commission on Labour (Industrial Relations, 26; Shannon, 1970), session 3558, p. 63.
[89] Gordon Phillips and Noel Whiteside, Casual Labour (Oxford, 1985), 63.
[90] Ibid. 254.
[91] Lovell, Stevedores and Dockers, 136.
[92] Phillips and Whiteside, Casual Labour, 44.   [93] Ibid. 33.

describe it as the revival of 'Chartism at its best'.[94] What he sought to emphasize by this remark was the new awakening of the working class as a class. New Unionism which was now spreading among the unskilled was bound to be class-conscious and class-based.

[94] *Labour Elector* (28 Sept. 1889).

5. New Unionism and Class Conflict

BORN out of an industrial battle, the Dockers' Union was bound to be a class-based union from the start, and it was soon caught in a series of disputes that became fierce as recession set in in the winter of 1890–1. Public sympathy was replaced by class conflict in the years of employers' offensive that followed. Eric Hobsbawm once wrote that 'the "New Unionism" of 1889 . . . became uncomfortably like the "old unionism" it had once fought', for from 1892 to 1910 it took the form of a 'cautious, limited, and conservative "sectional" unionism'.[1] This is to ignore the seriousness of the employers' offensive which began with the formation of the Shipping Federation, and drove the unions, new and old, into the defensive position which should be distinguished from mere conservative sectionalism. Hugh Clegg also suggested that the epithet 'New Unionism', 'militant, class-conscious, and socialist', was a 'myth . . . too far from the truth to be sustained for long'.[2] Both Hobsbawm and Clegg, though from opposite points of view, maintained that New Unionism with its legend or myth of solidarity and militancy had been ephemeral and transitory. Hobsbawm in his later study,[3] however, revised his position and has come to regard the labour unrest of 1911–13 as 'a continuation . . . of the process initiated in 1889'. He now points out that 'the shock of 1889 . . . precipitated permanent changes in attitudes not only among unions but among employers, politicians and government administrators'. To examine the 'permanent changes' in the light of working-class experience; to see what problems Mann, Tillett, and Burns among other 'New Unionists' (and Wilson in so far as he related to the 'trio' of 1889) had to face in the years of confrontation between capital and labour, with the latter taking the defensive position; to see how they gradually built up a strategy for labour in class struggle—these are some of the issues to be dealt with in this chapter.

[1] Eric Hobsbawm, *Labouring Men* (London, 1964), 191.
[2] H. A. Clegg, Alan Fox, and A. F. Thompson, *History of British Trades Unionism since 1889*, i (Oxford, 1964), 96.
[3] Eric Hobsbawm, *World of Labour* (London, 1984), 152, 157.

For about one year after the London Dock Strike, the organization of unskilled workers went almost unchecked, and about 200,000 new men found themselves in some trade unions. Shortly after the end of the strike, Burns along with Jack Williams and several others, ventured on an ambitious scheme to form a National Federation of Labour Unions. Their manifesto called upon the skilled workers to 'join with the labourers' for 'greater security from combination among masters'. 'The time has come when we meet combination with combination', it declared: 'At present, the great Army of Labour is split up into sections and divisions, whose leaders are, in most cases, the tools of political parties'. It aspired to set up a 'great "Parliament of Labour"'.[4] The scheme did not come to much, but it illustrates well the aspirations of New Unionism. Burns, who rivalled Tillett in the strike leadership, was now in great demand among the Dockers: he was asked not only to address branch meetings, but to accept an honorary branch membership (Wapping), to unfurl a new branch banner (Tidal Basin), and to allow a branch to call itself 'The John Burns Branch' (Dundee No. 2).

In the meantime the Liverpool TUC of September 1890 became the scene of challenge by the New Unionists against the old unionist leadership. Union opinion had been moving rapidly away from the stance taken at the 1887 congress, when Henry Broadhurst who was secretary to the TUC's Parliamentary Committee and had served in Gladstone's Liberal administration, championed individualism and self-reliance for the workers. The presence of the New Unionists at Liverpool ensured the passage by 198 to 158 of a motion in favour of an eight-hour labour law.[5] Two New Unionist leaders, Havelock Wilson and John Burns, were elected to the Parliamentary Committee.

On 8 September, on his way home from Liverpool, Burns delivered a speech at a meeting organized by the Stove-Grate Workers at Rotherham. He emphasized that the workers' victory in a dispute was due simply to 'a well-drilled and well-disciplined organization' among themselves, not to philanthropic sentiment nor even to mass processions of the strikers. He predicted that the TUC would grow into 'a parliament of skilled and unskilled labourers': should the 'Imperial Parliament' refuse legislation recommended by the TUC, the workers'

[4] Manifesto (20 Sept. 1889), Newspaper cutting, BL Add. MS 46289, JBP.
[5] A. E. P. Duffy, 'Eight-Hour Day Movement in Britain 1886–1893', *Manchester School of Economic and Social Studies*, 36 (1968), 214.

parliament would have to expel such a legislative body and establish itself as the 'Imperial Parliament'. His exultant rhetoric was greeted with cheers and applause. He also stated his views of the role of a new union: sickness, old age, and unemployment benefits should be dealt with by legislative measures, especially by progressive taxation on the upper and middle classes, while trade-unionism itself should remain 'pure and simple', chiefly concerning itself with getting higher wages and shorter hours, and possibly better housing. Hence, the New Unionists should try their best to 'invoke the aid of the state' and should be 'socialistic' in its aims.[6] His views on the New Unionist tactics were further clarified in a speech delivered at Battersea later in the same month. He was in favour of an eight-hour day by legislation. If trade unions should seek to achieve an eight-hour day by voluntary combination alone, he argued, they would be forced to resort to a general strike, civil war, and revolution, and the contest between 'the bright steel sword of political action' wielded by the rich and 'the leathern scabbard of trade unionism' would simply be unequal and one-sided. They ought to fight, said Burns, through the ballot-box and in Parliament.[7]

Mann and Tillett, for their part, were defending New Unionism with a slightly different accent in their joint pamphlet on the subject. They asserted that the old unionist view of new unions as being dependent upon legislation was 'bunkum', an unworthy prejudice, and that methods to change the industrial system should be 'on a strictly trade union basis': the 'sturdy spirit of independence' should be encouraged and undue reliance on Parliament should be avoided; 'the key-note is to organize first and take action, in the most efficient way, so soon as organization warrants action, instead of specially looking to Government'.[8] They quite optimistically believed that 'the political machine will fall into our hands as a matter of course, so soon as the educational work has been done in our labour organizations'. Like Burns, they emphasized the need for organizations, 'dealing with trade matters only', concerned primarily with reduced working hours and higher wages. 'Poverty, in our opinion, can be abolished', they declared,

and we consider it is the work of the trade unionist to do this. . . . Our trade unions should be the centre of enlightenment. . . . The

[6] J. Burns, *Trades Unionism, Past, Present, and Future* (Rotherham, 1890).

[7] Id., *Liverpool Congress* (London, 1890), 15.

[8] T. Mann and B. Tillett, *'New' Trades Unionism: A Reply to Mr. George Shipton* (London, 1890), 14–15.

organization of those who are classed as unskilled is of the most vital importance. . . . The man or the woman who honestly toils, no matter in what capacity, is of the most vital concern to the community; and his or her surroundings should be equal to those of any other citizen.[9]

Indeed, New Unionism was presented as 'a new enthusiasm', 'a real religious fervour', a new crusade to promote 'a cosmopolitan spirit', 'brotherhood', and thus the precursor of a co-operative commonwealth. It placed a special emphasis on the dignity of labour and of man and created a tradition that has aptly been called 'an emancipatory trade unionism'.[10]

A similar 'religious fervency that demands as a right the happiness of the toilers' was prominent in the secretary's report to the Dockers' first annual congress held in September 1890.[11] A year later when they held the second annual congress at Hull in increasingly difficult circumstances, the spirit of buoyancy still remained with the leaders. At a banquet held at the Queen's Hotel, Tillett declared: 'Labour is an eloquent theme; Labour will rule. It becomes us to see the toiler shall rule, not only in the factory, but shall improve until we govern every institution which is for the people'.[12] Tom Mann, for his part, at a reception given by the mayor of Hull, made an eloquent speech 'on the right of culture':

It is culture we are striving for; it is culture we are yearning for; it is culture we must have—(applause). We don't admit that the men of Oxford and Cambridge should have the monopoly of culture—(hear, hear). . . . There is a dignity in labour. We won't talk much about it, we will prove it—(applause).[13]

Many years later Tom Mann recalled that it was William Morris who enabled him to 'get a really healthy contempt for Parliamentary institutions and scheming politicians'.[14] It is not easy from this brief reference to trace the genesis of Mann's non-governmental, proto-syndicalist orientation, but we can safely conclude that the 1889 London Dock Strike was a real watershed in his socialist thinking. His first pamphlet on a 'compulsory' eight-hour day and his activities in Champion's

---

[9] Mann and Tillett, *'New' Trades Unionism*, 4–5, 9.

[10] Ibid. 15; Ken Coates and Tony Topham, *New Unionism: The Case for Workers' Control* (Harmondsworth, 1972), 31.

[11] *Dockers' Record* (Oct. 1890).

[12] Dock, Wharf, Riverside, and General Labourers' Union, *Ben Tillett's Address on 'Man's Individual Responsibility'* (London, 1891), 18; *Trade Unionist* (26 Sept. 1891).

[13] Dock, Wharf, Riverside, and General Labourers' Union, *Tom Mann's Presidential Address* (London, 1891), 20.

'Shop Hour Regulation Committee' indicate that he was thinking of the question in social democratic terms at least until the strike. In a pamphlet written in May 1889, he expressed the hope that the TUC would bring pressure on the Government to limit working hours.[15] Two years later another pamphlet appeared on the same subject in which Mann referred to the discord after the Liverpool congress between the 'legalists' and the 'voluntary men' on the eight-hour issue, and suggested 'a middle course': the eight-hour day should be established by law and put into optional effect by the trade and locality. He had arrived at this position partly because of a split in the voting of the members of the ASE on the question, there being a two to one majority in favour of trade-union effort as against legal enactment. He was now firmly convinced that 'local autonomy in these matters is right in principle, and beneficial in practice, whereas to encourage the notion that Parliament is an all-wise institution, and capable of dealing with the details of our complex industrial system is wrong in principle, and bad in practice'.[16] An amendment in favour of trade option on this issue was carried at the Newcastle TUC of 1891. No wonder John Burns the 'legalist' wrote in his diary that Mann had 'done more harm to 8 hours than any other man since [the Liverpool] Congress'.[17] This was perhaps one of the earliest revelations of the serious difference between Mann and Burns on many issues of the Labour movement.

In fact, Burns became increasingly critical of the Dockers' leadership for pushing themselves forward on many fronts, including the publication of the *Trade Unionist* their new newspaper, which replaced the old *Dockers' Record*. 'Saw Mann, told him and Tillett about expenses £480 for *Trade Unionist*', read an entry in Burns's diary;

and urged him not to use it even though Executive passed it. Told both that they were hedging on political action, had a stiff talk. Both determined not to work with us. Positively sure that before long the Dockers Union will collapse unless greater economy is practised and the leaders devote more time to organising their own men instead of spreading themselves over districts where no permanent work is done.[18]

[14] T. Mann, 'Recollections of Morris', *Daily Worker* (24 Mar. 1934).
[15] Id., *Eight Hours Movement* (London, 1889), 19.
[16] Id., *Eight Hour Day: How to Get It by Trade and Local Option* (London, 1891), 17.
[17] J. Burns, Diary, 13 Apr. 1891, BL Add. MS 46311, JAP.
[18] Ibid., 31 July 1891, BL Add. MS 46311, JBP.

The crucial issue of New Unionism was how to cope with the employers' offensive which became increasingly open and well organized. The first new union to score a considerable success, the Gasworkers, was the first to retreat: at the South Metropolitan Gas Works non-unionists were brought in to replace the 2,000 strikers who were out in the winter of 1889–90. 'I haven't seen Will Thorne since I was with you,' wrote Mann to Burns: 'They had better compromise pretty quickly or very few of the two thousand will get back again.'[19] Soon it was the Dockers' turn to suffer. 'The membership in London is still shaky, but quite safe for all that,' wrote Mann towards the end of 1890: 'The total membership now stands at 57,000 against 61,000 10 weeks ago. This must not surprise or dishearten us. The men haven't got the money & can't pay. All will be well by Spring.'[20] The peak of their strength had apparently been reached by the summer of 1890. In fact, no sooner did the great strike of 1889 come to an end than fresh trouble began on London's waterfront.

Part of the trouble came from the fact that the Dockers failed to persuade foremen and permanent employees to join their union. Indeed, it was decided that union men should refuse to work in any department where the foremen and clerical staff had not become members of 'a union',[21] but these men soon organized themselves in company unions of their own and would not accept the Dockers' leadership. Another vexed question was that the dockers south of the Thames, on whom Mann had had a certain influence during the strike, were now entrenched in a separate union, the South Side Labour Protection League, and Burns's flirtation with them caused 'great dissent among our men', wrote Mann and Tillett.[22]

Then the problem of 'examination of tickets' became serious by the summer of 1890. As early as February that year Mann wrote to Burns: 'The Dock Company is making strenuous efforts to get us in a serious difficulty. They are now determined not to recognise the men's representatives & are taking on non-Union men. This means serious trouble.'[23] The agreed practice of union representatives checking union cards of men at the

[19] T. Mann to J. Burns, 4 Jan. 1890, BL Add. MS 46285, JBP.

[20] T. Mann to J. Burns, 19 Dec. 1890, BL Add. MS 46285, JBP.

[21] T. Mann to Mr. Cop, 9 Nov. 1889, Dock Companies Joint Committee Documents, National Museum of Labour History.

[22] T. Mann and B. Tillett to J. Burns, telegraph, 11 Nov. 1889, BL Add. MS 46285, JBP.

[23] T. Mann to J. Burns, 13 Feb. 1890, BL Add. MS 46285, JBP.

calling stations outside the docks was now thrown overboard by the Dock Company. A police officer wrote to the manager:

After the men out at the London Dock left this morning, they proceeded with Tom Mann to Tower Hill where a meeting was held of about 1200 men. Mann told the labourers that all they asked was that they should be allowed the practice of showing their Union tickets at the London & St. Katherine Docks, the same as they now did at the East & West, and South West India, & the Victoria & Albert Docks.[24]

The men's resistance, though apparently successful at the time, only lasted as long as trade remained prosperous.[25]

The problem was also related to the substitution of piece-work for contract work: the company's 'Proposed Scheme of Piecework' for a gang of men to work 'on co-operative principle', one of the terms of settlement of the Dock Strike, was soon withdrawn, and it was announced that only the company's foremen would take on the men. Mann and Tillett protested in vain against what they regarded as a breach of the agreement.[26] Moreover, the Dock Company handed over the discharging operations in the large downstream docks to the shipping companies from early 1891, and concentrated on the upstream docks where they relied mainly on the permanent men organized in a company union. As Lovell pointed out, this 'virtually killed the Dockers' Union' in that area.[27]

Mann had a difficult time even with the men. The Mansion House Settlement of September 1889 had actually settled very little but rather encouraged the dockers to resort to some form of industrial action to remedy various grievances. The union leaders were sometimes overwhelmed by the men's demands. 'We have decided to stop strike pay so as to choke off those who would gladly hang on for months', wrote Mann to Burns;

so we reduced strike pay to 8/- this week & 6/- for two following weeks giving the £1 in a lump to those who are to take it. About 400 have done so but we have had a hell of a time. I am obliged to carry a revolver. They threatened all kinds of nice things, going to make soup of me, & so on, but I reckon I'll come allright in the end.[28]

Already at the first annual congress of the Dockers' Union Mann had had to emphasize 'discipline of the strictest kind'.

[24] B. C. Child to the Managers, 24 July 1890, Dock Companies Joint Committee Documents, National Museum of Labour History.

[25] John Lovell, *Stevedores and Dockers* (London, 1969), 131–2.

[26] Dock, Wharf, Riverside and General Labourers' Union, Circular to the Members, 27 Nov. 1890, Webb Trade Union Collection, BLPES.

[27] Lovell, *Stevedores and Dockers*, 135.

[28] T. Mann to J. Burns, 30 Apr. 1890, BL Add. MS 46285, JBP.

What they needed was 'not extension but solidification'. 'Already we have a number of distinct trades', said Mann, 'such as copper smelters, cement workers, coopers, millstone makers, &c., besides those engaged in the ports, and we certainly do not require any others.' Apparently the union had to set its house in order so as to make it less vulnerable to the attacks from the employers, and there was all the more reason for this as the formidable Shipping Federation had just come into existence with the declared purpose of destroying union power on the waterfront. John Burns, equally aware of the grave situation, said to the delegates: 'They are meeting at a crisis not only in the history of their union, but of the great Labour movement.' He strongly urged them to be cautious in their policy. 'They had not too much money, and if they would permit him to say so, he thought they should be "off" with strikes for a time.'[29]

It was at the downstream docks, where the strength of the Dockers' Union now largely concentrated, that a dispute between the Sailors' and Firemen's Union and the British India Line developed into a head-on clash of the two opposing forces: the United Labour Council of the Port of London, an offspring of the Wade's Arms Strike Committee of 1889, and the shipping companies backed by the Shipping Federation. The Sailors and Firemen, Wilson's union, had the same difficulty as the Dockers, for so-called 'free crews' had been signed in on board ships. On 3 December, the day announced for a general strike, not only the sailors of the fleets concerned, but also the coalies, the shipworkers, carpenters, painters, and various other trades represented on the council, came out in support of the sailors. The Dockers' Union, which was not yet represented on the council, did not join in the fray at this stage. There is extant a copy of a Post Office telegraph, though without date, sent from Burns to Mann at the Dockers' Union, Mile End Road, telling him 'Don't be drawn by East End London Manifesto, all Trades court defeat for one union'.[30]

The Shipping Federation took immediate steps through agencies round the country to get free labour to replace those on strike. The nucleus of free labour came from Kent. 'We brought up from there about 150 men', later boasted George Alexander Laws, general manager of the federation, before the Royal Commission on Labour;

[29] *Dockers' Record* (Jan. 1891).
[30] J. Burns to T. Mann, telegraph, n.d., BL Add. MS 46285, JBP.

probably the finest workmen you could see anywhere, men from Rye, Romney, Lydd, men of splendid physique—nothing like it in London—men accustomed to seaside work, to canal work, to loading and unloading barges, men who had also been accustomed to coaling in London in a strike which had taken place the year before at one of the gasworks in London, and the same agents who supplied these men to the gasworks also supplied me in this case.[31]

Apparently these were mostly agricultural labourers used as semi-professional scabs. The Shipping Federation further approached the Commissioner of Police to obtain protection for the 'free labourers'—'the most effective arrangements were made by the police. They adopted our plans for putting them on board, and everything was done in the most quiet and orderly way, possibly rather helped by an extremely dense fog which held the city of London for three days at that time'. When 'a mob of the coalies' began to throw stones at the scabs in the barges, it was the Metropolitan Police who cleared the docks and let the work go on.[32]

The presence of the Kentish 'free labourers' on the London waterfront caused tension. It was at this time that the Dockers' Union decided to start a campaign among agricultural labourers to enrol them in the union with a reduced entrance fee and to demand 'small holdings with fair rents' for them, a strategy obviously intended to cut off a major source of the supply of blacklegs.[33] In February Mann and Tillett decided to 'black' all ships of the offending shipping companies,[34] but remained cautious not to extend the dispute too far, while the stevedores were divided among themselves over the issue of joining the strike. In March the dispute ended in a defeat for the men.

Meanwhile, the Shipping Federation extended its operation early in 1891 to the Bristol Channel. Cardiff became the storm centre where dock companies, shipowners, coalowners, and railway interests were mobilized in a concerted attack on the seamen and then on the dockers who came out in sympathy with them. Harry Orbel, Tillett, and then Mann came to help Havelock Wilson who, charged with 'unlawful assembly and riot', was imprisoned: the seamen's strike collapsed, and the Cardiff dockers gave in; the Shipping Federation now freely

---

[31] *British Parliamentary Papers*, Royal Commission on Labour (Industrial Relations, 26; Shannon, 1970), Evidence, Group B, Q.4954 [p. 345].

[32] Ibid.   [33] *Dockers' Record* (Jan. 1891).

[34] T. Mann and B. Tillett, Notice to the Members of the Dockers' Union, 12 Feb. 1891, BL Add. MS 46285, JBP.

enforced its 'tickets'.[35] In the course of the Cardiff struggle John Burns had occasion to see Tom Mann. He wrote in his diary:

I told him to localise strike at Cardiff to be beaten there rather than be drawn to London to be smashed by masters. Told him also that he was unconsciously being used by Wilson and as there was no direct issue to fight on, a compromise to extricate themselves must be decided upon. Predicted collapse of Unions if they did not mark time and consolidate position won by strike.[36]

Burns's advice was not acted upon immediately by Mann, largely because he had a more aggressive union policy, and in this he was closely allied with Wilson.

During the shipping dispute in London in the winter of 1890-1, when the Shipping Federation was able to open free labour establishments in each of the downstream docks, an attempt was made on the workers' side to set up a more viable federal body to deal with events. One such body comprising the Dockers' Union, the Sailors, and the South Side Labour Protection League came into existence in January 1891, and in September it was merged with the United Labour Council. The 'Federation of Trades and Labour Unions connected with the Shipping, Carrying and Other Industries', as it was called, of which Havelock Wilson became president and in which Tom Mann played an active part, was soon called to help the 300 dockers at the Wapping wharfs who in October 1891 went on strike against a wage cut due to non-payment during mealtimes. The blacklegs introduced by the Shipping Federation at once began their work under police protection. Some of the 'free labourers' were armed with revolvers and threatened to shoot the pickets, but the police officers in charge refused to interfere.[37]

The Wapping struggle became the scene of a direct confrontation of the two federations, of the employers and of the workers, but the balance of power was heavily tipped against the unarmed and unprotected workers. Thus Burns advised Mann to 'try in the interests of the preservation of the Unions to bring about a settlement, even at the cost of giving up the interests of the 300 men, to defend which may—I believe,

[35] Dona Torr, *Tom Mann and his Times 1890-1892* Our History Pamphlet, 26-7; (summer-autumn 1962), repr. in *Luddites and Other Essays*, ed. M. Mumby (London, 1971).

[36] Burns, Diary, 11 Feb. 1891, BL Add. MS 46311, JBP.

[37] *British Parliamentary Papers*, Royal Commission on Labour (Industrial Relations, 26; Shannon, 1970), Evidence, Group B, Q.8640 [p. 547].

will—jeopardise the Riverside Unions and through them the whole labour movement'.[38] Tom in his reply apparently mentioned the possibility of a general strike, and Burns immediately wrote back, saying 'You have nothing to gain by extending the dispute except to finish yourselves.'[39] As there was little hope of winning the strike, Mann had to accept Burns's advice, and spoke in favour of terminating the dispute. 'Dear Jack. It is not quite so simple a job as your letter would imply', wrote Mann:

I have had three hours with the strike committee. I urged the necessity of closing after getting every fact in connection with the business. They are not willing to close believing they can yet score if they get support of other Unions. Now I have been one to encourage the formation of the Federation and now that it exists it must at least be recognised or we shall not be able to federate after. Perhaps you know it has taken years to bring so much about. Well, last night the Executive of this Federation met, a decent set of fellows too, & *I was unable to bring them to my views.* They believing it possible to do great good, & of course there is this chance at any rate that determined action will prevent a *general reduction* which is contemplated if this goes down.

He would try again to 'close it' but such an attempt would 'sectionalise & antagonise'.[40] The strike dragged on and at the end of the seventh week it was finally abandoned. At a meeting held on this occasion, Tom Mann addressed the defeated men: referring to the pressure to end the strike 'weeks ago', he declared: 'the Dockers' Union was essentially democratic and would not yield its guidance to any autocracy'.[41]

Sometime before the end of the Wapping strike, Burns had warned Tillett against his and Mann's ineffectual leadership:

I tell you frankly that this conduct on your part [to prolong the strike] is almost criminal when at the same time you are spending your time and energy and the Dockers' money in going to religious conferences and addressing meetings in different parts of the country, where dockers' interests cannot be served. As a trustee of the Union I protest against it and as a man I am compelled to say that the conduct of this dispute is the saddest blow that your Union has received. If it is a case of rats leaving a sinking ship, say so candidly.[42]

[38] J. Burns to T. Mann, 5 Oct. 1891, BL Add. MS 46285, JBP.
[39] J. Burns to T. Mann, 9 Oct. 1891, BL Add. MS 46285, JBP.
[40] T. Mann to J. Burns, 11 Oct. 1891, BL Add. MS 46285, JBP.
[41] *Morning Advertiser* (2 Nov. 1891), quoted Dona Torr, *Tom Mann and his Times 1890–1892,* 217.
[42] J. Burns to B. Tillett, 17 Oct. 1891, BL Add. MS 46285, JBP.

The stricture of 'rats leaving the sinking ship' was evidently directed against Mann's candidature for the general secretaryship of the ASE. There was always a certain discordance in the relationship between Mann and Burns owing to their different stance on trade-unionism and political power. But why had Mann decided to stand for the leadership of the Engineers at this stage? Certainly he was not leaving the sinking ship of the unskilled workers. His answer to the Shipping Federation or the organization of the employers in general was to confront it with a better organization of the workers, which was not an easy task. In view of the perilous and exposed situation in which the new unions found themselves, Mann must have thought of mobilizing the strength of the oldest and most powerful trade union.

There was a rumour that Burns also had decided to stand. Though Burns did not actually stand, he refused to help Mann. 'Dear Tom', wrote Burns, 'I have carefully considered your request for my name on your Committee for Engineers and after the most anxious thought and deliberate consideration have decided not to take any part in the election whatever.'[43] Apparently Burns was not willing to bring the ASE into confrontation with the employers: he was in full favour of tactical retreat on the industrial front, though politically he was prepared to make an advance. There may have been an element of jealousy at the back of his mind. At any rate, Mann's election committee, with George Barnes acting as secretary of its London committee, started an active campaign, and Mann himself in his election manifesto urged the need for the ASE to enlarge its basis so as to admit electricians, for instance, in response to technological progress and thus to lead the labour movement as its vanguard. He was narrowly defeated by a candidate of the old school, John Anderson, who won 18,102 votes as against Tom Mann's 17,152. Mann wrote in a letter of thanks to his supporters: 'I entered the contest in the hope of assisting others in stimulating some of the latent energies of our members to increased activity', and the heated campaign did bring to the ASE 'a new lease of life'.[44] At the delegate meeting of 1892, full membership was opened to wider sections of the industry, low-paid and unskilled workers were allowed into special sections, and the way was opened to raise the necessary funds to participate in national politics. Ironically, John Burns elected as MP for Battersea in the general election

[43] J. Burns to T. Mann, 24 Oct. 1891, BL Add. MS 46285, JBP.
[44] James B. Jefferys, *Story of the Engineers* (London, 1945), 113, 136.

of July 1892 was to receive an annual grant of £100 from his union.

Shortly after the ASE election, Burns wrote in his diary:

Went to Dockers union, inspected books. The office seemed stricken with despair and helplessness. . . . Saw Mann and told him to pocket his pride and stay with the men who made him and Tillett. He was displeased at my refusing to assist his candidature. Told him to make his position clear on legal 8 hours. If Mann leaves Union Tillett must go as he is not capable of the detailed work and that continuity of common sense necessary for the post. Mann is disenthused to a great extent. The Laws, Nashs, Hollands and others have damaged the Tom Mann in him. Told him plainly my views of his economic hobbling.[45]

We have already noted the roles played in the London Dock Strike by Vaughan Nash and by Miss Margaret Harkness, who used the pseudonym of 'John Law' for her writings on East End workers. Canon Scott Holland who became aware of the crucial importance of the industrial problem was the leader of the Christian Social Union that came into existence in 1889. The agnostic Burns thus deplored the increasingly religious bent in Mann which we shall examine more closely in the following chapter. Apparently Mann found himself in an impasse as regards the Dockers whom he did appear to be 'deserting' by aspiring to assume the leadership of the ASE. At the annual conference of the Dockers' Union held at Swansea in September 1892, he resigned his post. Thereafter the Dockers under Tillett's leadership fought losing battles against the employers' offensive which became formidable and culminated in the men's defeat at Bristol in 1892–3 and another at Hull in 1893.

These two defeats, in fact, provided a heroic epitaph for New Unionism which was about to be crushed in relentless class warfare. The Bristol dispute arose in November 1892 when timber merchants in the city hired non-union men and the members of the Dockers' Union walked out in protest; they were replaced by blacklegs supplied by a Shipping Federation representative. In the absence of Tom Mann, Tom McCarthy, now the organizer for the Dockers, took charge and organized the strike. At a meeting held on 18 December, Tillett allegedly made a violent speech: 'if it came to a fight', he cried out, 'they fight too, with fists or clubs, and if it came to guns they could pick them up also. . . . I will if necessary, defend my home and

45 Burns, Diary, 26 Apr. 1892, BL Add. MS 46312, JBP.

wages by any means, violent or pacific'.[46] Tillett in his memoirs recalled: 'I made it clear in the most emphatic and definite terms that if organised violence was directed against the strikers, similar measures would be taken on our side.'[47] For this speech he was charged with sedition and tried at the Old Bailey, but found 'Not Guilty'. The Bristol struggle however dragged on and ended in a defeat of the men. Tom McCarthy prepared a petition signed by 12,000 men asking the Lord Chancellor to appoint worker–magistrates in Bristol: 'The very employers who are fighting the men sit on the bench & try cases arising out of present dispute. We have 25 men in jail more than half of whom are absolutely innocent of even the intention to break the law', he wrote to Burns, asking him to introduce 'our deputation', to an appropriate member of the House.[48]

Then came the strike at Hull in March 1893 when the Shipping Federation opened a 'Free Labour Bureau' in the docks along the Humber. In April Tillett sent an urgent appeal from Hull to John Burns:

The position here is damnable, damnable, for the bench of magistrates not only have the soldiers with 40 rounds of ball cartridge, but two gunboates. . . . I dont want any of you to act in any undignified [way], but this silence is killing in the face of the grave danger to the men here. With you new bloods we ought to have a different set of conditions in the House. It is a case of sheer brute force against our common right to combine.[49]

Tillett came to London the following day. With him Burns went to Toynbee Hall, which had provided a meeting-place for strike leaders at the time of the London Dock Strike, and there he moved 'a resolution calling for Funds for Hull, advising settlement on best terms possible to keep Free Labourers out, and a national conference to discuss the whole situations'.[50] Three days later Clem Edwards, formerly the Dockers' assistant secretary, then prominent in the Federation of Trade and Labour Unions on the waterfront, came to see Burns on the question of a possible national strike. He advised Edwards to urge the men not to strike unless called out by their union. At the same time they could 'show their resentment of Shipping Federation by burning the S.F. Tickets as would lead the S.F. to

[46] Quoted in Jonathan Schneer, *Ben Tillett: Portrait of a Labour Leader* (London, 1982), 82.   [47] B. Tillett, *Memories and Reflections*, 162.

[48] Tom McCarthy to J. Burns, 26 Apr. 1893, BL Add. MS 46285, JBP.

[49] B. Tillett to J. Burns, 11 Apr. 1893, BL Add. MS 46285, JBP.

[50] Burns, Diary, 12 Apr. 1893, BL Add. MS 46313, JBP.

keep their reserve Blacklegs in London for probable use'.[51] The following day, Sunday, Havelock Wilson called on him: he was definitely for a general strike. 'Sitting there with his open handsome sailor face, full of fight and energy', wrote Burns, 'I quietly combatted [*sic*] his arguments for the strike being extended to all ports. I urged him to continue his skirmishing at different ports, as it would keep the S.F. busy, raise the Sailors' wages, increase membership of Union but would not appreciably help Hull.'[52] Mann was also involved in the Hull dispute. He was present at a national conference held on 22 April to discuss a national strike to help Hull. 'I moved amendment against it', wrote Burns, 'and spoke vigorously against the policy of attempting for so small an issue so great a risk. Thorne seconded, and at end of debate Mann supported. Carried by 45 to 27. . . . Judging by Mann's report Hull men were not pleased with intervention for settlement of strike.'[53]

In the crisis of the trade-union movement Burns was convinced that the proper tactics to be adopted would be to avoid a strike as far as possible, to settle it quickly once it had started, and to contain the influence of the Shipping Federation by other means, possibly political, including industrial guerrilla warfare on a national scale. Somehow he 'prevailed upon C. H. Wilson [the Hull employer] to negotiate direct with Strike Committee and thus terminate strike'.[54] It is difficult to say whether Burns's tactics did not play into the hands of the employers and the Shipping Federation. The latter and its 'free labour tickets' triumphed in Hull in five weeks.[55]

Burns believed that 'trade unionism had in the past only been successful in so far as it had invoked the aid of the State'.[56] While urging the unions to be cautious under the circumstances, he would fight inside the State apparatus and strive to back them up from within the State. Tillett, on the other hand, saw how the Shipping Federation actually operated on the waterfront. At the second annual congress of the Dockers (Delegate Meeting), he attacked the federation, 'an aggressive body who, whining about the brutality of Trade Unionists, have yet armed men with bludgeons, revolvers, and supply of intoxicants, to be guilty of the worst ruffianism—

[51] Ibid., 15 Apr. 1893, BL Add. MS 46313, JBP.
[52] Ibid., 16 Apr. 1893, BL Add. MS 46313, JBP.
[53] Ibid., 22 Apr. 1893, BL Add. MS 46313, JBP.
[54] Ibid., 15 May 1893, BL Add. MS 46313, JBP.
[55] Lovell, *Stevedores and Dockers*, 122.
[56] J. Burns, 'Eight-Hours Day', *Daily Graphic* (3 May 1890).

gangs of half-drunken men who have resisted with violence men fighting for dear life [and for] the principle of fair remuneration'.[57] Pugnacious as he ever was, he was ready to fight back, provided that he was armed with sufficient organization. The dilemma with him was that the very organization, his only support, had been handicapped and languished in what Burns would call 'an unequal fight'.

In May 1890 when New Unionism was at its height of strength and Tom Mann was busy organizing the first May Day in London, he boldly declared the beginning of class war in an article in the *Nineteenth Century*. He emphasized an attempt recently made by the employers in the shipbuilding and engineering trades to form themselves into a national federation with the object of providing 'mutual support in resisting interference by workmen's associations with free contract work'. He went on:

Thus we shall shortly witness national federations of capitalists and workmen facing and fighting each other in a manner that will make the struggles of the past insignificant by comparison. It is no use any crying peace when there is no peace; it is of small use preaching moderation to workmen while employers are changing their old 10-pounders for '81-tonners'. Correspondingly we workers must do the same.[58]

His argument was double-edged: it emphasized an urgent need for strengthening workers' organizations and fighting capacity, while at the same time he felt that 'more extensive organisation on both sides' would facilitate settlement of disputes by conciliation and arbitration.[59] Events that followed, however, were not of the nature that would encourage his optimism.

Later as a member of the Royal Commission on Labour, Mann had occasion to ask George Alexander Laws of the Shipping Federation about the use of 'free' labourers in the Cardiff dispute of early 1891. In Cardiff, said Laws, 'we kept them [free labourers] on board a steamer called the "Speedwell", and fed them like fighting cocks'.[60] Mann also asked about the advisability of establishing a joint board between the workers and the employers: Laws answered that it would be useless and hopeless because 'the time would be

[57] Dock, Wharf, Riverside and General Labourers' Union, *General Secretary's Report to the Annual Delegate Meeting* (London, 1891), 11.

[58] T. Mann, 'Development of the Labour Movement', *Nineteenth Century*, 27: 159 (May 1890), 713–14.

[59] Ibid. 715.

[60] *British Parliamentary Papers*, Royal Commission on Labour (Industrial Relations, 26; Shannon, 1970), Evidence, Group B, Q.5169 [p. 362].

taken up in discussing utopian subjects'. 'Then', said Mann, 'that would mean that there is nothing for it but to fight it out', and Laws agreed. Mann's faith in a sort of corporatism, as it was, was badly shaken, but he was a member of the Royal Commission on Labour. As such he made some more efforts to see whether Fabianism or some species of socialism other than naked class conflict would provide any satisfactory solution to industrial warfare.

6. Labour Politics

New Vistas and Labyrinths

THE New Unionist leaders, Mann, Burns, and Tillett among others, while engaged in a series of disputes with the employers, were searching for a way out of costly confrontation. The enthusiasm and confidence born out of conflict were now channelled into a succession of ventures, moral and political: Fabianism, the Labour churches, and the Independent Labour Party (ILP), itself the political expression of the ethos of New Unionism and the progenitor of the Labour Party. Labour politics, as it emerged in the 1890s, like SDF politics before it, was fraught with internal discord and feuding on matters of tactics which also involved personalities, and Mann and his friends were entangled, often deeply, in almost all these vendettas and squabbles.

Municipal socialism was in the air in the early '90s. John Burns represented it on the London County Council and promoted it at its committees dealing with highways, bridges, and main drainage. The Battersea Labour League gained the support of the Liberals in the constituency, and Burns's success at the general election of 1892 with a large majority against his Conservative opponent was a landmark in his political career. On the polling day telegrams of good luck came from Engels, Kautsky, and Eleanor Marx; and after the election congratulations and invitations to lunch and dinner arrived from Dilke, Buxton and other Liberals and Radicals. Joseph Chamberlain, now 'a colleague', sought Burns's advice on the current situation of the socialist movement. In his reply Burns emphasized that a large majority of the workers 'are drifting into Socialism'. He bluntly told him that the Webbs's collectivism was much more useful for municipal socialism than Chamberlain's individualistic approach. The SDF was of no account as it remained 'a small sect, independent but impotent'. He mentioned some of his friends as socialists: 'Mr. Graham and myself are socialists as are Mr. Mann and Mr. Champion. Mr. Tillett is not altogether that far yet.'[1] In an

[1] J. Burns to J. Chamberlain, 20 Sept. 1892, BL Add. MS 46290, JBP.

interview given shortly afterwards to a *Figaro* correspondent, he declared that 'We English are not so much in a hurry as they are on the Continent', and added that 'the trade unions are the horses which drag the cart of Socialism'. As for municipal socialism, he proudly pointed to the achievements of only 12 socialists out of 139 members of the LCC. 'No more contracts, no more middle-men!', he said;

And, besides, we have already taken from the companies 32 miles of tramway lines which are managed by the Council, and . . . at the expiration, very shortly, of the existing contracts, the Council shall take over the whole of the lines. . . . We shall bring into force the eight hour working day for all the employees! . . . But we don't stop at this. We shall also take the water. We shall let the gas alone, because it is a dead industry, but we shall take up electricity, in which the future is embodied.

Asked about his views on a general strike he answered: 'I think no more about it', but he was not altogether against industrial action. As to strikes in general, he said: 'I am opposed to them when trade is bad; that's not the time to commence. On the other hand, I am altogether in favour of strikes at times when business is good; Oh, then the psychological hour has come! Everything is permissible,—and you must make use of your advantage.'[2] That 'psychological hour' when business circumstances were propitious and the workers were on the move did not come to him for about twenty years until 1911, when he was to lament his own position and lack of freedom as a minister of the Liberal Cabinet.

Tom Mann was passing through a phase of Fabian socialism early in the 1890s. He seems to have been more open to new ideas and experiences than Burns, as he was perhaps more consciously trying to develop and elaborate a socialist strategy in the struggle against the organized employers. His own Fabianism evolved largely from his own work on the Royal Commission on Labour, set up early in 1891 as one of the immediate reactions to the Dock Strike by the Government. Mann was one of the six working-class members of the commission and belonged to Group B which dealt with Transport and Agriculture. Lord Derby was his chairman and his fellow members included Professor Alfred Marshall the economist, Jesse Collings the Liberal MP known for his

---

[2] *Figaro* (2 Nov. 1892), tr. and quoted in William Edford to J. Burns, 18 Nov. 1892, BL Add. MS 46291.

campaign for 'three acres and a cow' in Parliament, and Samuel Plimsoll 'the Seamen's friend' famed for the load line, while Gerald Balfour, a Tory MP of Group A, often put in an appearance.

Ben Tillett was one of the first witnesses who gave testimony before Group B. He proposed 'some form of municipal control' of the docks in order to achieve certain regularity in the work; he added, 'I want an absolute popular control of the docks'. He extended his idea to a proposal of 'municipal workshops' and 'municipal factories' to be undertaken by the State in co-operation with local bodies so as to provide employment as well as technical education for the youth and the men. He advocated the adoption of a minimum wage and forty-eight-hour week, and suggested a ministry of labour and an arbitration board. He wanted 'some pension scheme'—'The State has given us the hint', he said, 'She provides pensions for her soldiers, who have less to do with the making of a great country than the workers.'[3] The following exchange with Professor Marshall was characteristic of him, and his senti-ments expressed here, not being Fabian enough in spite of his Fabian membership, did not enter into the Minority Report, a Fabian document, of which more later. Marshall mentioned the existence of 'a very peculiar class' in the docks, pointing to 'an extremely Irish temper' that would rather enjoy irregular work. Tillett replied:

I have a drop of Irish in my own composition, and I have seen a lot of Irishmen at regular work, and they have been most punctual and sober; but the same class of men when they get into irregular work, do develop that spirit, and if they did not they would eat their hearts out. They have got to make themselves happy. Under proper circumstances an Irishman as much as anybody else likes regular work.[4]

Apparently Marshall did not fare better with Tillett than Beatrice Potter had done before.

Tom Mann had submitted two memoranda, 'State and Municipal Control of Industry' and 'The State Regulation of the Hours of Labour' with his pamphlet *The Eight Hour Day: How to Get it by Trade and Local Option*, whose arguments we have already noted. In the first memorandum Mann made a proposal of interest from the standpoint of 'social engineering'. His plan was to 'dockize' the horseshoe bend in the Thames known as

---

[3] *British Parliamentary Papers*, Royal Commission on Labour (Industrial Relations, 26; Shannon, 1970), Evidence, Group B, Q.3568, 3573, 3594, 3600, 3602 [pp. 253–8].   [4] Ibid., Q.3650.

Limehouse Reach, Greenwich Reach, and Blackwell Reach, and
to cut a straight tidal channel for coasting traffic. A new
London Port Authority should be set up to administer the whole
area, to introduce the newest machinery, and to decasualize
employment in the Docklands, a proposal which was described
as 'the logical sequel of the Dock Strike'.[5]

Mann himself gave evidence before the Royal Commission on
Labour and quoted John Stuart Mill in order to justify his
position on socialism and 'municipal control' of the docks. This
led Alfred Marshall to launch a cleverly contrived attack on
Mann's position, Mann was made to agree that the triumph of
public spirit should come before the abolition of private
property, and when he said that men would 'gradually learn to
work for the common good', he had to emphasize the word
'gradually'. Indeed, he was no match for Marshall in the field
of moral philosophy and of academic sophistry. The worst was
still to come, however. When Gerald Balfour asked him which
would come first: an improvement in public morals or
government control of industry, Mann replied in an authentic
Fabian fashion: 'The improvement in public morals comes
first from a section of the community and not from the mass,
and then that section endeavours to influence Government in a
wise direction and helps the Government'—in short, élitist
'permeation'. He was in favour of employers' combinations,
because they would encourage subdivision of labour and the
adoption of more effective methods of production. When the
evils of the salt ring and the sugar syndicate were pointed out
to him, he declared: 'I am quite prepared that people shall
suffer till they learn to do that which is wiser'—that is, by
better organization of themselves.[6]

The Royal Commission on Labour reported in May 1894 that
industrial evils could not be remedied by legislative action, but
should be left to 'their gradual amendment by natural forces'.
It denounced 'the Socialist idea' as 'an encouragement to new
conflicts'.[7] Mann, in conjunction with James Mawdsley of the
Operative Cotton Spinners, William Abraham of South Wales
Miners, and Michael Austin an Irish nationalist and trade-
unionist, prepared a Minority Report. It dealt with the
problems already touched on, ranging from an eight-hour day

[5] *Trade Unionist* (5 Dec. 1891).

[6] *British Parliamentary Papers*, Royal Commission on Labour (Industrial
Relations, 43; Shannon, 1970), Evidence (Whole Commission) Q.2249, 2257,
2259, 2262, 2282, 2285, 2315, 2359, 2373, 2376 [pp. 187-90, 192, 196-7].

[7] *British Parliamentary Papers*, Royal Commission on Labour (Industrial
Relations, 44; Shannon, 1970), 120-1.

to a Ministry of Labour, minimum wages to a Court of Arbitration, old-age pensions to labour colonies for the unemployed, and its distinctively Fabian character was expressed once more in a recommendation that the 'unfortunate residuum' be treated as 'a case of disease', while suggesting that 'captains of industry' and the manual workers would find 'their proper position as servants of the community' in the progress of industrial evolution.[8] In a letter to Sidney Webb who throughout acted as his mentor, Mann described how the use of the term 'Minority Report' shocked some members of the commission (Collings among others), who became 'rather passionate in their protests', and Thomas Burt, the leader of the Northumberland miners and a Liberal or 'Lib–Lab' MP since 1874, had to state that he was not a party to it.[9] The signatories to the Minority Report sent Webb a letter, expressing their indebtedness to him for his help in preparing a report which would be of great value in the future as 'a guide to the industrial & political policy to be endorsed by the workers'.[10]

Tom Mann's Fabianism had further repercussions: his proposal for the 'municipal control' of the Port of London attracted the attention of the members of the LCC and several MPs, with whose support a London Reform Union came into existence with Mann as its secretary. This was largely a Fabian body, to which churchmen whose conscience had been roused by the Dock Strike also gave their blessing. *The Times* of 5 October 1893 rather prematurely reported that Mann had been recognized as a candidate for deaconship in the Church. There is no doubt, however, that he was deeply involved—as was Tillett—in certain phases of the new awareness in the religious world of the problems of labour, and they both willingly co-operated, from its inception, with the 'Labour Church' organized by John Trevor.

Indeed, it was Tillett who gave Trevor the inspiration he needed to start the movement. In April 1891 Trevor, then a Unitarian preacher at the Upper Brook Street Free Church, Manchester, came up to London to attend the National Triennial Conference of Unitarian Churches, where he heard 'Tillett's Titanic appeal'. The working class were not

[8] *British Parliamentary Papers*, Royal Commission on Labour (Industrial Relations, 44; Shannon, 1970), 154.

[9] T. Mann to S. Webb, 17 March 1894, Passfield Papers, BLPES.

[10] Mann, Mawdsley, Austin to S. Webb, 27 Apr. 1894, Passfield Papers, BLPES.

irreligious, declared Tillett: 'if they followed the lead of secularists and atheists, it was because these men understood and sympathized with their sorrows, and could point to a remedy beyond the knowledge of the churches'. 'He made', recalled Trevor, 'a heart-breaking appeal to his hearers to provide churches where the people could get what they needed, and warned them that if they did not do it, workers would provide churches for themselves, and invite the upper classes to them.'[11] Trevor, with encouragement also from Revd Philip Wicksteed and others, took steps to found a Labour Church shortly afterwards. Some seven months later Tillett came and spoke at one of the early services of the Manchester and Salford Labour church.

Now it was Tom Mann's turn. In the first issue (January 1892) of the *Labour Prophet,* the paper of the Labour Church movement, he published an article 'The Labour Movement: Is it inspired with an Ethical Principle?' His arguments were in line with Tillett's: churches and chapels were 'alien institutions' to the mass of the workers. Instead of encouraging the ideas of truth, justice, and brotherhood, the church upheld privilege and monopoly.

With regard to religion, as with politics, it is for workers to vitalise their own faith by drawing direct from the fountain head, and living daily and hourly a truly religious life. Doctrinal hair-splittings we do not want, and cannot have. ... The keynote of a religious life is to live for others. It is altruism as against egoism, and the basis of the Labour Movement is Altruistic.

He concluded by saying that 'the Labour Movement needs its own church. Not that we want sectionalism, but we do want Realism', and he emphasized that both co-operative societies and trade unions were broadly based on the principle of the Brotherhood of Man.[12]

In the following issue of the *Labour Prophet* appeared another article by Tom Mann, 'The Workman's Wife', the tone of which was as high-minded as his first article. He pointed out that the workman's wife with a family of three to six to look after had enough work to do for seven days a week and sixteen hours a day; though she would be glad if her husband should obtain an eight-hour day, she was sure she would not get increased leisure for herself. All this drudgery 'completely knocks idealism out of a woman'. Mann's solution for this state

[11] John Trevor, 'Founding of the Labour Church', *Labour Prophet* (Mar. 1893).   [12] *Labour Prophet* (Jan. 1892).

of affairs was a common kitchen and a common dining-room. 'The subject of associated home' was being discussed in London, and he optimistically expected that it would soon be put into practice.[13]

We do not know how his wife Ellen liked his ideas or how she would have co-operated with him in this new socialist utopia. The life of an agitator's wife was surely harder than that of the average workman's wife. During the London Dock Strike, which lasted five weeks, Tom Mann stayed at the house of Jem Toomey chairman of the strike committee and rarely went home.[14] At the time of the Shipping Dispute of 1890–1 Tom Mann's family moved from Kennington where they had lived to 82 Malmesbury Road, Bow, presumably in order to be near the scene of the actual confrontation.[15] In spite of his very heavy public commitments Mann was not oblivious to the welfare of his wife and daughters. He snatched time for a holiday and brought his family 'by trip train on a run to Scotland' in August 1894.[16] Nevertheless, there is little doubt that according to generally accepted standards, even among the working class, Mann had neglected his family. To the tragic outcome of this we shall shortly return.

Tillett's eloquent appeal was also featured in the pages of the *Labour Prophet*. 'The great Goliath, Greed, armour-plated from head to toe, with all the effective and powerful weapons of Government in his hand, becomes terror-stricken when the Labour Daniel [sic], stripped of any power but justice, challenges to combat those who possess the Land and Government power.'[17] This was a good summary of his experience as a labour agitator for the last few years. Mann and Tillett frequently visited Lancashire to speak at the services of Labour churches there. Mann established his fame as the foremost writer on the subject, and his article 'Preachers and Churches' came out in a collection of essays entitled *Vox Clamantium* in 1894. He now declared that 'the Socialist agitator and the Trade Union organiser [are]doing far more than the preachers and the Christians, the Missionary Societies and the Bible Societies to make Christ's gospel

---

[13] *Labour Prophet* (Feb. 1892).

[14] T. Mann, *Tom Mann's Memoirs* (1923; London, 1967), 66–7.

[15] T. Mann to J. Burns, 19 Dec. 1890, BL Add. MS 46285, JBP.

[16] T. Mann to Keir Hardie, 2 Aug. 1894, ILP Papers, BLPES.

[17] B. Tillett, 'World's Will-O'-The-Wisp', *Labour Prophet* (Apr. 1892), see also id., 'The World, the Church and the Agitator', *Trade Unionist* (11 July 1891).

prevail'.[18] The three sources he cited in his argument for socialism were Carlyle, Ruskin, and J. S. Mill. His religious fervour was soon to consume itself in circumstances which we shall examine later, but in the meantime, he recalled, he hoped 'not immodestly, to use the world as my parish'.[19]

Henry Pelling holds the view that it was in the field of politics that New Unionism had its most important and lasting impact.[20] It gave birth to the ILP, and the ILP in turn brought into existence the Labour Party. Naked class war at last found layers of cushions in parliamentary politics. Even the Fabian Society became politicized and undertook a 'Lancashire Campaign' in which Tom Mann, then a member of the Fabian Executive Committee, was also involved. His letters written to Sidney Webb in these days were mostly reports of his own organizing work in the North.[21]

Working-class Fabians recruited in the North were soon to join in the movement to launch an independent labour party. A central role for such an attempt was played by the Bradford Labour Union, itself the child of the Manningham Mill strike which lasted nineteen weeks in the winter of 1890–1 and in which Tillett played a leading role. He described the end of the strike as 'a model of organised retreat'.[22] Indeed, Tillett was a key figure in the development of New Unionism into independent labour politics. His hot-blooded orations during the strike made him a favourite among the Bradford pioneers who invited him to contest the Eastern Division of the city, but he declined by saying that 'I am convinced that my work *outside* the House of Commons is the most important, more valuable than any work *inside*.'[23] Tom Mann later confessed that Tillett had acted on his advice on this occasion.[24] In the end, however, the Bradford Labour Union won him over, and Tillett fought a three-cornered fight at the 1892 general election at West Bradford with an impressive vote in his

[18] T. Mann, 'Preachers and Churches', in Andrew Reid (ed.), *Vox Clamantium: The Gospel of the People* (London, 1894), 305, repr. as Mann, *Socialist View of Religion and the Churches* (London, 1896), 10.

[19] Mann, *Memoirs*, 95.

[20] Henry Pelling, *Origins of the Labour Party* (1954; London, 1965), 90.

[21] T. Mann to S. Webb, 3, 5, 7 March, 7 and 21 Apr. 1894, Passfield Papers, BLPES. Tom Mann was engaged in organizing work for the ILP.

[22] *Trade Unionist* (9 May 1891).

[23] Tillett to James Bartley, 4 May 1891, quoted by J. Burgess in *Clarion* (24 Sept. 1909).

[24] *Clarion* (24 Sept. 1909).

favour.[25] Tillett had the consolation of being elected to the LCC in that year and took special interest in housing problems, especially the clearance of the slums in the Bermondsey area.[26]

A Labour union similar to the one at Bradford was started in Colne Valley which extended from Lancashire to Yorkshire into the Pennines. The Union invited Tom Mann to stand for Parliament, but as might be expected, he declined, giving his reason that he would not concern himself much about parliamentary politics. 'My aim is to spread amongst workmen a knowledge of industrial economics, and the channels for the diffusion of this knowledge are the trade union and the co-operative movement, especially the productive branch of co-operation.'[27] This view was at once criticized by the *Workman's Times* as 'fanciful as well as [too] theoretical'.[28] Mann's anti-parliamentary bias was fairly widely known by this time. 'The fight out of the labour question', he declared, 'would take place in the municipalities, not in Parliament', and he urged decentralization of parliamentary functions.[29] Nevertheless, after the general election of 1892 at which Burns along with Havelock Wilson at Middlesbrough and Keir Hardie at West Ham, South, had been elected and Tillett fought well, Mann began to emulate his friends: his visits to Colne Valley became more frequent, and his emphasis on industrial action was expressed in slightly more flexible terms: 'Parliamentary effort should follow upon, not precede, trade union effort',[30] and this maxim was further qualified in his pamphlet *An Appeal to the Yorkshire Textile Workers*, published in April 1893. There he wrote that the task of trade unions was only preparatory and once new energy had 'permeated' among the constituents, they would demand 'the complete democratisation, not only of the governing institutions of the country, but of the entire industrial system'. 'With us it is not a case of Conservative, Liberal, and Labour', he added: 'it is rather Aristocracy, Plutocracy, and Democracy.'[31] Apparently he was concerned not with parliamentary politics as such but with political forms of class domination.

[25] The election results were: Alfred Illingworth (Lib.) 3,306, E. Flower (Con.) 3,033, Tillett (Lab.) 2,749.

[26] Tillett, *Memories and Reflections* (London, 1931), 167.

[27] *Yorkshire Factory Times* (28 Aug. 1891), quoted in David Clark, *Colne Valley: Radicalism to Socialism* (London, 1981), 30.

[28] *Workman's Times* (28 Aug. 1891).

[29] Ibid. (29 Aug. 1891).

[30] *Yorkshire Factory Times* (8 Jan. 1893).

[31] T. Mann, *Appeal to the Yorkshire Textile Workers* (London, 1893), 11.

The ILP was formed at Bradford in January 1893. British working-class leaders for the first time attempted serious preparation for the control of Parliament on a national scale. Tillett, one of the delegates from Bradford, took part in the discussion concerning the name of the party, whether it was to be called the Socialist Labour Party or the Independent Labour Party. 'In spite of all that had been said about the Socialists', he declared;

he thought English Trades' Unionism was the best sort of Socialism and Labourism. . . . With his experience of unions, he was glad to say that if there were fifty such red revolutionary parties as there were in Germany, he would sooner have the solid, progressive, matter-of-fact, fighting Trades' Unionism of England than all the hare-brained chatterers and magpies of Continental revolutionists.[32]

Was Marx 'a chatterer or a blatherer?' someone asked. Apparently his reference to the German party annoyed Eduard Bernstein, the fraternal delegate, and some other people present at the conference, but he merely emphasized the solid rock of working-class experience of organization upon which, he believed, any edifice political or otherwise should be erected.

Neither Burns nor Mann attended the inaugural conference of the ILP. Mann, however, represented the Colne Valley Labour Union at the second annual conference held in Manchester in February 1894. At this conference the ILP set up an apparatus of leadership, with Keir Hardie as president, Tom Mann succeeding the rather ineffectual Shaw Maxwell as secretary. John Lister, an Oxford-educated Halifax squire, became treasurer, and the National Administrative Council included Ben Tillett and Pete Curran, national organizer of the Gasworkers' Union and another prominent New Unionist, among its members. The secretary's job was really demanding: at a meeting of the NAC held shortly after the annual conference, it was resolved that he should issue a monthly report, supplying a copy to each of the Labour papers and to the Press Agencies, and that he should be instructed to draft a scheme for the organization of the ILP branches upon a county or district basis.[33] In one of his first monthly reports Mann gladly stated that the party was 'rapidly becoming a National one, in fact as well as in name'.[34] Years later in his old age, he

---

[32] ILP, *Report of the First General Conference* (Bradford, 1893), 2.

[33] ILP, Minutes of the NAC, 26 Feb. 1894, ILP Papers, BLPES.

[34] Ibid.

recalled: 'Forty years ago I became Secretary of the I.L.P. which I hoped would become a mass revolutionary Party. Those hopes were not fulfilled because the influence of reformism was too strong.'[35] The impact of 'reformism' was indeed subtle and corrupting as we shall soon see.

His first task as the ILP secretary was naturally to strengthen organization. 'On Sat & Sunday I had six meetings all I.L.P. in Bradford', he wrote to Hardie; 'On Monday I was at Barrow while you were with Fred Brocklehurst [an NAC member]. Pete [Curran]'s chances are not rosy nor will they be unless the Branch works better. ... I tried to put a little backbone in. Tuesday at Wolverhampton I found them equally flatly. Not enough pluck & no advertising.'[36] He had 'a rattling good meeting at Bootle with the I.L.Pers. At least Liverpool is moving. The dull dead lifeless democracy of that city is really indicating the possibility of revivification. 6 branches in L'pool, 1 in Bootle & one in Birkenhead.'[37] He attended the Co-operative Congress held at Sunderland in May 1894 and was pleased to find the ILP members—no less than 47 of them—'well in evidence' among the delegates. 'I am strongly persuaded', he wrote, 'that in a couple of years we would have so considerable a body as to be quite strong enough to make the movement a real live Democratic one instead of the Commercial affair it is at present.'[38] He naturally set great store on the independence of the ILP. 'For myself', he wrote to Hardie, 'I c'd not & w'd not get returned by any money from Labouchere & count it an indignity to have their moral? support. ... I sh'd be sorry to have Stanhope or Dilke connected with us. They are Plutocrats to the backbone & religiously disposed though I think I am I obey and feel inclined to say *Damn them.*'[39]

The London ILP, relatively weak, decided to boycott all non-socialist candidates including Progressives (i.e. Fabians) at the LCC election in January 1895. At a dinner organized by Sidney Webb after the election, to which Mann and Hardie for the ILP as well as Pease and Shaw for the Fabians were invited, Mann 'gushed out his soul', wrote Beatrice:

He would not support John Burns (or presumably Sidney), 'because Jack played to get the vote of the mere Liberal'. No one should get the

---

35 T. Mann, *Tom Mann and the I.L.P.* (London, n.d.), 12.
36 T. Mann to Keir Hardie, 10 May 1894, ILP Papers, BLPES.
37 T. Mann to Keir Hardie, 20 May 1894, ILP Papers, BLPES.
38 T. Mann to Keir Hardie, 17 May 1894, ILP Papers, BLPES.
39 T. Mann to Keir Hardie, 27 June 1894, ILP Papers, BLPES.

votes of the I.L.P. who did not pledge himself to the 'Nationalisation of the Means of Production and *who did not run overtly in opposition to all who were not Socialists'*. . . . It was melancholy to see Tom Mann reverting to the old views of the S.D.F. and, what is worse, to their narrow sectarian policy. Keir Hardie, who impressed me very unfavourably, deliberately chooses this policy as the only one which he can boss. . . . But with Tom Mann it is different. He is possessed with the idea of a 'church' of a body of men all professing exactly the same creed and all working in exact uniformity to exactly the same end. . . . And, as Shaw remarked, he is deteriorating. This stumping the country, talking abstractions and raving emotions, is not good for a man's judgement, and the perpetual excitement leads, among other things, to too much whisky.[40]

There are certain exaggerations in Beatrice's remark, especially on the nature of Tom's religious faith, since his idea of brotherhood on his own showing was well compatible with J. S. Mill's liberal co-operative socialism. Her reference to whisky may have been true: his work for the ILP, which required extensive organizing tours, may well account for this newly acquired habit. His drinking caused rumours and comments about his behaviour. It most likely affected his relations with his family. The evidence is not forthcoming, but one gets the impression that poor Ellen may well have been at the end of her tether and the four girls—some of them now teenagers—may have grown sensitive and critical.

At the 1895 annual conference of the ILP, the secretary's report emphasized that 'the Progressives [in London] were part and parcel of orthodox Liberalism'.[41] He had begun preparation for the selection of ILP candidates for the forthcoming general election. His pamphlet *The Programme of the I.L.P. and the Unemployed* was published in June in time for the election. It stated a view of socialism that was free from his former Fabian ambiguities. He was opposed to imperialist expansion in the overseas market and advocated domestic growth and adjustment so as to achieve a harmonious balance between 'the food-producing workers [and] the industrial workers of the nation'. He would also introduce 'scientific supervision of the nation's work' that would solve the unemployed problem. In order to do all this, he argued, it would be necessary for the workers to 'take from the capitalist the power to decide when, [and] on what conditions trade should be conducted'. In short, workers' control of industry was now

[40] Beatrice Webb, *Diary of Beatrice Webb*, ed. Norman and Jeanne MacKenzie, ii (London, 1983), 65–6, entry for 23 Jan. 1895.
[41] ILP, *Conference Report* (1895), 18.

declared to be the aim of the ILP policy. The ILP endorsed twenty-eight parliamentary candidates including Hardie for South West Ham, Mann for Colne Valley, Tillett for West Bradford, Lister for Halifax, Tom McCarthy for West Hull, Pete Curran for Barrow-in-Furness, and Ramsay MacDonald for Southampton, but all were defeated.

Mann also contested two by-elections, one at North Aberdeen in 1896 and another at Halifax in 1897. At the former, which was a straight fight against a Liberal, he was very narrowly defeated: 'a moral victory' which was reported also as 'a stunning blow to the Gladstonian enthusiasts'; but at the latter the result was 'a blow to the ILP' as Mann obtained only 15.5 per cent in a three-cornered fight. This was a poor showing compared with 25.4 per cent polled by Lister in a similar contest at a Halifax by-election in 1893.[42]

In the meantime, the simmering discord between Mann and Burns came to the open over another contest for the ASE general secretaryship. The rank and file of the ASE, as we have seen, roused by Mann's challenge for the same post in 1891, succeeded in restructuring the ASE, and this was followed by 'the development of a spirit of militancy greater than had been seen in the Society for twenty years'.[43] In May 1895 George Barnes, now the standard-bearer of the new militancy, resigned the assistant secretaryship to oppose John Anderson as general secretary. Mann strongly supported Barnes's candidature, declaring at a meeting of the ASE at Sunderland that 'a policy of drift' had characterized the present ASE and that 'the biggest "blackleg district" in the trade . . . was at Battersea'.[44] To this Burns responded vehemently. He called Mann's allegations 'so grossly unfair to our great society, its policy, its great development and work', defending the present union officials including Anderson. He was especially touchy about Battersea. 'How can Mr. Mann say that Battersea is a blackleg district, when a trade-unionist [Burns himself] represents it in Parliament and on the London County Council, and it has 67 trade-union workmen members upon its local Town Council?' As for the Government's policy of introducing a forty-eight-hour week in government factories and dockyards, he said that it was not 'the Independent Labour Party rip-and-tear brigade', but the 'officials and prominent members' of the

---

[42] David Howell, *British Workers and the Independent Labour Party 1888–1906* (Manchester, 1983), 170, 192.

[43] James B. Jefferys, *Story of the Engineers* (London, 1945), 136.

[44] *Sunderland Daily Echo* (6 Mar. 1985).

ASE who secured it.[45] At the general election of the same year, John Burns was re-elected at Battersea, but as we have seen, all the ILP candidates and Hyndman, who had attacked Burns's 'treachery', were defeated. 'This desperate result', wrote Burns,

was mainly due to the fact that the poor themselves weary in well doing: whilst some of their leaders are under the impression that the best way to reach the millennium is to kill their best friends and colleagues on the road. I was fortunate in running the gauntlet and surviving the attacks made upon me. How I held my own is to me now a marvel.[46]

Upon his election to the secretaryship of the ILP, Tom Mann began negotiations with the SDF for 'harmonious working relations' between the two socialist bodies.[47] The SDF, too, had been favourably affected by the tide of New Unionism: its membership doubled and even tripled in these few years. Tom Mann must have felt that the new unions and the revitalized old unions could provide a common basis for a united socialist party. The electoral disasters in 1895, however, brought many lessons especially to the ILP which undertook to overhaul all its apparatus and policies. The party now weakened its ties with New Unionism, which now appeared to be a lost cause, and sought to turn itself into a party of practical socialism led by such semi-professional politicians as Ramsay MacDonald and Philip Snowden and self-righteous moralists like Bruce Glasier and Russell Smart. Middle-class or white-collar elements became increasingly prominent in the leadership.[48] It no longer promised to be a party for Tom Mann and Ben Tillett, the New Union evangelists. This naturally had an adverse effect on the negotiations Tom had started with the SDF for an understanding between and even for a possible amalgamation of the two parties.

After the electoral setback of 1895, however, the negotiations made such progress that when the issue of unification was submitted to a vote of the membership of the ILP and the SDF, the result was overwhelmingly for amalgamation. Hardie was not enthusiastic about the result and complained that the voting had been 'rushed'.[49] Bruce Glasier, a new NAC member

45 Ibid. (13 Mar. 1895).
46 J. Burns to Mrs Barrett, 24 Oct. 1895, BL Add. MS 46295, JBP.
47 ILP, *Conference Report* (1895), 16–17.
48 Howell, *British Workers*, 330–1.
49 Referred to in T. Mann to Keir Hardie, 21 Dec. 1897, ILP Papers, BLPES.

formerly of the Glasgow Socialist League, 'the most dedicated opponent of all things SDF',[50] complained to Tom Mann that he (Tom) had not sent out 'the NAC note of advice', apparently a cautious note, 're voting on proposed fusion with the SDF'.[51] It was indeed Glasier himself, supported by Hardie and Mac-Donald, who killed the attempt at *rapprochement* with the SDF at the 1898 annual conference of the ILP. He now read a paper of his own, denouncing the idea of fusion with the SDF, a body 'more doctrinaire, more Calvinistic ... than the ILP' and decrying the advocates of unity which, he said, was 'the pretext of the tyrant and the inquisitor'.[52] By making the issue ideologically obscure and confused, the clever new leaders succeeded in frustrating Tom Mann's efforts for socialist unity.

It was not a mere coincidence that along with this drastic change of front in ILP strategies went an underhand campaign to smear Tom Mann's personal character. Indeed, he had sacrificed his family life for a succession of causes, the SDF, the dockers, and the ILP. Now his critics ransacked his private life for a pretext to discredit him. In 1897 when Tom Mann was for a while adopted as the prospective ILP candidate for Leicester, Russell Smart, another NAC member, who was connected with the Labour Press of Manchester, told Bruce Glasier that 'rumours affecting Mann's character are bound to give trouble at Leicester. ... Mrs Mann told him [Smart] all long ago'.[53] Smart had only recently sought to help Mann start a new Labour journal. His *volte-face* was as complete as it was sudden. In the course of conversation with Glasier, he said that 'Tom Mann had turned up at Socialist meeting held ... at Birmingham in connection with Trades Congress—and Mann was drunk and said very stupid things'.[54] Apparently Smart and Glasier were spreading unsavoury rumours about Tom Mann's private life. 'Smart again opens the question of Tom Mann's conduct', wrote Glasier shortly afterwards,

Tells me he has had a talk with Hardie on the subject. Hardie agrees that Smart should speak to Mann and advise Mann to retire from the Secretaryship. Smart says Mann's conduct at Birmingham during Trades Congress was very foolish. He went about with Joe Tanner's sister who is regarded as a prostitute. He brought Mimie Palmer into the Gallery of the Congress, and altogether seems anxious to flaunt his profligacy before the public. Smart thinks we must do something. I

[50] Howell, *British Workers*, 316.   [51] Glasier Diary, 6 Dec. 1897, LUL.
[52] ILP, *Conference Report* (1898), 27–8.
[53] Glasier Diary, 30 Aug. 1897, LUL.   [54] Ibid., 11 Sept. 1897.

agree. . . . The movement has treated him as a prince—and he has behaved as princes commonly do.[55]

Then in December 1897 when the problem of balloting on fusion with the SDF was annoying the new leaders of the NAC, Glasier had a talk with MacDonald on the issue of Tom Mann at the ILP offices at Fleet Street. 'We both agreed', he wrote in his diary,

things could not long continue without some action being taken, as already it seems the London Executive of I.L.P. have resolved by a majority of one not to countenance his proposed series of meetings at Lambeth Baths. Finally we thought that if the London Executive pressed its objection to the Lambeth Baths' meetings, this might afford Mann an excuse for retiring from I.L.P.

Obviously their aim was to induce Mann to withdraw from their party. On entering the outer room in the offices they unexpectedly met Tom Mann who came up to them. MacDonald shook hands with him and left. Glasier and Mann then went into the inner room. 'I then acting on a sudden impulse raised the matter about the trouble concerning the Lambeth Baths meetings', continued Glasier:

I told him I could not defend his course of action, as I feel that propaganda work should not seem to be undertaken for private gain. Tom strongly defended his action. He said he had tried over & over again to get London Executive to organise a series of meetings of the kind & that they had refused to undertake the responsibility. Two years ago he had under similar circumstances arranged a series of meetings at Holborn Town Hall. I confessed that his statement of the refusal of the London Executive to act, certainly placed the matter in a different light.[56]

Amid the hard work for organization as general secretary, Tom had found time to organize a series of lectures, in part apparently for his own benefit. 'I am running that series of six addresses at the Working Class College & they are going very well', he had written to Keir Hardie about a year before.[57] C. S. Quinn of the Associated Anarchists who had attended all his meetings, expressed the feeling of 'general satisfaction among the Anarchists' at the stand Tom had taken with regard to the problems of anarchist communism (communitarian anarchism associated with the name of Kropotkin).[58] Evidently Tom's lectures were not of the kind that would go on without being challenged by some political socialists. 'Then I asked him to bear with me while I raised another matter', runs the entry in the Glasier diary on the same day:

I thereupon told him how much we all were troubled concerning the scandals that were growing up round his name. I said that whatever true or false they were doing great harm & that if they became public, it would mean serious disaster to the movement & himself. At first he chafed a little, but soon listened calmly. ... For a time we talked together: he asking me for particulars of the charges which I gave him frankly admitting that I gathered them all from hearsay. I said we did, not feel it our duty to sit in judgement on his conduct, but we did feel responsible to prevent if possible any disaster coming to the movement that reposed trust in us. He showed no resentment at what I said & indeed he seemed touched as indeed I was with emotion. He admitted that perhaps so far as his public behaviour was concerned he had perhaps made mistakes, but said that he had a standard of his own which he adhered to & which he had not broken in his private conduct. I said it did not matter how much he felt free from self-accusation—we had the public opinion, not his to deal with.[59]

In other words, Tom Mann's personal standard of conduct, his conscience, was to be ignored and even suppressed in the name of party exigencies and 'the public opinion' which was admittedly based largely on 'hearsay'.

At the following NAC meeting held in Sheffield in January 1898 Tom Mann handed over to Hardie a letter of resignation as secretary, in which he gave the need to attend to the International Federation of Dockers, his new creation, as the reason for this step. Apparently this was similar to or even the same as the one he had presented to the NAC meeting one year before and probably was withdrawn later when John Penny was appointed as assistant secretary to help him. 'Hardie and all of us pressed him kindly not to resign but to wait till our Easter Conference', wrote Glasier;

We felt that his sudden resignation would create all manner of gossip & have a bad effect on the movement. After a curiously constrained conversation, Smart in a blunt way said we were all speaking with masks on; and that but for other reasons than T.M. had given, we would not think of allowing him to resign at all. T.M. then challenged Smart to speak out. Smart in a difficult way laid the whole nature of the charges before him: but indeed they were all mere rumours, and the recital of them seemed curiously like mere stupid gossip. T.M. affected alternately amusement and indignation.[60]

---

[59] Glasier Diary, 6 Dec. 1897, LUL.   [60] Ibid., 8 Jan. 1898.

So the ILP's new leaders threw out Tom Mann the prince of British socialism. Indeed, his strategy for workers' emancipation—workers' control of industry with the socialist politics of the ILP allied with the SDF to support it—proved incompatible with theirs: independent but traditional party politics, with trade-union support in terms of votes and funds, or the so-called 'Labour Alliance', which was even more cautious than John Burns's idea of a trade-union socialist party which he aspired to lead if he could. And the smear campaign, though not designed as such, played its part. But none of the ILP leaders involved in this undignified business apparently knew the real difficulty Tom Mann had in his private life at the time.

It was during the days of his commitment to the Labour Church movement that Mann came to know Miss Elsie Harker, the daughter of a Congregational clergyman, twelve years younger than himself. Elsie was born on 28 November 1868 at Rhos Llandrim, presumably a country house in Llansaintffraid, Montgomeryshire, to Bailey John Harker, an Independent minister, and his wife Amy, formerly Smith. Her father was then preaching on the English side of the border. In due course the family moved to Grassington, Wharfedale, one of the charming Yorkshire dales, which so enchanted the Revd Harker, himself 'one of a long line of Yorkshire dalesmen',[61] that he wrote several guide books, such as *Rambles in Upper Wharfedale* and *A Complete Guide for Tourists to Grassington*, which he called 'The Buxton of Yorkshire'.[62] He was also interested in local history, published a booklet entitled *Philip Neville of Garriton: A Yorkshire Tale* in 1875, and became Fellow of the Royal Historical Society. He had one other interest, which was socialism. His sermon given at the Duke's Alley Congregational church (the Labour church) at Bolton in July 1892 came out as a booklet under the title *Christianity and the New Social Demands*. He noted with approval the workmen's 'unwillingness to be associated with hypocrisy . . . their revulsion of feeling against class partialities and the want of humanity and brotherhood in the churches that has estranged them' and advocated the kind of socialism that 'demands no more than its right to the spring of God's

---

[61] Dona Torr, 'Mrs. Tom Mann is Eighty', Newspaper cutting (n.d.), TMP.
[62] Bailey John Harker's *Complete Guide for Tourists to Grassington* was published in 1890 and reissued in 1903.

bounty'.[63] He now invited Ben Tillett and Tom Mann to speak in a chapel at Bury with which he was connected, an incident which annoyed the agnostic John Burns.

Elsie had been trained as an opera singer and had taught at a school at Bury; she came up to London, where she joined the ILP shortly after its formation, helped Tillett with her songs in his election campaigns, and assisted Hardie in his office work. This was before Tom Mann joined the ILP, and in London she stayed with Tillett and his wife. She even began to display literary talent by writing in the *Labour Leader* a report of her visit to the Burnley Workhouse and a short story with a motto from Kingsley, 'Men must work, and Women must weep'.[64] Early in 1896 Mann received a letter from Tillett disapproving of his actions with regard to Elsie among other things. This letter apparently was not kept, but Mann's long reply is extant among the Mackay Papers at Warwick. 'Your long delayed letter arrived at last, & what a dose it is', read his reply:

It's necessary to be told that one's faithless, cowardly, selfish, mean &c & that to the dearest comrade I ever had or otherwise I certainly sh'd not have known it; I must have gone down hill somewhat rapidly too to be exhibiting such qualities as these & to be deprived of your friendship for ever without any intimation other than this one explosive bomb of a letter. Ben old man, if I am guilty of the things you allege against me I think you would be acting wisely in giving me the cold shoulder once for all, as you declare you have done, & if I am never to talk with you again or receive another letter from you I shall put it down as the result of a queer set of circumstances in which, if I played a guilty party at least I wasn't conscious of it.

The first complaint made by Tillett in his letter was related to some internal trouble of the Dockers' Union, and it was not too difficult for Mann to deny any responsibility for disclosing certain secrets about it. The second point was much more serious, as it directly affected their mutual friendship. 'Then you refer to "my avoidance of you" ', wrote Mann:

This is not true in the slightest particular. I have no difficulty on reflection in thinking how easy & naturally [sic] it w'd be for you to so conclude when your mind has been undergoing so heavy a strain, but I will readily admit that I ought to have sought you out; in any case you may reasonably complain that I did not, & that I did not I now really express my regret. You do not do an old pal justice in saying you had to

---

[63] Harker, *Christianity and the New Social Demands: A Reply to the Rev. J. Dawson* (Manchester, 1892), 15.

[64] *Labour Leader* (19 Jan., 1 Mar. 1895).

conclude that I 'wanted to get out of obligations I wrongly imagined you wished to impose'. The crowning point of the whole matter I clearly see is Elsie leaving Leytonstone & going to Willesden. I did express my strong conviction that it was the right course to take, but by Christ I did not say so out of regard to any 'fancied peril to myself'. If I didn't exist it would have been wise; that's my judgment now, & yet Ben lad I understand how it would appear to you to be careless & selfish on my part or any one else's to advise such a course. I am not disposed to comment upon this in a letter but I may ask that you shall allow yourself to think that I might have so advised from motives other than purely selfish ones. You declare all friendship off now; well let it be so, but not with my endorsement. I plead no virtue, I lay nothing against you, & I shall continue to love and admire you. To Ben from Tom.[65]

Tillett was then living in Culworth Road, Leytonstone, and apparently his ire against Tom was related to Elsie's decision to leave his house and his personal tutelage, and this meant greater freedom for her to move around and to associate more closely with Tom Mann. Mainly for health reasons, Tillett was to spend several months in Australia and New Zealand in 1897–8. It is quite likely that Mann became more deeply and inseparably attached to Elsie while Tillett was away.

In a letter he wrote many years later to Elsie, Tom recalled the beginning of their joint life:

I think Saturday of this week, the 25 Nov. is the anniversary of our trip to Brighton in 1898—24 years ago, and Monday next the 28th is your birthday, please use a couple of pounds extra for a new hat or whatever you require most for a little present. 54 eh? quite a juvenile compared to 66. Glad to say I'm in excellent health.[66]

The 25 November 1898 must have been the day of their 'union' which they could not publicly celebrate nor officially register. In the following year, 1899, their first son Thomas was born, to be followed by Robert in 1900. Mann had to sort out his tangled family relations somehow. The idea of a journey to Australasia may have been suggested by Ben as a chance to cut the Gordian knot with one stroke. Ellen and her four daughters would remain in England; Elsie and her two boys would follow him. Apparently family circumstances were not the only reason for his decision to leave the country, for he found himself increasingly in a political impasse at the time. His Australasian years, which we shall examine later, helped him reconstruct his life. There Elsie bore him another son Charles in 1905 and a

[65] T. Mann to B. Tillett, 30 Jan. 1896, IMP.
[66] T. Mann to Elsie Mann, 21 Nov. 1922, TMP.

daughter Elsie in 1908. He loved his wife Elsie with all his heart; his tender feeling for her pervaded innumerable letters he wrote to her from South Africa, America, Canada, Scandinavia, Russia, and China, and from Britain whenever he was away from home on a lecture tour. A loving husband, he wanted to share all his experiences and impressions with her. He rarely talked about Ellen and the four daughters, and Charles recalled that only once had his father told him that the music-hall singer Effie Mann who was somewhere on the stage was his half-sister. Now and then, however, Tom did send a photo of himself to some of his daughters, such as one with 'Love to Emmeline from Dad' sent during his speaking tour in the United States in 1913.

From the days of his advocacy of an eight-hour day, Mann saw himself as a strategist. As such he made mistakes in public life, as he confessed; but he was honest and upright throughout in his private life, adhering strictly to his own moral standard. His connections with the Fabians and especially with the ILP were not so rewarding as they should have been, and sometimes even humiliating. He was far happier as the president of the International Federation of Ship, Dock, and River Workers. To this aspect of his work towards the close of the century we shall now turn.

7. International Trade-Unionism

THE Second International founded in Paris in 1889, unlike its predecessor, had no general council, no secretariat, not even a title until 1900. Its continuity was ensured only by congresses held at irregular intervals. The title of each congress varied: the Zurich congress of 1893 was called the 'International Socialist Labour Congress', and the London congress of 1896 the 'Socialist Workers' and Trade-Union Congress'. 'Labour' and 'Trade-Union' were dropped altogether from its title after 1900 when it adopted the regular title of the 'International Socialist Congress'.[1] Unlike the First International which had heavily relied upon the support of trade unions, especially those in Britain, its successor depended largely on the socialist parties that had come into existence in Europe and America in the course of the 1880s with some sort of Marxist principles. Not only were the anarchists, its old adversaries, denied membership, but also the trade unions, its possible allies, were not welcomed because they were not socialist enough. Yet trade-unionists for their part carried on their attempts to draw together internationally for mutual support. The Glass Workers and the Miners had each set up an international body of their own, and the lead thus given was soon to be taken up by the Transport Workers under the initiative of Tom Mann and his friends.

Tom Mann, as we have seen, attended the International Trades Union Congress held in London in 1888. His name again appeared among the 180 British 'delegates, adherents and visitors' to the first International Co-operative Congress held in London in August 1895. It was attended by over 30 foreign delegates from 12 countries, and Earl Grey [4th Earl], the president of the congress and a patron of the co-operators, gave an opening address in which he welcomed some of the prominent members of the trade unions, 'notably Mr Thomas Burt and Mr Tom Mann', identifying themselves with the co-operative movement, which Grey chose to equate with

[1] Julius Braunthal, *History of the International 1864-1914* (London, 1966), 243.

profit-sharing.[2] In an article published in one of the co-operative journals, Tom Mann enlarged on the subject of 'co-partnership'. He would support 'the efforts of the labour co-partnership workshops' or attempts to start co-operative production based on the co-partnership of the workers. He would support the movement started by the large wholesale co-operative undertakings based on the non-dividend-paying principle. He made a plea for toleration and mutual encouragement from those who were engaged in various aspects of the co-operative movement.[3] We have seen how Tom sought to extend the ILP influence in this movement. His interest in a variety of co-operative projects, remarkable for a socialist of his day, was one of the sources which led him later to commit himself to the idea of workers' control or what he called 'democratic ownership and control' of industry, and this was in fact the theme of his forecast for the coming century.[4] For the moment, however, he was more deeply involved in the work of preparation for the London congress of the Second International which had to settle the issue of toleration for the anarchists.

Early in December 1895 Tom Mann was at Sunderland, engaged in a speaking and organizing tour in the North-East among the miners and engineers. From there he wrote to Keir Hardie on the coming London congress of the Second International, telling him that he was on the Zurich and Conjoint Committees and would 'specially watch our interests'.[5] The Zurich Committee set up at the previous congress held in Zurich managed to preserve an uneasy alliance between continental Marxists and the Hyndmanite SDF, while the Conjoint Committee, including representatives of trade unions, was more broadly based. The role Mann played in watching 'our interests' was obviously not pleasing to Eleanor Marx, who complained that he and Keir Hardie were doing all they could 'to get the anarchists in on the usual ground of "fair play"'.[6] On the second day of the London congress held in July 1896 Mann spoke against the Zurich

---

[2] International Co-operative Association, *Report of the First International Co-operative Congress held in the Hall of the Society of Arts on 19–23 August 1895* (London, 1895), 47–8.

[3] T. Mann, 'Socialist View of Co-Partnership', *Labour Co-Partnership*, 1: 17 (Dec. 1895).

[4] Id. in Edward Carpenter (ed.), *Forecasts of the Coming Century* (London, 1897).

[5] T. Mann to Keir Hardie, 5 Dec. 1895, ILP Papers, BLPES.

[6] E. Marx to W. Liebknecht, 11 July 1896, quoted in Chushichi Tsuzuki, *H. M. Hyndman and British Socialism* (Oxford, 1961), 121.

resolution to exclude the anarchists: 'Let us try to be as many-sided as possible. . . . A man may be a trade unionist as well as a Socialist. Any shade of opinion can come under the head of trade unionism. . . . Non-Parliamentarians they are, but Socialists all the same.'[7] He was on the commission dealing with economic and industrial questions. Hyndman, another British member of the same commission, recalled that Mann expressed his fury on the exclusion of the anarchists not only at the Queen's Hall where the congress was held but also at a separate anarchist meeting held at the Holborn Town Hall where 'Mann . . . declared that he did not differ materially from them as to methods, and gave them his heartiest welcome'.[8]

Mann was really more interested in the prospect of forming international links between trade unions than in the theoretical controversy among the Marxists over the issues of anarchism and revisionism which were to vex the Second International for the years to come. In those days probably he did not even think of himself as a Marxist. Some time after the London congress in October 1898, he took the chair at the opening meeting of the Tottenham Socialist Church which he said would provide 'a cosmopolitan platform on which anyone who had anything worth saying to the people would be welcome. While on some occasions and on some platforms it was necessary to raise the flag of "no compromise!" yet, here, anything like dogmatism or sectarianism would be fatal'.[9] Dogmas should be avoided as far as possible, as these would prejudice and constrain free human development and action, especially industrial action. The outcome of the London congress further convinced Tom of the need for an international organization for trade unions free from sectarian restraint.

In spite of Tillett's declaration of the termination of his friendship with Tom Mann at the beginning of 1896, these two soon found themselves closely collaborating in their joint work of promoting an international federation of port and transport workers. The third partner in this project was Havelock Wilson who continued his vendetta against the Shipping Federation and was interested in the prospect of cutting off the supplies of foreign strike-breakers. An international organization of port workers, Tillett believed, was 'the only force counteracting the

[7] Report of the Congress, *Justice* (19 July 1896); International Socialist Workers and Trade Union Congress, London, *Report* (London, 1896), 10.
[8] H. M. Hyndman, *Further Reminiscences* (London, 1912), 110.
[9] *Labour Prophet* (Nov. 1896).

interlocking shipping interests'.[10] Mann expressed similar sentiments in more impressive terms: 'Every year shows more clearly to the ordinary observer how thoroughly International the capitalists are as regards the use of the capital they control. . . . What we do now stand in urgent need of, is AN INTERNATIONAL WORKING ALLIANCE AMONG THE WORKERS OF THE WHOLE WORLD.'[11]

The early moves to form an international transport workers' federation preceded the London congress by several weeks. The Dockers' Union which was to provide its main corps sent through Tillett an assurance of international solidarity to the Swedish dockers in Stockholm who were on strike in May.[12] By the beginning of July 1896 an organization called the Central Council of the International Ship, Dock, and Waterside Industries had come into existence with Tillett as its secretary. He indicated to Charles Lindley, the leader of the Swedish dockers, that the British trade union connected with transport industries were about to launch a movement that would unite 'all the interests that are kindred in the European & American ports' as a counter-measure against the powerful Shipping Federation which was also spreading its influence abroad.[13] A meeting of delegates from the 'kindred' unions in Britain and the Continent was held in London on 13 July, and soon the International Federation of Ship, Dock, and River Workers was launched. It started publishing a series of leaflets, urging the men to wear the federation button and exhorting them to claim not a 'living wage' but 'the full value of the work performed'.[14] Organizing activities across the Channel soon began. Tom Mann, who became the chairman of the central council of the federation, together with Havelock Wilson, visited Antwerp to help organize the Belgian port-workers by setting up a branch of the National Sailors' and Firemen's Union there.[15]

The new agitation alarmed the Belgian authorities. On 19 August Tillett, secretary of the federation, who had been sent to Antwerp to strengthen and extend the contact, was arrested on arrival in spite of an innocent-looking dress of shorts and neat shoes worn for a planned cycling tour in

[10] B. Tillett, *Memories and Reflections* (London, 1931), 176.

[11] T. Mann, *International Labour Movement (Socialist and Trade Unionist)* (London, 1897), 5–6.

[12] B. Tillett to Charles Lindley, 20 May 1896, ITWFA.

[13] B. Tillett to C. Lindley, 7 July 1896, ITWFA.

[14] International Federation of Ship, Dock, and River Workers, *What We Want, Why We Want It, and How We Mean to Get It* (London, 1896), ITWFA.

[15] *The Times* (25 Aug. 1896).

Belgium. The little Ben had duly attracted a crowd of dockers and sailors at the harbour and hence the attention of the Belgian police. Released from police detention, he at once joined a procession of the unemployed, marching prominently at its head, and was arrested again. He was sent to gaol where he knocked down a bullying warder who had puffed the smoke of his cigar in his face, an incident which led to his confinement in a cell which, inhabited by drunkards, was in a filthy condition. As an act of protest, 'for at least twenty hours I sang all the revolutionary songs I could remember', he recalled.[16] The matter, however, became so desperate that his influential friends such as Lord Rosebery, his colleague on the LCC, and Sir Charles Dilke intervened on his behalf; he was released and expelled from the country on 21 August. His open challenge had unfortunate consequences, for what he experienced at Antwerp had a serious effect on his health: for many months he was in a state of nervous exhaustion. Moreover, he tried to obtain compensation for damage done to him by the Belgian authorities and secured the assistance of Henry Broadhurst who wrote on his behalf to George Curzon, Undersecretary of State for Foreign Affairs:

I have the greatest faith in the accuracy of all the statements he has made of complaints as to his treatment. He assured me that for eight days after his liberation he vomited every day, that the stench of the cell and its receptacle for human excrement had such an effect upon his health that he still suffers from it.[17]

John Burns took a keen interest in the matter.[18] Charles Dilke also assisted him: soon the Foreign Office made contact with the Belgian Government on Tillett's case, and was 'consulting the law officers of the Crown on difficult points'.[19] A few years later, however, an award was given in favour of the Belgian Government against the British Government who supported Tillett's claims for compensation.[20]

In the absence of Tillett who was temporarily incapacitated because of his Belgian experiences, Tom Mann undertook organizing work which took him to several Continental ports. He was expelled from Hamburg in November 1896, in spite of the British Consulate's intercession on his behalf with the German officials, who were far better informed of the nature of

16 Tillett, *Memories and Reflections*, 176, 180.
17 Henry Broadhurst to George Curzon, 19 Sept. 1896, IMP.
18 *The Times* (8 Sept. 1896).
19 Charles Dilke to B. Tillett, 29 Oct. 1896, IMP.
20 F. H. Villers, Foreign Office, to B. Tillett, 31 Dec. 1898, IMP.

his propaganda work. Notwithstanding his formal expulsion, he returned to Hamburg six weeks later when 800 blacklegs were imported from Britain during a strike of the port workers there.[21] He even managed to address the men but was soon arrested and expelled again. On his arrival in London he was pleasantly surprised to find in the *Daily Graphic* a sketch of cell no. 28 of the Hamburg Stadthaus, where he had been detained, which was reported to have been 'well heated' and 'perfectly clean throughout', probably to the chagrin of Ben Tillett.[22]

Tom now called for an international conference to discuss international action to enforce a certain uniformity with regard to working hours and wages among the port-workers of various countries. The scheduled conference was duly held at the Holborn Town Hall from 24 to 26 February 1897, attended by 32 British, 4 French, 3 German delegates, and 1 each from Spain, Holland, and Belgium. Tom Mann represented the Seamen of Nantes. The British delegation, in which the Dockers' Union and the National Sailors' and Firemen's Union formed the largest contingents, had decided prior to the full conference that the most opportune time for the enforcement of the men's demands would be Monday 19 July 1897. They also agreed that the central council should have power to declare an international or national strike 'when the consent of the majority of the Federated Unions [had] been obtained', Tom Mann having emphasized that 'the basis of action was local autonomy all round'. At the full conference the chairman Mann made it clear in his opening speech that in the event of 'a general International Strike of Port Workers and Seagoing Men' it would be quite impossible to provide the usual strike pay as the unions involved could not afford it, and 'we could not rely upon any large amount of public sympathy'; hence the only course open to them was to 'conduct a dispute on such extensive lines that the carrying trade of the world would be crippled'. A French delegate, though in favour of an international strike, pointed out the need for a year's organization before any such attempt be made. The Germans were against the proposed general strike in July, while the Dutch wanted such an international strike to be arranged as quickly as possible.[23] Although Mann

[21] T. Mann, *Hamburg Dockers' Strike: Help Urgently Needed* (n.p., 16 Dec. 1896), ITWFA.
[22] *Daily Graphic* (23 Dec. 1896); Tom Mann, *Tom Mann's Memoirs* (1923; London, 1967), 109.
[23] International Conference of Ship, Dock, and River Workers, *Minutes of Proceedings* (London, 1897), 6–8, ITWFA.

had to vacate the chair to Havelock Wilson owing to an engagement for his own candidature at a by-election at Halifax, he summarized the debate in a pamphlet written on the subject:

Germany declared strongly in favour of complete organisation, but was by no means enthusiastic in favour of striking. The French were very pronounced in favour of a general strike as soon as the organisation were sufficiently perfect in the respective countries. The Belgian and Dutch declared themselves ready for action immediately the signal should be given.[24]

It was decided at the conference that 'a conjoint international effort' should be made in July 1897 to obtain better wages, shorter hours of labour, and generally improved conditions for the port-workers of the world connected with the International Federation, and that the central council should be asked to convene another international conference in June to decide on the 'conjoint' action by ascertaining the courses separate unions would have chosen to take in the following month.[25]

A certain Fenton Macpherson, chief correspondent for the International Federation in Paris, made arrangements with the Confédération Générale du Travail (CGT) and several dockers' and seamen's unions in Paris, Le Havre, Nantes, and Marseilles for the president of the International Federation (Mann had become president at the February conference) to visit Paris and several port-towns and to address trade-union meetings under their auspices with a view to forming a national federation for France which in turn would confederate with the International.[26] A *Report Sheet* from the central office for May reported the expulsion of Macpherson from France, and the following month announced the expulsion of Mann but commented that

the work done [by him] had been of a most satisfactory character. The information gained about French Trades Unionism by the President while in Paris, has been of exactly the right kind and will be of immense benefit to the International Federation. From the French newspapers we learn that the expulsion has been the means of drawing much attention to the Federation.

In fact, in the Municipal Council of Paris, a vote of censure was passed on the prefect of the Seine for prohibiting the meeting arranged for Mann, and his speech thus suppressed was read

[24] T. Mann, *Position of Dockers and Sailors in 1897* (London, 1897), 13.
[25] International Conference of Ship, Dock, and River Workers, *Minutes of Proceedings*, 10.
[26] T. Mann in Central Office of the International Federation of Ship, Dock, and River Workers, *Report Sheet* (Apr. 1897), ITWFA.

in the council chamber.[27] Moreover, Tom in Paris was able to address 'private' meetings organized by the Allemanists, and his direct contact with Jean Allemane, an old Communard, aroused his interest in the latter's syndicalist principle which insisted that all who joined his party should be members of a trade union.[28] As he was served with an order of expulsion, he made last-minute arrangements for his message to be read at a public meeting. He was convinced that 'a good lift' had been given to trade-unionism in France.[29]

The June conference of the International Federation was held at the Club and Institute Union at Clerkenwell Road. Tom Mann represented a French union, this time the Syndicat National des Ouvriers des Ports, Entrepôts et Magasins Généraux de France. Difficulties surrounding the International Federation came to the open at this conference. The Dockers' Union (British), though it presented a most elaborate statement of demands, was not prepared to take action at this time. The German law which did not allow international association complicated the matter of affiliation in that country, while some of the Russian sailors who had sought to help the federation had already been deported to Siberia. A strong ally, however, had emerged in Sweden; in fact, the Swedish labour movement, a late comer in the field, was experiencing a period of rapid union growth from 1895 with the beginnings of the substantial industrialization of the country and the resulting upward price trend, while Swedish socialism, though strongly influenced by German Marxism, was inclined to promote industrial action. When the reduction of the federation fee (one penny per member per quarter decided at the conference) was urged by a delegate from the Thames Steamship Workers, it was Charles Lindley of the Swedish Dockers who exhorted the British delegates 'not to be too stingy'. Indeed, the Swedish Transport Workers' Federation was willing to take action that year for a wage increase and a ten-hour day, and the International Federation decided to 'render all possible assistance'. This was in fact the utmost the federation could aspire to do. Although 'the Scandinavians have forced the pace more than any other',[30] the planned international action for July failed to materialize. The scale of the British engineers' lock-out which began in July 1897, the same month, dwarfed anything planned

---

[27] T. Mann, *Report Sheet* (June 1897).   [28] Id., Memoirs, 110.

[29] T. Mann to C. Lindley, 24 May 1897, photostat in Frow Collection, Salford.

[30] B. Tillett to W. H. Hughes of Waterside Workers' Federation of Australia, 7 June 1904, ITWFA.

by the International Federation, the future of which now appeared uncertain and even bleak.

Tom Mann sent a fortnightly letter to the *Social Demokraten* and *Arbetel* the two working-class papers published in Stockholm, reporting the progress of the lock-out,[31] in which his strategy of confrontation and emulation between the organized employers and the organized workers was severely tested. His energy was now momentarily directed to domestic industrial action. On 9 January 1898 Mann issued a manifesto in which he declared that the ASE, 'this powerful union', after twenty-six weeks of the struggle had not only failed to obtain its one demand, an eight-hour day, but had been asked to accept employers' terms of settlement. He urged the union not to sign any such agreement and instead 'to go back to work as best as they can when their final resources are exhausted'. He regretted that there was no adequate organization to sustain the men for twelve months and pleaded for setting up a national federation of trade unions, 'a cosmopolitan union including skilled, semi-skilled, and unskilled of both sexes'.[32] Mann followed up the manifesto with a letter advocating 'a Union of a general character', having 'for its objects the enrolling of all sections of the workers into an organisation, for the purpose of fighting on political and Trade Union lines'. The proposed union would have financial arrangements similar to the Dockers' Union. 'Labour is not beaten; on the contrary, it is just learning how to assert itself', and the union would 'avenge the Engineers' defeat'.[33]

These statements by Mann were issued from the London headquarters of the International Federation of Ship, Dock, and River Workers at 181 Queen Victoria Street. There still stands a solid five-storey building called Bridge House at this address, on the western extremity of the street, on the south side, squeezed between the entrance to Blackfriars Station and Blackfriars Bridge. The building used in multi-occupancy was completed at about the same time as the opening of the station in 1886. We have already noted that Tom Mann mentioned the place when the central office of the SDF was located there in 1887. When Tom started the International Federation, he obviously remembered that Bridge House would provide a good, cheap, centrally located office. The building had forty-seven occupants in 1899, mostly trading and commercial

---

[31] T. Mann to C. Lindley, 21 Dec. 1897, photostat in Frow Collection, Salford.
[32] *Weekly Times and Echo* (9 Jan. 1898).   [33] Ibid. (30 Jan. 1898).

organizations, and none other with a labour or political purpose.[34]

It was in this same office at Bridge House that a preliminary meeting of what was soon to be known as the Workers' Union was held in February 1898. In April Mann, inspired with a new prospect of trade-unionism, was seen at Bilbao, having visited the French ports of Le Havre, Nantes, St Nazaire, and Bordeaux on behalf of the International Federation.[35] He may well have wished to co-ordinate two trade-union federations, one national and the other international, from his office at 181 Queen Victoria Street. But his endeavours for the rebirth of New Unionism on a grander scale, as Richard Hyman has pointed out, were greeted with 'widespread suspicion and resentment' by the leaders of the existing general unions, Will Thorne among others. On his return from Bilbao Mann revised his plan for the Workers' Union, which he now stated, 'is not, and will not be opposed to any other Union of workers. . . . Our desire is to organise the at present unorganised, and so remove the cause of present-day weakness from which the workers suffer'.[36] The plan became far more modest than originally contemplated. The International Federation, on the other hand, changed its name to 'The International Federation of Transport Workers' so as to include all the workers connected with the carrying trades.[37] At any rate, the failure of the Workers' Union to become a mass organization at this stage and the difficulty of organizing the port-workers on the Continent, coupled with his more or less forced resignation from the general secretaryship of the ILP which, as we have seen, had taken place earlier that year, were perhaps sufficient to draw Mann's attention to various other directions in those days of *fin-de-siècle*.

Before turning to Tom's other activities, however, we should trace the development of the International Federation (ITWF) after the turn of the century. As late as October 1901 Tom sought to strengthen the ITWF by attending the annual conference of the Amalgamated Society of Railway Servants held in London, in an attempt to win their support. He was accompanied by Harry Orbell of the London Dockers' Union and Tom Chambers, formerly the secretary of the Workers' Union and then the secretary of the ITWF. 'In these days', said Mann,

[34] I owe the detailed information on Bridge House to Mr Andrew Whitehead who kindly undertook a search through the annual Post Office directories.

[35] *Weekly Times and Echo* (10 Apr. 1898).

[36] Ibid. (24 Apr. 1898).   [37] Ibid. (19 June 1898).

'when the operation and organisation of capitalism covered almost every country in the world, it was vitally necessary that Labour for its own protection should have an international organisation as well.' Chambers boasted that the membership of the ITWF had reached 100,000, but the conference was not impressed and appeared even hostile to the deputation. Some of the delegates went so far as to protest against Tom Mann speaking.[38] Tom Mann, as we shall see, was about to leave for New Zealand.

During the Boer War the ITWF organized a meeting to boycott British war-efforts, but by then the British commitment to the ITWF had considerably weakened. The Dockers' Union suffered a heavy blow to its strength in the summer of 1900 when they were defeated in a strike demanding a conciliation board and a return to the practice of hiring the men outside the dock-gates. Tom Chambers, secretary of the ITWF, resigned or was dismissed, leaving a mess behind him, including the un-answered application of the International Longshoremen of America for affiliation which caused embarrassment to Tillett who now sought to revive the ITWF.

Tillett found the organization in a state of utter neglect and bankruptcy, and complained that for three and a half years the books had not been audited. This was early in 1904, and his immediate aim was to hold an international transport workers' conference about the same time as the Amsterdam congress of the Second International fixed for a week from 14 August 1904. Thus the Transport Workers' International held its own con-gress on 10 August at Amsterdam, attended by nineteen del-egates representing more than 200,000 members from nine European countries (Holland, Italy, France, Belgium, Great Britain, Germany, Portugal, Sweden, and Austria). Tillett regretted that 'a lot of damage' had been caused by the last secretary's fault and inaction. Paul Mueller, the German delegate, reminded Tillett that the last conference in London had been organized by the Germans because all international links had been broken. 'Not Tom Chambers only but the whole London Management were to blame': the allegation can be seen as a repercussion of the Anglo-German discord over the Boer War. He declared that 'for all respect for Tillett and Orbell the Management cannot be left with England'. Harry Orbell protested against obvious German insinuations, and Mueller

---

[38] *Railway Review* (11 Oct. 1901). I owe this reference to Prof. Takao Matsumura.

remarked: 'it looks as if there was a fight between Germany and England'.

In Amsterdam the German fought another battle: Lindley, the Swedish delegate, defended the principle of the international strike and boycott by extending it to include demands for a large wage increase for the work on black-listed ships, whereas J. Doering of Germany found the whole thing impracticable. As for the federation fee Tillett pointed out that so far the Dockers' Union (his union) had paid about half of the amount of assistance money paid out by the federation, i.e. fl. 1,700 out of fl. 3,450. 'The English Dockers will not pay a penny as long as the other organisations will not pay defined and increased contributions'. The French presented a draft resolution making a general strike dependent on the strength of the organizations and on support by international sentiment; Tillett was sceptical of the effect of such a resolution. There was a Dutch resolution on machines; Harry Orbell was 'surprised that there is still opposition against the improvement of tools. Machines must be brought under the control of the community'. Lindley was of the view that the workers should bring the machines into their own hands by political action. 'In Sweden every T. U. member is a Social Democrat.' Another Dutch resolution advocating workers' solidarity against militarism was given the cold shoulder by Mueller who, on behalf of the German and Austrian delegations, expressed surprise and doubt at a trade-union conference dealing with 'such a highly political question', while the French maintained that the army was 'a tool in the hands of the bosses', and the Italian delegate felt that the fight against militarism was 'not party but class politics'. The resolution was adopted by 8 votes to 7, with the British Dockers voting in favour. In spite of British objections a German draft constitution was adopted as the basis for debate and the pro-British Lindley only kept his chairmanship under protest. Tillett doubted whether the Germans could accommodate the federation as Tom Mann and himself were on the wanted list of the German police, whereupon Schumann for Germany commented: 'You will not leave a visitor's card with the police?' All national delegations except the British and the Swedish voted for Germany to be the seat of the ITWF.[39] The Boer War had not yet been forgotten, and Tillett withdrew his union from the federation shortly afterwards. His Dockers' Union, numerically weak after the failure of the 1900 strike,

---

[39] International Transport Workers' Federation, 'International Dockers' Congress', Typed report of the proceedings, 1904, ITWFA.

remained in the wilderness of international labour until it rejoined the ITWF in 1908.[40]

We have already examined the circumstances in which Mann had to resign from the ILP general secretaryship and have traced his activities especially in connection with the International Federation of Ship, Dock, and River Workers (later ITWF) in its early days. At Bilbao he attended the meetings of local dockers and came to know Pablo Iglesias the socialist leader. In April 1898 on his return from Spain he became treasurer of the Spanish Atrocities Committee which organized a meeting in Trafalgar Square to protest against 'the barbarous manner in which the Spanish authorities have conducted Cuba and the Philippine Islands'.[41] This was on the eve of the Spanish–American War in which Spain proved no match for the emerging new imperial power, but the committee was not sufficiently informed or prepared to criticize the spread of new American imperialism.

The secretary of the committee, Joseph Perry, was a member of the Freedom Anarchist Communist Group, and Tom Mann remained on friendly terms with anarchists and cosmopolitan groups. It was about this time that he became the tenant of the *Enterprise*, a public house in Long Acre, Covent Garden, which was used as a lecture room and meeting-room for various organizations such as the Young Italy Society, the SDF Central Branch, the Friends of Russian Freedom, and the Cosmopolitans. There Enrico Malatesta opened a debate on anarchism, and John Morrison Davidson lectured on 'Winstanley the Digger'.[42] The *Enterprise* stood at the corner of Endell Street and was generally patronized by 'the better class of those whose business calls them to London's great market' for a hasty lunch or for a drink and chat with a friend. A reporter, sitting in his corner, watching 'the strong characteristic face of the man who engineered the Dock Strike, whose voice has rung so defiantly from Labour platforms', and who was now 'flitting amid bottles, jugs and glasses', had to chuckle at 'Providence's little joke'. But he was by no means lost to the workman's cause, added the reporter. 'He recognises that, from an independent position, he can best voice the woe of the descendants of Ishmael.' Surprisingly he was still a teetotaller, and served

---

[40] Douglas J. Newton, *British Labour, European Socialism and the Struggle for Peace 1888–1914* (Oxford, 1985), 90–1.
[41] J. Perry to J. Burns, 15 Apr. 1898, BL Add. MS 46297, JBP.
[42] Mann, *Memoirs*, 121.

drink because he felt that the cause of temperance should be well served by selling good beer and running a public house in a clean, healthy way. 'There is not the slightest truth in the assertion that I have quitted the ranks of Socialism', he said to the reporter;

If anyone regrets my step in becoming a publican, he is welcome to his opinion. That it has made no difference is shown by the fact that a few days ago I was up North addressing labour meetings. There is a lull just now in labour politics, and I had to regard my responsibilities. But I shall never change my political creed. Never![43]

It was about this time that Tom assisted the founding of the Waiters' Union. He had participated in an SDF demonstration held in Trafalgar Square in July 1899, protesting against an impending war with the Transvaal Republic.[44] Further, in conjunction with Ben Tillett, he planned to start the *British Socialist News* as 'the paper for the Movement', and the first issue was projected to come out on 27 October 1899 from the office of the International Federation at Bridge House.[45] But by then war in South Africa had begun and apparently nipped their effort in the bud.

One of the many ventures at which Tom tried his hand was the National Democratic League of which he became organizing secretary. This was a body founded by W. M. Thompson editor of *Reynolds's Newspaper* who sought to coalesce all radical left-wing forces on a minimum programme of political democracy in the tradition of Chartism. Although it was formed in the midst of the Boer War—launched as it was at a conference held on 27 December 1900—it was not an offshoot of any anti-war campaign,[46] nor had it anything to say on the war which divided the ranks of both socialists and Liberals. Tom Mann, in his pamphlet *Why I Joined the National Democratic League*, pointed out that the general election of 1900 had brought about 'an enormous Tory majority in the House of Commons, a general and wholesale support given to the War party, a bolstering up of the forces of reaction and privileges', but his major concern was the lack of unity among the left which, he felt, could be remedied by the Democratic League. Ben Tillett co-operated for a while. It is true that some of its branches organized anti-war meetings, but its own programme

---

[43] *Labour Chronicle* (Liverpool) (July 1899).
[44] *Justice* (15 July 1899).   [45] Ibid. (14 Oct. 1899).
[46] Richard Price, *Imperialist War and the British Working-Class* (London, 1972), 246.

for radical reform quickly lost its attraction, and it soon faded away. The SDF which had participated in its formation came round to denounce the body as 'chiefly Liberal decoy ducks and marionettes'.[47] Mann resigned from the National Democratic League in May, and by the end of the year he was on his way to New Zealand with his new family. He must have felt that he had been led helplessly down a blind alley in the British working-class movement as his ventures, one after another, had been foiled and frustrated.

[47] *Justice* (5 Jan. 1901).

8.   An Australasian Interlude

ON 5 December 1901 Tom Mann, accompanied by Elsie and the two infant boys, left England for New Zealand, travelling on SS *Ruapehu* of the New Zealand Shipping Line. For this sudden departure for the Antipodes he gave various reasons in his memoirs: the reading of a book on New Zealand called *Newest England* by Henry Demarest Lloyd, the American advocate of the rights of labour and co-operation; his shared common interest with Robert Blatchford's brother who was obsessed with things about New Zealand; and an acquaintance he had made with a visiting New Zealand MP, E. M. Smith. All these events either separately or taken together do not appear to explain sufficiently why Mann had to leave the country in the midst of the Boer War, at a time when the need for a powerful labour organization with an international orientation was all the more keenly felt. The key to his decision to leave the country should be looked for, as suggested above, in his family circumstances and also in the impasse he apparently felt he had come to in his work for the working class. We have noted the dismal failure of his attempt made only two months before to win the support of the railwaymen for the ITWF. The National Democratic League was indeed a poor substitute for the ITWF, work on which had been disrupted and made practically impossible by the outbreak of the Boer War.

Tom and his fellow passengers on board SS *Ruapehu* were not allowed to land at Cape Town which was under martial law. The boat took on Australian soldiers who had served in the war against the Boers, sailed on, and arrived at Wellington on 21 January 1902. Indefatigable as he always was, Tom addressed the Wellington Trades Council shortly after arrival, and two days later spoke at a local branch of the ASE. The following day he was a speaker at a crowded Sunday gathering at the opera house.[1]

New Zealand, under Liberal government from 1890, had established a reputation as the 'Land without Strikes' and 'the small man's paradise'. 'Digger' Richard John Seddon, the Prime Minister from 1893, had been responsible for such measures as

[1] T. Mann, *Tom Mann's Memoirs* (1923; London 1967), 133.

the break-up of large landholdings, loans and transport facilities for small farmers, protective tariffs and state trading,
female suffrage, industrial conciliation and arbitration, and
old-age pensions. In spite of all this, Tom was struck by the
great number of unemployed members of the ASE who complained about the dilution of their work by the introduction of
cheap labour of young people, and he was interested to know
that the ASE branch was solidly against the Arbitration Act of
1894. When he visited the Waihi gold mining area in the north,
he found the miners on strike against the Act. They were soon
outmanœuvred by the management, however, who had no difficulty in founding a company union to be registered under the
Act.[2] On the South Island he spoke to the miners at Coalbrook-
dale, an isolated village on a high plateau, 'the most completely
shunted off from civilized society and from humanity generally
of any I had ever seen',[3] which he reached on horseback. Practically the whole village attended his meeting which provided
an occasion for rare diversions for the miners and their
families in their dull, monotonous life. While he was in New
Zealand, he met some of the 'Clarionettes', the readers of
Blatchford's *Clarion*, who had come to this land of promise
before him with the object of settling on a co-operative plan.
They had drifted apart, however, giving up their hopes that
practical socialism would be started in the colony.[4]

After a hectic nine months in New Zealand, Tom travelled to
Australia. He arrived in Melbourne towards the end of September 1902, and was at once drawn into the Victoria state
election. By noon of the day of his arrival he was in touch with
the Trades' Hall Council, and under its auspices addressed 'six
meetings that afternoon and evening, and six more the next
day'.[5] He spoke in favour of the Labour Party, which had come
into existence in the wake of a series of unsuccessful strikes in
1890–1 by the Shearers as well as by the Maritime Workers
who had been threatened with the imposition of 'free contract'.
In fact, the close of the century witnessed not only the formation of the Australian Labour Party which was to grow within
two decades into a ruling party both in state legislatures and in
the federal government, but also the formation of the system of
compulsory arbitration in which Australian trade unions had
to operate. Moreover, an eight-hour day, the first item in Tom's

[2] Ibid. 136; [Dona Torr], *Tom Mann in Australasia 1902–1909* (Our History
Pamphlet, 38; summer 1965), 5.   [3] Mann, *Memoirs*, 138.
[4] *Clarion* (21 Aug. 1903).   [5] Mann, *Memoirs*, 142.

programme for the emancipation of the working class, had been achieved in Australia even before Tom became aware of its supreme importance for trade-unionism in England, and the Australian practice of holding an annual gala to celebrate it had begun in Sydney sometime in the 1870s. In high spirits Tom attended one such celebration in Sydney in October, and on his way he spoke at the Broken Hill Trades Hall, the foundation stone of which had been laid by Ben Tillett during a visit he made in 1898.[6]

Tom at first spoke at the major cities in New South Wales, Victoria, and South Australia on an independent basis; then he was asked to do organizing work for the Victorian Labour Party. In order to break the ice with the indifferent people in the agricultural districts, he once performed the part of the bellman as well as that of the speaker at a meeting. He spent three weeks at the shearing sheds for the Shearers' Union, sometimes driving a horse and buggy along all day. Australia, in spite of her eight-hour day and apparent high standard of living, was still dominated, he felt, by a capitalism as ruthless as in Britain. For the benefit of the Labour Party, therefore, he produced a pamphlet early in 1903 to show the present position of Australian socialism in the context of the international working-class movement. In this survey of world socialism, Tom took a sympathetic view of Alexandre Millerand, the French independent socialist, who had entered the bourgeois Cabinet of 'Republican Defence' led by Waldeck-Rousseau, for 'it shows clearly the great power of the movement there when, to ensure stability of government, Socialists are requested to take office'. He was, however, quick to point out that the Allemanists in France were now opposed to all parliaments and were bent on establishing socialism 'by means of "La Grève Générale"—The General Strike, or, as they picturesquely put it, "The War of the Folded Arms"'.[7]

Melbourne remained the centre of his organizing work, which took him among other places to Ballarat and Bendigo, the gold-mining towns in Victoria, and to Moonta in the copper-mining district of South Australia. While travelling through western Victoria, he observed that most of the land was in the hands of the squatters who were cutting up their big estates and exacting high rent from the farmers who were engaged in the 'dairying industry' newly developed in that area. At Hamilton

[6] John Laurent, 'Tom Mann, R. S. Ross and Evolutionary Socialism in Broken Hill 1902–1912', *Labour History*, 51 (Nov. 1986), 57.
[7] T. Mann, *Labour Movement in Both Hemispheres* (Melbourne, 1903), 7, 12.

he was greatly impressed with 'a freezing works devoted exclusively to rabbits', putting through 50,000 to 60,000 of them a week. Still he remained optimistic about the prospect of setting up a co-operative colony, because good land had not entirely been alienated by the State. By adopting intensive cultivation of the type advocated by Kropotkin in his *Fields, Factories, and Workshops*, he felt it should be possible to start a settlement not far from Melbourne, to be inhabited by persons with knowledge of garden and farm work, who were also 'thoroughly imbued with co-operative principles'. 'I do not think it too sanguine to hope to see a settlement here in Victoria', he wrote to the Clarionettes at home,

where all main essentials shall be produced for the adequate maintenance of the settlers, and, of course, a surplus of some things must be produced, to admit of the purchase of such requirements as could not conveniently be produced. I think it quite possible that a thousand or two thousand acres could be obtained under reasonable conditions, and the requisite capital obtained to admit of maintenance until results could be obtained. I think both sexes would be able to do more effective work, and have much more variety of recreative amusement, living under disciplinary co-operative arrangements, than is possible either in town or country under the existing customary arrangements.[8]

Probably the failure of the first co-operative settlement of the Clarionettes in New Zealand damped any enthusiasm that had remained for Tom's project.

In 1904 he undertook a lecture tour in Western Australia, from Perth to Coolgardie, Kalgoorlie, and Boulder City, visiting the mines as well as the miners. 'Once more I'm doing a bit of travel', he wrote to Ben Tillett while he was travelling on board SS *Kanouna* for Adelaide after his Western Australian propaganda tour:

I've had two months in W.A. running about nearly all the time, I have not had a successful time financially as I'm returning not a shilling better off than when I came. As you will know there is a Labor ministry in power, and politically the Labor vote is able to dominate but the movement is very superficial, it would be terribly disappointing to an English Socialist to have put time in W.A. What passes as alright for a decent Laborist there is the most flimsy twaddle imaginable, nor are they at all familiar with Socialist economics nor do they desire to know anything about it, at least judging by my recent experience. I should say there are not more than five percent that give any thought to the subject in a general & cosmopolitan sense.

[8] Id., 'Co-operative Settlement in Australia', *Clarion* (21 Aug. 1903).

Moreover, the timing was bad. His arrival coincided with the beginning of an industrial slump. 'About half of the Jarrah timber cutters were unemployed. And the Collie Coal Miners came out on strike, and there was the usual lack of organisation re my meetings, and an intense interest in Boxing & Racing & what else—Lo Lo—'. Having been away from home for quite some time, Tom Mann longed for news of his old friends. 'Well Ben old man', he continued, 'how are you with your own share of troubles. I see you come up smiling time after time no matter what happens. Why haven't you told me anything about your candidature? Eccles Division isn't it, Miners largely eh?' Ben was to contest Eccles in 1906. Tom went on to ask what chance Hyndman would have for Burnley, and what had happened to John Burns, whether he would sign the constitution of the Labour Representation Committee, the future British Labour Party. He asked about new roads and new railways in London, and about the docks.

Tell me exactly what stage has been reached re the control of the Docks of London? Is that matter still in the enquiry stage; and is there likely to be any reconstruction of the Docks or diversion of the Thames? I saw a report a couple of years ago that the proposal to cut the Channel I talked about was revived. I sh'd like to know if it is to be acted upon.

It was not to be, although the Port of London Authority created in 1908 was to tackle the problem of modernizing the old system. 'Kind regards to any of the lads you meet', he concluded, 'but not to any girls, I leave them all to you in the earnest hope that all may have a good time here & hereafter.'[9] In the following year he made an extensive tour of Queensland from Brisbane as far north as Townsville and Cairns, speaking for the miners and the engineers as well as for the sugar growers, and was astonished to learn that the white men who poured in while the Kanakas were being deported under the 'White Australia' policy, were casual workers on the move, housed temporarily in rough barracks, ready to work long hours for small wages.[10] In fact, Tom spent nearly twelve weeks from March to May visiting several mining centres such as Charters Towers, Gympie, Mount Morgan, and Mount Perry, where he found only a handful of miners organized in a union. At Bundaberg, a local centre for growing and manufacturing sugar, he visited a plantation where

---

9 T. Mann to B. Tillett, 6 Sept. 1906, IMP.
10 Mann, *Memoirs*, 162–3.

they have in their employ about 500 Kanakas, about 50 Chinamen and 50 Hindoos, and about 100 white men at the more responsible jobs and as casuals at the ordinary work. All the regular jobs are given to the coloured men, who are as much slaves as any humans ever could have been. Through the outrageously unhealthy conditions under which these men are herded together quite a number of them fall ill and have to go to hospital.

Usually there was no pay for the sick. At another plantation he visited, the Kanakas deported were being replaced by the Hindus, keeping out the white men who were 'not quite so docile as the coloured fellows'.[11]

He found Brisbane 'very dull and uninviting' from a socialist standpoint in spite of its magnificent record in the working-class movement including the substantial donations made by the dockers and seamen of the city to the London Dock Strike of 1889.[12] He attributed the weakness of the Labour Party in Queensland to the existence of the Liberal–Labour Alliance. He cited the anecdote of Mr Kidston, the State Treasurer and 'a fighting member of the Labour Party', as typical of the ranks of Labour. Mr Kidston was once asked at a public meeting if he was a socialist:

He replied that Lord Salisbury had said, 'We are all Socialists now' (of course meaning Harcourt), and added: 'If I'm asked if I'm a Socialist like Lord Salisbury I reply "Yes"; but if I'm asked if I'm a Socialist like Karl Marx I reply "No".' And this no doubt correctly indicates his attitude—i.e., he is neither Liberal, Tory, nor Labour, but a bit of each as it may serve.[13]

On his way south Tom spent a few days at Sydney, making the acquaintance of Samuel Smith, the workers' representative on the Court of Arbitration, and attending a meeting of the un-employed.[14]

Back in Melbourne in June 1905 Tom started a lecture series on social problems in the Gaiety Theatre every Sunday after-noon.[15] This dispelled the rumours that 'Mr. Tom Mann . . . the dictator of the Labour Party in Victoria has at last come to the conclusion that he has been "called" to the pastoral industry, and has definitely resolved to give up politics and go in for

---

[11] Id., 'Slavery in Queensland', *Clarion* (30 June 1905).
[12] Id., 'Queensland Labour Party', *Clarion* (5 May 1905).
[13] Id., 'Liberal–Labour Alliance', *Clarion* (9 June 1905).
[14] *Clarion* (14 July 1905).   [15] *Socialist* (Melbourne) (8 Sept. 1906).

farming'.[16] He may have actually longed for 'a nice little holding well watered and fertile, where he can turn his energy to growing crops or raising stocks',[17] as he was to try his hands in a similar occupation in Kent years later.

In one of his occasional reports he sent to *Clarion* in those days, he examined the social and political conditions of Victoria.

The standard obtaining here in Victoria is, for some sections of workers, a distinct advance upon the standard in Britain for similar workers; but a large proportion have exactly the same struggle to make ends meet financially; the proportion of unemployed is much the same as in England; charitable agencies are at work in a similar fashion; orthodox politicians grumble at the Labour Party, and call out for fair play for capitalism; and the two principal papers in Melbourne, the 'Argus' and the 'Age', attach chief importance to the fiscal question.

The Tories generally being for Free Trade and the Liberals for Protection, the Tory *Age*, 'fed by writers in London', sought to create the impression that Britain was 'impoverished owing to her Free Trade policy', while the Free Trade *Argus* was thoroughly wedded to the interests of the squatters and capitalists. (Incidentally, the Federal Labour Party, which duly emerged, was nationalist enough to emphasize 'the cultivation of an Australian sentiment' and adopted the policy of 'New Nationalism' that accepted protective duties as a factor affecting the wages and conditions.) Tom acknowledged the yeoman's service Ben Tillett had done for socialism during his visit in 1897. Indeed, Tillett had left behind him Australian 'Tillettism' and a weekly socialist newspaper *The Tocsin* (Melbourne). Tom, however, had to admit that 'whilst a small section battled well for Socialism, the vast majority of the rank and file and of the leaders were Labour men of the very moderate Liberal–Labour type'. The Victorian Labour Party was 'very much like the Labour Representation Committee with you in the old land', though efforts were being made, again like in the 'old country', to have it declare for socialism.[18]

Tom led that small section battling for socialism. The Gaiety Theatre lectures proved a success: Sunday evening lectures were now given at the Queen's Hall, Bourke Street, while open-air meetings were held on the Yarra Bank. At a meeting held in the Furlong's rooms, Royal Arcade, the Social Question Com-

---

[16] 'From the Platform to the Plough', Newspaper cutting, Jan. 1905 (details unknown), attached to the copy at the Rhodes House, Oxford, of Mann's *Labour Movement in Both Hemispheres*.   [17] Ibid.

[18] T. Mann, 'Socialism in Australia', *Clarion* (14 Apr. 1905).

1   Tom Mann's four daughters by his first wife Ellen: Emmeline, Effie,
Rosalind, and Gertrude (from left to right)

2   Tom Mann, his second wife Elsie, and four children: Tom, Robert, Charles, and Elsie

(b) John Burns

(a) Ben Tillett

3. The Men of 1889

4 Tom Mann addressing the strikers in Liverpool, 1911

5 Tom Mann addressing a meeting, probably of the Minority Movement

6 Tom Mann, Earl Browder, Jacques Doriot, and Syder Stoler, the RILU delegation to
China, at Hankow, 1927

mittee was set up with the declared objects of collecting and making use of information on social questions, with special reference to the proper feeding of children, the claims of the unemployed, and the housing question.[19] The committee undertook house-to-house visits in the industrial districts of Melbourne and proved that over five thousand adults and a similar number of young people were unemployed. They pressed for various schemes of relief work to be undertaken by the authorities. The committee duly developed into the Victorian Socialist Party (VSP), membership of which had reached 1,500 by September 1906 and 2,000 by April 1907.[20]

The *Socialist*, the newspaper of the party, was started in April 1906. The first number announced Tom's Sunday lecture in the Queen's Hall, 'a Socialist sermon taking his text from the Epistle of St.James [sic], Chap.V.1–4':

Next a word to you who have great possessions. Weep and wail over the miserable fate descending on you. Your riches have rotted; your fine clothes are moth-eaten; your silver and gold have rusted away, and their very rust will be evidence against you and consume your flesh like fire. You have piled up wealth in an age that is near its close. The wages you never paid to the men who mowed your fields are loud against you, and the outcry of the reapers has reached the ears of the Lord of Hosts.

This was to be followed a week later by his speech on the leading European socialists he had known: Liebknecht, Engels, Bebel, Bernstein, Singer, Jaurès, Millerand, Vaillant, Allemane, Louis Michel, Elisée Reclus, Paul Lafargue, William Morris, Hyndman, Quelch, and Bax, a mixed lot with strong anarchist elements in it. In the same number Elsie Mann's article 'Evolution and Revolution' was featured prominently. This provided the keynote to the controversy on the same subject, as there had been proposed an amendment to the party constitution, which read 'that evolutionary (not revolutionary) Socialism is the true remedy for the ills of labor in Australia'. Elsie now maintained that 'Marx and Engels were revolutionary Socialists, and were the first to express the theory of social evolution'. What she meant by a sort of jugglery of words was that a revolution was social change due to class struggle, itself brought about by the clash of class interests occasioned by the conditions of production and social institutions, while evolution

[19] *Socialist* (8 Sept. 1906).
[20] Ibid.; Robin Gollan, *Radical and Working Class Politics: A Study of Eastern Australia 1850–1910* (Melbourne, 1960), 210.

was 'the process leading to such a change'. She concluded by saying that the remedy was not in the process but in its completion, that is to say, 'Revolution when not only labor will be freed from the domination of a class, but all humanity will be emancipated.'[21]

Tom Mann's interest in evolution and revolutionary theories has attracted attention, and his socialism has been called 'evolutionary'.[22] As a matter of fact, Elsie's 'revolutionary' article was adopted as the common basis for the VSP, and Tom's party in a review of its own work for the first year stated that it upheld 'Socialism of the scientific school, that is, the recognition that the evolutionary development of Capitalism renders Collectivism of Socialism imperatively necessary. . . . While of necessity it [their socialism] is evolutionary, it is equally of necessity revolutionary.'[23] The VSP did not specify how to achieve a revolution, but a constitutional method was taken more or less for granted, and its attitude to the Labour Party was still one of influencing its members with their own socialist views.[24] At the Zion Hall, Swanston Street, Melbourne, Tom Mann started regular Sunday evening lectures on such varied topics as 'Sociology, History, Ethnology, Mythology, The Development of Humanity through Savagedom into Wagedom, now on to Freedom, Religion and Moral, Economics and Politics'.[25] His encyclopaedic interest was well suited to the purpose of enlightening the people. His consistent support for co-operation naturally led him to look up Kropotkin and his *Mutual Aid* as much as Marx and his 'evolutionary–revolutionary' theory of class struggle, but he was increasingly caught in a struggle against class domination, first of all in a free-speech fight in Melbourne.

Prahran was one of the Melbourne suburbs south of the Yarra, where public meetings were held by various organizations in side-streets adjacent to the main thoroughfare. In the autumn of 1906 the borough council and the police launched a campaign against socialist speakers which led to the arrest of over twenty VSP stalwarts including Tom Mann. He was charged with obstruction in the street and with resisting the police, and was sent to the Old Melbourne Gaol on 9 November for five weeks.[26] He somehow enjoyed a period of rest at the

---

21 *Socialist* (Apr. 1906).
22 Laurent, 'Evolutionary Socialism in Broken Hill', 57–61.
23 *Socialist* (8 Sept. 1906).
24 Gollan, *Radical and Working Class Politics*, 211.
25 *Socialist* (28 July 1906).   26 Ibid. (10 and 17 Nov. 1906).

expense of the State, reading Shakespeare and Dickens. Ramsay MacDonald, now MP for Leicester, and his wife Margaret visited him in prison on their tour through the Antipodes.[27] In prison Tom wrote a 'Catechism for the Children' for the socialist Sunday school.[28] When he came out, he resumed his Zion Hall lectures, his subjects ranging from Confucius to Joseph Dietzgen, from the Paris Commune to the need for a six-hour working-day.[29] He advocated the six-hour day as a representative of his Melbourne branch of the ASE on the Trades Hall Council, and the same ASE connections brought him over to Tasmania where he visited Hobart, Launceston, and Devonport among other places. Tom, interested as he always was in agriculture, was duly impressed by the 'deserved reputation' of the island for fruit-growing, though he found the growers largely at the mercy of the London market.[30] In Melbourne the Socialist Co-operative Store was started with a board of directors including Tom himself and H. H. Champion who had come to Australia before him. Champion also acted as Treasurer for the *Socialist* and was on the executive of the VSP.[31]

The old world continued to send out to the youthful continent some of its veteran champions of the cause of the people when they had become overwhelmed by an unfavourable turn of events or physically too weak to tackle the new situations. To the list of Champion and Mann was now added Ben Tillett. After his defeat in 1895 as an ILP candidate Tillett had fought no parliamentary election until 1906 when he unsuccessfully contested Eccles, Lancashire, as an LRC candidate. He was not included in the electoral deal Ramsay MacDonald had made with Herbert Gladstone of the Liberal Party and fought a three-cornered fight gallantly.[32] There followed a period of political flirtation with Horatio Bottomley, the political and financial trickster, when Tillett wrote occasional notes and articles for his *John Bull*. Then Tillett's health suffered another relapse, and Bottomley was 'instrumental' in raising a fund to enable him to take a holiday in Australia.[33] In March 1907 Tillett

[27] Ibid. (1 Dec. 1906). [28] Ibid. (9 Feb. 1907).
[29] Ibid. (19 Jan., 9 and 23 Mar. 1907). [30] Mann, *Memoirs*, 177–8.
[31] *Socialist* (16 Mar. 1907); Mann, *Memoirs*, 159.
[32] Tillett won 3,985 votes as against 5,841 for his Liberal and 5,246 for his Conservative opponents.
[33] Jonathan Schneer, *Ben Tillett: Portrait of a Labour Leader* (London, 1982), 131.

wrote to Tom Mann, asking him to organize a series of meetings
for him 'throughout Australia'. 'I shall be doing all that is best
to get well', he added, 'and believe my health will be restored
when I reach Australia.'[34] Another letter followed telling Tom
about himself: he had joined the SDF; so had his wife and two
daughters. Mrs Tillett, who was assistant secretary of the
Bristol branch of the SDF, had just been elected a member of
the Bedminster (Bristol) Board of Guardians 'as a Socialist,
beating the forces of reaction'.[35] Tillett actually sailed from
Liverpool on 30 April on board SS *Essex*, and arrived in
Melbourne in the middle of May. He was welcomed by J. P.
Jones, president of the Socialist Party, and was duly 'fixed up
with' Tom Mann.[36] His first lecture at the Guild Hall was
enlivened as of old by Elsie's solo.[37]

Tillett's arrival coincided with a new move among the Australian socialists. Just as the Prahran 'class war' for free
speech had been a factor which moved Tom Mann and the
Victorian Socialist Party away from the Labour Party, so did
the movement for unity among the socialists provide an occasion for them to go further away from the Labourites and from
Labour politics. The initiative for such a move came from the
Socialist Propaganda Group of Broken Hill, a group that had
been strongly influenced by the VSP. Having received a communication from the Broken Hill socialists in favour of united
action, the VSP called the first inter-state socialist conference
which was held in Melbourne in June 1907 with the representatives of the Socialist Labour Party of Sydney, the Internationalist Socialist Club of Sydney, the SDF which had recently been
revived by Champion in Sydney, the Broken Hill Socialist Propaganda Group, the Social Democratic Vanguard of Brisbane, the
Social Democratic Association of Kalgoorlie, and the VSP.[38]
Tom Mann welcomed the delegates, and the need for 'a class
conscious United Socialist Party' was recognized by all
present, except for those from the Sydney SLP who withdrew
from the conference boasting that they were the only such
party already in existence. A resolution from Broken Hill in
favour of 'the reorganisation of the Australian working class
on the lines of the Industrial Workers of the World' was unanimously carried; the preamble of the IWW was agreed to; and

[34] B. Tillett to T. Mann, 5 Mar. 1907, *Socialist* (13 Apr. 1907).
[35] *Socialist* (4 May 1907).   [36] Ibid. (25 May 1907).
[37] Ibid. (18 May 1907).
[38] *The Flame* (July 1907), quoted in Gollan, *Radical and Working Class
Politics*, 211.

the name of 'The Socialists' Federation of Australasia' was adopted for the new organization.[39] The American IWW, after which it was modelled, had been created in Chicago in 1905 with a syndicalist preamble expurgated of a political clause after a debate, which foreshadowed the later controversy and schism that weakened the revolutionary organization. In the meantime IWW clubs sprang up in Sydney, Melbourne, and Adelaide. Tom Mann had decided that the Labour Party was no longer a workers' party but the party of the middle class, and the Socialist Federation at its second conference in 1908 declared that industrial unionism was a logical development from trade-unionism.[40]

While Tom Mann was away in Sydney organizing work for this new federation, Tillett filled his place as a regular evening lecturer at the Guild Hall, Melbourne: 'Mrs. Mann, with her beautiful voice at its best, could not escape an encore. . . . Ben spoke with the orator's power.'[41] On 21 July Tom Mann chose 'John the Baptist' for the theme of his lecture at the Guild Hall, when the first service of dedication to the socialist cause of six children took place. Mrs Mann sang 'Listen to the Children'. Two members of the VSP stood on the platform, each holding a red flag archwise. As the parents came up two at a time, Tom Mann, standing under the red flags, confirmed their wishes. 'It is their desire and hope, in which we all most heartily share,' he said, 'that the child shall grow up with a sound knowledge of ethical and economic principles, and become truly balanced, physically, mentally and spiritually.' Kissing the infant and handing it back to its mother, Mann fastened on it a scarlet ribbon with a bow with the name of the child, the date of dedication, and 'Socialist Party, Melbourne', printed on it. The fourth child thus dedicated to socialism on that day was his own son Charles Benjamin Mann.[42] Apparently Tom Mann the socialist minister, with the help of Elsie, had by now successfully built up a great socialist parish in Melbourne with its own Sunday school, library, choir, brass band, dramatic society, and orchestra, and its newspaper, speakers' class, and callisthenics.[43]

Tillett was recuperating at Hobart, Tasmania in the autumn of 1907, regaining his cheerful spirit, and putting on weight.[44] He now wrote for the *Socialist* a series of personal sketches of

[39] *Socialist* (15 and 22 June 1907).
[40] Gollan, *Radical and Working Class Politics*, 212.
[41] *Socialist* (6 July 1907).   [42] Ibid. (27 July 1907).
[43] T. Mann, 'Two Years' Work', *Socialist* (31 Aug. 1907).

British socialists: Quelch, Hyndman, Hardie, Blatchford, and
Lady Warwick. Tom Mann was involved in an industrial
struggle again. A Miners' strike in the Newcastle district of
New South Wales at once affected the coal-lumpers in Sydney,
on whose behalf he, accompanied by Tillett, proceeded to New
South Wales. The Industrial Disputes Act weighed heavily
there not only against the sympathetic strike of the coal-
lumpers, but also against the original strike action by the
Miners. On this occasion Mann addressed many meetings on
the Sydney Domain, the 'Hyde Park' of that charming city.[45]

On 4 January 1908 Mann emerged from an overcrowded
second-class carriage at Broken Hill after a weird, 'almost
Siberian' journey from Adelaide, and addressed no less than
five meetings in this mining centre. He was back in Melbourne
in time to take the chair at the farewell meeting for Keir Hardie
who had been visiting Australia since December. Tillett and
Champion sat on the platform, but Tom in his speech appeared
far more interested in the Broken Hill campaign that had been
carried on vigorously by the Barrier Socialist Group.[46] In
March Tillett left for England, thanking Victorian socialists for
the 'health and strength' they had given him.

In the following month Mann visited New Zealand for the
second time, arriving in Wellington by SS *Moeraki* on 15 April.
He was to spend a few months there, engaged in organizing
work mainly for the Socialist Federation of Australasia. He
attended the annual conference of the New Zealand Socialist
Party held in Wellington in May, at which it was decided to
affiliate the party to the Australasian Federation, and a
special emphasis was placed on 'increased economic organisation and no political action for the present'.[47] Industrial unionism was in the air. No sooner had the coal miners' strike at
Blackball on the west coast of South Island come to an end than
a tram strike began at Auckland. Tom also spoke at open air
meetings in support of a bakers' strike in Wellington.[48] The
official apparatus for the 'Land without Strikes' had become
oppressive as well as cumbersome for the workers on strike.
Tom, however, found time to enjoy the beauties and wonders of
nature of the islands; he climbed Mt. Egmont (8,360 feet) to the
height of about 7,800 feet, saw the Maori women cooking in the
holes in the rocks in the Hot Lake District, and was fascinated

[44] B. Tillett to a person unknown, 23 Nov. 1907, IMP.
[45] Mann, *Memoirs*, 179.   [46] *Socialist* (25 Jan. 1908).
[47] [Torr], *Tom Mann in Australasia*, 12.
[48] *Socialist* (12 June, 17 July 1908).

by the sight of a pilot fish known as 'Pelorus Jack' in Pelorus Sound off the northern coast of South Island.[49] In July he left New Zealand and returned to Sydney, where a tram strike had just ended in a defeat for the workers. Tom Mann made an earnest appeal to all the workers employed in the transport industry to organize, federate, and unite.[50]

Tom's active mind was now fully attuned to a period of Herculean effort in the great industrial struggle that was in store for him at Broken Hill. When he returned from his second visit to New Zealand, he apparently entertained the idea of going back to England, there to start a new movement of industrial unionism, possibly among the transport workers, with the assistance of Ben Tillett who had seen some of the new moves in Australia. His acceptance, however, of the job as organizer for the Miners' Federation of Broken Hill, who had been threatened with a wage reduction of 12.5 per cent, changed all this and completely altered the nature of the industrial struggle at the mining town. Tom Mann arrived at Broken Hill on 30 September, and within three weeks he had succeeded in augmenting the union membership by 1,600.[51]

Broken Hill, a mining city flanking the eastern side of the Barrier range, was proud of its rich mines of silver, lead, and zinc and also of its imposing civic buildings, including the spacious red-brick technical college and museum. The Broken Hill Proprietary, the chief mining company, had its furnaces at Port Pirie in South Australia, to which the crushed ores were taken from the mines for smelting and refining and from which the finished metals were shipped out. There the working conditions were extremely harsh; the furnacemen, for instance, worked seven days a week under the most intolerable, unhealthy conditions. R. S. Ross, a socialist journalist and the editor of *Barrier Truth*, came over to Melbourne and joined with Champion to take charge of the work for the VSP and the *Socialist* while Tom was away. At Broken Hill Tom with his usual eloquence stressed the need for solidarity, and new members came 'in wholesale'. At Port Pirie his task was harder, but he sought to inculcate the sense of self-respect in the most indifferent and sometimes even hostile men. After two or three weeks' strenuous effort, 'we obtained a ninety-eight per cent organisation, and unanimity in the demand for a

[49] Ibid. (15 and 29 May, 26 June 1908); Mann, *Memoirs*, 138–41.
[50] *Socialist* (7 Aug. 1908).
[51] Laurent, 'Evolutionary Socialism in Broken Hill', 66.

six-day week'.[52] The Broken Hill men had decided to have recourse to the Federal Court of Arbitration in the hope that this
would prevent a lock-out threatened by the company. But the
court delayed its adjudication, and when it gave an award in
favour of the men, it did not terminate the lock-out which had
already begun at the end of the year. There were some hitches
and flaws in dealing with the demands of the Port Pirie men,
and their claims were quashed in the High Court when an
appeal was made by the company lawyers who took advantage
of technical faults. 'This experience of the admittedly most
perfect Arbitration Court in existence, with a Labour Government in power', wrote Mann, 'damped any enthusiasm I might
have felt for such an institution!'[53]

The Mines had been at a standstill since the beginning of
1909. The Combined Trade Union Committee of the ten unions
involved in the dispute now acted as a dispute committee. The
scenes of the Docklands in London in 1889 were now reproduced at this Barrier city in a more intense atmosphere of class
struggle. Co-operative stores and communal bakeries were
successfully set up, an elaborate system of picketing was maintained, and a daily procession of the men headed by a band and
a group of union officials was organized through a section of
the town and along a thoroughfare near the pit-heads. The
police behaved differently from the London policemen in 1889,
however, and an additional body of armed police, foot and
mounted, was brought in from Sydney. On Saturday 9 January,
the day of their arrival, the marchers found their way blocked
by the police who seized the union banner and used its pole as
a weapon to attack the men. Tom Mann was walking at the
head of the procession and was caught in the midst of the fray,
at the end of which he was taken to the police station together
with twenty-seven others: he was bailed out on the 11th by the
mayor of the city. 'History is being made here', read an urgent
message from Broken Hill: 'The workers were putting up a
gallant fight. . . . Tom Mann is at present the centre of capitalist
attack.'[54] At the Bijou Theatre Mrs Mann made an appeal to
'the workers of Australia' to 'rally to the aid of the fighters for
freedom at the barrier'.[55]

Tom was committed for trial at the quarter sessions to be
held in April at Albury. As the conditions of his bail compelled
him to refrain from public activities in New South Wales, he
held mass meetings at the border town of Cockburn, to which

[52] Mann, *Memoirs*, 186, 188-9.   [53] Ibid. 190.
[54] *Socialist* (15 Jan. 1909).   [55] Ibid.

special trains with a banner inscribed 'Tom Mann Train' on
the front of the engine, carried 4,000 people from Broken Hill.[56]
It was at this stage that Tom Mann severed his official connections with the VSP. An announcement in the *Socialist* read:

Tom Mann has decided not to again stand [sic] for re-election as secretary . . . In a very special way our comrade has been the pivot of the
Socialist Party. . . . He feels called up to operate in other domains for
the time being. The Broken Hill upheaval has revived and brought to
flame all his standing loyalty to, and belief in, industrial organisation.[57]

At the trial held at Albury in April, though charged with
sedition and unlawful assembly among other counts, Tom was
acquitted. A number of other leaders, however, were sent to
gaol for alleged rioting. By the end of May after twenty-one
weeks of strike–lock-out, the unions finally won their case. Tom
returned to Melbourne, and spent the latter part of the year,
devoting himself to the new mission of spreading industrial
unionism abroad. It has been pointed out that 'the strength of
the revolutionary socialists in the Australian labor movement
has never been their doctrines, but their organizing skill, their
ruthlessness, and the appeal of the immediate gains they have
won for the rank and file of the unions'.[58] Tom Mann symbolized such gains and skills in his devoted work for the Australian
workers.

Broken Hill left him with an important lesson. The armed
police had been transported from Sydney by the organized
railwaymen of New South Wales, themselves in full sympathy
with the Broken Hill men. The painful thought that working-
class solidarity did not exist among the organized workers led
Tom to write a pamphlet, *The Way to Win*, in which he set forth
the desirability of more complete industrial organization and
advocated such alterations in the existing unions as would
enable them to set up 'a genuine federation of all organisations,
with power to act unitedly for industrial purposes'.[59] This was
written for the use of a conference of trade-unionists to be held
in Adelaide in July 1909. He was generous enough to recommend to the conference a pamphlet by James Connolly as a
'better' exposition of the same subject. Connolly, who had been
in America, organizing his compatriots in his Irish Socialist
Federation, had been an earnest supporter of the IWW. After

---

[56] Mann, *Memoirs*, 191–2.   [57] *Socialist* (19 Feb. 1909).
[58] Kenneth F. Walker, in Walter Galenson (ed.), *Comparative Labor Movements* (New York, 1952), 236.   [59] Mann, *Memoirs*, 194–5.

having attended the 1908 convention of the IWW which witnessed the splitting away of the doctrinaire leftist De Leonites, he remained in Chicago, where Kerr & Co. published his articles on industrial unionism under the title *Socialism Made Easy*. In it he advocated industrial unity and also the need for securing 'a commanding position on the field of economic struggle', in other words economic hegemony by the workers.[60] E. J. B. Allen, who was later to emigrate to New Zealand, also sent Tom his own pamphlet *Revolutionary Socialism*. Allen had been one of the leaders of the non-political faction of the British Advocates of Industrial Unionism, a British IWW. Apparently Mann was anxious to return home to join in the new ferment of the British labour movement.

His farewell address was delivered at the Oddfellows' Hall, Port Adelaide, early in January 1910. On this occasion Tom spoke on 'The Outlook of Labour'. 'While believing in the wisdom of parliamentary action', he declared, 'there were tasks to be accomplished by the workers that could not be done by the Parliaments of the civilised world, which were essentially capitalistic in character. He was there to preach class war to the knife.' The audience generously contributed something in the shape of a New Year's gift for Mann and his family who, it was said, were 'not in the best circumstances'. Mrs Mann contributed a solo for the last time.[61] They left Adelaide by SS *Commonwealth* and after having stopped at Perth reached Durban on 21 February 1910. At the request of the Transvaal Miners' Association Tom launched an organizing campaign, advocating industrial unionism at Johannesburg, Pretoria, Kimberley, and Cape Town. He soon found that out of 21,000 white miners only 4,000 were organized, while 189,000 natives worked in the mines under most abject conditions of slavery.[62] From Cape Town Mann and his family sailed for England on 13 April and arrived in London on 10 May, after a long absence of eight and a half years. His years in Australasia and especially his experiences in the Broken Hill dispute forged out of him a devoted advocate of industrial unionism and syndicalism, a new industrial gospel that was to provide an alternative to the New Liberalism of Edwardian England.

[60] Reference in J. Connolly, *Workers' Republic: A Selection from the Writings of James Connolly*, ed. Desmond Ryan (Dublin, 1951), 75.

[61] Newspaper cutting, n.d. [Jan. 1910], attached to the copy at the Rhodes House, Oxford, of Mann's *Labour Movement in Both Hemispheres*.

[62] T. Mann, *From Single Tax to Syndicalism* (London, 1913), 63.

9. Syndicalism and Labour Unrest

THE years preceding the First World War were marked by a new ferment in the labour movement. The novel feature of labour unrest in this period was the spread of industrial union-ism and syndicalism, and Tom Mann, the syndicalist, was certainly a major influence in this new unrest. These were the years of a decline in real wages and of disillusionment with the newly created Labour Party especially over its inability to exact from the government adequate measures to cope with the unemployed problem. Tom Mann must have had mixed feelings about John Burns, now a Liberal Cabinet minister, who was largely responsible for the discomfiture of Labour MPs over this issue. Moreover, the situations of socialist politics were still fluid: both the SDF, now called the SDP (Social Democratic Party) and the ILP contained many who were thoroughly dis-satisfied with parliamentary politics. It is little wonder that Tom was welcomed into the SDP when he returned from the Antipodes.

The steamer *Narrung*, delayed by fog, brought Tom Mann, now almost a legendary figure wearing the revolutionary halo of the Broken Hill struggle, back to England to his old friends and new admirers, 230 in all, awaiting him at a London quay-side on 10 May 1910. Tillett and Guy Bowman, Tom's syndical-ist friend, walked to the boat to welcome him. 'Hi, boys!' said Tom, as he saw them. There were H. W. Lee and others from the SDP as well as several officials from the Dockers' Union. He rejoined the SDF (SDP), and 'an enthusiastic reception' presided over by Harry Quelch was held three days later at the Holborn Town Hall. R. B. Cunninghame Graham; Charles Duncan, MP, of the Workers' Union; H. W. Lee; and Tillett were among the hosts who greeted him. Tom said in his speech that he had gone to Australasia with 'a rosy view on conditions there', but he had met 'no attempt to encourage Socialism—the one idea was trade. . . . The Labour Parties really were Radical Parties'.[1] Ten days later Hyndman took the chair at St James's Hall at another reception for Tom. The old man was to write

[1] *Justice* (21 May 1910).

some kind words on him in his autobiography shortly to be published. In his usual condescending tones he reminisced:

For a good deal more than a quarter of a century, since Tom Mann came up to our house in Devonshire Street in 1884, he has been carrying on in the same way, not only in Great Britain but in Australia and elsewhere. There is no end to him. And his knowledge and charm of manner are equal to his marvellous vitality. Moreover, of all the Labour Leaders I have met, Tom Mann is the one who, however successful he may be, puts on the least 'side'. After a speech which has roused his audience to the highest pitch of almost hysterical enthusiasm, down Tom will step from the chair in the open air, or from the platform in the hall, and take names for branch or organisation, and sell literature to all and sundry as if he were the least-considered person at the gathering. Even those who differ most widely from him cannot but respect him, for he has assuredly gained nothing personally by his stupendous efforts.[2]

Tom reciprocated the same kindly regards in his memoirs, though he could not quite stomach Hyndman's 'bourgeois mentality'.[3]

Tom Mann's momentary *rapprochement* with the SDP was made easy at least in part by the presence of Guy Bowman among its active members. In spite of Hyndman, the SDF–SDP had by and large identified itself with the anti-militarist and anti-war cause. Bowman, who came from the Free Thought movement, was known as the translator of Gustave Hervé's anti-war book *My Country: Right or Wrong*. He wrote on 'the need of an armed nation' or a citizen-army. He accused many of the working-class leaders of being 'English jingoes' and 'allowing themselves to be carried by the current of anti-German feeling side by side with the capitalist class'.[4] Bowman had been appointed business and financial manager of the Twentieth Century Press, the SDF's publishing house. He, however, failed to secure the additional capital which he had promised for the press, and resigned.

But who was Guy Bowman? Two years later when he fell out of favour with the SDF because of his militant syndicalism, he was described as a Frenchman with an English name, a struggling journalist whose ability to supply money remained doubtful.[5] Certainly he was not a success as the TCP manager; the new press, called the TCP (1912), bought the assets of the old company which had been liquidated by a court order. But this

[2] H. M. Hyndman, *Further Reminiscences* (London, 1912), 464.
[3] T. Mann, *Tom Mann's Memoirs* (1923; London, 1967), 27.
[4] *Justice* (8 Aug. 1908).   [5] Ibid. (1 Feb. 1913).

is to anticipate. When Tom Mann returned home, Bowman apparently sought to make full use of his fame and enthusiasm as well as his own foothold in the SDF–SDP in order to promote the cause in which he believed. He proposed that Mann should visit Paris to study French syndicalism. Charles Marck, Tom's old friend in the days of his international work for the dockers and seamen, who was then an executive member of the CGT, acted as an intermediary, and Tom, accompanied by Bowman, went to Paris and 'examined thoroughly the principles and policy of the CGT, the Syndicalists of France'.[6] Before we set out to investigate the development of Tom's own syndicalism at some length, we shall review the current of labour discontent which provided a background for it and which was curiously embodied in Tillett himself, and was reflected in a devious way in Burns as well.

Tillett, who had returned to England two years before after a sojourn in Australia was also in a militant mood. His pamphlet *Is the Parliamentary Labour Party a Failure?*, published in 1908, presented the Dockers' challenge to the Labour MPs who appeared to have accepted the claims of 'the Temperance Liberal Party' at the expense of the unemployed problem which seemed to them all-important. It ran parallel to an earlier protest made in the House by Victor Grayson, the independent socialist MP, on the same subject. Indeed, Tillett, who had once been a temperance man himself, was one of the most vociferous among the critics of the Government Licensing Bill which, though killed in the Lords, attracted much support from Labour MPs. Echoing the sentiments expressed by Bishop Magee in a Lords' debate on a Licensing Bill in the 1870s, Tillett now declared: 'I would rather have England drunk, but free, than sober without freedom'.[7] He objected to MacDonald 'making a scape-goat of the President of the Local Government Board' (John Burns), while he himself denounced Henderson, Shackleton, and Snowden as 'hot-gospellers', 'betrayers', and 'Press flunkeys to Asquith'.[8]

He was certainly tender to Burns his old friend for whose vigorous personality he always had profound admiration. Years before when Burns attacked the young ILP as a 'bogus' organization largely because of his own fear of Champion's influence in the new party, Tillett sought to exhort him to a

[6] Mann, *Memoirs*, 203.   [7] *Justice* (6 Feb. 1909).
[8] B. Tillett, *Is the Parliamentary Labour Party a Failure?* (London, 1908), *passim*.

more sensible course of action.[9] At the founding conference held in 1900 of the Labour Representation Committee (the LRC, which became the Labour Party in 1906), Burns went out of his way to scoff at the appellation 'working-class'—'working-class' boots, trains, houses, margarine, and by implication parties—which in his view had become a symbol of inferiority for the workers who should be elevated as citizens.[10] Tillett, who represented the Dockers at the conference, might have fully endorsed Burns's view of the workers as men and citizens.

Meanwhile, the Taff Vale Decision of 1901, which frightened the trade-union world by making unions liable as a corporation for the damages caused by their officers, and which induced some of the larger trade unions such as the Engineers and the Textile Workers to join the LRC, proved a decisive factor for Burns to identify himself more closely with the Liberal Party, since his pet idea of a trade-union Labour Party with himself as its possible leader now visibly crumbled. He was not even sure of his own Battersea Labour League.[11] On the other hand, his friendship with Liberal politicians, which had been strengthened by his bold criticisms of the Boer War, was extended and consolidated, and he was offered the presidency of the Local Government Board in the new Liberal Government formed in December 1905. This 'popular' decision on the part of Sir Henry Campbell-Bannerman was indeed useful for 'Sir Enry' the new prime minister to counterbalance the weight of the Liberal imperialists in his Cabinet and also to appeal to the working-class electorate at the general election of January 1906,[12] which, in fact, resulted in a great landslide for the Liberals.

This is not the place to record the progress of the 'working-class' minister of the Crown, and it suffices to say that Burns's policy of retrenchment on the relief of the poor and the unemployed incurred the wrath of the Labour Party which now emerged as a force in Parliament, while a series of events and issues drove the Labour Party increasingly into the arms of the Liberal Party: the Licensing Bill of 1908 which we have already noted, the Osborne Judgement of 1909, and the National Insurance Act of 1911. Indeed, the parliamentary position of the Labour Party and its prestige among the rank and file of the

[9] B. Tillett to J. Burns, 6 Sept. 1893, BL Add. MS 46285, JBP.

[10] LRC, *Report of the Conference on Labour Representation* (London, 1900), 11, 13.

[11] J. Burns, Diary, 27 Jan., 20 Oct. 1904, BL Add. MS 46322, JBP.

[12] John Wilson, *Life of Sir Henry Campbell-Bannerman* (London, 1973), 436.

trade unions were evidently weakened. *Justice*, with a tinge of Schadenfreude, declared: 'The rank and file of the Labour movement is ahead of its leaders; the Government is ahead of the Labour Party, taking the wind out of their sails and pinching all the best goods out of their bags, while they stand aghast at the thieves.'[13] Referring obviously to his opponents in the Labour Party, Tillett told Burns: 'I am at war John with some of the poltroons abasing the Movement we gave our youth and manhood to.' He sent him a medal commemorating the London Dock Strike of 1889.[14] Burns, too, perhaps for the first time since he had become a Cabinet minister, began to pay more serious attention to 'Tillett, Dock, Port Labour'.[15] At the general election of January 1910, Tillett fought a three-cornered contest at Swansea and was badly defeated. It was at this juncture that Tom Mann, one of the old triumvirate of 1889, was returning to England after nine years' absence. Ben was anxiously awaiting Tom's home-coming so as to throw in his lot with him in his work for industrial unionism, which, he certainly hoped, would grow into something to outflank MacDonald's Labour politics.

Tillett's union offered facilities, including its newspaper *Dockers' Record*, for Tom's new propaganda and enabled him to speak at various meetings held all over the country, in London, Sharpness, Port Talbot, Middlesbrough, Hull, Southampton, Cadishead, Avonmouth, and Bristol.[16] Tom Mann, also in conjunction with Guy Bowman, founded a paper of his own: the *Industrial Syndicalist*. The first number came out in July 1910, and this apparently was the cause of Bowman's trouble with the TCP at the time. In this number Tom wrote a stirring appeal entitled 'Prepare for Action', declaring himself to be 'a common soldier in the People's Army'. Many sops, from 'bread and circuses' to 'profit sharing and old age pensions', had been thrown to 'the snarling Demos', whereas 'organisation is the one thing that the capitalist dreads more than the Ballot box', since a few years in Parliament could turn some revolutionary socialists into apologists for the existing state of society. He dwelled on 'the curse of sectional unionism' and proudly pointed to the past examples of direct action, especially those

---

[13] *Justice* (29 May 1909).
[14] B. Tillett to J. Burns, 31 Jan., 10 Aug. 1909, BL Add. MS 46285, JBP.
[15] Burns, Diary, 3 Feb. 1909, BL Add. MS 46311, JBP.
[16] Clegg *et al.*, *History of British Trade Unionism since 1889*, i (Oxford, 1964), 451.

of 1889. He also made it clear that industrial unionism was what he had in his mind for the ideal type of unionism, and his visit to the CGT had convinced him of its viability:

Their plan is to organise first in the syndicates or Unions; then for each Industry a federation of syndicates is formed; then, over all these Industrial federations is the General Confederation. . . . They declare themselves revolutionary. They favour resorting, when advisable, to the General Strike. But while working for the Revolution they do not neglect to do all possible to secure general betterment. They are, for the most part, anti-patriotic and anti-militarist. . . . They are 'non', not 'anti' Parliamentary.

The French policy, he felt, would 'suit us best' and at this stage he found a possible CGT for Britain in the General Federation of Trade Unions which had been set up for financial co-operation among the unions after the defeat of the Engineers twelve years before. The supreme aim of the new movement was to 'secure to the workers full fruits of their labour', and he concluded his appeal with a slogan borrowed from Marx:

'Unite' was Marx's advice long ago, but we have never thoroughly acted upon it. Now is the time to do it, and we will do it right here in England. . . . 'Workers of the World Unite. You have a World to Win. You have Nothing to Lose but your Chains'.[17]

In an article in *Justice*, Tom declared that 'economic or industrial organisation is the "right arm" of the workers' movement'. He was opposed to rival or dual unionism, and was determined to strive for 'the welding together of the existing unions by industries'. The same sentiment was repeated in his article 'Forging the Weapon' in the *Industrial Syndicalist*.[18]

In the same paper, Tillett had published a circular for setting up 'The National Federation of Transport Workers' and invited fourteen unions in the transport industry to a conference shortly to be held for that purpose. In it he drew attention to the fact that the introduction of new machines such as the suction elevator or the new and more efficient cranes did not alter the casual state of work in the Port of London. Meanwhile, the organization of the Dockers remained partial and sectional, and sectionalism weakened their potential strength. The executive council of his union now authorized Tillett to go on with his plan for a national federation. At the TUC held in Sheffield in September a resolution in favour of organization by

[17] T. Mann, 'Prepare for Action', *Industrial Syndicalist* (July 1910).
[18] *Justice* (10 Sept. 1910); *Industrial Syndicalist* (Sept. 1910).

industry on the basis of amalgamation and federation was carried by a large majority. The conference of the Transport Workers held at Compositors' Hall in the City on 27 September was also a great success. The delegates all declared amalgamation to be desirable but preferred federation as a more practical approach. Harry Gosling, the Watermen and Lightermen's secretary, took the chair, and was 'deeply impressed by the genuine desire for closer relationship shown by all'.[19] Will Thorne, representing the portion of the Gasworkers connected with transport, Charles Duncan, general secretary of the Workers' Union, and J. Havelock Wilson of the Seamen urged the need for action. Tom Mann was there as a delegate from the Dockers' Union and found it encouraging to see James Sexton of the National Union of the Dock Labourers (based in Liverpool), Joe Cotter of the Ship Stewards, and Ben Tillett of the London Dockers 'all declaring for common action'.[20] The first meeting of the council of the National Transport Workers' Federation was held on 10 November. Tillett acted as secretary until the federation was made to stand on its own by the affiliation of the Stevedores' Society; then Gosling on Tillett's recommendation became president of the federation and Anderson of the Stevedores its general secretary.

In the meantime Tillett presided over an anniversary meeting of the 1889 Dock Strike at the Boulogne Restaurant, where Tom Mann made 'a fighting speech' and Harry Quelch heartily responded to it. Bill Haywood of the Western Miners' Federation, an affiliate of the American IWW, was on his way back from Copenhagen where he had attended the congress of the Second International and was present at an SDF reception where he endorsed the remarks made by Tillett, one of the speakers, on industrial unionism. 'Parliament', said Haywood, 'could only assist the workers in organising for democratic management. He worked for the democratic management of things collectively owned.' At a meeting held in Burnley, the new trio of Haywood, Tom Mann, and Hyndman attracted a large audience; Mann emphasized the need for 'better organisation, both political and industrial, of the working class, urging closer solidarity among the workers'. Tillett reported on the Boilermakers' lock-out and the assistance given by the General Federation of Trade Unions, Tom Mann's CGT. Labour unrest had already begun and was gathering momentum.[21]

[19] Harry Gosling, *Up and Down Stream* (London, 1927), 147.
[20] T. Mann, 'All Hail Solidarity', *Industrial Syndicalist* (Oct. 1910).
[21] *Justice* (29 Oct. 1910).

'It is no exaggeration to say that the spirit of industrial dis-content was never so widespread as it is to-day', read a report in *Justice* from the South Wales coalfields.[22] A wage dispute at one of the Cambrian pits over the opening of a new seam led to the lock-out of the men involved, to a sympathetic strike, and finally to the great strike of all miners employed by the Cambrian Combine. Tom Mann was in Rhondda Valley early in September and in a 'very informative article'[23] pointed out the difficulty for the men arising out of the existence, apart from the South Wales Miners' Federation, of three other unions for the enginemen and the stokers who were still employed. 'Class solidarity by All leaving, and let the capitalists look after their property, or let it go to blazes, is the only sensible fighting policy', he declared.[24]

It was in such a fighting mood that Tom convened a con-ference on industrial unionism, or what he now chose to call industrial syndicalism, at the Coal Exchange, Manchester, on 26 November 1910, which was attended by 198 delegates in-cluding Noah Ablett of the Rhondda Miners and Jim Larkin of the Irish Transport Workers. Albert A. Purcell of the Man-chester Furnishing Trades took the chair and recommended amalgamation rather than federation. Tom Mann in his opening speech declared that the time was ripe 'for industrial action as distinct from trade action', and moved a resolution in favour of setting up 'a Syndicalist Education League to propagate the principles of Syndicalism throughout the British Isles, with a view to merging all existing unions into one compact organisa-tion for each industry, including all labourers of every industry in the same organisation as the skilled workers'. 'Capitalist organisations have travelled much faster than the workers', he added: 'They have syndicated their forces. We are called upon to do the same on the basis of class, and not to act sectionally.' Noah Ablett wanted the movement to grow sufficiently strong to 'paralyse industry', while Larkin desired Ireland to be left out of the resolution. A delegate from the sectarian Socialist Labour Party thought the whole venture mistaken. With two dissentients, probably one from the Industrial League (London) and the other from the IWW (Birmingham), who were in favour of dual unionism of the De Leonite type, the resolution was carried. Tom Mann reminded the delegates of a change that had taken place in the tactics of the American IWW, whereby

[22] *Justice* (29 Oct. 1910).
[23] R. Page Arnot, *South Wales Miners: A History of the South Wales Miners' Federation 1898-1914* (London, 1967), 184.   [24] *Justice* (12 Nov. 1910).

'they are throwing the A. F. of L. on to advanced lines'.[25] The close contact now formed between the Industrial Syndicalist Education League (ISEL) and the South Wales miners was due largely to their mutual rejection of dual unionism and to their efforts for radicalization of the existing trade unions.[26]

The 'whirl and swirl' of the general election in December 1910, wrote Tom Mann, tended to conceal the existence in the Rhondda and Aberdare valleys of 18,000 miners still locked out or on strike; moreover, the Aberdare men received no strike pay because of the 'unofficial' character of their strike, for the officers believed in 'Peace, sweet Peace, Conciliation, Arbitration'. And winter was not a good time for determined action. So Mann proposed a temporary cessation of warfare. 'I therefore say the fight should be stopped now, and all necessary action taken to secure unanimity of action over the whole of Britain; and not only with the Miners, but these should at once open up with the Transport Workers, and certainly with the Amalgamated Society of Railway Servants, to secure common action.'[27] It was indeed a prophetic advice in view of the future development of the Triple Alliance of the Miners, Transport Workers, and the Railwaymen, but the immediate prospect was grim. There had been violent clashes especially at Tonypandy between the men and the police led by the Chief Constable, an ex-major who regarded his forces almost as the 'Coalmasters' Army of Occupation in South Wales'.[28] As the situation deteriorated, Winston Churchill, the Home Secretary, intervened, and the military were used to reopen one colliery. Disturbances followed, the Miners' Federation of Great Britain decided to withdraw support, and the strike had petered out by August 1911.

Tom Mann had to concentrate on the industrial front, though he had repeatedly declared himself to be non-parliamentary, but not anti-parliamentary. When he was asked by the SDP committee on Parliament to contest North Aberdeen, he declined the invitation, stating as his reason that he had entered upon a task, 'a really big one' which 'demands all the energy I can put into it'.[29] This was followed by the announcement of his resignation from the SDP in May 1911. In a letter to H. W. Lee, the secretary, he wrote:

[25] *Industrial Syndicalist* (Dec. 1910).
[26] Bob Holton, *British Syndicalism 1900–1914* (London, 1976), 61.
[27] T. Mann, 'Class War in Wales', *Justice* (10 Dec. 1910).
[28] Arnot, *South Wales Miners*, 182.
[29] T. Mann to H. W. Lee, 7 Feb. 1911, *Justice* (20 May 1911).

I do so [tender my resignation] partly because of the endorsement by the recent conference of the official attitude of the Party on the issue of war, but more because, since rejoining the party a year ago on my return to this country, I find myself not in agreement with the party on the important matter of Parliamentary action. . . . I declare in favour of direct industrial organisation, not as a means, but THE means whereby the workers can ultimately overthrow the capitalist system and become the actual controllers of their own industrial and social destiny.[30]

Ben Tillett, for his part, had been elected to the executive committee of the SDP at its annual conference of April 1911, where the executive amendment in favour of 'the maintenance of an adequate Navy for national defence' was carried with a small majority.[31]

Trade was now good, having recovered from the depression of 1908, and the cost of living was rising. As John Burns had once said, 'the psychological hour' had come, and everything seemed possible. It was the same with Burns himself. He had been unpopular and frustrated as the head of the LGB, and had thought of resigning even at a very early stage. After a year and a half in office, he began to ponder over the cause of his depression: 'I am afraid I have too much pride for office. 16 months wrestling with fossils inside and fools and firebrands outside has taken much of the milk of human kindness from me.'[32] With the recovery of trade, the gospel of direct action began to appear attractive once more. He felt his life as a Cabinet minister was not exactly what he had desired, and wished to 'regain my freedom of action and speech'.[33] He wrote to Tillett, enquiring about the dockers, and asked him for precise information on casual labour in the docks.[34] The cause of the dockers became Burns's cause again, and he regretted that 'a long continued stay in office, over-routine work and overmuch detail has enchained my spirit and depressed my power'.[35]

As Gosling said, it was J. Havelock Wilson who 'set fire to the heather' by bringing his men into the Transport Workers' Federation and thereby strengthening his hand in his battle with the Shipping Federation. On 14 June 1911 the sailors at

[30] *Justice* (13 May 1911); reproduced in *Social Democrat* (Sept. 1911).
[31] *Justice* (22 Apr. 1911).
[32] Burns, Diary, 19 Apr. 1907, BL Add. MS 46325, JBP.
[33] Ibid., 5 Feb. 1911, BL Add. MS 46333, JBP.
[34] Ibid., 4 Mar., 20 Apr. 1911, BL Add. MS 46333, JBP.
[35] Ibid., 14 May 1911, BL Add. MS 46333, JBP.

Southampton went on strike unofficially and prevented the sailing of the new liner SS *Olympic*. Wilson's union now called for a national strike and asked for support from the federation. Nearly all the ports in the provinces were affected, Hull among others. At a Cabinet meeting held on 28 June, Burns spoke on the strike at Hull 'which I handled as to military and police in the light of their provocative use 18 years ago'.[36] The transport Workers' Federation called upon the London port-workers for a sympathetic strike. Tillett decided to take advantage of this situation to press for a minimum rate of 8d. and 1s. for overtime for a dock labourer, and on 29 June he presented the 'Dockers' Ultimatum' to 'the Port of London Authority, Ship, Dock Wharf & Quay Owners, and Managers of the Port of London', which led to negotiations with the employers. The 'Manifesto' Tillett issued on the following day complained that the Mansion House agreements of 1889 had 'in no way been honoured': the minimum period of employment or payment had not been respected, the proper call-time ignored, some of the places of hiring where a 'hunger battle' took place every morning being 'a disgrace to society and British freedom'.[37]

At a conference finally held from 25 to 27 July between the representatives of the PLA and of the NTWF, Gosling presented the men's case, stressing that 'we have every right to a fair share of any increased facilities and earning powers just as have the employers'. Discussions followed paths familiar to the 1889 strike on issues related to decasualization; and terms of settlement were suggested which would concede a penny or two less than the terms of the ultimatum. At a mass meeting of the Transport Workers held on the following day at the Assembly Hall, the largest hall in the East End, the men rejected the offer. 'It may be said', wrote Tillett, 'that the stopping of vessels of one or two of the big lines, particularly on the Surrey side, had had the effect of whetting the appetites of the men and rousing them to a new consciousness of manhood and strength.'[38]

Meanwhile, the main points at issue were submitted to arbitration: these were the Sailors' objection to the 'Shipping Federation Ticket', the rate of 8d. and 1s., and the payment of mealtimes. Before arbitration set to work, industrial war had been declared on 2 August in the great excitement started off

[36] Ibid., 28 June 1911, BL Add. MS 46333, JBP.
[37] Dockers' Union, Manifesto, 30 June 1911, ITWFA.
[38] B. Tillett, *History of the London Transport Workers' Strike* (London, 1911), 8, 14.

at the Assembly Hall meeting. At another mass meeting of the dockers held at West Ham on that evening, the leaders of the Dockers' Union and of the NTWF 'decided to bend with the wind and accept the inevitability of a stoppage',[39] and an official call was issued for a general strike throughout the port of London. By 4 August there were 20,000 men out. The dispute committee met for the first time on the 5th and took control of the movement which was 'spontaneous on the men's part'.[40] Surely the strike was another round in the struggle for the dockers' tanner and something more. At a great meeting, one of the largest ever held in Trafalgar Square on Sunday 6 August, the strike leaders were able to announce that arbitration had been made in favour of the men. John Burns took a cab and drove to the square to see 'a very large orderly crowd better dressed and of good appearance'. 'Sincerely delighted', he wrote, 'that our old friends had done so well in the recent negotiations and rejoice that such a step upward was possible as the result of 1889. I have frequently seen B. Tillett and Devonport [Lord Devonport, the chairman of the PLA] in the early stages of discussion of details and Tillett last week.'[41]

The favourable results of arbitration, however, did not terminate the strike, as the Coal-Porters' and Lightermen's claims were cropping up. The strike committee of the NTWF urged the men to stand firm and refuse to start work until a satisfactory settlement could be obtained. 'Strike proceeds vigorously, Continental ports must support', Tillett cabled to H. Jochade of the International Transport Workers' Federation.[42] The response was enthusiastic and excitement was spreading.

The Transport Workers had held up every service—coal and water, gas and electricity, meat, flour, ice and vegetables, materials for commerce, products of the workshops, the factory and the mill, the meadow and the field; the railway service, transport by road, water and river all ceased their hum,

wrote Tillett, taking an immense pride in the worker who was 'by far the superior person'.[43] On 9 August Tillett went to see Burns who 'told him to bridle his tongue and settle before what had been secured had frittered away. Gave him tea and had a pleasant chat and tried to drill some good advice into him.'

[39] John Lovell, *Stevedores and Dockers* (London, 1969), 168.
[40] B. Tillett to H. Jochade, 19 Aug. 1911, ITWFA.
[41] Burns, Diary, 6 Aug. 1911, BL Add. MS 46333, JBP.
[42] B. Tillett to H. Jochade, Cablegram, 7 Aug. 1911, ITWFA.
[43] Tillett, *History*, 20.

Burns also saw Devonport in the Lords about the same matters. 'Devonport showed agreement which Tillett had signed and so far as he was concerned that settled P.L.A. terms.'[44] On the following day when the Lords yielded to the Commons by accepting the Parliament Bill and when the payment of Members was carried in the Commons, Burns, encouraged by these events, went to the Home Office to confer on the strike situation:

Urged that situation not so serious as alleged, food not much dearer, the Press was lying about the matter, and advised coolness and the police alone dealing with situation. After Conference went to Smithfield, Billingsgate, Covent Garden, Cold Storage, Docks, Mile End Rd., Commercial Rd., Poplar, and back to NLC [National Liberal Club] and Home Office at 2. After this round Docks, Markets, Tower, and on telephone with Tillett and others, to LGB for business. A great day for people, Lords, Payment of Members, Dock Dispute. Carmen notorious. It moves.[45]

The carmen had paralysed the whole of London's street traffic. A warning had been given that 25,000 soldiers awaited the order to man the ships and clear the docks, and Burns worked hard to persuade his colleagues that there was no need for their use. The situation, however, remained tense. It was decided that no permits were to be issued, other than to supply hospitals, asylums, and public-health bodies with necessities, pending the result of negotiations. As in 1889, a great march through the streets of the City was organized, a march this time of 100,000 men.[46] By 11 August most of the claims of the Lightermen and the Carmen were met. On the following day recorded Burns: 'The papers are full of strikes, riots and veiled instigations thereto in the hope and wish they could occur. London has done very well. I am sincerely pleased that Carmen, Dock Labourers and Stevedores have done so well.'[47] The flame of the strike in the Port of London was rekindled when it became known that the PLA had failed to honour the terms of settlement on one important point: the reinstatement of the men. The 'Government on Tower Hill' continued. It became 'the hub of industrial England'. 'The seat of the mighty', wrote Tillett, 'had shifted to Tower Hill. . . . It was on the Hill

[44] Burns, Diary, 9 Aug. 1911, BL Add. MS 46333, JBP.
[45] Ibid., 10 Aug. 1911, BL Add. MS 46333, JBP.
[46] Tillett, *History*, 23–5.
[47] Burns, Diary, 12 Aug. 1911, BL Add. MS 46333, JBP.

our Strike Committee issued orders of war, of treaty; we governed more than the ten million people of the Thames Valley.'[48]
There followed a coolness between the Board of Trade and the strike committee. On 16 August Burns again found himself on Tower Hill, and at a Cabinet meeting on that day 'gave the real facts of situation, urged caution and that situation could be met by the normal conditions, that extraordinary safeguards would defeat their objects and provoke instead of pacifying. They agreed'. Then he attended a conference in the House of Commons with Churchill and Harry Gosling. 'A respite for at least 24 hours. Took H.G. home and was all night in cab at Docks, Stratford, N. Woolwich, Albert Docks, and struck with the tired . . . men and women in endless procession to their too early work.'[49]

Final settlements were reached by the Home Office agreement of 18 August in which Churchill and Burns played leading roles. On that day Burns took the chair at the conference between the Shippers and the Dockers:

We argued, persuaded, implored and after several abortive attempts to secure agreement managed to pull Scrutton over and convince Torrey and persuade Potter [*all on the employer's side*] to concede the question of *outside* place of call. This I know was to the men the vital point, convinced the men to abandon Foremen and Tally Clerks contention whom they do not need and whom they always suspect. Urged the masters to see the general situation, the Government's difficulties, their own position and the need of agreement in a friendly way with men. I could only get them our way by promising to see that the men accepted agreement. This settled it and we won.[50]

'John Burns redivivus', wrote Tillett:

He coaxed and bullied, reasoned and flouted, ever at the service of both sides. The war-horse, who was not killed by the atrophy of office, came out. The years have dealt more kindly with his strength than his appearance, but there was the old ring, triumphant, confident, swaggeringly confident; the toss of the head, the banter, were there, old memories crowded into conversations now and again when the halt came, as halts came again and again in painful weariness—it was the talk of the old times. Although the dock agitator was now a Cabinet Minister, he really forgot that at times.[51]

It was a repetition of 1889 in all its essentials, as Harry Quelch wrote, only with greater spontaneity and larger aims.[52] On

[48] Tillett, *History*, p. 29.
[49] Burns, Diary, 16 Aug. 1911, BL Add. MS 46333, JBP.
[50] Ibid., 18 Aug. 1911, BL Add. MS 46333, JBP.
[51] Tillett, *History*, 36.   [52] H. Quelch, Pref. to Tillett, *History*, p. iii.

19 August Burns visited ports of call near the docks and wharfs, and

addressed in happy hearty mood a really joyous throng of hard beaten, strong, lusty fellows who were very cordial to me. . . . Orbell took the chair, and after 15 minutes of speech from myself reviewing 1889, the present dispute and the need for discipline, good temper and adherence to their leaders and the joint agreement we ended a great gathering in a tempest of hearty cheers. A bold stroke for an arbitrator to address one side.

Thus he congratulated himself.[53]

Tillett and his associates pursued the contradictory tactics of arbitration and general strike, for which they were perhaps wrongly accused of 'duplicity'; and the real cause for this, it has been suggested, was that 'they had little control over the forces which they were supposed to be leading'.[54] Hyndman himself had expressed similar views with greater sympathy:

Tillett, who is one of the ablest organisers, as he is one of the finest orators in the Trade Union Movement, had his hand forced by the men themselves . . . he . . . referred every difficult question for decision to the men themselves at their public gatherings. He and they won; but he knew, if they did not, that it was a touch-and-go affair; that but for the fine weather and the hot sun, the strikers would not have stood out so long. . . . In my opinion Tillett . . . deserved the highest credit for the manner in which he kept his head and handled the situation in that most difficult time.[55]

The Transport Workers' Strike of 1911 was not simply a spontaneous revolt of the masses in the ports, but it was planned and premeditated as a counter-attack against the supremacy of the Shipping Federation for the previous two decades, and the convergence of these two elements produced the atmosphere of 'Syndicalism as a mood' for Tillett and even for Mann. According to Mann, June had been selected for the best month in the year for the struggle because trade was exceptionally busy and the coronation scheduled in that month would attract a number of overseas visitors. In fact, SS *Olympic* was to bring over a contingent of American millionaires who had come to the occasion.[56]

On the 14 June when the Seamen went on strike at Southampton, Liverpool had its own trouble, for 500 firemen refused

---

[53] Burns, Diary, 19 Aug. 1911, BL Add. MS 46333, JBP.
[54] Lovell, *Stevedores and Dockers*, 169.
[55] Hyndman, *Further Reminiscences*, 462.
[56] T. Mann, *From Single Tax to Syndicalism* (London, 1913), 68–9.

to 'sign on' for SS *Empress of Ireland* of the Canadian Pacific Line and for SS *Teutonic* and SS *Baltic*, both of the White Star Line. Tom Mann had arrived in Liverpool the day before; he formed a strike committee, and acted as its chairman. In fact, Liverpool was 'spearheading a national movement': it was the employers' weakest link, because some of its largest shipping lines were not affiliated to the Shipping Federation,[57] and Tom Mann was chosen to lead the strike there. Liverpool had shown considerable interest in syndicalism: eight delegates from the city had participated in the Manchester Conference to launch the Syndicalist Education League.

'War declared. Strike for Liberty.' This was the signal with which Tom Mann inaugurated the shipping strike in Liverpool. The District Joint Strike Committee led by Tom adopted a strategy which was to seek a favourable settlement with the large independent shipping companies who were prepared to concede and then to turn attention to the smaller firms that were supported by the Shipping Federation, 'the bitterest enemies of the workers', as Mann put it.[58] And it worked. In the wake of the old family firm of Alfred Holt granting the demands of the Seamen on the first day of the strike, there followed concessions made by the Canadian Pacific, the White Star, the Cunard, Booth, and others. The Stewards' Union also joined in the struggle, 'throwing sectionalism to the winds'. Dockers and carters were soon involved, and they acted in unison, though the dockers were largely Catholic and the carters Protestant.[59] Mann organized a demonstration at St George's Plateau on the evening of 25 June, where he distributed over 50,000 copies of a manifesto, calling upon all waterfront workers to refuse to handle the goods of the firm blacklisted. Some three to four thousand workers attended the demonstration to support the Seamen and listened to Mann who was described by a reporter as having 'a stocky figure, a deep, broad chest, and a voice which rings above the clamorous railway bells, the roll of the overhead trains, and the deep rumbles of the lorries'.[60] In his speech, referring to the conversion by the Shipping Federation of the *Friesland*, a 6409-ton steamer, into a depot ship for the

[57] H. R. Hikins, 'Liverpool General Transport Strike 1911', *Historic Society of Lancashire and Cheshire Transactions*, 113 (1961), 169.

[58] *Liverpool Daily Post and Mercury* (15, 22 June 1911); Eric Taplin, *Dockers' Union: A Study of the National Union of Dock Labourers 1889–1922* (Leicester, 1985), 85.

[59] Hikins, 'Liverpool General Transport Strike', 175.

[60] *Liverpool Daily Post and Mercury* (28 June 1911).

blacklegs, Mann called it a 'Leper Ship' which he would like to sink 'if he were able to'.[61] This was a violent speech for Tom.

He had been in close consultation with James Sexton general secretary of the Liverpool-based National Union of Dock Labourers, and the NUDL now put forward demands of their own: union rates of pay and union recognition. Mann and Sexton successfully negotiated with some of the small firms as well: sixteen shipping companies, large and small, had conceded the men's demands by 28 June. On that day 10,000 ship waiters came out to hold up transatlantic trade. The strike flared up again and spread to the dock labourers and coal-heavers. In spite of the growing unrest on the waterfront, Mann and Sexton continued negotiations patiently with companies that had not recognized all the unions involved, and a final settlement satisfactory to the men was signed on 4 August.

The spirit of revolt was such that there had been a rank and file defiance of the leadership towards the end of June when the strike committee gave instructions to resume work pending negotiations with the Cunard chairman. The committee, giving five shillings per week strike pay to all involved, knew its own weakness and was apparently concerned with the need to retain public sympathy by reasonableness of its demands. A Sunday meeting at St George's Plateau was turned into a mass meeting for the strike committee to explain the situation on the docks. 'I am going down to tell these men my honest opinion', said Mann, 'if, even, they should throw me in the dock afterwards. I have never been afraid of facing the employers and I shall never be afraid of facing workmen. No man shall ever accuse me of fear or insincerity.'[62] Trade-union discipline was thus enforced on the new recruits. In fact, the 'joining in the union' movement was such a success that Sexton could tell the Trades Council meeting in July that his union had grown in membership from 8,000 to 26,000 in five weeks.[63]

Now peace returned, but it was armed peace. In order to strengthen the syndicalist position in the struggle, Tom Mann founded the *Transport Worker*, a monthly paper edited by himself, priced at a penny a copy, the first number of which, in 2,000 copies, came out on 8 August. Its declared aim was 'to raise the standard of life of the workers by means of Industrial Organisation', the keynote was to be 'industrial solidarity on purely non-political lines', and its ultimate object 'to secure for

[61] Ibid. (16 June 1911).
[62] Hikins, 'Liverpool General Transport Strike', 179–80.   [63] Ibid. 182.

all workers the full reward of their toil', and achieve a syndic-alist commonwealth.[64] Indeed, peace had been broken even before the launching of the paper. On 5 August railwaymen employed by Lancashire and Yorkshire Railway began an unofficial strike, but their union, the Amalgamated Society of Railway Servants, advised them to refer their grievances to the Conciliation Board. The strikers were soon joined by the railway-goods porters on the quayside, but the company promptly introduced blackleg porters from outside Liverpool. The number of men on strike reached some 4,000, and Mann's committee took the matter into their own hands and pledged the support of all transport workers, the introduction of black-legs being 'an all sufficient reason' for it.[65] The *Transport Worker* issued a special strike edition in which appeared the declaration by the National Transport Workers' Federation (Liverpool District), dated 9 August, of a general strike of all transport workers of the Liverpool district to start at midnight of 14 August.

There had been little violence during the whole course of the strike since mid-June, but at this stage the situation deterior-ated as extra police arrived from London and Birmingham, and soldiers of the 2nd Warwickshire Regiment came to Seaforth barracks. 'The whole of Liverpool looked like an armed camp.' Apart from the Warwickshire Regiment, there were the North-umberland Fusiliers, the Scots Greys, the 2nd South Stafford-shire Regiment, and the Hussars; one gun-boat was moored in the Mersey near the landing place.[66] On Sunday 13 August, 'Red' or 'Black' Sunday as it was soon to be called, an estimated 80,000 people turned up for a demonstration organized by the strike committee in support of the railwaymen at St George's Plateau. A scuffle took place, and police were suddenly let loose on the crowd: a night of looting and battles with police and troops followed with some 350 wounded. 'I witnessed the savage attack', wrote Mann:

I saw men six feet high with long truncheons run off Lime Street into the thick of the crowd, and indiscriminately strike with full force, boys and men, on the head with batons, persons who had absolutely neither said one word nor performed any act other than stand as near as they could get to one or other of the platforms, and were listening attentively

---

[64] *Transport Worker* (Aug. 1911). By Oct. the paper had attained a circulation of 20,000 throughout Merseyside and the North-West. Holton, *British Syndicalism*, 103.

[65] T. Mann, 'Bravo Railwaymen', *Transport Worker* (Aug. 1911).

[66] Id., *From Single Tax to Syndicalism*, 79–80.

to the speeches being delivered. So dastardly an attack, such uncalled for brutality, has not been witnessed in England for over fifty years.[67]

'Ugly but exaggerated news from Liverpool', wrote Burns in his diary.[68] In the course of the next few days Liverpool came to a standstill. Two thousand extra troops were rushed to the city, as the strike committee decided on the transport of goods in the city by issuing permits. Their handling of permits for milk and for bread, like a similar situation created in the Port of London, might as well be described as 'working-class control of the means of distribution'.[69] In the struggle that ensued, two workers, one docker and one carter, were shot dead.

Meanwhile, the railway dispute in Liverpool became part of the national railway strike which began on 17 August and lasted three days. The Government intervened and brought both sides to accept a temporary solution—resumption of work with no dismissals while a government commission prepared a report on the dispute. The Liverpool City Corporation, however, decided against the reinstatement of 250 tramwaymen on strike; the strike committee threatened a national strike, and this forced the corporation to accept a compromise that all would be employed as vacancies took place. 'Tom Mann unsuccessful in his appeal to T.W.F.', commented Burns.[70] At any rate the great Transport Workers' struggle of 1911 came to a close with an agreement finally reached between the shipowners and the NUDL on 25 August. Work was resumed the following day.

Tom Mann believed that his experiences in 1911 had justified the resort to direct action. 'Fight on, Brothers, fight on, never have we [had] such good conditions under which to fight.' He chose an eight-hour day as the aim of the fight,[71] and carried on his agitation, visiting the men in dispute all over the country from Pontypridd to Glasgow and Belfast.

In January 1912 the first number of the *Syndicalist*, the new paper of Mann's Industrial Syndicalist Education League, came out. In it Mann declared: '1911 opened the eyes of many as to a few things that can be done when Solidarity is in the

[67] *Transport Worker* (Aug. 1911).
[68] Burns, Diary, 15 Aug. 1911, BL Add. MS 46333, JBP.
[69] Hikins, 'Liverpool General Transport Strike', 194.
[70] Burns, Diary, 24 Aug. 1911, BL Add. MS 46333, JBP.
[71] T. Mann, 'Looking Backward and Forward', *Transport Worker* (Jan. 1912); id., 'Eight Hour Day: Get Ready for the Fray', *Transport Worker* (Feb. 1912).

saddle. 1912 will show this in a much larger degree.' There followed an account of the league's New Year's Eve festivities held at Anderton's Hotel, Fleet Street, where George Lansbury, then MP for Bow and Bromley and a crusader for many causes, took the chair. Tom Mann gave an account of the Liverpool struggle, Elsie Mann contributed 'a musical prelude', and the Italian anarchist Malatesta congratulated the league on its libertarian ideals. Then on page three of the same number of the paper appeared an 'Open Letter to British Soldiers':

Men! Comrades! Brothers! You are in the Army. So are we. You, in the army of Destruction. We, in the Industrial, or army of Construction. . . . You are workingmen's Sons. When we go on Strike to better our lot, which is the lot of Your Fathers, Mothers, Brothers and Sisters, You are called upon by your officers to Murder US. Don't do it! . . . Don't disgrace Your Parents, Your Class, by being the willing tools any longer of the MASTER CLASS. . . . Help us to win back BRITAIN for the BRITISH and the WORLD for the WORKERS!

This was not the first time that the famous 'Don't Shoot' manifesto, written by a syndicalist mason, Fred Bower, had appeared in print. The previous publication of the same in Larkin's *Irish Worker* in July 1911 did not cause alarm or even curiosity. As Tom Mann said, no special importance was attached to it even when it was republished in the *Syndicalist*. But the embers of the labour unrest of 1911 again flared up early in 1912 when the Miners, demanding a district minimum wage, staged a national strike, 'the greatest till then of a whole industry in any country'.[72] The strike began on 1 March. Meanwhile, Fred Crowsley, a railwayman who distributed the manifesto among the soldiers at Aldershot, was arrested. Soon the printers, the two brothers Buck, and the editor, Guy Bowman, of the *Syndicalist* were in gaol. Tom Mann himself was arrested at his home at 23 Engadine Street, Southfields, Wimbledon on 19 March, on a warrant issued at Salford. It is noteworthy that the Government introduced its Minimum Wage Bill for the miners on the same day. The Welsh miners felt Mann was persecuted for their sake.[73]

'Don't worry Mam,' wrote Mann to Elsie from a superintendent's office at Scotland Yard, 'This won't hurt me & I shall be as right as pie. . . . I'm not a bit sorry on my own personal account. Kiss the Kiddies & give them their money on Saturdays; Charly & Elsie ought to have 2d each for stamps. Best love dear

[72] Arnot, *South Wales Miners*, 275.   [73] Ibid. 316.

Mamie.'[74] About midday he was escorted out from St Pancras Station to Salford. Excitement in Manchester was such that he was made to get off at Stockport where a detective had a taxi ready but 'photographers had got wind of it & quite a host were on the steps with cameras', he wrote from a cell at Salford Town Hall.[75] He was moved to Strangeways Prison, Manchester; from there he wrote to Elsie again: 'If you have time I wish you could do something for "Transport Worker" at once, as I cannot owing to regulations, also a note to "La Bataille" or Marck.'[76] The *Transport Worker*, however, came to an end with its March number, while the *Syndicalist* was kept going with the assistance by Gaylord Wilshire the wealthy American socialist.

Meanwhile, the Salford police made known the full charges against Mann. Thus 'as I understood it', he wrote to Elsie, 'I am charged with 1. Responsibility for publication [of the January number of the *Syndicalist*], 2. Inciting to Mutiny by speech etc. at Pendleton [near Salford], 3. For disposing of the paper contrary &c.'[77] The charge of 'Inciting to Mutiny' was related to the fact that the members of the Workers' Union at a meeting held at Pendleton on 13 and again on 14 March had cheered Tom Mann when he gave an anti-militarist speech quoting the manifesto, and defied the Government and the police by asking what was the purpose of the temporary barracks built around Manchester. He was tried at the Manchester assizes on 6 May and defended himself. He was sentenced to six months' imprisonment, but this was reduced to two, to be served in Strangeways Prison. A few days before the trial he spoke to a friend who came to visit him:

I desire to tell you that I would put forth all the mental and physical energy of which I am capable in fighting down poverty and in uprooting the causes thereof. In doing that I have received many criticisms, but I have no complaint to make. ... I am like unto John the Baptist in attitude. He believed the day of Lord was at hand. I believe the day of the people is immediately at hand, but I also know that our day of emancipation cannot come of its own accord. It must be ushered in by the workers without the help of the capitalist class.[78]

It is easy to see the great distance he had travelled since the days when he had argued with Alfred Marshall about Mill's

---

[74] T. Mann to Elsie Mann, 19 Mar. 1912, DTP.
[75] T. Mann to Elsie Mann, 20 Mar. 1912, DTP.
[76] T. Mann to Elsie Mann, 22 Mar. 1912, DTP.
[77] T. Mann to Elsie Mann, 27 Mar. 1912, DTP.
[78] *Syndicalist* (June 1912).

socialism and about the length of time it would take to achieve it. It is equally easy to note an element of millenarianism in his statement, but we should not put too great store on this aspect of his argument, for it largely reflected his own experience at Liverpool in 1911, when sixteen shipping companies, one after another, accepted the terms of the men under his leadership.

On 1 April while he was out on bail awaiting his trial, Tom Mann wrote an article on 'The Uprising of British Miners' in which he gave an account of the Miners' national strike. He deplored the fact that 'neither leaders nor rank and file (apart from a small but virile minority), had any real grasp of the true principle of industrial solidarity'. Thus the Miners' leaders declined the offer of assistance made by the National Executive of the NTWF. He especially commended *The Miners' Next Step*, a pamphlet recently published by the Unofficial Reform Committee of the South Wales Miners' Federation, Noah Ablett and W. H. Mainwaring among others, 'an exceedingly well written and well thought out product'. The young Welsh miners advocated 'a united industrial organisation' and 'a programme of a wide and evolutionary working-class character, admitting and encouraging sympathetic action with other sections of the workers'. The Coal Mine (Minimum Wage) Act which became law on 29 March, and which recognized only the principle of a minimum wage to be determined by district boards, Mann felt, was 'no great gain',[79] but the leaders' decision for a general return to work on this basis, though it led to further unrest in certain mining districts, found the Welsh miners overwhelmingly for resumption.

In the meantime John Burns was helping Lloyd George with his Insurance Bill. 'At 53 how different the outlook is as compared with 33,' he wrote at the time: 'And how little mere acts of Parliament affect the social and industrial life of the people except where they give the means of life and labour ... or reduce hours of overworked and thus spread available employment over large number.'[80] With reference to 'industrial unrest' among the miners, he commented: 'A nation whose workmen have ceased to strike has begun to die, and ought not to live. Strike but a symptom of large desire, better appetites, a larger share of wealth.'[81] 'Thought over Coal situation,' he wrote again; 'If they [the miners] were presciently wise they would avoid a legislative minimum because that will stereo-

[79] *International Socialist Review*, 12: 11 (May 1912), 711–16.
[80] Burns, Diary, 11 Feb. 1912, BL Add. MS 46334, JBP.
[81] Ibid., 20 Feb. 1912, BL Add. MS 46334, JBP.

type itself in their wage rate longer than they think. "The Dockers Tanner" stayed 10 years longer than it should have done because it was a fetish with men and a dogma with Employers.'[82] His position was thus remarkably close to Tom Mann's.

At a time when the prosecution against the *Syndicalist* began, Burns reflected in his diary: 'We are in for a very anxious time. Personally I have been anxious to resign and resume my place in the Labour movement.'[83] On 19 March when the Miners' Bill was introduced, he 'did his best to make it temporary ... experimental and to withdraw from it the elements of precedent of Compulsory Arbitration'.[84] Mann, as we have seen, was arrested on this day. Shortly afterwards Burns wrote: 'I am undecided as to immediate action. Personally I should like to be free of office and able to face the future of the Labour Movement which now wants guidance and lacks leadership.'[85] The same sentiment came back to him again and again: 'Thought over personal position. My own untrammeled view is to resign at once. I am tired of being a mere Civil Servant, denied the freedom and opportunity of influencing events which in Labour sphere is waiting and wanting.'[86] Burns, however, did not agree with syndicalism and was convinced that 'Labour by a General Strike could not hold up Society; when it did it was Civil War and then the other issues come in.'[87] In spite of his reasoned opposition to direct action, even he was affected by 'syndicalism as a mood', or it is perhaps truer to say that Tom's heroic struggle and sacrifice helped to revive his memories of the comradeship and rivalries of bygone days.

While Tom Mann was in his Manchester prison and Havelock Wilson was away in the United States, there took place another transport strike in London, which, Mann believed, had been caused by the treatment of one man, a member of the Lightermen's Union, a watchman formerly a foreman, who was used by the firms 'with the avowed object of breaking up the solidarity brought about by the Transport Workers' Federation'. 'No Syndicalist has had anything whatever to do with the

---

[82] Ibid., 3 Mar. 1912, BL Add. MS 46334, JBP.
[83] Ibid., 15 Mar. 1912, BL Add. MS 46334, JBP.
[84] Ibid., 19 Mar. 1912, BL Add. MS 46334, JBP.
[85] Ibid., 31 Mar. 1912, BL Add. MS 46334, JBP.
[86] Ibid., 14 Apr. 1912, BL Add. MS 46334, JBP.
[87] Ibid., 10 Apr. 1912, BL Add. MS 46334, JBP.

leading of this dock strike, which is the most preposterous and the most insane trade union action that has taken place for a long time,' commented the *Syndicalist*.[88] According to Tillett's report of the 'General Strike in the Transport Industry on the rivers Thames and Medway' which was officially declared on 23 May 1912, the dispute originated in an atmosphere in which a number of employers set out deliberately to violate the agreements reached in the previous year on matters principally concerning wages and union recognition. In the end 'between 70,000 and 80,000 men were called upon to leave their work to compel a man to join a Trade Union', in other words to oblige the watchman to join or stay in the Watermen and Lightermen's Union, while the Master Lightermen's Association had agreed to assist the firm hit by the original dispute.[89] It was certainly a preposterous but desperate fight.

John Burns was again in touch with Tillett and Gosling, leaders of the strike, in an effort to find a solution. 'Attended Masters Conference at H. of C. but before saw Orbell, Gosling and Tillett, and warned them that . . . they were risking their chance of being right with the public.'[90] Burns was against any legislative settlement:

I put strongly to Cabinet that we were Governors and not Strike Makers nor Strike Breakers as the convenience of Labour Leaders may decide who want Government to relieve them of their Liability and mistakes by shifting the venue from the Trade Unions and the Employers to Parliament and Downing Street.[91]

He was critical of each of the leaders of the strike: 'Tillett has allowed his tongue to run away with him. Gosling has lacked grit and courage in not subordinating Tillett. Thorne was heavy and useless. The rest are cargo.'[92] In fact, Tillett in one of his speeches at Tower Hill, challenging the chairman of the Port of London Authority, prayed: 'Oh God, Strike Lord Devonport dead'.[93]

Despite the negative attitude shown by the *Syndicalist* towards the London Transport Strike of 1912, Tom Mann felt instinctively drawn to the vortex of industrial action once it had taken place. On 3 July he made his first public appearance

[88] *Syndicalist* (Aug. 1912).

[89] B. Tillett, Report of the London Transport Workers' Dispute, 1912, to the Secretariat of the International Transport Workers' Federation, ITWFA.

[90] Burns, Diary, 7 June 1912, BL Add. MS 46334, JBP.

[91] Ibid., 11 June 1912, BL Add. MS 46334, JBP.

[92] Ibid., 16 June 1912, BL Add. MS 46334, JBP.

[93] *Daily Telegraph* (25 July 1912).

since his release from prison, and spoke at a meeting held on Tower Hill, declaring that 'his heart and soul were with the strikers in the fight for working-class redemption'. Tillett was reassured by 'the reappearance of Tom Mann on Tower Hill, bearing his years and his woes with all the courage of the Titan man'.[94] In spite of considerable financial support from the ITWF and also from the *Daily Herald* which had come into existence as a strike sheet, 'the misery and starvation ensuing from the protracted strike' forced the dispute committee to recommend the resumption of work from 29 July. Tillett attributed this to 'the folly of unpreparedness'.[95]

Mann's attention had been directed once more to his international commitments. Early in July he crossed the Channel to assist the French Seamen on strike, and upon his return he spoke in support of a resolution carried at a London meeting, protesting against the use made by Millerand, then the War Minister in France, of the soldiers and sailors as blacklegs.[96] In August he had 'a strenuous three weeks in Scandinavia, interminable travelling and addressing meetings, at a different town every night, with only one night free in the lot' under the auspices of the Swedish Workers Central Organization, a syndicalist body.[97] His letter to Elsie bearing no date but apparently written in the second week of his Scandinavian campaign gives some insight into his Herculean task and ceaseless effort:

Saturday morning changing trains travelled from 10.25 yesterday till 7.35 just in time for meeting, started again this morning at 6.35 & it will take all day, no meeting tonight but two tomorrow, at Billesholm at 2 o/c & at Helsingborg at 6 o/c. . . . The lakes & rivers are large & very numerous, especially the lakes. . . . I am not greatly impressed with their manufacturing towns. Eskilistuna has not much claim to be counted a Sheffield, except that they make cutlery best in Sweden. . . . I dreamt about you last night & somehow got you and George Barnes mixed up together, quite a fat headed sort of dream, not through over feeding or drinking as our last meal was at 3 o/c yesterday afternoon. . . . As usual I am with the hard up crowd, but I'm having compensation in variety, scenery, change of air & pushing Syndicalism.

Then followed an advice on books and other observations:

I wish you would get Bergson's book in Larne series. Six pence only. . . . I see no. 68 is on Nietzsche, it seems an excellent list. . . . The C.G.T.

[94] *Daily Herald* (4 July 1912).
[95] Tillett, Report of the London Transport Workers' Dispute, 1912.
[96] *Daily Herald* (4 and 18 July 1912).   [97] *Syndicalist* (Oct. 1912).

Conference begins on Monday I think. I will write Marck. Tom's birthday will soon be here & if he wishes still to have that telescope combination microscope will you please get it for him.[98]

In a train to Christiania he wrote to his son Thomas:

The meeting that I was to have had yesterday (Sunday) morning at Gotheborg I did not have. The chief of Police would not grant the permit . . . but a meeting of members of the Syndicalist body was held & it was declared to be a private meeting & I addressed that. . . . In the evening we travelled to another town named Boras, it is a textile town - cotton chiefly. . . . It was past midnight when I got back to the hotel at Gotheborg, & I had to be called at 3.30 this morning to catch this train at 4.30. The train reaches Christiania about 12 o/c. I expect a good meeting tonight, & tomorrow I start back home. . . . Anyhow I expect to reach Harwich about 5 o/c Thursday night [26 August] and shall be home on your birthday evening. I'm glad. Tell Mama I shall be disappointed if she does not meet me at Liverpool St.[99]

Gustave Hervé came over to England to carry on his campaign 'War against War' jointly with the English syndicalists. Tom Mann presided over an anti-militarist demonstration held at the Shoreditch Town Hall on 21 October, at which George Lansbury and Josiah Wedgwood, member of a Liberal foreign affairs group in Parliament (later a Labour minister), spoke against war. 'The only war we might gain anything from is the class war—civil war,' Tom added.[100] He addressed several meetings in the Birmingham district, speaking on a similar subject under the auspices of the Workers' Union and also of the British Socialist Party, formerly the SDP (SDF).[101]

The Industrial Syndicalist Education League held two conferences in the autumn of 1912, the first in London and the second in Manchester. At the London conference held at the Holborn Town Hall on 9 November, Tom Mann, commenting upon 'the growth of the British Fleet', suggested that solidarity and co-operation among the miners and the munition workers could 'at once put a stop to bloodshed'.[102] The Manchester conference held at the Coal Exchange on 30 November was made livelier by the attendance of Alfred Rosmer of the *Bataille Syndicaliste* and Leon Jouhaux, secretary of the CGT, as fraternal delegates. Jouhaux had made a tour of Britain in the previous year with Tillett, visiting Glasgow, Liverpool, and Manchester, and was surprised to find that the strike com-

[98] T. Mann to Elsie Mann, n.d. [14 Aug. 1912], DTP.
[99] T. Mann to Thomas Mann, Jun., 23 Aug. 1912, TMP.
[100] *Syndicalist* (Nov. 1912).   [101] *Daily Herald* (22 Oct., 13 Nov. 1912).
[102] Ibid. (11 Nov. 1912).

mittee in Liverpool was housed in a big hotel in the city.[103] Tom Mann, at the conference, moved a resolution 'Solidarity Reaffirmed' which once more emphasized the role of trade unions as a class organization.[104] A plan was made to hold an international syndicalist congress, the first of its kind, in London during 1913, but it was postponed and eventually abandoned. The ISEL held its 'first annual general meeting' on 1 February 1913 and retained Mann and Bowman as its president and secretary respectively. Thereafter the *Syndicalist* changed its name to the *Syndicalist and Amalgamation News*, putting a greater emphasis on the trade-union amalgamation movement. Several trade-union amalgamation committees had come into existence. A minimum-wage movement which Mann pushed at this time was also meant to serve the greater aim of trade-union amalgamation. He naturally welcomed the creation of the National Union of Railwaymen as a result of amalgamation of three separate unions. He wrote on 'the Greater Unionism' which would involve the severance of the industrial from the political forces,[105] and warned 'the industrial forces' against government intervention: 'Labour Exchanges, Insurance Act, and forecasted legislation to control industrial disputes, mean determination on the part of the governing class to get control (but they won't) of the working class organisations.'[106]

Riding the crest of the new industrial wave, Mann stood once more for the general secretaryship of the ASE. He was then living in Levenshulme, Manchester, and was a member of the Manchester 10th branch of his union. In a letter addressed to its members dated 8 April 1913, he wrote that he was in favour of 'the amalgamation of all sectional unions in the engineering industry into one amalgamation [sic]'. 'If I am returned', he went on, 'I shall devote the whole of my energies to the duties of the position, and believe that by so doing I could materially advance the essentials of Working-Class Solidarity and Direct Action.'[107] He was defeated, having secured only one quarter of the votes cast,[108] a disappointing figure which also showed the limits of syndicalist agitation. In the same year, 1913, his major book *From Single Tax to Syndicalism*, partly autobiographical,

[103] Bernard Georges and Denise Tintant, *Leon Jouhaux*, i (Paris, 1962), 114.

[104] *Syndicalist* (Jan. 1913).

[105] T. Mann, *Labourer's Minimum Wage* (Manchester, 1912), 10.

[106] *Daily Herald* (2 Apr. 1913).

[107] ASE, *Quarterly and Yearly Reports* (1913), 65; B. C. M. Weekes, 'Amalgamated Society of Engineers 1880–1914', Ph.D. thesis (Warwick, 1970), 347.

came out, in which he again enunciated the gospel of workers' control of industry.

In the autumn of 1913 Mann went on an extensive speaking tour in the United States, visiting seventy cities from Boston to San Francisco. He lectured under various auspices, the IWW, the American Federation of Labor, the Socialist Party of America, and industrial trade unions. The strike in the previous year of the textile workers in Lawrence, Massachusetts, had revealed the strength of the IWW at its best. Bill Haywood, who assumed its leadership, secured valuable assistance from the Socialist Party to bring the strike to a successful end. American socialism had made great strides in the first decade of the century, tackling, in short, 'the growing dichotomy between American democratic theory and practice'.[109] Yet the socialists were deeply divided over the matter of political and industrial action and also of craft and industrial unionism. In Chicago Tom Mann defended industrial action in a debate held at the Garrick Theatre against Arthur M. Lewis, an evolutionary socialist and advocate of political action.[110] While in Chicago, he came to know William Z. Foster, then an AFL leader who was soon to organize the stock yard workers, and later active for the Communists like Mann himself. In New York another debate took place in the New Star Casino between Tom and Louis B. Boudin, a New York attorney and a popularizer of Marx in the States.[111] A demonstration to welcome Tom Mann on his return from his successful American tour was held in the Memorial Hall, Farringdon, on 14 January 1914 under the auspices of the *Daily Herald*, now a veritable rebel newspaper. He told a *Herald* reporter that America was 'a country of long working hours', where 'the feed and speed system' was extensively applied, and added: 'I do not think the I.W.W. is destined to supercede the existing unions; it can, and I think will, do much towards enthusing and stimulating them to action.'[112] Indeed, labour unrest was not confined to Britain, and Tom was emerging as a crusader on the industrial front of world socialism.

[108] The results of the first ballot were Robert Young 14,532, Jenkins Jones 11,204, and Tom Mann 8,771.

[109] Ira Kipnis, *American Socialist Movement 1897–1912* (New York, 1952), 421.

[110] *Debate between Tom Mann and Arthur M. Lewis* [at the Garrick Theatre, Chicago, 16 Nov. 1913] (Chicago, 1914).

[111] *Justice* (1 Jan. 1914).

[112] *Daily Herald* (6 Jan. 1914).

Early in 1914 the South African Government deported to England nine active trade-unionists from the Rand in the Transvaal. The nine had been arrested on account of the prominent roles they had played in a railway strike earlier in the year, which was followed by an abortive general strike and the proclamation by the South African Government of martial law. On 1 March a protest demonstration was held in Hyde Park, and it was announced that 'our reply to Botha' was to send Tom Mann 'to South Africa to carry on the fight'. 'He will go as the Ambassador of the Rank and File of Great Britain and Ireland, and in their name will carry on the great work commenced by our deportee comrades.'[113]

On 7 March, the day of his departure for South Africa, Tom issued a statement, in which he said:

It is absolutely essential that our comrades in South Africa shall realise the full force of industrial action. . . . Brethren, it is not in the power of the Church, or the State, or the capitalist class, to rectify our economic wrongs. We ourselves must do it, and we ourselves shall be able to do it soon. The South African comrades have been confronted with a hard proposition. By and by, we of England shall also be confronted with the same. Get ready, therefore, prepare for action, and prepare now. Poverty is going, and misery with it, but not till robbery goes and class domination. A soldier in the workers' army, I encourage my comrades to work with increased vigour, for verily our day is at hand.[114]

In a speech he made at a farewell rally at Waterloo Station, he said he would tell South African workers that 'those he represented knew neither race nor colour, class nor creed, but were all one in the bonds of brotherhood'. He sailed from Southampton on board RMS *Edinburgh Castle*. As the ship moved away from the shore, cheers went up. Tom shouted 'One More Solidarity'. 'Look out for Botha and 14-pounders', someone cried, and Mann, with a wave of his red handkerchief, shouted back 'Righto!'[115]

He was somehow permitted to land at Cape Town when the boat arrived on 24 March, and at once proceeded to the Rand, where he was pleasantly surprised to find about 200 young Dutchmen with their trade-union banner, walking in the forefront of a procession of 10,000 people who had come to welcome him at Johannesburg Station.[116] He was said to have 'set the Rand aflame once more with the gospel of revolt' given

[113] Ibid. (2 Mar. 1914).   [114] Ibid. (7 Mar. 1914).
[115] Ibid. (9 Mar. 1916).   [116] Mann, *Memoirs*, 268–9.

in his first speech delivered at Johannesburg. His opening declaration was: 'I am a revolutionary. . . . My mission is to help you to overthrow, not only this tyrannical Government, not only the profit-mongers who run and control the politicians of both parties here or in England, but the whole capitalist system generally.'[117] Perhaps his gospel sounded too evangelical for the government to interfere. Indeed, he wrote that he had had 'the most uniformly successful series of meetings' he had ever had, but he had to admit that 'the drastic action of the Government, with its martial law, wholesale imprisonments, and deportations, coupled with the intensely bitter behaviour of the Rand bosses, has knocked out some of the Trade Unionists'.[118] He reported on the victims of miners' phthisis in the Rand mines: 'Five years is the duration of the working developer in the mines, but the Dutchman whose system is less inured to such conditions, dies much earlier. Natives die like diseased sheep.'[119] He then entered upon a two months' speaking tour through Natal and Cape.

Mann's pre-war work for working-class solidarity, industrial and international, thus culminated in his extensive campaign in South Africa which continued till August. Owing largely to his foreign commitments, his syndicalist work at home had begun to falter. The *Syndicalist and Amalgamation News*, still the newspaper of the ISEL, issued its last number in August 1914, when not only the Social Democrats but also the syndicalists were thrown into the whirlpool of national antagonisms. Hervé, one of the most extreme and most unreliable among the anti-war propagandists, changed the title of his paper *La Guerre sociale* to *La Victoire*.

By then syndicalism at home had played out its historical role by providing a sense of direction and *esprit de corps* to the years of labour unrest. British syndicalism has sometimes been described as a mood or a mode of behaviour, because it often lacked intellectual and theoretical content. As a system of ideas, indeed, it reaped the bitter fruits of romantic restlessness and anxiety widespread in the *fin-de-siècle* culture of Western Europe. It is interesting in this connection that Tom Mann suggested Elsie should read Bergson and Nietzsche. As a strategy of the working-class movement it reflected the basic experience of class struggle in the French CGT, the American IWW, and British New Unionism. Mann's 'home-spun folk-wisdom', which characterized his syndicalism,[120] was an asset

---

[117] *Daily Herald* (2 Apr. 1914).   [118] Ibid. (16 May 1914).
[119] Ibid. (6 June 1914).   [120] Holton, *British Syndicalism*, 68.

rather than a liability. He was always aware that his stra-
tegical views had to be tested by the actual experience of class
confrontation. Soon the war and a revolution came to open new
perspectives for the viability of his message.

10.   War and Revolution

A Responsible Patriot

WHEN the European war broke out in August 1914, Tom Mann had not returned from his propaganda tour in South Africa, and it was John Burns his erstwhile colleague, now a Cabinet minister, who made a dramatic gesture of protest against war by resigning his post. It turned out to be Burns's last public act, and it was popular with the anti-war Liberals and socialists. Even George Lansbury, who had been a victim of his retrenchment policy as regards Poor Law administration, sent him 'sincere and hearty congratulations'.[1] But the real cause of his resignation has remained obscure, as he obstinately refused to comment on it. Though a little Englander and a great admirer of Gladstone all his life, he was never a pacifist. His prominence in the pro-Boer cause earlier in the century did not mean that he was opposed to the continued existence of the British Empire in some form. There are indeed many signs that his real interest lay in the creation of a new model army or a citizen-army, as his frequent visits to Aldershot, home of a military camp, would reveal. Before we deal with Tom Mann's attitude to the European war and to its manifold repercussions at home and abroad, the circumstances that led to Burns's resignation will be examined in some detail.

'War news serious but not critical. . . . Fleet prevented from dispersing', wrote Burns in his diary on 25 July. He was then president of the Board of Trade, a new post assigned to him in the Government reshuffle of January 1914. Serbia had succumbed to Vienna's ultimatum, but her conciliatory reply was rejected, and Austria had begun mobilizing part of her army. The two alliances, Austro-German and Russo-French, were now aligned against one another. 'The outlook of war rather serious', he wrote again on the 27th;

Why 4 great Powers should fight over Serbia no fellow can understand. This I know there is one fellow who will have nothing to do with such a

[1] G. Lansbury to J. Burns, 6 Aug. 1914, BL Add. MS 46303, JBP.

criminal folly the effect of which will be appalling to the welter of nations who will be involved. It must be averted by all the means in our power. Apart from the merits of the case it is my special duty to dissociate myself and the principle I hold and the trusteeship for the working classes which I carry from such a universal crime as the contemplated war will be. My duty is clear and at all costs will be done.[2]

It has been said that 'John Burns was at once the most resolute and the least coherent of all the waverers. None of his colleagues ever quite understood why he decided to resign.'[3] Yet it is obvious that what he called 'the trusteeship for the working classes' or his belief that he represented the workers in the Cabinet dissociated him from his colleagues, from other 'waverers', and from the anti-war or neutralist group who counted ten or eleven in the Cabinet of twenty. No other Cabinet minister, not even John Morley, his closest ally, the official biographer of W. E. Gladstone and now Lord President, dared take the initiative in stemming the critical tide that was about to sweep the nation into war. Burns at last took the lead. On 1 August he

lunched with Grey, Haldane, Runciman at 28 Queen Annes Gate. After others had gone had a pleasant yet serious talk with Grey about situation. . . . I told Grey my fears as to Germany beaten allying herself with Russia and Japan. Urged him to press for the triumphs of Peace rather than the laurels of war. The one everlasting, the other withers and fades.[4]

At the Cabinet meeting that afternoon, according to Morley, 'Burns . . . intimated in his most downright tones that the warning to Germany not to try it on against French coasts or ships in the Channel was more than he could stand.' To this Burns himself added in Morley's Memorandum: 'not only because it was practically a declaration of war on sea leading inevitably to a war on land, but mainly because it was the symbol of an alliance with France with whom no such understanding had hitherto existed'.[5] The existence of any such understanding had not yet been disclosed.

The Cabinet meeting reopened at 11.30 a.m. on the following day 2 August, and lasted till 2 p.m. After a discussion it was decided to assure France that Britain would protect the French coast and shipping against attacks by the German fleet. 'Burns,

[2] J. Burns, Diary, 27 July 1914, BL Add. MS 46336, JBP.
[3] Cameron Hazlehurst, *Politicians at War* (London, 1971), 58.
[4] Burns, Diary, 1 Aug. 1914, BL Add. MS 46336, JBP.
[5] J. Morley, *Memorandum on Resignation* (London, 1928), 8.

with remarkable energy, force, and grasp, insisted that this was neither more nor less than a challenge to Germany, tantamount to a declaration of war against her. He wound up with a refusal to be a party to it.'[6] Asquith persuaded Burns to postpone his resignation until the evening Cabinet to be held at 6.30. Seven or eight waverers, including Morley himself, lunched at Lord Beauchamp's house at Belgrave Square. Morley later admitted that it had been 'in truth a very shallow affair', but 'the general voice was loud that "Burns was right"'. They felt that 'the Cabinet was being rather artfully drawn on step by step to war for the benefit of France and Russia'. 'The dissolution of the Ministry was that afternoon in full view', added Morley.[7] At the Cabinet held in the evening Burns affirmed his determination to resign. Morley wrote a letter of resignation on the following morning 3 August. The waverers' unity had been broken, and in fact no point of contention had been pressed at the evening Cabinet on 2 August. Arguments for the protection of British interests appeared to have disarmed them. In the meantime, the German violation of Belgian neutrality, the celebrated *casus belli*, took place; on 4 August Britain sent her ultimatum to Germany and by the following morning the nation found itself at war.

The strength of the opposition in the Cabinet, as Morley observed, had been only on the surface. Burns himself took the view that Lloyd George and four others 'could have kept Britain out and adjusted Russian French difficulties'. He added another cause of the war 'on our side'—'too large a Cabinet: too small a coterie inside and a Commons kept innocent of what was transpiring and a country ignorant of all that occurred'.[8] He finally pinned down the villain, Lloyd George, who 'more than any other living man has helped to plunge the credulous country' into the war.[9] He remembered the provocative speech Lloyd George had delivered at a Mansion House dinner at the time of the Moroccan crisis of 1911, and believed that he had been in the hands of clever bankers.

On 2 August when Burns tendered his resignation, Tillett was playing a prominent part in the huge 'Stop-the-War' socialist demonstration held in Trafalgar Square, though he was soon to join the horde of patriotic labour leaders. 'In reality this war will be fought in the main by the working classes, although they

---

[6] Morley, *Memorandum on Resignation*, 12.   [7] Ibid. 17.
[8] Burns, Diary, 23 Oct. 1914, BL Add. MS 46336, JBP.
[9] Ibid., 4 May 1915, BL Add. MS 46337, JBP.

had not power and neither were they consulted for or against war', wrote Tillett in *The Times*.[10] His devotion to the war-effort at once revived his old chequered relationship with Horatio Bottomley, who fanned the flames of patriotism years before the outbreak of the war, while engaged in bogus company promotion. His shady interventions in local politics in the East End of London are said to have 'roped in Ben Tillett'.[11] He and Bottomley had been friends when they were both young. 'Well Ben,' said Bottomley one day, 'you've been denouncing the thieves—I've been robbing them'.[12] Indeed, Tillett in the war presented a striking contrast to the 'Honest John' who had refused to take responsibility for slaughtering the men of his own class. Even so they were both committed to the cause of the working class, though each saw it from a different angle. Tom Mann, who appears to have shared the feelings of the two men, was to develop a radical strategy for labour in war. This, however, is to anticipate, and for the moment we shall follow and review the evolution of Tillett in his attitude towards war and labour.

When war-clouds gathered on the European horizon, Tillett and his National Transport Workers' Federation maintained a definite anti-war stance. The executive council of the federation submitted a resolution to an international congress of the ITWF held in Caxton Hall, London, in September 1913: 'In the event of international war being imminent in consequence of the criminal conduct of the war faction, and without the consent of the overwhelming majority of the people involved, we recommend a general stoppage of work among all transport workers who are engaged in the transportation of troops and munitions of war.'[13] As the German head office of the ITWF was not willing to expedite transactions including the publication of a congress report, Robert Williams, the young secretary of the NTWF, complained that the administration of the ITWF had been 'overloaded with German personality, German sentiment, German methods and control'.[14] In the early summer of 1914 Tillett found himself in Berlin, receiving medical treatment for his chronic illness, and took trouble to attend a congress of the ITWF held at Munich a few weeks before the war. He was urged by the German delegates not to move a

[10] 'Mr. Ben Tillett's Manifesto', *The Times* (20 Mar. 1915).
[11] Kenneth O. Morgan, *Keir Hardie* (London, 1975), 136.
[12] Jack Gill to Ian Mackay, 19 Jan. 1951, IMP.
[13] R. Williams to Hermann Jochade, 19 Mar. 1913, ITWFA.
[14] R. Williams to H. Jochade, 5 Jan. 1914, ITWFA.

resolution calling upon labour of all nations to strike if war was declared. He sought to persuade himself and Williams that all this was due to the 'Teutonic temperament' and that war was still avoidable.[15] At the 'Stop-the-War' demonstration of 2 August, referred to above, he proposed that the industrial Triple Alliance prepare concerted action to prevent war.[16]

Once war was declared, there was a drastic change of front for Tillett as for so many other labour leaders. In fact, the overwhelming mass of working-class opinion in Britain, as in other belligerent countries, was patriotic and strongly 'pro-war', at least throughout the early phase of the war. Tillett soon got in touch with Lloyd George and offered his co-operation in the war effort. In the pages of *John Bull*, Bottomley's paper, he openly declared his support for the war and urged the workers to fight. He adduced several reasons for his pro-war campaign, one of which was the sheer helplessness of the workers as opposed to the coercive power they had entrusted to the ruling classes.[17]

In the spring of 1915 Tillett went to the south of France for health reasons, and journeyed to the front on his way home. He again visited the front-line trenches over Christmas and also in the spring of 1916. In the summer of 1915 he started a speaking campaign delivering his patriotic message from music hall stages.[18] Willie Gallacher, the leader of the Clyde workers, recalled how Ben Tillett, 'the first of the big "Defend our Country" demagogues to visit Glasgow', fared at a meeting organized by the Clarion Scouts at the Pavilion Theatre: the audience simply 'hooted him off the platform'.[19] Even Hyndman, now the leader of the pro-war socialists, had to warn him not to blur the socialist distinction between military conscription and a democratic citizen-army in his campaign.[20] Tillett later recalled: 'just as in a strike when our starving people had to be fed I thought only of feeding and helping' the fighting man.[21]

Tillett felt that transport became 'the governing factor in the organisation of war', and was prepared to do his best to maintain industrial peace on the docks. In March 1915 he issued a

[15] B. Tillett, *Who was Responsible for the War—and Why?* (London, 1917), 8. R. Williams to H. Jochade, 26 Mar. 1914, ITWFA.

[16] *Justice* (6 Aug. 1914); *Daily Herald* (3 and 5 Aug. 1914).

[17] *John Bull* (10 Oct. 1914).

[18] Jonathan Schneer, *Ben Tillett: Portrait of a Labour Leader* (London, 1982), 187; see *Clarion* (17 Nov. 1916); *The Times* (22 June 1915).

[19] William Gallacher, *Revolt on the Clyde* (1939; London, 1949), 50–1.

[20] *Justice* (15 June 1916).

[21] B. Tillett, *Memories and Reflections* (London, 1931), 253.

'News Bulletin' on the war for the benefit of his union, in which he wrote that the Dockers' executive would do all they could to enforce 'fair play' in the matter of wages through conciliation, arbitration, and the use of every Government agency.[22] This was the time when the TUC Parliamentary Committee and more than thirty individual unions concluded with the Government the so-called Treasury Agreement that implemented an industrial truce offered by the official leadership of the movement. In a pamphlet published in 1917 Tillett declared that the trade unions had abandoned their fundamental claims for the duration of the war: 'the right to strike, the non-dilution of labour, the regulation of hours, the limitation of non-skilled work'.[23] The Dockers' representatives, including Tillett, Sexton, Gosling, and the newcomer Ernest Bevin, sat on the Port and Transit Executive to deal with the problems of port congestion. They were, however, often outnumbered by employers, and the unions on the waterfront were drawn into an alliance with the State especially with the introduction of mobile transport battalions.[24] This was exactly what Tom Mann feared when he resumed trade-union work in war-time Britain.

When war was declared, Tom Mann had been on the sea for several days after his South African mission. 'It has been an adventurous voyage', recalled Tom:

From the time the ship sailed—August 1—we travelled in complete darkness after nightfall. We got news by wireless that war had been declared by Germany when we were a day's sail from land, and, later that England had joined her Ally—France. Thenceforward the vessel was an armed camp, sentries posted at every vulnerable point. We had representatives of eight nationalities aboard, including a German consul.[25]

By the time he reached London, socialist protests against the war had been submerged by the tidal wave of nationalism. Even the French CGT had decided 'to drop the principles' and had renounced the idea of a general strike prior to the outbreak of the war.[26] 'As to the war', Tom continued:

I prefer not to make any definite pronouncement, as I have been somewhat out of touch with current home events, but I extremely

---

[22] *The Times* (20 Mar. 1915).
[23] Tillett, *Who was Responsible for the War*, 10.
[24] Gordon Phillips and Noel Whiteside, *Casual Labour* (Oxford, 1985), 121–2.
[25] *Daily Herald* (27 Aug. 1914).
[26] Georges Haupt, *Socialism and the Great War* (Oxford, 1972), 242.

regret that the workers of the world are at one another's throats, and that the International revolutionary movement will receive a severe set-back in the interests of dynastic houses and market monopolists. I stand where I have always stood with regard to all wars: they are never in the truest interests of the workers.[27]

Tom's fundamental opposition to the war never wavered, though he, too, played the part of a patriot, 'a "responsible" patriot, concerned to win the war, but also concerned to defend the interests of labour'.[28] In April 1915 Tom was present at a demonstration of the Clydebank men, about whom he wrote to his friend R. S. Ross of Melbourne:

I failed to find one man who exhibited any bitter hatred towards the Germans. . . . Yet it must not be supposed they are not opposed to Germany. . . . Many more thousands would join the Colour if they were allowed to leave the workshop and go. . . . My temperament is more anti-Governmental than your own. . . . I am very keenly alive to the true inwardness of the British governing class; I am under no delusion as to their real character and their diabolical behaviour to the workers. Even so, I am sure as a human being can be that it would be most seriously harmful if the ruling class of Germany should gain the ascendency in other countries, including this. . . . I am really of opinion that it [the war] ought and must be fought out.[29]

His eldest son Tom Mann, Jun., duly served in the Royal Navy and was stationed at Dover during the war.[30]

It seems that when he returned from South Africa Tom had no organizational basis for his trade-union work. The amalgamation movement especially in metal engineering and shipbuilding, in which he had a great stake, came to an end when the war broke out and for the moment cut off almost all unofficial activities.[31] Syndicalism appeared to be a spent force, having dropped its anti-war, anti-militarist edge. He apparently sought to inform himself of working-class opinion on the war through his friends old and new. Tillett, who was ready to help the Government with the cessation of normal trade-union practices, obviously disappointed Tom. Sexton, with whom he had fought an industrial battle in Liverpool three years before, was as willing as Tillett to co-operate with the Government in war-efforts. John Burns, who was assisting a London committee to

[27] *Daily Herald* (27 Aug. 1914).

[28] I owe the expression a 'responsible patriot' to Dr Ken Coates.

[29] T. Mann to R. S. Ross, 11 Apr. 1915, *Justice* (12 Aug. 1915).

[30] Interview with Tom Mann, Jun., 15 May 1982.

[31] Branco Pribicevic, *Shop Stewards' Movement and Workers' Control* (Oxford, 1959), 71.

deal with the problems of unemployment and poverty that appeared to command urgent attention in the initial stage of the war, was in a pensive mood. Tom probably found J. Havelock Wilson little changed: he was as patriotic, as daring as he used to be, and as yet singularly lacking in the racial animosity that he was to display in due course. It so happened that Tom Mann worked in the first instance with Wilson and his union, the National Sailors' and Firemen's Union.

'I went up to see Tom Mann last night,' wrote his friend H. Gibson in 1915; 'he and the family are keeping in the pink, he always seems to be bubbling over with vitality. He has been on the Clyde most of the time since the beginning of the year, he is working for the "Seamen & Firemen".'[32] Tom duly attended the Annual General Meeting of Wilson's union held in January 1915 at Caxton Hall, London, as one of its executive councillors. At the beginning of the war the union found itself in an awkward situation, because there were 5,000 to 6,000 Germans and Austrians on board British ships, loyal members of the unions, who, however, had to be interned as enemy nationals. Wilson, the chairman, announced that his union had bought an estate at Eastcote, Northamptonshire, to accommodate these unfortunate Germans and erected there a solid, permanent structure that would be used as a home for retired seamen once the war was over. He also pointed out that members of his union had joined not only in the Royal Navy but thousands of them were serving in the Army, and proudly declared that the seamen had got 'one of the best unions in the United Kingdom' with a respectable balance of union funds. Tom Mann joined in general congratulations for the chairman and looked back to the 'dark days' when they—he and Wilson—shared the hardship and trouble in building a sound, fighting union. His was indeed an impassioned speech: he was glad of the seamen's 'glorious achievement' and of 'the privilege of [his] being identified with the President [Wilson] in the years, knowing what took place before, knowing how he strove and how he yearned'. He was especially glad of 'a complete absence of any silly racial animosity' in Wilson's address and of 'genuine brotherly fraternity' shown by the seamen in general.[33] Tom was elected to a committee to look into the future Eastcote scheme. His service to the Seamen's Union was fully acknowledged, for he

[32] H. Gibson to a 'comrade', 27 June 1915, Frow Collection, Salford.
[33] National Sailors' and Firemen's Union, *Report of the Twenty-Seventh Annual General Meeting held at Caxton Hall, Westminster, 26 and 27 Jan. 1915* (London, 1915), 16–17.

had intervened successfully in a dispute over the local stand-ard rate between two districts: Dublin and Liverpool. He did not miss the opportunity to declare his syndicalist convictions at the meeting as he firmly believed that the Government was taking advantage of the war 'to get an increasing grip of the workers' organisations. ... If you will allow more and more provision to be made by the Board of Trade and other Govern-ment agencies, it will mean less and less provision made by you and therefore less and less control.'[34]

Havelock Wilson, who had a political career as a 'Lib–Lab' MP and who had not infrequently behaved like a syndicalist or an advocate of direct action at times of labour unrest, was certainly less than sympathetic with the demand made by some of the seamen for their union's affiliation to the Labour Party. The issue was discussed at this meeting, and Wilson repeatedly emphasized that the union had no money to spare for affili-ation. Tom Mann supported his friend's stance against the Labour Party with an orthodox syndicalist argument:

The industrial is a real force; the political could never be anything but the reflection of the industrial. ... Your concern is for an economic change, that is a change in the condition under which work is done. The value you create by your labour and the percentage you receive there-from; the way to get that change is by economic, by industrial action. ... I believe it to be a mistaken step to be identified with a political Party. We want not to hand work to the State; we want to take the work the State is doing now in our own hands.[35]

It seems that Wilson distrusted the Labour Party all the more for those whom he called 'international talkers', implying Ramsay MacDonald, prominent in the Union of Democratic Control, an anti-war body, and Keir Hardie, a crusader for peace in the Second International which was now defunct. Hardie was a sick man, and died in September.[36] At the annual general meeting of his union in the following year Wilson succeeded in lowering the amount of his union's contribution to a Keir Hardie Memorial Fund from the proposed £25 to £5 by dwelling upon Hardie's 'dastardly' attitude towards himself and his union. Tom Mann in a somewhat extravagant speech of praise moved a vote of thanks to the president for his opening address, but did not take part in the sordid debate on the Keir Hardie Memorial Fund. His own association with the ILP, as we

[34] National Sailors' and Firemen's Union, *Report*, 102.
[35] Ibid. 111.
[36] Ibid. 108; Morgan, *Keir Hardie*, 261, 272.

have seen, was none too happy an episode, but he refused to be a party to the spiteful.[37]

Tom was then living in Levenshulme, Manchester, at 18 Beech Range, and was working also for the National Transport Workers' Federation in the capacity of an honorary district secretary in the Liverpool area.[38] The NTWF in Liverpool and District comprised Sexton's Dock Labourers, Wilson's Sailors and Firemen, the Ship Stewards and Cooks, the Carters, the Gasworkers, and three other unions, and no doubt Tom found a broader outlook on many issues of war and labour there than in Wilson's union which was dominated by the autocratic personality of the President. Wilson's 'ultra patriotic views and deeds', in spite of Tom's earlier statement to the contrary, soon became apparent and led him to achieve reconciliation with his old enemy the Shipping Federation.[39]

'Compulsory military service' was one of the issues hotly discussed at the annual general council meeting of the NTWF held in Glasgow in June 1916. The debate provided the first public occasion for Tom to state his views on war and deserves a close examination. It took place some time after the failure of the Dardanelles campaign, though the greater disaster on the Somme was yet to come. Several millions of men had enlisted voluntarily, but it was announced on the New Year 1916 that the voluntary system had failed and in January the first Military Service Bill was introduced. A labour conference decided to oppose it, but apparently agreed not to resist when it had become an Act. Ernest Bevin now spoke in support of a resolution which would pledge the Transport Workers 'to oppose Conscription with all its power'. Referring to the labour conference against the Act, he suggested that those in charge of negotiations had been 'jockeyed into undoing the work of the conference', and above all he 'objected to the right of the military authorities to continue to call upon the country for more men while men were sacrificed through the bad strategy of the staff', an almost seditious statement. Sexton, speaking for himself as well as for his friends like Tillett and Harry

---

[37] National Sailors' and Firemen's Union, *Report of the Twenty-Eighth Annual General Meeting held at Caxton Hall, 26 Sept. 1916* (London, 1916), 24–5, 119–21.   [38] I owe this information to Dr Ken Coates.

[39] J. McConville and John Saville, 'John Havelock Wilson', in *Dictionary of Labour Biography*, iv (London, 1977), 204; Tom Mann's report on Liverpool District, in NTWF, *Report of the Sixth Annual General Council Meeting held in Glasgow, 8 and 9 June 1916* (London, 1916), 71–3.

Gosling, said: 'They changed their minds not because of any arrangements, but because of the facts of the situation. They went into the voluntary system heart and soul, because they believed it was absolutely necessary to have a large army to defeat the Germans and their aims', and he would trust Lord Kitchener who said that he had wanted to get soldiers voluntarily because the voluntary soldiers were the best, but he could not get enough of them. Tom Mann then spoke in support of the resolution. He disagreed with Sexton on the merit of Lord Kitchener's or any soldier's opinion on a matter that affected the liberty of the people. He maintained that Britain had special duties among the Allies and that these were to provide munitions and money. 'There was no military necessity for the conscription of men in this country', he declared, 'while the Allies were possessed of millions of men whose chief requisites were the arms and the money that this country alone could provide.' Russia alone had manpower as large as all the other enemy nations put together. Therefore there was no sound reason, he argued, 'for taking a few hundred thousand more men from the trades essential to the financing of the Allies'. Then he pointed out what he considered to be the real reason for conscription, which was 'the fear of organised labour', and he believed that 'conscription was the gateway to industrial compulsion'. This was perhaps a common syndicalist argument. It is to be noted, however, that Tom declared at the same time that he was 'in favour of a settlement [of the war] by negotiation as early as possible' though he wanted to see his country win the war.[40] Tillett was for conscription; he compared it to coercion or forced cohesion in a strike and replied to Tom Mann by arguing that 'all our allies were conscriptionists ... [and] the French looked upon conscription as the most democratic form of militarism'. He would say to Tom Mann that he should go and repeat his speech to the men in the trenches who, though voluntarily enlisted soldiers themselves, were conscriptionists at heart. The resolution was lost on a card vote by 100,000 to 81,000.[41]

At this conference Tom Mann proposed the setting up of a trade-union clearing house to deal with the unemployment that was to be expected with demobilization after the war. His plan was to collect necessary information and absorb surplus labour by shortening the working hours of those employed; in

[40] NTWF, *Report of the Sixth Annual General Council Meeting*, 100-1.
[41] Ibid. 102-3.

fact this was his pet idea from the early days of his eight-hour agitation.[42] It attracted some attention but aroused no enthusiasm, for there was no prospect of the war coming to a swift end. Nevertheless, Tom remained optimistic, and was finding a more congenial field of work in the rank and file or unofficial movement among the workers that had been strengthened as the industrial truce enforced by the leadership became increasingly unpopular.

The war was also a war of the engineers, the producers of munitions,[43] and Tom was an engineer by trade and a loyal member of the ASE. The union leadership, however, was tied to the State through the Treasury Agreement and the Munitions of War Act that followed, and the Government sought to exert direct pressure on the rank and file with a policy combining persuasion and coercion. Under the increasingly tight control of labour by the Government, a strong current of labour unrest continued. A major storm centre was on Clydeside, where the Labour Withholding Committee, so named in order to avoid the use of the term 'strike' in connection with an unofficial strike at the Weir's and the Albion works in February 1915, gave birth to the revolutionary shop stewards movement. (The committee was later renamed the Clyde Workers' Committee.) Tom Mann, as we have seen, was often found on the Clydeside in the early months of 1915, but being a patriot of a sort and working for Wilson's union at the time, it is unlikely that he played an active role in the strike which, Gallacher pointed out, though defeated, 'had broken the rotten atmosphere of war-jingoism'.[44]

Nevertheless, he soon found himself in a similar but less obviously rebellious movement among the engineers. This was the amalgamation movement which was given a new lease of life. He attended a series of rank and file conferences on amalgamation for his branch of the ASE, 'Manchester 10'. In November 1915 Mann, along with W. F. Watson of the Chiswick ASE and E. L. Pratt an industrial unionist, started a monthly paper *Trade Unionist*, which inspired the Amalgamation Committee with a new sense of direction.[45] A resolution adopted at the first conference held in London in August 1916 demanded that the executives of all the unions catering for engineering and shipbuilding workers should prepare a practical scheme of

[42] Ibid. 83–4.
[43] James B. Jefferys, *Story of the Engineers* (London, 1945), 174.
[44] William Gallacher, *Revolt on the Clyde* (London, 1949).
[45] Pribicevic, *Shop Stewards' Movement*, 74.

amalgamation 'having as its object the organisation of all workers in the Industry, regardless of craft and sex, and as its ultimate, the control of the Industry'. This was debated and reaffirmed at the next conference held in Leeds in the autumn, at which Tom Mann spoke successfully against an attempt to saddle the grand scheme of industrial unionism with the sectional issue of dilution: 'every worker was of equal value', he declared. The adoption of a 'Basis' of organization committed the conference to the foundation of an 'Engineering and Shipbuilding Workers' Industrial Union' with autonomy assured for each district branch and craft group, though Arthur McManus, the delegate of the Clyde Workers' Committee, managed to insert 'the workshop' as the basic unit in which 'control of policy and action should be vested'.[46] Tom Mann declared in a concluding speech:

The time had arrived ... when a Conference of the rank and file, untrammelled by officialism, should be held to lay down a definite policy for after the war. The Trades Union Congress recently held at Birmingham was ... a disgrace to Trade Unionism, and not a reflection of the views of the rank and file. Every resolution adopted was in humiliating terms asking Parliament to be so good as to do things for them. This is futile. What is wanted is a definite rank and file policy demanding a reduction of hours upon the cessation of hostilities to absorb all the workers.[47]

The same idea that he had suggested to the Transport Workers was repeated here perhaps with better effect.

By the time of the fourth National Rank and File Conference held in Manchester in June 1917, it had become clear that the executive of his union would remain hostile to the movement, and Tom Mann expressed the view that amalgamation 'could be achieved by closer workshop action' without the Executive or other officials to help. 'Maybe, inside a few weeks, we would be faced with demobilisation'—he was as optimistic as ever—'and we had no scheme prepared. We should demand six hour day and five day week. That is what the workers were doing in Russia. Then why not we?' This was after the February Revolution in Russia. 'What was wanted', he added, 'was not a breaking away from the present unions, but a new building up of the new methods inside the unions.'[48] Mann never favoured rival unionism, and he supported the unofficial rank-and-file move-

[46] Rank and File Conference on Amalgamation, *Report* (Leeds, 11 and 12 Nov. 1916), 20–5.   [47] Ibid. 27–8.

[48] Rank and File Conference on Amalgamation, *Report* (Manchester, 9 and 10 June 1917), 14.

ment mainly for its 'educational character'. However, he now identified himself and his syndicalist aspirations with the 'new method', the shop-stewards movement. Indeed, the shop steward had by now developed 'from a mere "card inspector" and membership recruitment officer into an aggressive strike leader'[49] and something more.

Although there was the rumour—partly justifiable—that Tom had 'buried the hatchet for the duration of the war', he was in fact in great demand as a speaker to address trade-union meetings up and down the country.[50] In a speech delivered at a mass labour rally at Smethwick, he attributed the success of the Workers' Union—whose vice-president he still was—to the movement of the shop committees.[51] The Workers' Union, according to its general secretary Charles Duncan, was 'the child of his [Tom's] brain'.[52] Tom for himself pointed out that Tom Chambers, the first secretary of the union, was now the 're-spected' general treasurer of Wilson's Sailors' and Firemen's Union. Charles Duncan, himself an engineer from Middlesbrough and an MP since 1906, found Tom as fiery and as volatile as ever and called him 'the Peter Pan of the Labour movement, who resolutely refuses to grow old', an apt description later borrowed by Stephen Sanders.[53]

Tom had written a brief history of trade-unionism in general and particularly of the Workers' Union, a union expected to organize 'any section in any occupation not already provided for by any Union', whose membership stood at the respectable figure of 195,750 at the time of his writing. He recalled how he had placed himself at the disposal of those members of the union in the Black Country who resorted to direct action in 1913. 'In the Black Country Strike for the Bottom Dogs of Labour he was everywhere, and performed wonders', wrote Duncan. Tom emphasized 'the way in which the skilled workers belonging to other Unions entered into the fight' at the time. The Workers' Union, he still felt, could provide a sound basis for solidarity of the workers, and the aim of the trade-union movement should be workers' control of the industries in which they were occupied. The Workers' Union, as we have seen, had remained weak for many years after its formation in 1898, and

[49] Sidney Webb and Beatrice Webb, *History of Trade Unionism* (new edn., London, 1920), 488.
[50] *Solidarity* quoted in *The International* (Johannesburg) (30 Mar. 1917), DTP.
[51] *Smethwick Telegraph* [8 Jan. 1917], DTP.
[52] Charles Duncan, 'Tom Mann', *Workers' Union Record*, 29 (Mar. 1916).
[53] Ibid.

it was only under the conditions created by the war that it gained in vigour and strength. The lack of funds had prevented it from even holding a conference, and it was in July 1916 that the 'First Triennial Conference' was held in Birmingham, at which Tom, an honoured guest, stressed the importance of 'organising the masses of workers in the most effective manner' and declared that they were 'on the eve of great changes in the direction of amalgamation'.[54]

Duncan's description of Tom is worth quoting for his intimate knowledge of his friend:

Tom is about five feet seven in height, and weighs about twelve stones. He is as dark as a Spaniard and as fiery, as lively as a Frenchman and as courteous, as cheerful as an Irishman, as cautious as a Scotsman and as persistent. He has the energy of a steam engine, the vitality of a lion, the brain of a Socrates, the tongue of a Demosthenes, and the health, physique, and iron will of a Red Indian.

Overstatement, if there was any, was made up for by his concluding remark: 'He is a great good-hearted Pal of the Poor'.[55] In spite of Duncan's adoration for Tom and of a remarkable increase in strength of his union from just over 140,000 at the beginning of the war to 379,000 at its termination, however, the Workers' Union did not allow Mann to play any part in formulating its policy, which tended to be more on the right than on the left of the trade-union world.[56]

The year 1917 witnessed American participation in the war and the two Russian Revolutions, while in Britain industrial discontent and war weariness gave rise to the persistent demand for a negotiated peace. Mann's address, given in January at the West Bromwich Town Hall for a local trades and labour council, in some way heralded the new awakening of political consciousness among the trade-unionists. 'Applying the methods used in the industrial struggle to the European war,' he declared that 'to refuse to listen when other nations made overtures was insensible, outrageous, and contrary to the spirit of workpeople to-day'. He believed that the American emphasis on war aims was 'very fair' and that 'the war would have to be settled by discussion'. He was certainly more emphatic now on this point than when he had brought out the

---

[54] *Workers' Union Record*, 33 (July 1916). Tom Mann's article 'Workers' Union' was published in three parts, *Workers' Union Record*, 29, 30, 31 (Mar., Apr., May 1916).   [55] Duncan, 'Tom Mann'.

[56] R. Hyman, *Workers' Union* (Oxford, 1971), 37, 39.

same argument for the Sailors and Firemen two years before. 'Like in an industrial dispute, I am favourable to negotiate at the very first opportunity that arises', he added.[57]

Negotiations were suddenly in the air among Labour and socialist circles, but very few noticed that negotiations were at variance with Lenin's slogan 'Turn the imperialistic war into civil war' and that the foundations for the Third International had already been laid at a small international conference of anti-war socialists held at Zimmerwald, a Swiss village, late in 1915. Now at an international socialist conference planned to take place at Stockholm in the summer of 1917, pro-war socialists on both sides of the battle-line as well as the anti-war socialists were expected to meet for the first time to consider the possibilities of a peace that would be just to all the peoples concerned. Meanwhile in Britain, cinders of labour unrest again flared up in the great engineering strike of May 1917, which, having been provoked, as Lloyd George recalled, by the 'stupid' action of a Rochdale firm to extend 'dilution' beyond war production, spread to forty-eight towns, involving nearly 200,000 men, and revealed the extent of genuine distrust and grievances among the workers.[58]

It was in this lively and somewhat heroic atmosphere that the Leeds Convention, itself a pale reflection of the February Revolution in Russia, was held at the Coliseum, Leeds, on 3 June, attended by 1,150 delegates. The galaxy of the British Left, from Ramsay MacDonald to Willie Gallacher, from Bertrand Russell to Mrs Montefiore, came to emulate the revolutionary Russians. Tom Mann, too, found himself in the gallery and stood up to support a resolution moved by Philip Snowden welcoming the declared foreign policy of 'no annexation and no indemnities'. He was keenly aware that there had been 'a vast change in the opinion of organised labour'.[59] 'Declare now whether or not you are favourable to those main principles contained in the [Russian] manifesto issued in May 1917,' he asked; 'He was an Internationalist when he was 30, and that day at 60, he was still an Internationalist.'[60] Ben Tillett and Ernest Bevin, the two delegates from the Dockers' Union, felt uneasy at this assembly which gave vent to the growing sentiment of internationalism and working-class solidarity.[61] Tillett

---

[57] *West Bromwich Sun* (7 Jan. 1917), DTP.

[58] David Lloyd George, *War Memoirs*, ii (London, 1936), 1149–51.

[59] *British Labour and the Russian Revolution: The Leeds Convention, A Report from the Daily Herald*, introd. by Ken Coates (Nottingham, n.d.), 27.

[60] *Leeds Citizen* (8 June 1917).

[61] Alan Bullock, *Life and Times of Ernest Bevin*, i (London, 1960), 194–5.

said little, while Bevin asked for evidence that the German Social Democrats were prepared to reverse their policy and commented that Snowden was indulging in 'dialectical cynicism'.[62] The resolution, however, was carried with two or three dissentients, one being 'Captain' Tupper of the Sailors' and Firemen's Union, who had wanted German reparations for reimbursing the widows and orphans of torpedoed merchant seamen. A resolution, perhaps most revolutionary of all, calling for the establishment of councils of workers' and soldiers' delegates in every town and district was supported characteristically by Arthur McManus, Willie Gallacher, and Noah Ablett among others.

The Leeds Convention, however, managed to complete its proceedings amidst hostile public opinion, under a government committed to fighting to the bitter end. It was held in Leeds, because the use of the Albert Hall, London, had been denied. Shortly after the convention, the Russian Council of Workers' and Soldiers' Delegates invited the Labour Party, the British Socialist Party (former SDP without Hyndman's patriotic faction), and the ILP to send delegates to Petrograd as a preliminary step to the Stockholm conference. Urged by Havelock Wilson, whose 'anti-Germanism' had now become morbid and obsessive, his union decided to call upon its members to refuse to sail ships carrying delegates to Stockholm and Petrograd unless they would consent to demand restitution and indemnities for the relatives of the seamen killed as a result of the submarine warfare. 'Captain' Edward Tupper who made himself notorious at Leeds was no captain at all but a bankrupt company promoter and ex-private detective, and he now acted as national organizer for Wilson's union.[63] Accordingly the seamen in Aberdeen refused to allow Ramsay MacDonald and Fred Jowett, two ILP delegates to Russia, to go on board a ship that was to take a Labour delegation to Petrograd, and this was generally regarded as the work of Havelock Wilson and his henchman 'Captain' Tupper. The latter went so far as to picket the Aberdeen hotel where the two ILP delegates were staying.[64] The seamen's actions were certainly embarrassing to Tom Mann and others who advocated peace by negotiations. Moreover, at the special conference of the Seamen's Union held the day after the Leeds Convention, Tom was elected as one of the

---

[62] *Call* (7 June 1917).

[63] McConville and Saville, 'John Havelock Wilson', 203.

[64] *Call* (21 June 1917); Fenner Brockway, *Socialism over Sixty Years: The Life of Jowett of Bradford* (London, 1946), 155.

two delegates to be sent to Petrograd and Stockholm to plead on behalf of the torpedoed seamen and their families.[65]

At the annual general meeting of the NFTW held in Bristol in the middle of June, however, Bevin compared the action of the seamen not unfavourably with the Leeds Convention which he felt was ill-advised. The central issue of the whole debate was the conduct of Robert Williams secretary of the NFTW who, in a letter to the *Daily News*, had criticized the seamen's decision and had contradicted their claims by arguing that compensation for the victims of the submarine attack should come from the employers first of all. His letter also contained the following controversial paragraph:

It is quixotic, to say the least, that Mr. Tom Mann is to be sent to Petrograd and to Stockholm as a representative of the National Sailors' and Seamen's Union. Mr. Tom Mann was the ablest supporter of the resolution calling for 'no annexation and no indemnities' who spoke from the floor of the Leeds Convention; so that the seamen will paradoxically prevent their own representative from sailing to Stockholm and Petrograd if he does not recant.

Wilson's union formally moved a resolution, demanding Williams's resignation unless he would give a pledge not to implicate the name of the NTWF in 'peace and bogus meetings' such as the one at Leeds, with which the secretary had been associated. The situation was delicate indeed for Tom Mann, because Williams was also blamed for having 'gone back on Tom Mann, one of his ablest supporters'. Sexton moved an amendment which rescinded reference to the secretary's resignation. Tillett spoke in favour of Williams in glowing terms, but called the Leeds Convention 'a fake conference'. Tom Mann then stood and explained the circumstances of how he had gone to Leeds. He and John Cotter of the Ship Stewards had been appointed at a meeting of the Mersey District Committee of the NTWF as their delegates to the convention. He offered a clumsy excuse, saying that his action at the convention would not clash with the wishes of the seamen, because the declaration of 'no indemnities and no annexation' (*sic*) only meant that no Power should come out of the war as a conqueror and there was nothing in the Leeds resolution that would prejudice the just claims of the seamen which included reparation for the evils inflicted by the Germans. There was no alternative for Tom Mann but to try to act as a mediator between Wilson and Williams: he hoped that both the original resolution and

[65] *The Times* (5 June 1917).

the amendment would be withdrawn, once Williams had made it clear that he was not representing the NTWF in his criticism of Wilson's union. Williams now spoke and emphasized that there was no 'double dealing' on his part in spite of differences of opinion with his colleagues. 'I can quite understand men with strong individualities', he went on:

I like Tom Mann and Ben Tillett retaining their belief in the underlying principles of libertarianism, which I fully appreciate, and I am grateful to them. But, as Tillett put it to me when I assumed office: Do you want me to be an automaton or a man? Tillett then advised me not to be an office-boy or even a secretary but to be a man. That I have been and shall, I hope, remain.

Williams refused to give pledges under duress, but admitted that there had been 'some lack of discretion' in his dealings with the seamen, and promised that such incidents would not be repeated. Wilson and Sexton withdrew the resolution and the amendment respectively, and Tom Mann as well as the Transport Workers avoided a crisis that might have led to an awkward situation.[66]

It was perhaps at about this time that Tom Mann began consciously to free himself from his former commitments to Wilson and the seamen whose hyper-patriotic acts now obviously annoyed him. Moreover, he was increasingly drawn into the movement for trade-union amalgamation and workers' control of industry. Under the new political setting created by the events both at home and abroad, especially in Russia, his new enthusiasm developed into a new conviction, communism. To the intricate process of this transformation we shall now turn.

[66] NTWF, *Report of the Seventh Annual General Council Meeting held in Bristol, 14 and 15 June 1917* (London, 1917), 25–44.

11. War and Revolution

The Road to Communism

THE Leeds Convention rediscovered in Tom Mann a crusader for labour's solidarity and internationalism. Soon the October Revolution in Russia gave the lie to the unity of radical forces in Britain achieved in Leeds. The coming to power of the Bolsheviks alienated the moderates such as MacDonald, Snowden, and Bertrand Russell, while giving a fillip to those who endorsed the establishment of the workers and soldiers' councils in Britain. Moreover, this was the one practical decision made in Leeds, and it inspired the Shop Stewards' and Workers' Committee (SSWC) movement, even though some claimed it had caused 'not the slightest ripple' in that direction.[1]

In fact it was in the wake of Leeds that the SSWC started a national movement of its own in August and merged with the amalgamation committees in February 1918. In this merger Tom Mann played a prominent role. Throughout the summer of 1917 he was seen spreading the gospel of Leeds. He expressed the conviction, when he addressed an audience of over 2,000 at Merthyr, that the only effective weapon in the hands of the workers was their power to withhold their labour, and 'the machinery to do this was in the workshop, in the Shop Steward and Committee for every 20 or 25 men irrespective how they were classified or graded'.[2] Arthur Horner, then a young miner of twenty-three living at Ynyshir, recalled how a conference for a Soldiers' and Workers' Council held in Swansea had been attacked by a group of soldiers and ended in a mêlée.[3] The Rhondda valley was ablaze. A series of 'monster meetings' were held there with Tom Mann as a main speaker. At a meeting organized by the South Wales Miners' Federation at Ynyshir, a resolution demanding a conference of belligerent governments which would negotiate an immediate cessation of hostilities along the lines of the Russian manifesto, was moved by Noah Ablett, supported by Tom Mann, and carried with great

[1] J. T. Murphy, *New Horizons* (London, 1941), 63.
[2] *Pioneer* (23 June 1917).
[3] Arthur Horner, *Incorrigible Rebel* (London, 1960), 23–4.

enthusiasm.[4] Mann was in great demand elsewhere as well. He spoke for the Joint Engineering Shop Stewards' and Workers' Committee in the Bradford district on 5 July and gave an address at a mass meeting at Nelson on 9 August for the Nelson District Branch of the Workers' and Soldiers' Council. 'I am occupied on Trade Union work almost exclusively', he wrote to an Australian friend: 'but I deliberately avoid official position. I can exert a greater influence on the rank and file by getting in contact with them direct, and at present I am helping the Warehouse Workers' Union.'[5] It was, indeed, the revival of the spirit not only of syndicalism but also of New Unionism.

Arthur Henderson had resigned from the War Cabinet because of the rude treatment meted out to him by the Government for his support of the Stockholm conference, which was in fact sabotaged by the Allied Powers. Henderson was now taking the lead in formulating Labour's memorandum on war-aims, which was duly adopted at a Labour congress; and Tom's hope for 'closing the slaughter' was about to be realized when Labour's campaign for a negotiated peace was overtaken by the events on the front which culminated in the military collapse of the Central Powers. It was probably in the last months of the war that Tom gave a series of lectures at a hall at Salford, his subjects ranging from 'The United States of Europe: No More Kaisers: Abolish the War Lords', 'The International Socialist Movement: Its Limitation and Prospects', 'State Socialism, National Guilds or Syndicalism—Which?' to 'The American and French Revolutions of 1776, 1789, and the Present War'.[6]

Sometime before the armistice Tom Mann applied for a passport to go to Australia. It was George Barnes, now in the War Cabinet, who conveyed to him the Foreign Office's negative decision. Barnes, on hearing Mann's new plans, sent him good wishes 'in your project of going to the land'.[7] Shortly after the armistice, the *Manchester Evening Chronicle* reported that Tom Mann, 'a stormy petrel for years', was now retiring. 'Having finished with industrial strife he proposes to settle down as a small holder. . . . The Sailors' and Firemen's Union have subscribed £250 to a testimonial on his behalf and the Transport Workers' Federation £100. The Amalgamated Society of Engineers, of which he is a member, is also contributing a

---

[4] *Pioneer* (17 July 1917).
[5] T. Mann to Frank Hyett, 29 Aug. 1917, Frow Collection, Salford.
[6] A handbill, n.d., Frow Collection, Salford.
[7] G. Barnes to T. Mann, 16 Oct. 1919, TMP.

goodly sum.'[8] Towards the end of January 1919 the vans carried furniture to the remote Kentish village of Biddenden in snow. 'I shall stay at Hill View tonight', Mann wrote to Elsie: '& be on my own. Glad you have fixed for the 9 o/c train. . . . You must not mind the mud, there is mud just now at every farm.'[9] Tom Mann, Jun., recalled that his father had bought a poultry farm at Hill View, Biddenden, paid £100 for it, and lived as a farmer for six months.[10]

Indeed, it was only for six months that he remained content with feeding chickens. The trade-union world was again stirred with new moves for reorganization and a new international alignment. With the restoration of the pre-war trade practice after the armistice, a demand for shorter hours—forty to forty-four hours per week—became a major issue for the ASE. Its membership had increased from 170,000 to nearly 300,000 during the war years. The amalgamation committees set up before the war were now linked with the Shop Stewards' and Workers' Committees; and the campaign for the new amal-gamation was greatly assisted by Tom Mann's third candidature for the general secretaryship of his union. It was inevitable perhaps that he should be called back from his semi-retirement to active trade-union work again.

From Biddenden, Mann issued an election address which stated his iron faith in one union for all workers in the engineering industry and his cherished idea that the aim of trade-unionism was 'the complete control of industry by the workers'. Referring to revolutionary events in Russia, Germany, Hungary, and Austria, he maintained that such 'great emotional and psychic waves' would also affect British workers and 'we must be ready to . . . control them and not be engulfed by them'. 'I am not afraid', he went on, 'of the terms Socialist, Spartacist, Bolshevist or Syndicalist. I know that in essense these all mean the thorough application of the principle and practice of *true co-operation*, and I unmistakably stand for co-operation and the wiping-out of the capitalist system.'[11] The result of the election announced in October was 31,449 for Mann as against 22,364 for his opponent James Kaylor of Coventry. A member-ship vote in the ASE for amalgamation in the engineering industry showed an overwhelming majority for it, with 163,181

[8] *Manchester Evening Chronicle* (11 Dec. 1918).
[9] T. Mann to Elsie Mann, 29 Jan. 1919, TMP.
[10] Interview with Tom Mann, Jun., 15 May 1982.
[11] T. Mann's address, 5 Apr. 1919, ASE, *List of Candidates* (London, 1919), 17.

votes cast in favour and 13,992 against, the total votes cast being well over the legal requirement of 50 per cent of the membership.

Thus it was Tom Mann, the new general secretary, who presided over the historical transformation of the ASE with nine other smaller unions into the new Amalgamated Engineering Union (AEU) which came into existence in July 1920 with a membership of 450,000. The larger unions like the Boilermakers and the Electricians remained outside it, but a beginning had been made, and it was a challenge just as Tom's leadership proved to be. Upon his election to the new post Mann had declared that his union would pursue 'a wisely militant policy. . . . We must march with heads erect to that better condition of true co-operation foreshadowed by those fathers of the A.S.E. who were responsible for the Preface in our Rule Book', an old Owenite statement of 1851.[12] In a pamphlet produced at the time, calling for a greater amalgamation, he commended, 'a substantial measure of control in shops, factories and mills' such as had been achieved by the Italian workers, and proposed a two-stage method for achieving such control in Britain: 'Our immediate object is control in conjunction with the employers. Our ultimate object is complete co-operative control on the basis of production for use and not for profit.'[13] An urgent note was struck, however, when he declared that 'we are part of the International Proletariat'.[14] Morris's idea of Fellowship and Tom Paine's famous maxim: 'The world is my country, and to do good is my religion' were invoked to support his renewed faith in internationalism.

The Allied intervention in Russia took a new turn with the armistice, as it virtually became a crusade against revolutionary Russia. The 'Hands Off Russia' movement in Britain which had begun early in 1918 gathered momentum. Tom Mann spent at least the first half of the year 1919 in his semi-retired seclusion on a Kentish farm, while Ben Tillett, now a Labour MP elected at a by-election in November 1917 and re-elected at the 'khaki election' after the armistice, and still secretary of the Dockers' Union, was making amends for his wartime excesses as a patriotic Labour leader. So we must call Tillett back to the scene, so that the role which he played in these

[12] ASE, *Monthly Journal and Report* (Nov. 1919), 50.
[13] T. Mann, *Required Now! One Big Union of Boiler Makers, Foundry Men, Engineers and Steel Workers* (London, 1920), 12.
[14] ASE, *Monthly Journal and Report* (Jan. 1920), 41.

turbulent post-war years, as well as that played by Tom Mann, can properly be assessed.

Tillett attended the annual conference of the Labour Party held at Southport in June 1919, where he critically appraised a resolution calling for consultation with the TUC to take effective action so as to enforce 'immediate cessation' of the Allied intervention in Russia 'by unreserved use of their political and industrial power'. He objected to dictation from the political side of the movement to the industrial side:

When industrial action was to be taken it must be taken with a full sense of responsibility by responsible bodies. . . . When they wandered blindly into revolution, led by the professional politicians and the middle-classes who had gouged out the eyes of the Samson, when the debt had to be paid, it was the middle classes and the professional politicians who benefited—it had been the workers who suffered.[15]

Earlier in the year the Triple Alliance adopted a resolution demanding immediate withdrawal of all British troops from Russia, and this sufficiently impressed the Government to give a pledge to that effect. 'There was too much talk of the Triple Alliance,' Tillett declared in his speech at the conference; 'The Triple Alliance was a body subordinate to discipline. Neither the miners, the transport workers, nor, he took it, the railway men, could be led by the nose. Their constituents must be consulted before any action was taken.' Then he turned his criticism to the Bolsheviks:

When they came to direct action in Russia to-day no Trade Union meeting could be held. In Russia to-day they had a Trotsky and Lenin Government. After all Trotsky and Lenin were mere accidents. They represented no power. The more terrible power was represented in the rank and file of the Russian peasantry and workers.[16]

Perhaps he made the mistake of applying British standards of labour and democracy directly to the Russian situation and of denying political importance to the professional revolutionaries. Again he showed the same dread of direct action and civil war as Burns had, and expressed doubts similar to those which Tom Mann apparently had not overcome, as we shall see presently, as to the nature of the Bolshevik Government.

Tom Mann was more forthright in his criticism of the Allied intervention in Russia which was one of the major issues dealt with at a special Trades Union Congress held in the Central Hall, Westminster, in December 1919. 'The unsatisfactory reply

[15] Labour Party, *Conference Report* (1919), 156, 158.   [16] Ibid. 159.

[by the Government] to the demand for the recognition of the Workers' Government of Russia roused the delegates,' read the ASE *Journal*, 'and the Parliamentary Committee were instructed, by special resolution, to again demand the cessation of war measures and withdrawal of the blockade. In this debate Tom Mann spoke splendidly.'[17] The national 'Hands Off Russia' Committee organized a series of demonstrations, and Tom Mann, who was one of the vice-chairmen of the committee, was invited to take the chair at a meeting held at the Albert Hall on 27 February 1920. The packed audience heard Colonel Malone, formerly a Coalition Liberal MP, then a propagandist for the BSP (which he joined after his visit to Russia), and others speak. Tom Mann was again in the chair at the Albert Hall on 21 March when Lansbury, having returned from a short visit to Russia, spoke against intervention.[18]

The cause of Ireland was now added to that of Russia, as the British Government brought in the notorious 'Black and Tans' to meet the challenges of the Irish Republican Army. At the special Trades Union Conference held in July 1920, a resolution protesting against 'the British military domination of Ireland' and demanding the withdrawal of British troops from Ireland and the cessation of the production of munitions destined to be used against Ireland and Russia was moved by Frank Hodges of the Miners' Federation and seconded by Ben Tillett. It was carried by 2.7 to 1.6 million votes. The resolution contained a characteristic phrase: 'in case the Government refuse these demands, we recommend a general down-tools policy, and call on all the Trade Unions here represented to carry out this policy, each according to its own constitution, by taking a ballot of its members or otherwise'.[19] Already at the annual conference of the Labour Party held one month before at Scarborough, Tillett had made an impassioned speech on Ireland. British rule there, he said,

had been disastrous. They had never understood the psychology of the Irish people. He would prefer that the Conference should give absolute freedom to the Irish people. He would withdraw every armed soldier from Ireland. Not that he believed in murder for he thought the Irishmen indulging in murder were doing wrong to themselves and to humanity. But he believed that if the Army of Occupation were withdrawn from Ireland the secret forces sheltering behind the dead bodies of murdered policemen, and sheltering behind the soldiers, would have

[17] ASE, *Monthly Journal and Report* (Jan. 1920), 45.

[18] R. Page Arnot, *Impact of the Russian Revolution in Britain* (London, 1967), 161–2.   [19] TUC, *Congress Report* (1920), 116.

to come out into the open and face a democratic nation. . . . He wanted them to respect the Irish nation.[20]

The Scarborough conference also discussed the Government refusal to admit the Russian trade-union delegation, and J. Havelock Wilson caused an uproar by suggesting that 'the Soviet Government are evidently waging some form of war against this country'. He was very ably answered by Robert Smillie and other delegates present. Then Tom Mann, ever loyal to his old friend, stood up and reminded the conference that he and Wilson had worked together in the trade-union movement 'in exceptionally trying circumstances'. 'I know, notwithstanding any views he is identified with to-day, that he has in days gone by worked in an exemplary fashion.' After this harmless compliment, he argued for the acceptance of Russian delegation from his own point of view:

When an invitation is sent in a dignified and becoming way from the organised workers of this country to those who have been passing through a most exceptional experience, and who, beyond any question, could be of the greatest value to us in enabling us to understand the particular set of circumstances with which they were confronted and the like of which we may be confronted with in the more or less distant future, it should be allowed acceptance. How to control industry, that is a question above all others—that is the concern of the organised workers of this country. There are people—in Russia, above all others —who have not only grappled with it, but, allowing for the astounding situation, they have come through so far with wonderful ability and exceeding great efficiency.

He concluded his speech by suggesting that his friends in Wilson's union should take good care not to carry 'fat-headed reactionaries' over here 'unless there is a fair chance of bringing the rank and file to teach us that which we desire to learn'.[21]

The defeat of the tsarist generals had not restored peace in Russia, as the new Allied intervention began in April 1920 with the Polish invasion of Soviet Russia. On 10 May the dockers in the East India Docks refused to load the *Jolly George* because they found munitions among the cargoes consigned to Poland. A manifesto issued shortly afterwards, calling on the TUC and the Labour Party jointly to bring about 'a national "down-tools" policy of 24 hours to enforce peace with Russia' was signed by

[20] Labour Party, *Conference Report* (1920), 167.   [21] Ibid. 293.

many trade-union leaders including Tom Mann.[22] Kiev fell in June, but by July the Red Army was driving out the Poles, and in August the British Government threatened to intervene on behalf of the Poles. Under Bevin's initiative a Council of Action was set up, and further preparations for direct action were made by the TUC and the Labour Party. The threatened action checked any further intervention by the Government for the Poles, and peace was concluded between Russia and Poland in October.

Bevin had won fame as the 'Dockers' K.C.' earlier in the year, when he with 'care' and 'cogency' pressed the Dockers' case for an increase in wages and made his own proposals for decasualization of the dock industry. There was no doubt that Tillett had been eclipsed by Bevin as the leader of the Dockers even before the advent in the course of 1921–22 of the Transport and General Workers' Union, virtually Bevin's creation, in the formation of which Tillett played little part. At the TUC held in Cardiff in September 1921 he joined in a debate on disarmament and spoke 'as an old revolutionary':

I am a revolutionary to-day; but a revolution without method, without order, without concept, and without consent, a revolution on the part of one section of the people would be a suicidal and criminal act which would defeat itself. If the Trade Union movement were without lines of demarcation and without its craft and class distinctions we might have a right to say to the nations: 'You shall agree'. . . . When 95 per cent. of my class constitute any movement for war or peace I am with them whether they are right or wrong; and 95 per cent. of our class constituted the fighting forces in the war. . . . War is dreadful. I have seen too much of it ever to want to see it again. I never supported war, but I supported the men who went into the war, as I have supported men who had gone into ill-considered strikes. Pass the resolution, and so give ourselves a fair chance of being understood by the Germans, the Americans, the Japanese workers—even the Chinese will understand that we are against war and those who make war.[23]

In fact, Tillett had spoken in favour of a resolution welcoming the Washington disarmament conference. His line of argument appeared a little confused, but it was an honest statement as well as the swan song of 'an old revolutionary'.

Tom Mann had been an energetic secretary of his union. When the engineers demanded a rise in wages in the period of post-war boom, he travelled to the affected areas. Thus he wrote to Elsie from Newport early in 1920: 'Had conference with the

[22] Arnot, *Impact*, 161.   [23] TUC, *Congress Report* (1921), 301–2.

District Committee yesterday in Newport. This morning we go to Cardiff to meet the Employers, & we hope to stick at it till settlement arrived at. The A.S.E. men are out at Swansea & Port Talbot & Barry. Cardiff, Newport & Bristol are involved.'[24] Shortly after the end of his term as general secretary we find him wandering outside Sheffield along the ridge to pay a visit to the Ebenezer Elliot Stone (commemorating the old Anti-Corn Law poet). A few days later he found himself in Newcastle-on-Tyne with a full schedule for lecturing: 'Last night I had a meeting at Sunderland. . . . Tonight I have a meeting at South Shields, tomorrow at Ferry Hill, on Saturday at Holden Colliery & Sunday in Newcastle: a bit trying for the throat, but I'm all right.'[25]

Mann's term of office as the general secretary of the ASE–AEU lasted about one and a half years until April 1921, when, in accordance with the rules of the union, he, having reached the age of 65, had to terminate his official connection. This was the period when, in addition to undertaking practical organizational work, he edited the ASE (later AEU) *Journal* and elaborated his theory of syndicalism as an ideology of class struggle with the Shop Stewards' and Workers' Committee as its core. He began to accommodate this notion to the rising tide of communism. The crucial issue was the nature and role of the State. He was critical of the Miners' demand for nationalization of the mines, for he felt that some of them were unaware of 'the risk of plutocratic State domination' involved in accepting State ownership and government control.[26] He protested against what he took to be an undue weight placed on parliamentary action as against direct action. Labour's wrongs, he felt, were fundamentally economic rather than political, and the capitalist who controlled the workshop, would control the men and their labour power; hence the need for workers' control of the workshop and industry. Parliament, on the other hand, even if it had been placed under Labour control, would be useless 'as the agency through which the working class can emancipate itself', and even after their emancipation, it would be 'useless for the co-operative control of industry'.[27] What distinguished him from other advocates of syndicalism was the emphasis he placed on the everyday struggles of the trade

[24] T. Mann to Elsie Mann, 19 Feb. 1920, TMP.
[25] T. Mann to Elsie Mann, 4 and 9 June 1921, TMP.
[26] ASE, *Monthly Journal and Report* (Jan. 1920).
[27] T. Mann, 'Trades Union Congress and Direct Action', ASE, *Monthly Journal and Report* (Apr. 1920), 50–1.

unions. Hence, direct action to him was not simply a means to effect revolutionary change by a general strike. It consisted rather of a series of industrial struggles over wages and hours of work pursued in a frame of mind that would perceive these struggles as events in the process of working-class emancipation. Commenting upon the acceptance by the NUR of the sliding scale in wages, he denounced it as the 'shoddiest form of unionism in the industrial world' especially for its implication that the workers' wages may or must be decided by the cost of living. This he called 'The Living Wage Stupidity'. 'A man in future', he now declared, 'must claim with his fellows on the basis not of what he can exist upon, but upon his productive capacity.'[28]

It was the same with hours of work. His new proposal on this issue was 'to saddle responsibility for unemployment upon the industry', in other words, those who controlled an industry should adjust the hours of work 'in such manner that all shall participate who are identified with the industry'.[29] At the Portsmouth TUC held in September 1920, he moved a resolution to make each industry responsible for unemployment with a special fund provided by a levy on the industry. Seconded by Tillett and supported by Bevin, this was carried.[30] Mann's idea was in part put into practice in the engineering industry with the Double Pay and Three Shift Agreement signed with the employers in December 1920, which was based on the principle that it was desirable to absorb some of the existing unemployment by three-shift working. A similar principle was applied to the piece-work system of wage payment, which had been extensively adopted during the war for the dilutees. The skilled engineers who had insisted on the time-work system had to turn to overtime work in order to make up for a considerable decline in real wages in the post-war years, and the piece-work system began to attract the attention of ASE workers. Tom Mann urged his fellow workers to consider the effects of mechanization in the industry, such as replacement of steam by oil which would make boilermakers redundant. He was 'entirely in favour of' production 'with the highest efficiency' which, however, should be matched by distribution 'with the truest equity'. Hence, piece-work or any plans of payment by results should not be taken up until a measure of equity was secured.

[28] Mann, 'Where are We with the Wage System', ASE, *Monthly Journal and Report* (Feb. 1920), 64–5.

[29] Id., 'Six-Hour Day', ASE, *Monthly Journal and Report* (Mar. 1920), 49–50.

[30] TUC, *Congress Report* (1920), 307–9.

Any fluctuations in the amount of work caused by such change in method should be met not by discharging workers but by the adjustment of working hours. Workers' control of industry was to secure such equity, and workers' committees and shop stewards were the means through which such control was to be exercised.[31] Indeed, Tom's millenarian aspirations, which we have seen fully displayed at moments of labour unrest and direct action, had an element of realism and practicability, and he was always ready to learn and adapt his tactics to new situations as they arose.

It was while he was acting as the general secretary of the AEU that the Communist Party of Great Britain came into existence, and his AEU *Journal* closely followed the process of its formation. He had rejoined the BSP probably after it had parted company with its pro-war faction, and at the annual dinner of its central branch held at the Restaurant Chanticler in May 1920 he praised the Bolsheviks for 'their ability to get to grips with production without the intervention of plutocratic parliaments'.[32] In its newspaper *Call*, he declared that he would 'emphatically and definitely' stand for the Third International.[33] He sent a message to the unity convention of the Communists held in the summer of 1920, and commended a book on direct action by William Mellor, who as representative of the Guild Communist Group actively participated in the convention. Communist unity was finally achieved in January 1921 at the second unity convention, when anti-parliamentary Communists led by Sylvia Pankhurst (herself then in prison) and a Scottish group prominent in the Workers' Committee Movement led by Willie Gallacher joined with the main body of Marxists who had come from the BSP and the SLP or Socialist Labour Party, itself an offshoot of the old SDF. One major obstacle had been the issue of Communist affiliation to the Labour Party. Lenin's admonition in *Left Wing Communism* and his interview with Miss Pankhurst and Gallacher in Moscow at the time of the second congress of the Communist International had paved the way for unity in Britain; but his famous aphorism, to support Henderson 'as a rope supports the hanged', whereby he described the attitude Communists should take towards the Labour Party, failed to commend the hangmen to those to be hanged and thus helped to deprive the young party of any

[31] Mann, *'Payment by Results': 'Piece Work and Time Work'* (London, 1920), *passim.*   [32] *Call* (27 May 1920).   [33] Ibid. (22 Apr. 1920).

prospect of becoming a mass party like some of its other European counterparts.

In the meantime, Tom Mann expatiated on workers' control of industry, which he deemed all the more urgent since a recession had followed the post-war boom by the summer of 1920. Indeed, he regarded it as the essential condition for communism and co-operation. He did not bother about the hangmen nor the hanged. At the time of the second unity congress of the Communists, Mann was addressing himself to the younger member of the AEU:

You will not be content with being capable mechanics. You will be citizens of the world; you will study HUMAN SOCIETY; you will chafe at the blots on society; you will arrive at conclusions as to how these can be removed. . . . Reason must prevail, and affection not only will, but ought to assert itself.[34]

He quoted a dozen past leaders of world opinion so as to elaborate his own idea of communism. Jean-Jacques Rousseau drew attention to 'the condition of the people question'. Tom Paine was 'the first man in England to grasp effectively the full meaning of government and its attendant evils'. Godwin was cited as another worthy advocate of 'the dissolution of political government'. He regarded St Simon's proposals for organizing industry as 'fanciful to a degree'. Robert Owen was far more important, for 'he saw the evils of the capitalist system [and] understood the cause of these evils. . . . He was the Father of the Co-operative Movement. He recognised very early on the necessity for the ONE BIG UNION. . . . Every British worker, at least, should raise his hat to Robert Owen.' After Owen came J. S. Mill and his socialist faith with an emphasis on individual liberty. Proudhon, 'an avowed Anarchist', would strengthen Tom's position with his argument that 'the government of man by man is slavery'. Bakunin was remembered for his plea for a 'free union of individuals into communes'. Tom admitted that Karl Marx had had an increasing influence in his own day, but regretted that 'his interpreters are often very doctrinaire, and not by any means in complete agreement'. His reference to Lassalle was extremely brief, while he praised Tolstoy in so many words. Lastly came Kropotkin, not Lenin. Tom Mann had known Kropotkin for thirty years, 'a most lovable personality, a genuine Russian and citizen of the world. I can understand', wrote Mann, 'that he would not concur with all that the Bol-

---

[34] Mann, 'To the Young Members of the A.E.U.', AEU, *Monthly Journal and Report* (Jan. 1921), 73.

shevists have found it necessary to do, and realising this it was noble of him to write lengthily and emphatically in their defence to let the world know where he stood'.[35] Probably he felt that his position was closer to Kropotkin than to Lenin or even to Marx.

Tom Mann has been regarded as one of the founding members of the Communist Party,[36] but he was not directly involved in its formation. His communism and internationalism were expressed in the simple terms of co-operation and world citizenry derived from Paine and Morris, Owen and Kropotkin. His farewell address to the 453,000 members of the AEU was written in a similar vein:

I think it well to remind the membership that it is essential for true success that the spirit of fraternisation must show itself in the workshops. . . . As we approach a co-operative condition of society engineers ought to be, and I think will be, as ready as any to effectively apply co-operative principles and methods. . . . Our reply [to the employers] should be, to accept the full responsibility for the management of industry, for ourselves to enter into relationship with the workers of other countries and exchange service for service or value for value. The Co-operatives and Trade Union movements agreeing upon such action could soon find the ways and means of carrying it out.[37]

The termination of his official connection with the AEU coincided with the collapse of the Triple Alliance on 15 April 1921; 'Black Friday', when a scheduled sympathetic strike by the Railwaymen and the Transport Workers was cancelled over the issue of the desirability of further negotiation by the Miners. Although Mann was not personally involved in these traumatic events, it was clear that the gospel of direct action had received a heavy blow. Moreover, it soon turned out that communism was a doctrine of political power rather than industrial action. The inevitable 'bolshevization' of the British party began under the dominant influence of the Russian party and the Communist International of which each national party formed a national section. A new situation was developing in which Mann was no longer able to sing a happy song cheerfully, reciting that communism was co-operation. Yet he was to embark upon his last missions which would fully occupy him as an old man for another decade and a half.

[35] Id., 'Men who have Changed the World's Thought', AEU, *Monthly Journal and Report* (Feb. 1921), 97–101.
[36] James Klugmann, *History of the Communist Party of Great Britain*, i (London, 1968), 79.
[37] AEU, *Monthly Journal and Report* (Apr. 1921), 59–62.

12. Last Missions

The RILU and the Minority Movement

LENIN'S hope for an imminent world revolution, expressed so forcibly at the founding congress of the Communist International (CI), had faded away, and his major concern at the second congress, of 1920, was the tactical issue of how to win over to the communist cause the main body of the working class in each country through parliamentary and trade-union action.

Revolutionary trade-unionists were among those who were invited to the second congress, but they apparently sobered down when a thesis was adopted, declaring 'Syndicalism and Industrialism' to be 'a step backward' in comparison with communism, though 'a step forward' compared with 'the old, musty, counter-revolutionary ideology of the Second International'.[1] It became obvious that communism, the ideology of the Communist International, would emphasize the idea of overthrowing capitalism by political rather than industrial means and would entail an 'iron discipline' to be imposed upon the member parties. Indeed trade unions, essentially democratic mass organizations concerned with wages and hours, were excluded from the revolutionary CI, but the trade-union problem was recognized as 'the most serious and important question facing our movement'.[2] The note of urgency reflected the grave concern among the CI about the lead taken by the Second International in launching a trade-union international, the revived International Federation of Trade Unions which claimed to represent millions of workers. The role to be played by the revolutionary trade-unionists for the CI was soon mapped out: it was through their initiative and active intervention under communist control that trade-union support was to be gained for communism, and it was for this purpose that the Red International of Labour Unions (RILU) was created at a special conference held in Moscow in July 1921 about the same time as the third congress of the CI.

[1] Roderick Martin, *Communism and the British Trade Unions 1924-1933: A Study of the National Minority Movement* (Oxford, 1969), 7.

[2] Julius Braunthal, *History of the International 1914-1943* (London, 1967), 174.

Preparations for launching the RILU had been going on for some time. J. T. Murphy, an engineer at Vickers and formerly secretary of the Engineering Amalgamation Committee in Sheffield and organizer of the Shop Stewards Movement in that area, had remained in Moscow after the second congress of the CI and had assisted the Russian trade-union leaders Alexei Losovsky and Michael Tomsky in forming a preliminary committee for a trade-union international. He returned to England in the autumn of 1920, and early in the following year the British Bureau of the Provisional International Council was set up with Tom Mann as chairman; Ted Lismer, president of the Sheffield Engineering Workers' Committee, as organizing secretary; George Peet, secretary of the National Committee of the Shop Stewards, as corresponding secretary; and Harry Pollitt as secretary of the London committee.[3]

It was Pollitt, a boilermaker by trade, who had secured Mann's whole-hearted co-operation for this new venture. He had been a prominent figure in a succession of radical movements: the Shop Stewards' Movement, the 'Hands Off Russia' Movement, the Socialist Workers' Federation led by Sylvia Pankhurst, and the Communist Party. He admired Tom Mann as a great revolutionary, and bought and treasured the whole of Tom's syndicalist library. He had recently visited his hero at the headquarters of the AEU at Peckham Road where Tom now lived. 'What a welcome he gave me', wrote Pollitt,

while he sized me up and wondered what surprise I was going to spring on him. He soon found out: I asked if he would become the first Chairman of the British Section of the Red International when he retired from his office as Secretary [of the AEU], and go as a delegate to the First Congress in Moscow in July. He agreed to my proposals, and thus began my long friendship with one of the most lovable comrades the working-class movement has ever produced.[4]

Indeed, Pollitt became Tom's great friend and most trusted assistant or perhaps manager in political and industrial work in his old age.

The task of 'the British Section' or British Bureau was to promote an effective alliance between the Communist Party and the revolutionary or leftist trade unions such as the Shop Stewards' and Workers' Committee to which Mann had been fully committed. Pollitt was entrusted with the work of propagating the cause of the Red International among the trade-union

[3] J. T. Murphy, *New Horizons* (London, 1941), 167; James Klugmann, *History of the Communist Party of Great Britain*, i (London, 1968), 109.

[4] Harry Pollitt, *Serving my Time* (London, 1950 edn.), 130.

branches and trades councils in the London area. In order to mobilize support for the forthcoming founding congress of the RILU, the British Bureau organized a London conference of trade-unionists early in May, at which the largest contingent of delegates came from the branches of Tom's own union the AEU,[5] and he was duly appointed to represent these London trade-unionists at the Moscow congress.

An account of his journey to Moscow has been provided by Pollitt himself who went with him. They started from the East India Dock on SS *Baltic* and called at Danzig, Libau, and Riga on the way. They took a walk on the sands at Libau where they saw a great many people sunbathing under the glorious sun, and finally disembarked at Reval. A railway journey from there to Petrograd in a wagon-lit coach 'all to ourselves' turned out to be a tedious, slow business, waiting hours at the frontier town of Narva for a new engine. The rest of the route was strewn with the traces of 'the dastardly work of the counter-revolutionary before they were driven off Soviet soil: blown-up bridges and damaged permanent way'. They were at last in Red Petrograd: 'Tom Mann's name was well known to the Party comrades, and a right royal fuss they made of us.' Black bread and tea offered to them seemed a banquet in their excitement over the Promised Land they had reached.[6] From Petrograd Tom Mann sent Elsie an account of his journey:

We have reached Petrograd alright, & expect to leave for Moscow at 2 o/c. It has been exceedingly interesting to watch all the time we have been travelling—people & land &c—At the frontier yesterday the train stayed a long time, the flowers I send [*Mann enclosed several dry flowers*] partly to show they are just the same as we have at home and partly because they are from the frontier of Russia & Esthonia. Besides the marguerites I saw red, white & speckled clover, wild parsley, vetches, buttercups, sorrel & the usual grasses. The weather was very stormy yesterday. . . . Quite a lot of German & Spanish delegates are also on this train going to the Congress.[7]

He reached Moscow on the following day with a group of trade-unionists. Fortunately for Mann and Pollitt, they missed a bus to the station on an excursion and escaped a train disaster which killed William Hewlett, the delegate from South Wales, and injured many others. At the third congress of the CI which preceded the RILU congress, Tom had occasion to speak to Lenin. 'How glad he [Lenin] was to greet Tom Mann!',

---

[5] Martin, *Communism and the British Trade Unions*, 21.
[6] Pollitt, *Serving my Time*, 133–6.
[7] T. Mann to Elsie Mann, 30 June 1921, TMP.

recorded Pollitt: 'His face lit up with pleasure as he told Tom how closely he had followed his activities all over the world.'[8]

The founding congress of the RILU was held at the Dom Siyosov, the First House of the Russian Trade Unions, formerly a banquet-hall of the Moscow nobility, attended by 342 delegates from 42 countries.[9] Mann was elected to the congress presidium. The chief resolution proposed was for a close relationship between the CI and the RILU by exchanging one executive member from each, but this was strongly opposed by the Spanish and German delegates, who were syndicalists, as well as by the American IWW. Mann found himself 'in hearty sympathy' with their argument that there must under no circumstances be any domination of the industrial movement by the political, but he persuaded himself that it would not actually amount to this. In fact, he had come round to the view that 'the capitalist state must be destroyed and that the Red Trade Unions must work for their destruction'. The First World War and the Russian Revolution had changed the whole situation so drastically that 'a readjustment of methods' had become necessary. The dictatorship of the bourgeoisie, 'the owners and controllers of industry', from which trade unions as well as parliaments proved powerless to deliver the workers, must be replaced by 'the Dictatorship of the Proletariat operating in the interests of social justice'. This is the essence of what he wrote in his report of the congress published shortly after his return to London.[10] Already at the congress Mann had spoken in favour of the Russian proposal for closer contact between the Red Trade Unions and the Communist Party and had even surprised his syndicalist friends 'by a limited defence of parliamentary action'.[11] All this was a drastic change of the front at least on the surface. His article, published in the *Labour Monthly* (October 1922), was aptly entitled 'From Syndicalism to Communism'. Yet a close examination of his arguments would give the impression that he was trying to defend syndicalists who 'aimed at depriving the State of its power to tyrannise'. And again, if the syndicalists limited themselves only to industrial struggle and ignored the State, 'this was a misunderstanding of the real Syndicalist view'. Thus he placed an emphasis on destroying the capitalist state machinery which could be used against the workers, an argument as much syndicalist as communist.

[8] Pollitt, *Serving my Time*, 137, 139.   [10] Ibid. 22.

[9] T. Mann, *Russia in 1921* (London, 1921), 12.

[11] Martin, *Communism and the British Trade Unions*, 13.

During the congress days of the CI, Mann patiently listened to the speeches made by Lenin, Trotsky, and Zinoviev, all intellectual revolutionaries, but he seemed to be more favourably impressed by President Kalinin with whom he came into close contact, a metal-worker like himself, and like him the owner of a plot of farmland. He also came to know Alexei Losovsky, a vigorous intellectual who had worked in Paris and was now the head of the RILU. After all, Mann's concept of a communist party was peculiar to himself—not a party of iron discipline but rather an ideal communist party which would allow a degree of loose federation. Commenting upon the Russian attempt to build 'a thorough Communist Society', he wrote:

it is utterly impossible to apply full-fledged Communist principle to all departments, and with all sections irrespective of their mental outlook and economic surroundings. Thus, with regard to the land of Russia, it is not complete Communism by a long way to allow each peasant to exercise full individual right to cultivate or control for a period of years.

He heartily endorsed the view that 'the Russian Communist Party never considered Communism to be a rigid formula'.[12] It is true that the Russia Tom Mann saw in 1921 was Russia under the New Economic Policy (NEP), which accepted 'detours' and 'bypaths'. The danger of totalitarianism was not apparent yet. With the NEP Russia threw overboard her dream of a world revolution and began to grope for a way to live in the hostile capitalist world, a world familiar to Tom Mann.

His report on his visit to Russia began with the expression of his joy in finding a country where the workers' right to the whole produce of labour was acknowledged for the first time in history, albeit only in principle. 'Reader!', he wrote, 'the great miracle has actually been performed!! The domination of the ruling class is no more!! The peasants produce the food, and it is theirs; theirs to actually eat, to enjoy, to satisfy themselves, not occasionally but regularly!!'[13] He had to qualify his glowing picture of the emancipated peasants and workers in Russia by an account of his three-week visit to the famine-stricken areas on the Volga; such qualifications, however, would only inspire the readers in their support of the new-born workers' republic struggling against all the odds. The launching of the RILU and the famine in Russia were the subjects he dwelled upon at a conference held in the Memorial Hall shortly after his return to

[12] T. Mann, *Russia in 1921* (London, 1921), 34–6.   [13] Ibid. 3.

London.[14] While in Russia, he had kept a diary, which tells us that on the boat down the Volga he learned to sing the Volga boat-song in Russian, an episode which shows him in high spirits, ready to fraternize with the people, while his account of the starving children begging at Samara, the centre of the famine area, was heartfelt and revealing.[15]

After the collapse of the industrial Triple Alliance earlier in the year, the labour movement in Britain, including the British Bureau of the RILU, remained at a low ebb. In order to put a stop to the state of 'workers' impotency' as Mann called it, the British Bureau furthered its work with the publication of a newspaper of its own: *All Power*, edited by Harry Pollitt. In its first number (January 1922) Mann sounded 'The Call to Action, Direct and Otherwise', Mann's old cliché 'and Otherwise' implying 'Political, Parliamentary, Municipal or Co-operative' according to what 'good sense' would dictate. Mann made another stirring call, this time for a general strike, 'the war of folded arms', to be conducted by the General Council of the TUC in order to remedy the consequences of the 'betrayal' of the Miners and turn the scale in class struggle, a half-fulfilled prophecy of events to come in 1926: 'one week would be enough and no strike pay would be wanted'.[16]

The British Bureau took an active part in the first national conference of trades councils in October 1922 and sponsored several rank-and-file trade-union movements, the most important of which was the Miners' Minority Movement (Miners' MM) launched in August 1923 in the South Wales coalfields and formally set up at a Sheffield conference in January 1924. The Miners' MM began a campaign to transform the Miners' Federation by demanding a wage increase and a six-hour day, and affiliation to the RILU.[17] Engineers, Shipyard Workers, and Transport Workers followed its lead. To this aspect of the movement we shall shortly return.

Tom Mann spent the winter of 1922–23 in South Africa, engaged in another bout of overseas propaganda work. A Tom Mann Tour Committee had been set up at the Central Executive Office of the Communist Party (South African Section of the CI), Johannesburg. This was his third visit to that country, and his task was to spread the gospel of the RILU. He reached Cape

14 Pollitt, *Serving my Time*, 142.
15 T. Mann, Russian Diary, 1921. I owe this to Dr Richard Hyman.
16 *Workers' Weekly* (14 Apr. 1923).
17 Martin, *Communism and the British Trade Unions*, 33.

Town on 2 October on board SS *Armadale Castle*, a Union Castle liner, and was met at the docks by a large number of trade-unionists and Communists with banners and bands. 'It is just a week since I arrived here', he wrote to Elsie;

You would see I had a demonstration on arrival, and same evening a gathering in the Trades Hall, the next night the City Hall 'Meeting', on Thursday a meeting at Somerset—Strand about 40 miles away. Friday at Claremont which you may remember is on the way to Wynberg. Yesterday afternoon at Salt River, evening at Grand Theatre. . . . However, it has not been all work. I had a fine motor run to Cape Point, part of it over a new road recently constructed. . . . Many have asked me about you & a lot of them remember Tom & Bob & Charly & Elsie.[18]

He arrived in Johannesburg on 15 October and was met by another great demonstration. On the following day he wrote to Elsie:

The feeling here is very good & they are looking to me to help them a lot, & I am expecting I'll make a change—but the sectional difficulties are as you heard in that talk we had on the Wednesday before I left: & so many are out of work & others short time that money is scarce. . . . Smuts [Boer general, then Prime Minister of South Africa] is genuinely hated here by the workmen, but of course backed by the other side. No need to try to describe in detail, I have deputations & callers every half hour. Bill [W. H.] Andrews is a good steady well balanced fellow held in great esteem, but the CP of which he is Sec is of course hard up.[19]

'The Johannesburg Town Hall was packed', read a report of his meeting,

and the reception the speaker received on rising and again at the conclusion of his magnificent oration, lasting over two hours, must have been as gratifying to him as it was encouraging to the committee responsible for the arrangements. At Pretoria, the next evening, the triumph was repeated, and at Vereeniging, Brakpan, and Benoni, the 'evergreen Tom' won his way to the hearts of the working men and women who crowded to hear him.[20]

On 7 November he found himself at Cape Town again. 'This is the 5th Anniversary of Soviet Russia,' he wrote to Elsie; 'They have withstood it now for full five years, and seem likely to weather the storm. Is that the way to put it? Good luck to them any way. . . . Tomorrow . . . to Bloemfontein.'[21] Back from Bloemfontein he visited the Fort (Gaol) in Johannesburg to see

18 T. Mann to Elsie Mann, 9 Oct. 1922, TMP.
19 T. Mann to Elsie Mann, 16 Oct. 1922, TMP.
20 *All Power* (Dec. 1922).
21 T. Mann to Elsie Mann, 7 Nov. 1922, TMP.

the men still awaiting trials; 'hundreds of them, the trials are on all the time, & three more have been sentenced to be hanged or hung!!' [22] The prisoners he met at the Fort were former strikers. The results of the British general election of October 1922 now reached him. He felt, 'Labour has done well. My estimate was 135 [*it was 142*]'. 'Sidney Webb had a thumping majority eh! 12000. Havelock Wilson out, Stanton out, Tillett in by skin of teeth, Jesson out, David Kirkwood in, & old Canky [*sic*] ... Newbold in, as straight out Communal [*sic* for Communist], very good for Canky!!' [23]

He remained on the Rand till 24 November when he left for Natal. On 4 December he wound up his meetings at Durban where the Social Democrats had been active in helping him. 'This is no country for young white people,' he wrote to Elsie from Durban; 'The natives do the labouring, & the colored people are in the Trades, & 60 per cent. of young whites from 16 to 21 cannot get any work at all. This is literally the case.' [24] By way of East London he reached Port Elizabeth; from there he sent 'everlasting flowers' including the passion flower to Elsie. He got on the same SS *Armadale Castle* on Christmas Eve at Port Elizabeth and duly returned to Cape Town after a three-month tour of the principal cities of South Africa, encouraging the change from sectional to industrial organization among the workers.

Tom had been sending home his lecture fees in South African notes and bankers' drafts. He advised Elsie to pay for two insurance policies with part of his remittance. At Cape Town he agreed to put in another month for the Communists there while he awaited a definite invitation from Australia which had been vaguely promised. Early in January he enjoyed an orchestral concert of Tchaikovsky and Bizet at the town hall. He even thought of staying in the Cape with Elsie. 'I believe I could fix up here in Cape Town & run the place like we did in Melbourne; if I thought you would like to do it I would try to fix it up!!' [25] Elsie, however, was too strongly tied to England by now, with her mother at Grassington and her choirs in London, to encourage Tom in his new whims. Moreover, the half-expected journey to Australia failed to materialize. The last stretch of his South African campaign included an address at the Grand Theatre at Cape Town on 'Four Hours a Day Week'

[22] T. Mann to Elsie Mann, 1 Nov. 1922, TMP.
[23] T. Mann to Elsie Mann, 21 and 28 Nov. 1922, TMP.
[24] T. Mann to Elsie Mann, 5 Dec. 1922, TMP.
[25] T. Mann to Elsie Mann, 11 Jan. 1923, TMP.

and a week's organization for the unions connected with De Beers' explosive works at Somerset West.

He left Cape Town on 3 February on board SS *Betana*, a P. & O. boat, sailing direct for Tilbury. One of his last acts as an agitator in South Africa was to deliver an opening address at the annual conference of the Industrial and Commercial Workers' Union of Africa, a four-year-old union consisting solely of African natives and coloured persons. His impression of the conference was published in *All Power* (March 1923) after his return home:

At present the South African native is literally the Beast of Burden, carrying the white man and his family, doing all the drudgery, all the heavy and all the dirty work, and paid only a wretched pittance by white persons, men and women, many of whom would indignantly denounce any such conditions in any part of the world for whites, yet here, they have no compunction in imposing unbelievable tasks upon the blacks, who go about their work without a murmur, and slave away and see good food in great variety and enormous quantities near them, but they do not share it, they must keep their position of dog-like readiness to obey the high and mighty 'baas' or Mrs., or children; and may not go into a public hall with whites, may not participate in many of the recreations, or frequent areas and spaces which they, the natives, have made and keep in order. I declare my heart has ached and my mind has been made sore at the behaviour meted out by whites to blacks. It is therefore a source of real joy to me to find the natives taking action. The union is ambitious enough to undertake the organisation of agricultural workers, the natives at the mines, and domestic workers of both sexes.

Mann's self-imposed task for the emancipation of the proletariat took on a really international dimension as he now declared himself to be on the side of the native workers, whereas he had so far restricted himself to the organizing work among the whites.

Back home, action 'otherwise' than direct was an immediate issue: the general election of December 1923 at which the Communist Party put forward two candidates of its own, J. T. Walton Newbold at Motherwell and Gallacher at Dundee. 'Walton Newbold's supporters are mainly drawn from Irish catholics', he wrote to Elsie from Motherwell, '—street workers —who as Catholics not only support him but work well for his return. It is odd that neither Newbold, Purcell or Vaughan mention the Six Hour Day.' But the real reason for his writing was not the Catholic support nor the six-hour day but Elsie's birthday. 'I will have a quiet lil drink & turn nice thoughts on you,' he wrote; 'We are not likely to have another 25 years together, but we will have an even nicer time whether it is long or short.'[26] A few days later he was writing from Dundee, telling Elsie that Willie Gallacher had 'no earthly chance of winning this time', but this was to keep him for a better chance at the next run. He went on:

You did not know Jack McLean of Glasgow [a Marxist school-teacher, formerly of the BSP, active in the anti-war movement] except by reputation . . . The poor fellow died last night, his finish is very pathetic. I think his death is due to the worrying anxieties largely brought about by what appeared to be his eccentricities, which were really caused by the hardship & strain consequent upon hunger striking in prison. . . . Jim Larkin is excellent here today & he & I and Gallacher are in evidence tomorrow.[27]

Walton Newbold was defeated by his 'Orange protestant' opponent, and Gallacher was at the bottom of the list of defeated candidates. Yet the Labour Party, winning more seats than the Liberal Party in opposition to the Tories in an election fought on the issue of Tariff Reform, was to form a Minority Government under the premiership of Ramsay MacDonald.

The Labour Government did much to improve Anglo-Russian relations by giving *de jure* recognition to the Soviet Government, but floundered on the terms of Anglo-Russian financial and commercial agreements and in the end fell a victim to a strong wave of anti-Soviet propaganda. Meanwhile, the leadership of the TUC became more leftist in its outlook as some of the reformist members of the General Council had left it to join MacDonald's Government; and it appeared to be willing to consider the Russian proposals for a United Front or even the merger of the International Federation of Trade Unions—of whom the TUC was a major prop—with the Moscow-dominated RILU. After the dismal failures and fiascos of communist revolutionary attempts in Europe, the defeat of the German rising in October 1923 among others, the Russian Government had to shape its policies more carefully than ever on two apparently contradictory premises: equilibrium of the two systems, socialist and capitalist, to enable its foreign office to make terms with capitalist governments, and the assumption of the instability of that equilibrium which was the basis of the

---

[26] T. Mann to Elsie Mann, 27 Nov. 1923, TMP.
[27] T. Mann to Elsie Mann, 1 Dec. 1923, TMP.

tactics pursued by the two Moscow Internationals.[28] The 'United Front' policy, the tactic to win over the reformist labour organizations, was to be strengthened, or replaced if need be, by the tactic of the 'United front from Below', which, in Britain, had assumed the form of the Minority Movement.

In the spring of 1924 Tom Mann made another visit to Moscow in response to an invitation to address the All-Russian Conference of Railwaymen. Apparently he travelled to Switzerland first, and proceeded from Berne via Frankfurt-on-Main to Berlin, where he had to stay at a hotel near the station while waiting for another train to his destination. 'Prices are high here,' he wrote to Elsie: 'The Mark is now 28 to the pound. The country of the paper money is difficult because of the various values, one bit of paper is one Mark, a similar bit worth 500 or it is worth a penny. . . . People here seem well fed & clothed, & shops well stocked with provisions. I haven't yet been in typical working class quarters.'[29] On 18 April, during the conference week of the Russian Railwaymen, he wrote a report to *All Power* in which he referred to an opening speech given by President Kalinin commenting 'pointedly' upon the Anglo-Russian conference sitting in London. He also mentioned his own visit to several meetings of the Metal Workers' International Propaganda Committee at which he had stated that the RILU was 'heartily endorsed by fully 25 per cent of the British metal workers of all trades'. 'Much satisfaction was caused', he added, when the report reached Moscow that A. J. Cook had been elected secretary of the Miners' Federation of Great Britain.[30] Cook, the Miners' agent in central Rhondda, had been elected to the secretaryship with strong backing from the Miners' MM which did its best not to split the left-wing vote.[31] Mann's next dispatch from Moscow was bluntly optimistic: 'Here in Russia with government absolutely resting upon the workers . . . I declare Russia to be really the Land of Hope, aye, and Glory.'[32] While in Moscow, he remained in close contact with the leaders of the RILU, which at its third congress held in July expressed its willingness for a *rapprochement* with the IFTU, though it emphasized the importance of international discipline for the revolutionary trade-unionists.

In the meantime, a solid basis for the National Minority

[28] Murphy, *New Horizons*, 176; E. H. Carr, *Twilight of Comintern* (London, 1982), 3.   [29] T. Mann to Elsie Mann, 30 Mar. 1924, TMP.

[30] *All Power* (May 1924).

[31] Martin, *Communism and the British Trade Unions*, 34.

[32] *All Power* (June 1924).

Movement (NMM) that was about to be launched under the aegis of the RILU was provided by the National Workers' Committee Movement, formerly the Shop Stewards' and Workers' Committee Movement, which had merged with the British Bureau of the RILU as early as June 1922.[33] The founding congress of the NMM was now held in the Memorial Hall, London on 23 and 24 August, attended by over 270 delegates. Tom Mann in the chair declared: 'We are not disruptionists. (Applause) We are not anti-trade unionists. (Applause)'. He went on to urge the TUC to be equal to the need of the hour by preparing the workers for the struggle with capitalism. It was virtually an attempt to form a 'United Front from Below' in order to bolster a similar front from above. Several resolutions were moved by Harry Pollitt on the aims of the movement, one of which emphasized 'wide agitation and propaganda' within the existing organizations 'for the principles of revolutionary class struggle'. The RILU's call for a world conference of the IFTU and the RILU to set up a united trade-union international was endorsed, and British trade unions were called upon to support it. Tom Mann was elected as president, Harry Pollitt general secretary. 'Left-wing Trade Unionists Unite' was the caption of a report of the conference published in the *Workers' Weekly*.[34] A week later a Russian trade-union delegation headed by Tomsky was accorded 'warm and sustained applause' at the Hull TUC,[35] at which members of the NMM 'put up a strong fight for International Trade Union Unity' and they found 'a big response in the Congress itself', wrote Pollitt.[36] From Hull Mann wrote to Elsie: 'The usual crowd are here, saw Mrs. Tillett who enquired very kindly about you & the Family.'[37]

The growth of the NMM owed a great deal to the initiative taken by Harry Pollitt, and Tom Mann remained a symbolic figurehead. He has been described as 'a more prominent but less important member of the Secretariat', playing little part in administration and policy-making.[38] It was certainly too much to expect detailed work from him now, but he was ideal as a symbolic figure: the NMM and its championship of a united front policy, both national and international, as well as its

[33] Martin, *Communism and the British Trade Unions*, 22.

[34] *Workers' Weekly* (29 Aug. 1924).

[35] Lord Citrine, *Men and Work* (London, 1964), 88.

[36] H. Pollitt, Foreword to Alexander Losovsky, *British and Russian Workers* (London, n.d. [1926]), 9.   [37] T. Mann to Elsie Mann, 2 Sept. 1924, TMP.

[38] Martin, *Communism and the British Trade Unions*, 46–7.

class unionism suited him well. Apart from obvious political implications, the new policy as he saw it may well have appeared as a natural development of his erstwhile New Unionism and syndicalism. He even accepted the political action involved, and allowed himself to stand as one of the eight Communist candidates at the general election of October 1924, which was tainted by the Zinoviev letter scare. Mann was also an AEU candidate, and in order to qualify himself for the financial support of his union, he endorsed the programme of the Labour Party, 'as I not only want all the Labour Party is asking for, but much more'.[39] Hé contested Nottingham East, met the local Labour Party executive, and had enthusiastic meetings. The result of his campaign was not encouraging: he obtained 2605 votes, the lowest figure among the Communist candidates. With this general election the Labour Government, too, came to an inglorious end.

Meanwhile Tillett, who lost his seat at Salford North at this election, had been doing his utmost to promote the cause of Anglo-Russian comity. He had been a member of the Labour delegation sent to Russia at the time of the Russo-Polish War of 1920.[40] As the international secretary of the TGWU, he played his part in the tortuous process of the Anglo-Russian trade-union *rapprochement*. When the Russian delegation came to London to negotiate with the MacDonald Government, the TUC invited trade-unionist members of the Russian team to a dinner, at which Tillett made a 'lavish, flowery' speech. The Hull TUC decided to send a ten-member delegation including Tillett to Russia in order to assist the cause of international trade-union unity. They attended the Sixth Soviet Trades Union Congress, at which Tillett made a fraternal address and 'waxed reverently and lengthily eloquent on the virtues of Lenin'.[41] Pollitt, who also attended the Russian congress, recalled that he 'heard Ben addressing meetings and did he let himself go', and added that 'you might have been tempted to call him a "Kremlin Agent"'.[42] Indeed, Tillett was very favourably impressed by the 'State-aided' Soviet mother, education in which more had been accomplished in seven years than under the Tsar in seven centuries, and the positive role of trade-unionism in the State, and went so far as to declare: 'Religious, social and political

[39] *Workers' Weekly* (24 Oct. 1924).

[40] Daniel Calhoun, *United Front: The TUC and the Russians* (Cambridge, 1976), 33.   [41] Ibid. 51, 100.

[42] H. Pollitt to I. Mackay, 21 Jan. 1951, IMP.

freedom, with economic security, is now established in Russia.'[43]
In an attempt to exonerate the delegation from hostile attacks
at home, he wrote on his return that 'perfect freedom and carte
blanche were allowed for interview, for inspection, for conference, for councils, for examination, and for report', and 'the
utmost secret archives of the Soviet Foreign Office were at our
disposal', from which he concluded that the Zinoviev letter
which had contributed to Labour's defeat and his own at the
general election was a forgery.[44] The composition of the left-
wing support for international trade-union unity, however, was
of a mixed nature. Along with Robert Williams and John
Bromley, Tillett was regarded as a 'skilled opportunist',[45] and
certainly he was not prepared to go the whole hog and support
Tom Mann and the NMM.

Nevertheless, the launching of the NMM was opportune. It was
the time of economic recovery, and the trade-union movement
sought to make up for the losses suffered in the years of the
post-war slump. The TUC, as we have seen, was favourably inclined to attempts at *rapprochement* with Soviet Russia, and its
left-wing leaders like A. A. Purcell, who had chaired the founding congress of Mann's Syndicalist Educational League, were
sympathetic with the NMM. The number of trade-unionists
represented at its annual conferences rose from 20,000 in 1924
to 957,000 in March 1926. Industrial unionism was revived
under the new slogan of 'organization by industry'.[46]

Meanwhile, the long-drawn-out crisis in the coal industry
had been sharpened by the adverse effects of the overvaluation
of the pound as Churchill made the return to the Gold Standard
at the pre-war parity in April 1925. The Miners scored a victory
on 'Red Friday' in July when united action threatened by the
railwaymen and the transport workers under the TUC leadership led the Government to appoint a Royal Commission headed
by Herbert Samuel and to continue subsidies temporarily.

In August Mann, from his house at 1 Adelaide Road, Brockley,
SE4, was writing a humorous letter to Elsie who had been away
for recuperation, possibly at Grassington, telling her about a
dozen sparrows that plumped down at the back-door, cheeping
out 'Aint Mother about; Aint Mother about?', and added a political note: 'There will be fully 600 delegates at the Conference,

[43] B. Tillett, *Some Russian Impressions* (London, n.d. [1925]), *passim*.
[44] *Sunday Worker* (29 Mar. 1925).
[45] Quoted in Martin, *Communism and the British Trade Unions*, 76.
[46] Ibid. 55–6, 64.

good eh?'[47] At the second annual conference of the NMM
held in the same month Mann commented on the Government's
temporary subsidy which had been offered to cope with the
coal crisis and said that 'the other side would use the nine-
month period of the subsidy to prepare their attack and therefore the trade union must also use the time in preparing to
defeat the attack'.[48] The temper of the Scarborough TUC that
followed was almost militant. The Conservative Government
began preparing for large-scale industrial action by the
workers by setting up the Organization for the Maintenance of
Supplies, and it prosecuted leading Communists, including
Pollitt and Gallacher, for sedition.

On 21 March 1926, shortly after the Samuel Commission had
published its report, the NMM convened a Special National
Conference of Action in Battersea Town Hall, at which Tom
Mann, the chairman, criticized the report for being an attack
upon wages, hours, and national agreements. He deplored the
activities of the OMS, which was in fact an unofficial body for
the recruitment of strike-breakers: 'Let us have our industrial
machinery ready for *action*. The real central body through
which we must function is the General Council of the Trades
Union Congress. All unions should be loyal thereto and co-operate loyally therewith.'[49] The conference urged the formation of
a Council of Action through the trades councils to mobilize the
workers in each locality. For its proposals and for 'the spirit of
combativity', the conference is said to have marked the highest
point in the history of the NMM.[50] It is true that the NMM's
call for action made little impression on the trade-union leadership, but it met encouraging response especially from trades
councils, and local councils of action were actually established
in Glasgow, Edinburgh, Barrow, Liverpool, Doncaster, Sheffield, and elsewhere.[51]

The General Strike to support the Miners, who had rejected
Samuel's recommendations including a reduction in wages,
began on 4 May, led by the General Council of the TUC. The
NMM, however, was not in a position to exert significant
influence upon its course. Its office at 38 Great Ormond Street
was raided by the police and badly damaged early in the strike,
while prominent Communist leaders were still in prison and a

---

[47] T. Mann to Elsie Mann, 26 Aug. 1925, TMP.
[48] Wal Hannington, *Never on our Knees* (London, 1967), 186.
[49] Special National Conference of Action, *Report* (London, 1926), 15.
[50] Klugmann, *History of the Communist Party*, ii (London, 1969), 104.
[51] Martin, *Communism and the British Trade Unions*, 69.

large number of party members were in custody throughout the strike. Local councils of action were strongly under Communist influence, and the Communists 'maintained a strictly "Constitutional" attitude throughout'.[52] Indeed, it was not a revolutionary struggle nor even such direct action as Tom Mann had contemplated, and in spite of its impressive scale and degree of solidarity, as a political strike—as it was in the eyes of the Government—its failure was inevitable. On 13 May, the day after the General Council had issued a statement to terminate the General Strike, Mann wrote to Elsie from a London hotel where he was staying 'in charge for the present':

You will perhaps have had a B.W. [*British Worker*] but I enclose one in case, also I enclose the AEU decision which shows why many of them seemed late in taking action. [*The engineers were among the 'second line' workers to be called out in the second week of the strike.*] The situation now depends largely upon what the Miners Conference will do on Friday but the General phase of it will soon disappear.[53]

Mann may have not been informed that the Miners had issued a statement that they would not agree 'in any shape or form' to the calling off of the strike, since the *British Worker*, the strike sheet, dared not reveal it.[54] The Miners decided to continue their lonely fight, in the course of which they suffered disunity and breakaway as well as hunger and starvation which finally broke their resistance in November.

After the defeat of the General Strike, the NMM continued for some time as a major centre of the militant trade-union movement. At its third annual conference held in August 1926, solidarity with the Miners was the theme of Mann's presidential address. The Communist Party at its own conference held in October attacked 'the treacherous policy of the General Council' of the TUC and stated their own view of the situation in the following terms: 'In many districts, the Strike Committees were the germs of an alternative Government. The great importance of the trade unions in the British Labour Movement makes the creation of a mass Minority Movement imperative.'[55] Late in October Tom Mann wrote to Elsie from Newcastle on his work for the Miners and for the NMM:

I reached here alright & then went further in North'land to a district called Hazlerigg, where some miners re-started yesterday. Had

---

[52] Ibid. 71–2.   [53] T. Mann to Elsie Mann, 13 May 1926, TMP.
[54] Tony Cliff and Donny Gluckstein, *Marxism and Trade Union Struggle: The General Strike of 1926* (London, 1986), 248.
[55] Klugmann, *History*, ii. 224, 251.

meeting alright & in spite of a few Labour Party men doing their best to oppose us, got a Committee formed to take action re trying to stop those who had started. . . . I am fixed for two meetings today & also for each day up to & including Monday next. This afternoon I shall be at Wallsend—North Side of Tyne, evening at Wardley, South Side, close to Pelow where the coop have their works. The C.W.S. have a mine at Shilbottle, & the men yesterday decided to start today. Gallacher is at Ashington, that is some 20 miles further north.

He was paying 5s. a week as levy for the Miners.[56] In spite of an ambitious programme adopted at the August conference of the NMM, its decline had begun with the defeat of the General Strike which also brought the Anglo-Russian trade-union *rapprochement* to an end.

The NMM published an angry pamphlet by Losovsky who accused the General Council of the TUC for having 'surrendered all its positions and sold both General Strike and the miners' struggle'. The General Council had refused to accept the Russian money, contributions made by the Russian trade-unionists levying themselves two hours' wages, 'on the ground that it did not want to rouse the capitalists'. His attack was then directed against the left wing of the General Council: A. A. Purcell, George Hicks, Ben Tillett, John Bromley, and others, who were 'consistent in one thing only—in their inactivity. . . . They, too, approved the General Council's refusal of the "Red Gold". With that they vanished from the political horizon.'[57] At the 1927 Edinburgh TUC the painful episode of the Anglo-Russian trade-union co-operation was officially wound up, and the TUC severed whatever relations it had had with the NMM. At the fourth annual conference of the NMM held in August 1927, Tom Mann stressed that the Miners had been confronted by 'the organised Capitalist State', while denouncing the new Trade Union Act as 'the Blacklegs' Charter'. He pleaded for 'one real world-wide international of the organised workers of all lands' and referred to his recent visit to China where he said trade unions were 'growing notwithstanding the terrible obstacles opposing them'.[58] To the nature and scale of the revolution and counter-revolution he had seen in China we must now turn.

[56] T. Mann to Elsie Mann, 27 Oct. 1926, TMP.
[57] Losovsky, *British and Russian Workers*, 20, 22–3.
[58] NMM, *Fourth Annual Conference: Chairman's Address* (London, 1927), *passim*.

13.   Last Missions

The Chinese Revolution—A Journey to Wuhan

THE Communist International, after the bungling of revolutionary attempts in Germany and the total failure of the General Strike in Britain, found cause for hope, if not for a world revolution, at least for greater security in the Soviet Union, in the new political developments in China. The Revolution of 1911 which drove the Manchu dynasty from power altered little of the country's social and economic life. The second Chinese Revolution of 1919 arose out of the protest of the nationalist students in Peking, helped by the city workers, against the terms of the Versailles Treaty which had failed to apply the principle of self-determination to China and against the weak-kneed politicians who had accepted the unsatisfactory settlement. With revolutionary ferment spreading elsewhere, Sun Yat-sen, the founder of the Kuomintang the nationalist party, set up a government in Canton in 1920 and made contact with the newly organized trade unions there. He soon accepted Russian help in order to secure national unity and independence against the imperialist powers. In 1923 Michael Markovich Borodin, a Communist agent educated in America and known as 'George Brown' to the British, who had recently spent a term of penal servitude in a Glasgow prison for distributing Communist pamphlets, was sent by the Politburo of the Russian Communist Party to act as adviser to Sun Yat-sen. The Chinese Communists who had set up their own party in 1920 began to join the Kuomintang in great numbers. Chiang Kai-shek, Sun's staff officer who had returned from study in Moscow, became Borodin's special favourite and was appointed director of the Whampoa Military Academy, Russian-funded and Russian-staffed.[1]

The death of two men—Lenin on 21 January 1924 and Sun Yat-sen on 12 March 1925—accentuated disturbing elements in the revolutionary politics of the two countries as well as in their delicate mutual relationship. In Moscow Stalin began to consolidate his power against his rival Trotsky, and his—and

[1] Harold R. Isaacs, *Tragedy of the Chinese Revolution* (Stanford, 1951), 82.

for that matter Borodin's—policy towards China was to turn the Chinese bourgeoisie (in the bourgeois stage of revolution preceding the proletarian) into an ally of Russia against the imperialist powers. Chiang for his part was harbouring an equally ambitious plan to seize the leadership by manœuvring between Russia and the imperialist powers. In the meantime, unrest spread among the workers of the great cities of China. In the wake of unrest in Shanghai, during which a British officer ordered the shooting of demonstrators, a boycott of British goods and a general strike were declared in Canton in June 1925; Hong Kong business came to a standstill, deserted by all the workers. Aided by the strikes and boycotts, the Kuomintang strengthened its hand and by the end of July 1925 it had organized a new National Government of China. In Britain a 'Hands Off China' movement was launched by the Communist Party, and the NMM played an active part in it. Ben Tillett, who was again acting in close contact with Tom Mann, moved a resolution protesting against the murder of the Chinese workers and students at a meeting organized by the NMM.[2] Tom Mann too was prominent in this new anti-imperialist campaign.

Mann's interest in the Asian labour movement was not new. He had known Sen Katayama the Japanese socialist, now one of the Comintern leaders, from the pioneering days of the 1890s. At the founding congress of the RILU an incident took place which was quite characteristic of him. He headed a deputation to see Lenin and to plead for the release of the anarchists who had been imprisoned. 'I was eager to hear from Tom the results of his interview,' wrote Tom Bell, a delegate at the congress: 'To my amusement he was quite excited, not at the rebuff over the anarchists, but because he had been asked to make a report on the Eastern question!' Tom Mann worked all night and presented a long report on the colonial question the following day.[3]

In China, as the workers' movement in major cities became a serious threat to the bourgeoisie, both foreign and Chinese, a new situation soon developed: the Chinese bourgeoisie began to conspire with the imperialist powers against the workers especially in Shanghai. In Canton there was an uneasy alliance between Borodin, Chiang Kai-shek, and the left-wing Kuomintang, but Chiang soon made himself master of Canton by unexpected attacks on the strongholds of the Communists and the workers in the city on 20 March 1926. The Kuomintang Left

[2] James Klugmann, *History of the Communist Party of Great Britain*, ii (London, 1969), 309.   [3] Tom Bell, *Pioneering Days* (London, 1941), 239.

capitulated, and Chiang became the head of the party and the commander-in-chief of all the expeditionary armies. Stalin and the Kremlin strategists accepted the *fait accompli* for the sake of a strong China as an ally against the imperialist powers, and suppressed all the accounts of the coup in Canton in the communist press.[4] The Northern Expedition of the Kuomintang forces was launched soon afterwards so as to consolidate the new right-wing leadership with successful military operations and territorial expansion. The Russians supported the expedition, and because of this the Russo-Kuomintang alliance survived and the suppressed Communists were reinstated. A new revolutionary wave, however, surged across the provinces of Kiangsi, Hunan, and Hupei as Chiang's troops advanced northward. In fact, they were welcomed as an army of liberation as their route had been cleared by an advance guard of Communist-trained propagandists who organized strikes and peasant revolts behind the lines.[5] Agricultural revolution on a colossal scale backed up the advancing troops.

The Wuhan cities (Wuchung, Hanyang, and Hankow) were liberated in October, and there in December, the left wing of the Kuomintang organized a temporary government which was to function until the main body of the party and government leaders could arrive. The Kremlin had sent a telegram directing the Chinese Communists to check the revolutionary peasants so as not to antagonize the Kuomintang generals, many of whom were great landlords. Meanwhile, the workers' spontaneous action took over the British concessions in Hankow and Kiukiang, and this encouraged the Wuhan Left to stiffen their attitude to Chiang Kai-shek who had established himself at Nanchung, capital of Kiangsi, with right-wing Kuomintang politicians around him. After a short visit to Wuhan in January 1927, Chiang openly declared his intention to crush the Communists. It was in this tense and grave atmosphere surrounding the great Chinese cities that Tom Mann as a member of the International Workers' Delegation arrived in China.

'Dear John'—it was to John Burns that Mann now sent an appeal from the luxurious Versailles Hotel on Lenin Street, Vladivostok, where he was staying early in February:

---

[4] Robert C. North and Xenia J. Eudin, *M. N. Roy's Mission to China: The Communist Kuomintang Split of 1927* (Berkeley, Calif., 1963), 24; Isaacs, *Chinese Revolution*, 96-7.

[5] North and Eudin, *Mission to China*, 28.

By the address you will see I'm a long way from London. Came through Warsaw & Moscow, over 7000 miles so far, 6000 of it through snow. I'm on my way to China to try & help in their struggle. This splendid manifestation of courage & determination on their part is the biggest thing that has happened in our lives, and I reckon you & I ought to be with them.

The spirit of 1889 dawned once more upon him.

400 millions of them subjected to such treatment, and a percentage now really alive and proving their earnestness & capacity, but what formidable forces against them! . . . The more I think of it the more I am enthused with the glorious possibilities. You have tons of energy, & ability: I hope you will.[6]

Mann said, he was travelling with 'an American workman friend', who evidently was Earl (Russell) Browder, then twenty-five years old, one of the founders of the American Communist Party, who was later to coin the slogan 'Communism is 20th century Americanism'. He represented the Trade Union Educational League of America.[7] It has been said that the Indian Communist M. N. Roy, who had attended the seventh plenum of the Comintern in November and had been elected to the Chinese Commission, was travelling to China by way of Vladivostok with Mann and Jacques Doriot.[8] Doriot, one of the most popular Communist leaders in France at the time, was to advocate a United Front 'at the top' in 1934. When it was disavowed by other Communist leaders, he was expelled from the French party, and founded his own party, the Parti Populaire Française, which collaborated with the Nazis. The delegation consisted of three, Browder, Doriot, and Mann himself. A Russian, Sydor Stoler, acted as secretary. The three-man 'International Workers' Delegation', as it was called, was sent as a fraternal delegation, probably at the suggestion of the Chinese Commission of the Comintern with the support of the RILU, to attend the first Pan-Pacific Trades Union Conference and various other conferences scheduled in China such as the fourth all-China Trades Union Congress and the fifth congress of the Chinese Communist Party.

Vera Vladimirovna Vishnyakova-Akimova, a young graduate of the Far Eastern State University in Vladivostok, who worked as a translator–interpreter with the Soviet mission in China

---

[6] T. Mann to J. Burns, 7 Feb. 1917, BL Add. MS 46285, JBP.

[7] Earl Browder, *Civil War in Nationalist China* (Chicago, 1927), 9.

[8] North and Eudin, *Mission to China*, 44.

and also with the International Workers' Delegation, wrote in her memoirs:

On March 31 [30], an International Workers' Delegation headed by Tom Mann, one of the most popular workers' leaders of the time, arrived in Wuhan. He was a handsome, sturdy old man, small in stature, with an amusing tuft of hair on his grey head, long moustaches, and an eagle eye. So straight and self-assured was his bearing, so enthusiastic and bold his speech, that no one would have guessed that he was already seventy-one. . . . Tom Mann came to China as a representative of the National Minority Movement whose honorary chairman he was.[9]

The published aims of the delegation were as follows:

1. To bring greetings and the expression of sympathy and solidarity to the National Revolutionary Government of China and the Kuomintang from the international proletariat.   2. To study the situation in China and to acquaint themselves intimately with the problems, aims, aspirations and obstacles to be overcome in the great struggle of the Chinese people against world imperialism.   3. To establish contact and a lasting militant alliance between the revolutionary labour movement of the world and the Chinese revolutionary liberation movement.   4. To encourage the Chinese people in their historic struggle and to do everything possible to render moral and material aid to the Chinese revolutionary cause.   5. To utilise all the knowledge and information gathered by the Delegation in China for the purpose of mobilising the international labour movement to come to the aid of revolutionary China by preventing the imperialist powers from carrying out their predatory plans.[10]

The delegation sailed from Vladivostok, arrived in Canton on the evening of 17 February, and stayed at the Oriental Hotel on the Bund, spending 'sixteen active days' in the city.

Two days later, on 19 February, they visited the offices of the revolutionary and working-class organizations in Canton including the All-China Labour Federation and the Hong Kong Strike Committee, and each of the three delegates and M. N. Roy the Comintern representative spoke at a reception banquet organized in the evening by the Provisional Government and the Provincial Committee of the Kuomintang. 'It is 8.15 a.m. & I am to start off to Whampoa in ten minutes to a Military School,' wrote Mann to Elsie from his hotel on the morning of 21 February; 'We are full every hour. . . . I am going strong &

---

[9] V. V. Vishnyakova-Akimova, *Two Years in Revolutionary China 1925-1927* (Cambridge, Mass., 1971), 29.

[10] *International Press Correspondence* (28 Apr. 1927).

I mean to let the mealy mouthed ones do as they will . . . but we are here. . . . Say we have a military escort all day & night, no worry: Vive la Revolution.'[11] At the Academy the cadets assured the visitors that they would fight on the side of the workers and peasants. 'At the end of the reunion', wrote Doriot in his report to *L'Humanité*,

the old Tom Mann sang the song of the Kuomintang, the *Ta Tau Li Chan* [Down with the Great Powers], in Chinese. He unleashed an unforgettable demonstration: stamping of the feet, cries, raised arms, caps thrown into the air. Then came the *International*, and again *Ta Tau Li Chan*, and ovations were repeated in such a proportion as we rarely see in Europe. It was a demonstration of gratitude to Tom, representative of the British workers, who came from the most brutal imperialist country which crushes hundreds of millions of human beings; a splendid demonstration of revolutionary faith and enthusiasm.[12]

On the following day, 22 February, they paid a visit to the Hong Kong Strike Committee, which was, as expressed by Tom Mann, 'a real treat to the eyes, hearts and minds of the Delegates'. They were present at a review of the Hong Kong strike pickets and of the Canton Workers' Defence Corps. A ten-year-old boy, representing a thousand uniformed pioneers, greeted the delegation with an eloquent speech. 'Tom Mann was moved to tears by the sight of this young representative of revolutionary China addressing the mass meeting and calling for world unity of all exploited classes and peoples.' Tom was apparently in a state of constant agitation and wonderment. He was 'a conspicuous and popular figure' again at the Sun Yat-sen University campus on the 23rd, when he led the cheers and shouted the slogans in chorus with the masses he addressed.[13] On Sunday 27th the three delegates were the special guests of the two unions, the Seamen's and Railwaymen's, at a mass meeting. Browder, in a report to *Inprekor* the journal of the Communist International, described the organization of the Railwaymen in great detail and emphasized its revolutionary role.[14]

On 1 March Tom wrote to Elsie from the same hotel in Canton:

[11] T. Mann to Elsie Mann, 21 Feb. 1927, TMP.

[12] *L'Humanité* (26 June 1927).

[13] *International Press Correspondence* (18 Apr. 1927).

[14] Earl Browder, 'Brief aus China—Über den chinisischen Eisenbarnerverband', *Internationale Presse Korrespondenz*, 40 (14 Apr. 1927).

I have been (like the rest of the delegation) occupied all the time since arrival, & if the day was twice as long they would keep us at it all the time. It is now 2.30 p.m. We have had a meeting this morning of the Photographers Union, & I was presented with a bouquet so I am sending you a few specimen leaves.

The Revolution is in evidence everywhere, it characterises all sections. I was at a military dinner last night invited (the delegation) by Gen. Li in charge of the Canton Garrison Staff: speeches clear emphatic to the point, as men who are ready on the hour to take the field. Their first objective is Drive out the Imperialists, & the second to realise the Revolution in China. The weather is cold, only two warm days since we arrived 12 days ago. ... I'm alright, we have a military guard constantly, as we are in a country where things are happening: but I'm as right as a trivet.[15]

Tom Mann and his colleagues came to China to learn, observe, and to encourage. The split within the Kuomintang leadership that had already begun still escaped their watchful eyes. It is only with the advantage of hindsight that one could argue that 'they [the delegation] inspected the outer shell of the mass movement that still remained [in Canton]'.[16] They even sent their greetings to Chiang Kai-shek who wired back his welcome.

On 6 March the delegation left Canton for a 25-day journey of about 800 miles to Hankow, 'through mountainous country and typical agricultural country, through rice fields and wheat fields, and through tea-growing districts', and talking to the peasants with the aid of interpreters, wrote Mann laconically in his published report.[17] We get a more detailed picture of the journey from writings by Browder and by Doriot, and especially from Mann's letters to his family. There is also a report published in *Inprekor* on this journey.[18] Early in the morning of the day of their departure, delegates of the unions, government, and army came to their hotel to bid them farewell; they embarked in a tug-boat to reach the station; as they passed an English ship, Tom Mann waved his large red scarf. A spontaneous mass meeting was held at the station to send them off on a special train which stopped at every station on the way to receive the greetings of local trade-union and peasant representatives.

Shiuchow (now Kukong) was then the terminus of the southern section of the Canton–Hankow Railway. Tom wrote to Elsie:

15 T. Mann to Elsie Mann, 1 Mar. 1927, TMP.
16 Isaacs, *Chinese Revolution*, 109.
17 T. Mann, 'My Visit to China', *Labour Monthly* (Aug. 1927).
18 *International Press Correspondence* (23 May 1927).

We reached the terminus about 9 p.m. [on the same day] & I felt very tired, I had been bothered with stomach trouble & caught cold at the same time & I had the greater part of 2 days in bed, then after a dose of castor oil was all right . . . We stayed 3 nights at this place Schichew [*sic*], & the next stage had to be done in small boats on the West River [North River or Pei Kiang] against the stream which was strong & in places very strong. Only coolies to propel the boat, some—usually about six—were on shore pulling with ropes . . . & others on the boat with shoulder poles. . . . We had 4 boats which included a military escort of 50 or more soldiers, about 12 or 15 cooks for each boat, some Chinese companions & our own little group of 4. . . . On the boats on the West River it took three days to do the journey. Then the next stage had to be on foot across a mountain—the dividing range—a stretch of about 40 miles. We had coolies to carry all the baggage & also several sedan chairs & when I got tired I could & did take a spell in the chair, but I climbed the summit on foot alright & walked over & down a very rough road till we again reached fairly level land when I popped into the chair again. Some experience eh? [19]

As Tom Mann said, they walked across the mountain on foot from Namyung to Nananfu through the Meiling Pass, and the use of the sedan chair or palanquin was recommended, 'but we had no enthusiasm for being carried on the shoulders of men', wrote Doriot, 'and we decided to proceed on foot except for old Tom for whom we engaged 6 porters'. [20]

On 17 March they came to Nankang, the next town on the River Kan Kiang, and were told that at Kanchow, the town about 40 miles down the river, 'conditions are very reactionary'. Arriving there on 19 March they were met by nobody from the local trade union, the secretary of which, Chen Chang-shu, had only recently been brutally murdered. [21] 'We had learned before reaching this place that the Trade Unions were in a bad way,' wrote Mann to Elsie from Kanchow on 20 March:

they only formed since last September after the Cantonese Revolutionary Army passed through the district, & although the Kuomintang was formed, i.e. the People's Revolutionary Party very soon, the merchants & middlemen called Compradores & landlords got control of it & soon showed they were bitterly hostile to the formation of unions by the workers or to the Kuomintang being a revolutionary body. It resulted 2 weeks ago in the assassination of the most responsible man in the TU movement & the unions were forcibly put down. . . . [On arriving at

[19] T. Mann to Elsie Mann, 20 Mar. 1927, TMP.

[20] *L'Humanité* (6 July 1927).

[21] An account of the journey by Browder was published in the *Min Kuo Jih Pao* early in Apr. 1927; see Doriot in *L'Humanité* (8 July 1927). The best account will be found in Browder, *Civil War in Nationalist China*.

Kanchow] we decided to go on to the Quay & I briefly acknowledged the welcome & said we had investigations to make. . . . Back to the boat with the magistrate & others & had 2 hours talk. They urged we should stay if possible 2 days. . . . We questioned them on the real trouble & did not consider their replies satisfactory. Leaving them we had an interview with Trade Unionists who could not appear because of the reaction, from these we obtained &c. &c. too long to recite . . . got grip of the situation, having used influence effectively in conjunction with a contingent of the Revolutionary Army & have just had a three hours demonstration in the sunshine. . . . The guards are on each boat all the time with rifles in hand & bayonets fixed and wherever we go a group goes with us, we have part of the personal body guard of General Li, head of the revolutionary forces at Canton. . . . There is no sitting accommodation in the boat I am on, but we have camp beds & washing & shaving is a business, but for a youngster like me it doesn't matter. . . . The scenery is truly magnificent, on that walking job we stayed one night in a Taoist Temple & I went up to several smaller ones on a hill including the highest, & this was called 'The Gate of Heaven', so I was getting close eh? but retraced my steps.[22]

The 'three hour demonstration in the sunshine' was a moral victory for the delegation, but as Browder said, 'it was the support of the bayonets that really changed the situation'. After thirty-six hours in Kanchow, the boats resumed their journey down the River Kan Kiang: 'counter-revolution had for the time being been overcome'.[23]

Then took place what Browder called 'an idyllic interlude' in the civil war which had already been smouldering here and there along the path of their journey northward. At the village of Liangko they visited a school used as local headquarters of the Kuomintang. 'While Doriot and I were talking to the teacher', wrote Browder,

I noticed that the shy, timid youngsters who had been so quiet on our entrance were making quite a noise in the next room. I looked thru the door. There was Tom Mann the 71-year-old dean of our Delegation, in the center of a regular riot; two boys of about eight years were perched on his shoulders, and he was leading the rest in song. He was singing a nursery rhyme in English: 'London's burning! Look yonder, look yonder! Fire, fire! Fire, fire! Pour on water, pour on water!' With shining eyes and joyous faces the boys were joining in the song, especially the line 'Fire, fire', which they had quickly caught. Tom Mann had made 40 fast friends who will never forget him, I'm sure. The ice was broken, and we were all at home.[24]

[22] T. Mann to Elsie Mann, Kanchow, 20 Mar. 1927, TMP.
[23] Browder, *Civil War in Nationalist China*, 17.   [24] Ibid. 18.

For three weeks the delegation had been cut off from all connection with the outside world, but no doubt they had by now come to realize the heavy odds the Chinese workers and peasants had to overcome before completing their revolution. Indeed, as they journeyed through the Kiangsi province, the political scenery of revolutionary China presented kaleidoscopic changes. On 10 March the Wuhan radicals, in defiance of Chiang Kai-shek, convened the third plenary session of the Kuomintang Central Executive at Hankow at which they decided to strengthen the Government by accepting two Communists, T'an Ping-shan and Su Chao-cheng, for the newly created portfolios of agriculture and labour respectively; Tom Mann had come in close contact with the latter in Canton since he was chairman of the All China Labour Federation. Anticipating a split in the Kuomintang, Chiang had set up his rival nationalist centre at Nanchung, the headquarters of his army. Chiang apparently was 'steering for Shanghai to come to terms with the imperialists' and he could succeed only if he would be ruthless as well as tactful in suppressing the mass movement.

It was in this suspended state of conflict and tension that the delegation continued its journey through Nanchung, Kiukiang, and on to Wuhan. They arrived in Nanchung on 25 March, and on the following day Tom Mann and Earl Browder, on behalf of the delegation, visited the general headquarters of the Nationalist Army and the Provincial Government. A banquet was held in the name of Marshall Chiang, who on that very day entered Shanghai which had fallen into the hands of the workers at great cost to themselves. One general at the banquet bluntly told the delegation that 'our problems are entirely peculiar to China. . . . The Chinese Revolution is not a part of the world revolution', and what they needed was 'a strong military leader'.[25] At Kiukiang Tom Mann was hard at work, taking notes of an account given by a Chinese official of how the British concession in the city had been taken over by the Chinese through direct action.[26] The delegation reached Hankow on 30 March, after a journey through inland China fraught with incidents of revolution and the counter-revolution.

On arriving at Hankow, Tom Mann wrote, 'I personally counted the ships of war that were lined up two abreast over a space of two miles, and there were ten British, ten American, three French and seven Japanese . . . [with] guns trained ready for

[25] Earl Browder, 'Chinese Revolution Turns Left', *Labour Monthly* (July 1927).
[26] *L'Humanité* (16 July 1927).

action . . . only the ships of foreigners, on the Yangtze River, six hundred and fifty miles inland from the coast'.[27] On 2 April Mann sent home a copy of the *People's Tribune*, an English daily, of the same date in which appeared his article denouncing British imperialism for its support of the counter-revolutionary movement in China: they knew very well that 'revolutionary China is the vanguard of all oppressed peoples' in India, Africa, Egypt, and elsewhere.[28] In a letter addressed to his son Tom, he said he had just been to a meeting of peasants held in Hankow—in the whole of China there were eight million peasants and two and a half million workers organized—'China is in the throes of a new birth, changing wonderfully rapidly & showing great courage and ability'. He confessed that he was 'a bit tired just now' but 'I am, like the rest, busy everyday & evening. I close this to go to another meeting.'[29] He went to the reception given by the Central Executive Committee of the Kuomintang at which Madame Sun Yat-sen greeted the delegation. They had just published an appeal 'To the Troops of the Imperialist Powers in China', dated 2 April. 'The ruling class of your country has sent you to China,' it read;

It is the very same ruling class which exploits you, and your brothers and sisters, in your country. . . . Like you the Chinese people suffer from this exploitation. Like you, they aspire to Liberalism. Like you, they struggle to improve their miserable condition. . . . It is your duty and in your own interests that you who are yourselves being exploited should not fight against the Chinese people, but on the contrary, you must aid it in its struggle for liberation.[30]

This was in fact an international version of the 'Don't Shoot' manifesto of 1912. On the following day the delegation issued another appeal which blamed British imperialism for trying to destroy the Chinese revolution by 'shameless provocations'.[31] On this same day 50,000 people filled the race-course of Hankow to greet the delegation. At each of the four platforms erected at four corners Mann, Browder, Doriot, and Stoler addressed the masses. These events at the beginning of April marked the peak of the high hopes entertained by the Wuhan Left as well as by the delegation.

The delegation has been taken to task for the 'conspiracy of silence'. Through what they had seen and heard during their

[27] T. Mann, *What I Saw in China* (London, 1927).
[28] *People's Tribune* (Hankow) (2 Apr. 1927).
[29] T. Mann to Tom Mann, Jun., 2 Apr. 1927, TMP.
[30] *International Press Correspondence* (28 Apr. 1927), German trans. in *Inprekor*, 60 (10 June 1927).   [31] *Inprekor*, 36 (5 Apr. 1927).

overland journey, they 'were in a position to warn the workers of Shanghai that Chiang was not their saviour but their mortal enemy. . . . The fact is that they did not'.[32] No doubt they had come to know that Chiang was the enemy of the workers, and Browder, as soon as they arrived in Wuhan, wrote an account of their journey for the *Min Kuo Jih Pao*, warning against Chiang. Writing on 10 April, Browder clearly stated that 'the strategy of reaction was the production of a Chinese Napoleon'.[33] It is true that the delegation was concerned more about the armed intervention of the imperialist powers than about Chiang's ability to set up himself as a military dictator, of which Browder himself appeared only half convinced. Nevertheless, there was no 'conspiracy of silence' on their part at least. When they urged the European soldiers not to fire on the Chinese workers, they were certainly not under the influence of the new machiavellianism pursued by Stalin but were genuinely inspired by the sense of international brotherhood and solidarity of the working classes.

At this crucial moment Moscow gave fatal instructions to the Chinese Communists to hide arms and avoid open military conflict with the Right. On 12 April Chiang's troops launched an overall attack against the headquarters of the working-class organizations in Shanghai. Cold-blooded massacres of the workers continued till the following day, while the bankers and merchants rallied to the government which Chiang had set up in Nanking. The Wuhan radicals began to quake: they became more dependent upon the local militarists than ever, and launched another northern expedition, hoping to capture Peking. Encouraged by Chiang's coup in Shanghai, General Li Chi-shen who had ruled Canton since 1926, now staged an even bloodier coup later in April. Tom Mann kept a diary while he was in Wuhan and wrote on the tragedy in Canton: '3000 arrested, 400 pickets killed, 400 soldiers—all principal T.U. leaders killed, those with whom we were fraternising'.[34]

Tom Mann attended the fifth congress of the Chinese Communist Party held in Wuchung early in May as a fraternal delegate, but he was apparently more interested in a meeting of the 'Oppressed Peoples of the East' held about the same time: 'formerly it was only India & China, now it includes Korea, Formosa, Mongolia, Armenia, Burma. Excellent speech from

---

[32] Isaacs, *Chinese Revolution*, 158-9. A similar criticism was made by Jane Degras in Degras (ed.), *Communist International 1919-1943: Documents*, ii (Oxford, 1960), 359.   [33] Earl Browder in *Labour Monthly* (July 1927).
[34] T. Mann, Diary, 10 May 1927, DTP.

the chairman covering the whole international situation'.[35] On 5 May he moved to the Hankow Hotel where he shared a room with Earl Browder. On 7 May it was finally decided to arrange the Pan-Pacific Trades Union Conference: Mann and Browder were to remain and participate, but Doriot departed from Hankow on the following day to return to France via Moscow. In Moscow Doriot attended the eighth plenum of the Executive Committee of the CI where he sought to justify the official policy of a Communist–Kuomintang alliance or a popular front for China, though he appears to have privately admitted errors of the Comintern policy for China.[36]

It was only on 10 May that the date for opening the Pan-Pacific Conference was decided and Browder was to take charge of press publicity. On 13 May Losovsky arrived and 'Eugene Chen, Minister [of] Foreign Affairs, interview to Reuter—". . . before 3 months are ended, we shall conquer our way across Honan to Peking, where in the name of Nationalist China & the Kuomintang I will speak a language which cannot be ignored"'. 'If I read Sir A[usten] C[hamberlain] rightly', wrote Mann on 14 May, 'British eyes are glancing at Chiang Kai-shek as a new dictator. But the latter will not outlast the summer for his troops must soon obey the real master-government in Wuhan'. His reference to Chamberlain, then British Foreign Minister, was based on the latter's speech in the House of Commons on 9 May in which he said: 'in Shanghai, Canton and other towns the extremist organisations have been broken up and their leaders executed' and the Wuhan government was 'little more than the shadow of a name'.[37] Like Browder, Mann was still unable to grasp the situation which was moving fast. The lack of sufficient communication, due partly to language difficulties and partly to his isolated position, evidently sustained his optimism.

It was not long, however, before he was forced to accept the precarious state of the Wuhan Government. On 18 May he learned that Mr Newton, the British representative at Hankow, had informed Eugene Chen that he was instructed to leave. 'Many rumours also as to the advance of troops in various directions on Hankow. Uneasiness on [the] part of Chinese &

---

35 Ibid.
36 Jean-Paul Brunet, *Jacques Doriot: Du communisme au fascisme* (Paris, 1986), 90. The author mentions 25 articles by Doriot entitled 'A travers la Révolution chinoise' in *L'Humanité* (25 June–13 Aug. 1927), but there are several factual mistakes in his account: the delegation apart from Doriot, for instance, did not leave Wuhan early in May.   37 Isaacs, *Chinese Revolution*, 206.

showing disposition to take up all available houses on French concession.'[38] Shops and factories were closed, and workers were locked out, while land reform was delayed. Local war lords revolted against the Wuhan Government on all sides. Wuhan became a besieged city. It was in this tense atmosphere full of foreboding of doom that the Pan-Pacific Trades Union Conference was opened at the People's Club, Hankow, attended by 35 delegates representing China, Russia, Japan, Britain, USA, France, Java, and Korea. Losovsky chairman of the RILU gave the leading speech, in which he once more emphasized that the Chinese revolution was part of the world revolution and should be aimed against world imperialism as a whole. As for 'revolution from below', the task for the proletariat in Hupei and Hunan, he added, was not the establishment of the dictatorship of the proletariat but 'democratic dictatorship' in which the proletariat would take part.[39] Li Li-san the Chinese delegate spoke next, and reports on each national labour movement followed. Losovsky's was indeed a political speech which faithfully followed the Comintern policy on China even at this late hour. Li Li-san, by contrast, tackled the problem of imperialism or capitalism as a world system from below; in order to effect unity of the working classes of the world, he wrote shortly afterwards, the living conditions of the colonial labourers should be improved by the adoption of a shorter working day, a social security system, the right to organization, and even the right to set up a workers' police force to resist Fascism. 'The working classes of the coloured races appeared for the first time on the scene of the world labour movement', said Li,[40] and in this lay the major historical importance of the Pan-Pacific Trades Union Conference.

Yet the days of revolutionary Wuhan were numbered. 'I am at the Conference (Pan-Pacific), it has been on a week & will be over in a couple of days,' Mann wrote to Elsie on 25 May. 'I shall then immediately prepare to leave Hankow via Siberia, for home. The Revolutionary situation here has kept matters in a state of flux. I have been alright, and active althrough.'[41] The Pan-Pacific Conference closed its sessions by setting up a secretariat, the first meeting of which Mann attended on

[38] T. Mann, Diary, 19 May 1927, DTP.

[39] Ibid., 20 May 1927, DTP; Japanese Institute for the Study of International Problems (Chinese Section) (ed.), *Sources of the History of the Chinese Communist Party*, iii (Tokyo, 1971), no. 16, pp. 87–117 [in Japanese].

[40] Japanese Institute, *Sources*, no. 24, pp. 155–9.

[41] T. Mann to Elsie Mann, 25 May 1927, DTP.

27 May. On 1 June SS *King Wo*, a British ship, left Hankow with Tom Mann on board.

In his report 'My Visit to China' Mann wrote: 'We spent seven weeks in Hankow and a few miles around, and had an intensely interesting trip to Changsha, the capital of Hunan Province, and had many meetings en route. Altogether we had 188 meetings in China and many interviews.'[42] This reads like a report of a trade-union organizer. His diary written while in Hankow does not reveal any detail of his visit to Changsha where on 21 May a counter-revolutionary coup opened 'the bloodiest chapter in the history of a bloody year'.[43] When the fourth All-China Trades Union Conference was held in the middle of June, the delegates felt that they were 'in a reign of white terror'. In July all the Communists were expelled from the Kuomintang, and Borodin too left Wuhan. The Wuhan government was duly swallowed up by that in Nanking. The Communists' attempt to avenge themselves with the establishment of the Canton Soviet in December had cost them dear.

[42] Mann, 'My Visit to China'. [43] Isaacs, *Chinese Revolution*, 235.

14. Last Missions and the Unemployed March

Militant Trade-Unionism

BACK in England Mann soon found himself on a lecture tour. He reported back to Elsie on 'a splendid meeting' in Manchester and a 'not so good' one at Blackburn.[1] Tom was a family man as much as he was a public figure. On 'Commune Day' in 1928 he wrote to Elsie from Birmingham about a visit he had made to his brother George, now seventy-six years old, who was living at Wythall, milking cows and repairing broken roof tiles. He made a trip with Elsie through the West Country to visit the place where Elsie had spent her early days as a small girl. From Eccleshall, Staffordshire, he wrote to his son Tom:

Mam & I came along (all along down along) from Homeland's [the Manns's new home] on Monday to Coventry and went around Foleshill, my native haunts, staying the night at Coventry & came yesterday via Birmingham & Stafford to Eccleshall & Mam—although absent 50 years, found old playmates. Mother is very interested in this little trip, finding the place much as she left, the Father's chapel, & the House they lived in being—she says—'just the same'. We return today Mam to her Choirs & myself to Biggin Hill direct.[2]

Tom Mann had recently moved from Adelaide Road, Brockley, to 'Homelands', Sunningvale Avenue, Biggin Hill, Westerham, Kent, about twenty miles from central London. To his son Tom he wrote again: 'This place was awfully cloggy and messy yesterday while the rain was on, that paving job not yet finished, give a call as often as you can but as far as practicable avoid wet days'.[3]

Tom made for his own use a book of photographs including many he had taken while in China. As Stoler, the secretary of the delegation to China, had expressed the view that the Museum of Moscow ought to keep it in their custody, Mann

[1] T. Mann to Elsie Mann, 12, 14 Sept. 1927, TMP.
[2] T. Mann to Tom Mann, Jun., 25 Sept. 1927, TMP.
[3] T. Mann to Tom Mann, Jun., 1 Aug. 1929, TMP.

decided to send it to Losovsky, asking him to accept it as a gift.[4] The fate of the precious album is not known. Shortly after this he wrote to Browder, telling him about the album he had sent to Moscow and about the musical feat achieved by Elsie whom Browder had met on his previous visit:

Speaking of Mrs. M it will interest you to know that . . . she manages to attend both Choirs every Wednesday. In case this is not clear let me explain that for some years she has been a member of the Philharmonic choir, one of the very best in London. She has also been the conductor of a Choir at Deptford, and both these meet on a Wednesday, the first at six o'clock and the second at eight, and she regularly attends both.

I may add that the Deptford choir belongs to the London Choral Union which have an Annual competition and this year Deptford came out highest; later follows a concert where the Certificates are handed out and the winning choirs disport themselves under the conductorship of their own conductors, Madame was on this of course, and it was at the Queens Hall, Regent St.[5]

Elsie was still interested in radical politics, but as a spectator rather than an agitator, remaining a willing recipient of letters from her husband telling her about the development of his agitational work.

The upshot of the General Strike of 1926 was to push the union leadership to the position of 'class collaboration', illuminated as it was by the Mond–Turner talks early in 1928, while the National Minority Movement (NMM) was driven to the other extreme of upholding militant trade-unionism, the nature of which soon became clear. 'The tenuous united front bridge' between the NMM and the orthodox Left had collapsed. By the end of 1928 the NMM had been reduced to 'an organized ideological pressure group'[6] which was to implement the Comintern's new policy involving 'dual unionism', the principle of split and division which was anathema to Tom Mann.

The Comintern's hopes for some tangible results from a united front policy in Britain and perhaps for more striking strategic gains from an application of a similar principle in China had been destroyed in a disastrous failure in both cases. The sixth congress of the CI (Comintern) which met in the summer of 1928 only revealed 'the bankruptcy of Bolshevik

---

[4] T. Mann to A. Losovsky, 20 June 1929, TMP.
[5] T. Mann to E. Browder, 8 Oct. 1929, TMP.
[6] Roderick Martin, *Communism and the British Trade Unions 1924-1933: A Study of the National Minority Movement* (Oxford, 1969), 93, 100.

strategy',[7] out of which was created the new tactic of 'Class against Class'—supposedly suitable to a revolutionary era when it could treat the reformist parties and trade unions as class enemies. Confusion, however, continued on trade-union policy, and the fourth congress of the RILU supported the slogan of 'United Front from Below'. Soon the new principle of independent leadership and opposition to the union establishment was proclaimed as the new official line. The NMM 'old guards' like Pollitt and Jack Tanner of the AEU, formerly a syndicalist, refused to surrender, arguing for a flexible policy for strike strategy.[8] Although Losovsky and the RILU sought to enforce the new line, emphasizing the need to replace 'all reformist unions', the British NMM adhered to its traditional policy of 'not splitting unions'.[9] The young activists such as John A. Mahon, the son of John L. Mahon of the old Socialist League, however, were more amenable to the new line, and the temporary absence of Pollitt, who visited the United States early in 1929, helped the advocates of the new official line dominate the movement.

Tom Mann was obviously not committed to this new line. At the annual conference of the NMM Mann delivered his customary chairman's address. He was as sensitive as ever to technical, structural changes in capitalism and once more emphasized the need for working-class solidarity. 'With coal, iron and steel, and textile trades all declining, and no prospect of any general revival, and no proposals from the boss class except those of "rationalisation",' he declared, 'we . . . ourselves go full steam ahead for workers' control of industry and for sound international trade union relations with the workers of other countries.' He referred to the formation of the Pan-Pacific Secretariat which would secure concerted action of the workers in that region one day.

We are living in a period when the industrial system is changing rapidly. World finance has changed in a manner that has made America imperialist. . . . The U.S.A. is acting as the competitive rival against Britain on the one side and against Japan on the other. These three capitalist powers are each aiming at world domination, but they show a united front against any force or agency making for the economic emancipation of the workers.

[7] Julius Braunthal, *History of the International 1914-1943* (London, 1967), 337.   [8] Martin, *Communism and the British Trade Unions*, 113.

[9] Noreen Branson, *History of the Communist Party of Great Britain 1927-1941* (London, 1985), 39–40.

Only at the very end of his long speech did he mention the new Comintern line: all the best fighting elements in British trade-unionism would march 'under the slogan of "no industrial peace—but Class against Class"!'[10] Indeed, he appeared to have succumbed at last to the pressure from the RILU, but he only paid it lip service for the sake of Communist unity. Moreover, 'class against class' for Tom Mann meant no more than a confirmation of the old slogan of class struggle and no compromise.

In August 1929 the NMM annual conference endorsed the principle of 'independent leadership'. 'It signified the beginning of the end of the Minority Movement', writes Noreen Branson.[11] The NMM leadership submitted a report to the conference, in which the new line was presented as 'repudiation of company unionism, and non-political unionism, and the whole treacherous policy of the General Council of the Trades Union Congress'.[12] The dilemma of 'independent leadership' or rival or dual unionism was especially acute for some of the prominent union leaders in the NMM. Arthur Cook did break with the Communist Party at this point, and Jack Tanner never joined the party in spite of his strong link with the NMM.[13] The RILU had started its own newspaper, the *Red International Labour Unions*; although Tom Mann was mentioned as one of the regular contributors, he does not appear to have played an active role in it. It is true that he denounced 'the reformist trade union leaders and the tame rabbits of Labour politicians' and went so far as to attack 'the social–fascist leaders of the national reformist miners' unions' in an article written in support of a proposed Militant Miners' International.[14] His 'frank' explanation of 'our New Policy' was 'to take the leadership of the workers out of the hands of the reactionary unions' and to organize 'groups in all shops and factories, mills and mines . . . who recognise and are ready to engage in the Class Struggle'.[15] Ambiguities still remained as to his commitment to the new policy.

During the campaign for the general election of May 1929 Tom Mann was in the Glasgow area, speaking in support of

[10] NMM, *Report of the Fifth Annual Conference* (London, 1928), *passim*.
[11] Branson, *History of the Communist Party*, 43.
[12] NMM, *Another Year of Rationalisation: Report presented to the Sixth Annual Conference of the NMM, 24 and 25 Aug. 1929* (London, 1929), *passim*.
[13] Martin, *Communism and the British Trade Unions*, 50–1.
[14] *Worker* (9 May, 6 Sept. 1929).   [15] Ibid. (18 July 1929).

Communist candidates Helen Crawford at Bothwell and Isabel Brown at Motherwell. But the election turned out to be 'a major set-back' for the Party. Gallacher, elected at West Fife, was the sole Communist MP.[16] The Labour Party, however, emerged from it as the largest party in the House, and a Communist application for affiliation was again turned down.

As the Labour Party kept its door firmly shut against Communist influence, the Comintern pressed hard for vigorous application of the 'Class against Class' tactic. In the summer of 1930 Mann visited Moscow with Elsie. He attended the fifth congress of the RILU at which the NMM was severely criticized; Mann attempted 'a highly unrealistic defence of the NMM' and claimed that it represented 200,000 workers.[17] The German delegate F. Heckert, a Comintern hard-liner, attributed its errors to 'the old leadership', and the resolution adopted emphasized the need for a broad united-front tactic such as a workers' charter movement as well as support for the principle of 'independent leadership' embodied in 'Red trade unions' such as the United Mineworkers' Union in Scotland and the United Clothing Workers' Union in London.

On 12 April 1931, when MacDonald's second Labour Government was tackling the effects of the Great Depression by setting up a committee dominated by leading capitalists, the NMM held 'the first National Convention for the Workers' Charter' in Bermondsey Town Hall. It was preceded by a series of local and district conferences just like the Chartist rallies in 1838, and the convention itself was attended by 788 delegates, 'quite a number of whom', Tom Mann chuckled, had been active shop stewards.[18] In his opening speech, however, Mann faithfully followed the RILU line. In the early days 'we worked mainly in and through the trade unions', said Mann, but, in view of the failure of union leaders as reflected in the hardship suffered by the two and three-quarter million unemployed, 'there must be a new leadership of class-conscious militants'. The resolution prepared had to be modified, said Pollitt, because of the Open Letter of the RILU published the day before, in which the NMM was again criticized for being 'dangerously isolated from the mass of the workers' and for having failed to provide 'class leadership' in the strikes.[19] In his speech Pollitt emphasized that 'those honest rank and file who are still under the influ-

---

[16] T. Mann to Elsie Mann, 20 May 1929, TMP; Branson, *History of the Communist Party*, 38.

[17] E. H. Carr, *Twilight of Comintern* (London, 1982), 209.

[18] *Worker* (25 Apr. 1931).   [19] *Daily Worker* (11 Apr. 1931).

ence of the Social Fascists' should be won over to the Charter. 'We are welcomed as a ginger group, as good fighters, but we are not welcomed as the alternative leadership.' This was the gist of the RILU criticism rendered into more intelligible English, which the convention was asked to adopt. The Charter itself was a programme of practical demands: its original six points, including increased unemployment benefits and repeal of the Trade Disputes Act, were expanded to nine, the last being 'For the Defence of the Soviet Union against Imperialist War'.[20]

The RILU was not satisfied, and the same charges against the NMM as in the Open Letter were repeated in a resolution adopted at the eighth session of its central council. Even so there was a significant change in its tone, owing in part to a successful challenge that Pollitt had made to Losovsky, stressing the need to 'encourage every manifestation of revolt *inside* the existing unions'.[21] The resolution adopted at the eighth session recommended 'a fighting united front of all miners' and the unemployed movement to go 'in the direction of a united front movement'.[22] With the revival of the United Front tactic in 1932, the British party began to extricate itself from the fetters of the 'Class against Class'–'Independent Leadership' line of the Moscow Internationals. With it the history of the NMM came to an end. Apparently the Charter movement failed to secure mass support. In fact, a new rank-and-file movement had been growing outside NMM influence, notably among the miners, engineers, railwaymen, and London busmen.

Trade-union militancy, however, was not always apparent. Early in 1931 Tom Mann was writing from Ammanford, South Wales, to Elsie: he had been in the district for some time, assisting the miners on strike, but he said, 'I am not sure where I shall go from here, this is a weak centre because at one mine there is not one member of the MFGB—all belong to the non. pol. affair of Spencer's & they are pace setters in opposition sense'.[23] In the summer he was writing from Belfast where the figures of the unemployed in the shipbuilding and the linen industries were unusually high: 'but there is a brightness about

---

[20] *Worker* (25 Apr. 1931). According to Martin, the large total of 788 was misleading: only 67 trade-union branches and 22 factory groups elected delegates. The vast majority came from London, only 213 from the provinces: Martin, *Communism and the British Trade Unions*, 160.

[21] Branson, *History of the Communist Party*, 88.

[22] RILU, *Position of the Minority Movement and its Immediate Tasks: Resolution of the 8th Session of the Central Council of the RILU* (London, n.d.), *passim*.   [23] T. Mann to Elsie Mann, 11 Oct. 1931, TMP.

the place & a cheeriness about the folks. They are far from knocked out, & will react to what may be necessary'.[24] In October he was in Germany, attending the congress of WIR (Workers International Relief, or Internationale Arbeiterhilfe) held in the Berlin Lehrervereinshaus. 'I am on platform (Presidium) sitting next to Mrs Despard,' he wrote to Elsie; 'there are 1000 delegates. . . . There has been no police interference & none is expected.' Clara Zetkin, the veteran German Communist and feminist, spoke but looked 'fat and weak'. 'Several have asked about you who met you at Moscow last year.'[25]

We have a glimpse of his heavy lecture schedule for the following year from a letter he wrote to his son Tom from Cambridge: 'I return tomorrow & get to Woolwich at night to the Engineers Branch meeting. Next weekend I am at Norwich and am fully fixed up for a month ahead.'[26] It seems that he was assisting the rank-and-file movement all over the country with his speeches. One of his favourite topics at the time was 'Capitalist Aggression in China'. He deplored the futile attempts by the League of Nations to check the ruthless aggression of the Japanese in China and also the 'hypocrisy' of the British Government in expressing 'indignation at the Japs' and actually taking 'all necessary steps to do exactly the same by concentrating battleships in the neighbourhood of Shanghai'. He added prophetically: 'We shall soon find that munitions of war will be required by the BOSS CLASS to be made and transported by the workers and used by the workers to destroy other workers.' So he had to fall back on the simple formula: 'solidarity of the workers of all countries against the capitalist class of all countries'.[27]

Tom Mann's one other major preoccupation was unemployment, which remained a major chronic sore of the capitalist economy. The official figure of the unemployed, which never went below one million throughout the 1920s and which jumped to three million in the worst years of the world depression early in the thirties, needs to be doubled, since the published numbers related only to insured workers. Workers in the staple industries—textile, steel, shipbuilding, and mining— were the main victims of mass unemployment, and they formed the echelons of the workforce who enjoyed the solid tradition of

[24] T. Mann to Tom Mann, Jun., 18 July 1931, TMP.
[25] T. Mann to Elsie Mann, 11 Oct. 1931, TMP.
[26] T. Mann to Tom Mann, Jun., 25 Sept. 1931, TMP.
[27] T. Mann, 'Capitalist Aggression in China', typed note, 1932, TMP.

trade-union organization and who now provided leadership for the unemployed workers' struggles.[28] The National Unemployed Workers' Movement (NUWM) was launched in 1921 under the initiative of Wal Hannington, a young Communist and toolmaker by trade. Tom Mann, in spite of his age, had been prominent in the marches organized by this body. In November 1929, when the South Wales Miners led by Arthur Horner and Wal Hannington marched from the Rhondda Valley to London in order 'to draw attention to the chronic destitution affecting unemployed and employed miners, arising out of the failure of private enterprise in the mining industry', Tom Mann along with A. J. Cook came to meet them at Reading. After a rally in the town, Mann shared the hard boards with the marchers in one of the halls where they were accommodated.[29] Horner, active in the Miners' MM and the Miners' International, was the leader of the militant party at Mardy, sometimes known as 'Little Moscow', but was opposed to the party (or Moscow) line of 'independent leadership' in industrial action.[30]

The National March of 1932, 'the largest, best-organised march to date',[31] was a huge protest in itself against the Government which had introduced a family means test. A big battalion of 1,500 marchers in 18 contingents took to the road in September and October of that year; though warmly supported by local people, they met police brutality on the way and in London: the police guarding Hyde Park and afterwards Parliament far outnumbered the marchers. The *Daily Worker* of 9 December announced that 19 December had been fixed as a national day of demonstration and mass action by London workers to support a million-signature petition to Parliament for the abolition of the means test, and other demands. Along with Hannington, Sid Elias, chairman of the movement; Emrys Llewellyn, secretary; and Tom Mann, treasurer, were all arrested. The latter two were tried together at Bow Street Police Court on 17 December. Tom, by now an old man of seventy-six, declined to bind himself by a surety to keep the peace and 'be of good behaviour'. 'If I am to be tied up', he declared,

[28] Richard Croucher, *We Refuse to Starve in Silence: A History of the National Unemployed Workers' Movement* (London, 1987), 13–15.

[29] Wal Hannington, *Unemployed Struggles 1919–1936* (London, 1979), 163.

[30] Stuart Macintyre, *Little Moscows: Communism and Working-Class Militancy in Inter-War Britain* (London, 1980), 39.

[31] Peter Kingsford, *Hunger Marchers in Britain 1920–1940* (London, 1982), 139.

if my mouth to be closed, if I am not to participate in ventilating the grievances of those who are suffering while the incompetency of those responsible cannot find work for them and is knocking down their miserable standard lower—then, whatever the consequences may be—if I am to be shot in the next five minutes,—I would not consent to any undertaking.[32]

Sir Charles Biron the magistrate refused to release him, saying that this was 'merely a preventive measure'. Thus Mann and Llewellyn were sent to Brixton Prison for two months.

A memorial asking for the release of Mann and Llewellyn and presented to the Prime Minister Ramsay MacDonald contained an impressive list of ex-ministers, MPs, Lords, and members of the General Council of the TUC and National Executive of the Labour Party.[33] Harold Laski sought to prove that the Government had had recourse to 'obsolete Statutes' by quoting relevant sections of Acts of 1360 and 1817. Sir J. Gilmour, the Home Secretary, in his letter to Lansbury who had made a special appeal to the premier, denied that the right to free speech had been infringed.[34]

In his first letter to Elsie from Brixton Prison Tom gave her instructions as to payments for a loan club and other matters: 'I am wearing my own clothes, so will you please send me by the end of week clean combinations, socks or stockings & scarf, the white one would do well.'[35] He was a dandy even in prison. A week later he wrote to her again:

I had fully one hundred Xmas letters & cards. I would like you to take them home with you, also my soiled underwear, and will you please bring me a suit of pyjamas, and 1 pair stockings, also 1 suit underclothing—not combinations—one woolen collar ... one linen Collar, small wing—one white hanky & one large coloured one—the latter really for neck wear—If stockings not handy, bring a pair of footless ones that I can wear with socks, I must keep the knees warm to keep back the synovitis, I'm bothered with it and don't want give it a chance. Sorry I'm bothering you with so many requests enough to load a donkey. ... Glad of the mild weather but it's best to be ready for any sort, Frost, Snow, Hail, Storms, let 'em all come, we can face the lot & laugh at them when gone.[36]

He was anxious about his friend Arthur Horner, who had gone through a period of imprisonment and after release had been

---

[32] *Manchester Guardian* (19 Dec. 1932). [33] Ibid. (30 Dec. 1932).
[34] Ibid. (7 and 10 Jan. 1933).
[35] T. Mann to Elsie Mann, 19 Dec. 1932, TMP.
[36] T. Mann to Elsie Mann, 27 Dec. 1932, TMP.

re-elected locally to the position of checkweighman. But the owners closed the pit concerned so as to keep Horner out. Tom was very much worried, and asked Elsie to enquire. 'It is just 26 years since I was in Melbourne Jail and two of my then visitors were J. Ramsay MacDonald and his wife. You of course remember that alright', he wrote to Elsie.[37] Visitors this time included Jack Tanner, Harry Pollitt, and Ben Tillett.

It was while he was in Brixton Prison that he began preparations for a new working-class paper. When he came out he started the *Militant Trade Unionist*, a monthly paper, with the support of several trade-union branches which formed the core of the rank-and-file movement. The first number came out on 1 May 1933, and 30,000 copies were on sale. By then the climate of the labour movement had considerably changed with the rise of Hitler to power in Germany. In his editorial address Mann did not conceal uneasiness as to the prospects of the future. Trade unions should be 'fighting weapons for the defence of wages and conditions'. 'Only a mighty movement as could beat back every attack of the employing class . . . will prevent a repetition in this country of the terrible fate being meted out to the German working class by Hitler.'[38] He ventured to suggest a 'Militant Trade Unionist' conference to be held in September, but by then the paper had gone out of circulation. It was in the *Eye*, Martin Lawrence's paper, that he wrote an appreciative account of Georgi Dimitroff, the hero of the Reichstag trial.[39]

He had, however, put all his energy and enthusiasm into the new campaign. Late in February, shortly after he had come out of Brixton Prison, he was found among the miners at Llanelli. He also helped Arthur Horner in his election campaign at a by-election at Rhondda East shortly afterwards. A week later he was in Glasgow and was to visit Dundee and Edinburgh; the Meerut conspiracy trial in India was one of his topics.[40] In April he was in Chesterfield: 'Got the meetings—all good—heavy job but all such work is'. In September he was on Teesside, again fully occupied with a series of meetings. ' "Poverty will be driven out"—Tom Mann looks forward to time of peace and plenty', read a newspaper cutting reporting his meeting at Borough Hall, Stockton-on-Tees. 'I am now on the Billingham Estate. The big chemical combine. Mond's affair—where they

[37] T. Mann to Elsie Mann, 3 Jan. 1933, TMP.
[38] *Militant Trade Unionist* (May 1933).   [39] *Eye* (17 Oct. 1935).
[40] T. Mann to Elsie Mann, 4 Mar. 1933, TMP.

make the poison gases & extract the nitrogen from the air &c. Glad to be here & get close contact with them.'[41]

Part of the reason for his abandonment of the *Militant Trade Unionist* was the speaking tour across the Atlantic which he undertook in the autumn of 1933. On 28 September he wrote to Elsie shortly after he had left Southampton on board RMS *Majestic*, a White Star liner: 'Glad to report my leg is quite better, & I've enjoyed the sea water baths very much—just what I wanted but if I continue to get health trips like this I can't see what chance I shall get of turning my toes up!'[42] He reached New York on 3 October. 'We arrived Tuesday—with [Henri] Barbusse. He is working hard & well but he is not strong, suffering I think from War efforts.' His lecturing tour was sponsored by the American League against War and Fascism. 'Earl Browder has been very attentive & very kind. They have a far greater movement than we have. They run 9 Daily papers in about half a dozen languages, have a big school', he wrote to Elsie.[43]

Tom had a very heavy schedule for lecturing. After having addressed a huge gathering at Madison Square Gardens at 8 o'clock on the night of 6 October, he took the train for Philadelphia where he addressed another meeting at 11.30 the same night; and returning to New York on the 7th, spoke at Paterson, New Jersey, on the 8th. A hand-bill dated 8 October read: 'Unite in the Struggle against Imperialist War! Demand the withdrawal of U.S. Battleship from Cuba. . . . Tom Mann'. On the 12th he spoke at Pittsburgh along with Barbusse. After returning to New York where he got his permit extended for another month, he then headed towards the West. Via Buffalo and Detroit, he came to Milwaukee, 'a Socialist Town, not Communist', he said: 'Socialist Mayor—been in office 18 years, 11 Soc. Aldermen out of 33, all reactionary'.[44] 'Next War Being Prepared, British Labourite Warns. 1000 Hear Tom Mann Declare NRA [National Recovery Act] is Fascist Plan', read a local newspaper.[45] On the train to California Tom wrote to Elsie:

I left Chicago last night . . . I am in Pullman. . . . I had 95 miles car run yesterday from Milwaukee to Chicago. There is a big strike of Farmers

[41] T. Mann to Elsie Mann, 31 Aug., 23 Sept., 1933, TMP.
[42] T. Mann to Elsie Mann, 28 Sept. 1933, TMP.
[43] T. Mann to Elsie Mann, 6 Oct. 1933, TMP.
[44] T. Mann to Elsie Mann, 23 Oct. 1933, TMP.
[45] *Milwaukee Sentinel* (23 Oct. 1933), Newspaper cutting, TMP.

on in several States. ... 40 to 50,000 are refusing to operate their Farms under the National Recovery Act of Roosevelt. Several hundred thousand miners & steel workers are out also, all poorly organised or connected with AF of L (the equivalent or worse than the TUC crowd).[46]

After four days in San Francisco and a day in Seattle, he was allowed to visit Canada, starting from Vancouver. He wrote to Elsie from Winnipeg:

I was at Calgary ... had a very heavy day last Sunday. Snow every-where like Siberia, set out at 8 a.m. in car for a 90 mile run to a mining place called Drumheller, met Committee & fiddled about for 3 hours, had only a cup of tea & a wee bit bread & meat for dinner, a 2 hours meeting, back again Calgary just in time for a big meeting in Theatre—another 2 hours & then a meal: that's alright for the young un's, it's the old folks can't stand it.

At Winnipeg he met many people who reminded him of bygone days: 'Several Aberdonians came to me last night—telling me how they remember the election contest, you will remember it too, won't you? 1895 I think. Another man said "I worked with you in North Eastern Engineering works at Wallsend on Tyne". That was in 1887.' 'Most of the active men with an international outlook', he added, 'are from Ukraine, Germany or Scandinavia —most of the British retain the old outlook & stick in the old ruts—of course with exceptions.'[47] 'There is room in an anti-war movement for men of differing opinions' was the keynote of his speech at Winnipeg.[48] He had 'a very fine meeting' in Toronto on the 11th and left Canada on the 15th, again on board the *Majestic*.

There were two more national hunger marches after his American tour. Early in 1934 the Government issued warrants for the arrest of Tom Mann and Harry Pollitt, both members of the March Council of that year and of a Congress of Action to be held at the Bermondsey Town Hall on 24 and 25 February. They were charged with delivering seditious speeches (allegedly made in connection with the above congress) at meetings held in Glamorgan. They were released on bail, and the congress wel-comed them on arrival with acclamation. They were tried at the Swansea assizes in July. 'Am still on bail—was in "dock" all yesterday,' he wrote from a Swansea hotel. The judge showed no hostility, and D. N. Pritt, the counsel for Mann and Pollitt,

---

[46] T. Mann to Elsie Mann, 24 Oct. 1933, TMP.
[47] T. Mann to Elsie Mann, 8 Nov. 1933, TMP.
[48] *Winnipeg Free Press* (8 Nov. 1933), Newspaper cutting, TMP.

'did exceedingly well'. So, he felt, the verdict would 'not be more than 8 months . . . possibly less'.[49] The following day they were acquitted. It was probably on this occasion that he and Pollitt visited Owen's grave and the Owen museum in his native town of New Town. In a lecture note prepared later, he wrote:

I learned enough about him [Owen] and his work in my early life that I became convinced there was no real necessity for the evil of Unemployment. . . . Learning of his teachings and of the great efforts he made over so long a life, I revered the man as a great Teacher and in my turn determined to do a share of this great and vitally necessary educational work.[50]

The last march, that of 1,500 men and women in six contingents from the Depressed Areas, was welcomed by a crowd of 250,000 as they entered Hyde Park on Sunday 8 November 1936. Ellen Wilkinson and her Jarrow marchers also joined in. At their farewell rally held in Trafalgar Square a week later Tom Mann and Ben Tillett 'represented past struggles', Harry Pollitt the Communist Party, and Aneurin Bevan the Labour Party.[51] After 1936 the National Unemployed Workers' Movement began to falter, since unemployment itself declined with the rise of new industries and the acceleration of rearmament. Tom Mann was still alive and kicking in spite of his old age, but somehow he had become a symbolic figure representing the challenges of labour in bygone days, and Tillett was certainly living on memories of his heroic past.

[49] T. Mann to Elsie Mann, 3 July 1934, TMP.
[50] T. Mann, Lecture Note [1934?], TMP.
[51] Kingsford, *Hunger Marchers*, 218; Harry McShane and Joan Smith, *Harry McShane* (London, 1978), 217–19.

15. Twilight Years

ON 21 October 1936 a unique dinner party was held in the Thames House Restaurant for 164 veterans of the London Dock Strike of 1889. The youngest guest was seventy, the oldest eighty-seven. 'The Trinity represented here tonight of Tom Mann, John Burns and myself', said Tillett, 'affords a basic dynamic expression of social amelioration and change.'[1] A seat, however, remained vacant throughout the evening in the hope that Burns would turn up, though he had previously declined to do so. His rumoured antipathy to Tillett, probably on account of the latter's addiction to drink, was not the real cause for his absence. The tragic death of his only son Edgar had made him bitter. Edgar, against his parents' wishes, had enlisted in the army in 1916, suffered shell-shock, and died a lonely death in 1922 while serving as clerk for the Imperial War Graves Commission at Rouen. And Burns had been out of the limelight for nearly two decades. He persistently refused to be drawn in to the arena of politics on any terms. He knew that he would have been the odd man out, the object of curiosity and faint admiration even at the happy reunion of the veterans of 1889 from whom he had estranged himself for so many years, though he also felt that his natural place was among them.

Moreover, at the time of the reunion, Mrs Burns was not well. She died on 30 October after a short illness. 'Let me share your sorrow as an old comrade and one who once knew Mrs. Burns in the early years', wrote Tom Mann in a letter of condolence.[2] The twilight of life had brought the two friends closer once more, but there remained a degree of artificiality and even distance created by time in their renewed friendship. 'I saw, & probably you did that Mrs. Tillett has just died, cremation I think tomorrow', he wrote to Burns on 23 December, only two months after the death of Mrs Burns. In his speech delivered at the reunion in October, Tillett had called his wife Jane 'my best friend and colleague' and 'the mother of the Dockers' Union' (she having been the assistant secretary of the Tea Operatives' Union!).[3]

---

[1] Anon., *Ben Tillett: Fighter and Pioneer*, memorial vol. (London, n.d.), 6.
[2] T. Mann to J. Burns, 31 Oct. 1936, BL Add. MS 46285, JBP.
[3] Anon., *Ben Tillett: Fighter and Pioneer*, 6.

Old age brought family misfortunes and comparative insecurity. As for insecurity, Burns, having been a Cabinet minister for nearly ten years, was perhaps an exception, and there has been an argument that he had never entirely given up his ambitions. John Wilkes, Burns's prototype in many senses, dubbed himself 'an extinct volcano' in his later life, but 'Burns was never willing to admit extinction, and waited the recall that never came', wrote his biographer Kent.[4] This is exactly what Tom Mann felt about his friend at the general election of 1924. Burns 'does not seem to have fixed upon a constituency. I think he was disposed to but probably not approached'.[5] But neither Kent nor Mann was wholly on the right track. Kent, in particular, assumed his vanity and egocentricity to be the cause of his reticence.

It is true that Burns did not comply with Tom Mann's request to send him an article and a photograph of himself to be inserted in the ASE journal edited by Tom as general secretary of the union.[6] In May 1922 Asquith urged him to return to politics: 'Can't you see your way (now that Bottomley is disposed of) to go to Hackney and by that route re-enter the House? You need not pledge yourself to any party and, you would have the warm support of all who believe in clean politics and honesty in public life.'[7] He was not persuaded. At the general election of 1923 he was asked to speak for the Liberals in support of Free Trade, but he said he had 'strong political and real liberal reasons for declining'.[8] When the Battersea Labour League invited him to speak at a demonstration at Clapham Common in September 1924, he refused. When the assistant editor of the *Sunday Express* told him that now was 'the psychological moment for you to break your silence', his reply was 'No to Tory'.[9] The Conservative Government after the General Strike sought to restrict trade-union practices by a Trade Dispute Act, and Tillett on behalf of the National Trade Union Defence Committee urged him to take part in a demonstration in Hyde Park, 'your old battleground', but he did not move a finger.[10] After the collapse of the first MacDonald Government, Burns wrote to an American friend:

[4] William Kent, *John Burns: Labour's Lost Leader* (London, 1950), 383.
[5] T. Mann to Elsie Mann, 20 Oct. 1934, TMP.
[6] T. Mann to J. Burns, 8 Nov. 1920, BL Add. MS 46281, JBP.
[7] H. H. Asquith to J. Burns, 31 May 1922, BL Add. MS 46281, JBP.
[8] J. Burns to (Herbert Gladstone), 27 Nov. 1923, BL Add. MS 46304, JBP.
[9] Battersea Labour League to J. Burns, 3 Sept. 1924; Arthur David to J. Burns, 9 Oct. 1924, BL Add. MS 46304, JBP.
[10] B. Tillett to J. Burns, 20 June 1927, BL Add. MS 46285, JBP.

As you suggested in your letter my worst suspicions as to what would happen if office was prematurely taken by the Labour Party have been realised. . . . I am less concerned however with those who disregarded my advice and have damaged and set back their cause several years. The common people, Lincoln's people, Cromwell's people, John Brown's people are however marching on, wiser, braver and more disciplined than their leaders.[11]

As the world depression set in, the common people were visibly suffering 'for the follies of their politicians who were not and are not statesmen', wrote Burns: 'Super nationalism, Militarism, and Protection have burdened the people with almost intolerable liabilities which are reflected in Unemployment, and indebtedness with Rentiers who too often are warmongers and profiteers.'[12]

In his later life Burns had one obsessive idea—that war was the greatest tragedy for the common people and he had tried his best to prevent it in August 1914. When Edgar died, he wrote: 'we must dutifully share our sorrow with all those who suffer from a war that I did my best to avert'.[13] Even his remedy for the unemployed was stated in the same vein: 'Short & simple remedy for Unemployment is keep out of war, avoid Imperialism, shun Jingoism and all its evils.'[14] He remarked that the Second World War, when it broke out, was 'the result of the last war', and by inference he meant that he, alone among the ministers, had tried all he could to avoid it. Thus he could morally justify himself before all the calamities befalling the common people, and indeed could afford to be an onlooker. Herein lay his real vanity which had the innocence and inconsistency of a child who could say 'what a good boy am I',[15] and which provided excuse and inducement for inaction.

By the time of the 'reunion' in 1936, Tillett, too, had been reduced to a shadow of his former active self. He had been a member of the General Council of the TUC from its inception in 1921 till 1929. In that year he was returned to the House of Commons at North Salford at the general election, and took the chair at the TUC held in Belfast in September. He lost his seat at the general election of 1931, and his performance in the House for the period of 1929–31 had not been outstanding. His last speech was on the unemployed disturbances in Liverpool,

[11] J. Burns to Judge, 14 Dec. 1924, BL Add. MS 46304, JBP.
[12] J. Burns to Stella M. Franklin, 24 Aug. 1930, BL Add. MS 46304, JBP.
[13] J. Burns to Reading, n.d. [July 1922], BL Add. MS 46304, JBP.
[14] J. Burns to Pentland, 23 Apr. 1923, BL Add. MS 46304, JBP.
[15] Kent, *John Burns*, 194, 358.

and in it he repeated what he had been saying for the last two decades against the use of the Army and Navy in matters of industrial dispute. Long after he ceased to be a member, he used the privilege of 'access to the Lobby' where he was often found with his large sack trilby, chatting with his old colleagues. All this while, Baron Beaverbrook, the Unionist politician and budding tycoon of journalism, replaced Bottomley as a source of encouragement, both moral and pecuniary, especially during his ill-health.[16]

J. Havelock Wilson, who might perhaps, with some justification, be counted among the men of 1889 and among Tom's circle before 1917, had gone against the main current of the British labour movement. Not only had he reconciled himself with the Shipping Federation under war conditions, but also he supported the mineowners rather than the miners during the post-war disputes in the mining industry. He withdrew his union from the NTWF in order to evade the stigma of expulsion. He went so far as to support the Conservative Government in the General Strike of 1926 which he regarded as a 'revolutionary plot'. By now Mann and Wilson were poles apart in labour politics. The ignominy of the expulsion of his union from the TUC was followed by his death on 16 April 1929 after a lingering illness. 'He was looking forward eagerly to devoting himself to a new organisation which he started in 1926, the Industrial Peace League of the British Empire', read an obituary in *The Times*.[17]

By the time of the last hunger march of 1936 Tom Mann had become a symbolic but legendary figure. One could write a substantial history of the Communist Party of this period without mentioning his name. However, a group of Britons who formed one of the first volunteer forces against Franco in the Spanish Civil War called themselves the 'Tom Mann Centuria'. Nat Cohen and Sam Masters, two garment-workers from London, had cycled down France at the time of Franco's revolt, crossed the border and joined in an abortive attempt to capture Mallorca from the Nationalists. Back in Barcelona, they had formed a centuria consisting mostly of Spaniards.[18] They probably named it after Tom Mann because he was a man who

---

[16] I. Mackay, Notes on Tillett, IMP. See also B. Tillett to Beaverbrook, 2 Feb. 1939, IMP.

[17] J. McConville and John Saville, 'John Havelock Wilson', in *Dictionary of Labour Biography*, iv (London, 1977), 206; *The Times* (17 Apr. 1929).

[18] W. Rust, *Britons in Spain* (London, 1939), 20.

could represent the British working class in action. In a letter
to John Burns, Mann wrote: 'the terrible struggle in Spain is
our job too & we must have them ever in mind and heart'.[19]

Tom was still active in mind and body. He apparently sup-
ported himself with the fees for his speeches and lectures
delivered at home and abroad. In the summer of 1934 he and
Elsie were invited to Russia for a few weeks. Bob McIlhone, the
British Communist who was then in Moscow, took them to the
Red Army gathering on the day of their arrival.[20] In the early
spring of 1935 he made a speaking tour in Denmark where a
Socialist–Liberal coalition was in power. On his arrival at
Esbjerg he was welcomed by a crowd with a band and trade-
union banners, and a mile-long procession followed. At Copenhagen he made a radio broadcast, and on the whole he found
that 'Social Democrats are bitterly anti-Communist'.[21] The rest
of the year he spent mostly speaking for the Communist Party
at home—at a big open-air demonstration at Blantyre near
Glasgow with Gallacher and Moffat—and then for the Fife
miners in June, at Manchester and Rochdale in October, again
in Fife and also in the Rhondda in November. Towards the
end of the year Tom Quelch wrote him asking if he had been
'gathering together the materials for your later "Memoirs"'.
'You ought to do that during these winter months', he added,
'and reserve your agitational efforts for the warmer', an
appropriate advice for an old man seventy-nine years of age.[22]
Yet he continued his lecture tour in that winter, and wrote to
Elsie in January 1936 from a cottage at Bryn Mor Rhosgadfan
about a meeting held at Caernarfon the day before and about
his car getting bogged down in icy mud on the way.[23]

Meanwhile, the Tom Mann 80th Birthday Celebration Committee was set up with Tillett as chairman at the National
Trade Union Club at New Oxford Street, which he also chaired.
'How are you—and how is the family? We shall be making
history again lad, for the world is not finished with us of the
"Old Brigade"', he wrote to Tom, 'for there is spirit left still—
as well as the fires of life—are still young enough.'[24] The
celebration dinner was held on 15 April at the Royal Hotel,
Bloomsbury, attended by over 700 socialists and radicals:

19 T. Mann to J. Burns, 23 Dec. 1936, BL Add. MS 46285, JBP.
20 T. Mann to Elsie Mann, 3 Nov. 1935, TMP.
21 T. Mann to Elsie Mann, 3 Mar. 1935, TMP.
22 T. Quelch to T. Mann, 16 Dec. 1935, TMP.
23 T. Mann to Elsie Mann, 19 Jan. 1936, TMP.
24 B. Tillett to T. Mann, 10 March 1936, TMP.

Henry W. Nevinson, Fenner Brockway, Edith Summerskill, J. F. Horrabin, Jennie Lee, G. N. Barnes, Clem Attlee, and George Lansbury among many others. Bernard Shaw excused himself as he had had some teeth extracted the day before. Alan Findlay, president of the TUC, and Harry Pollitt, secretary of the Communist Party, appeared together 'at the same microphone', wrote Ian Mackay for the *News Chronicle*. Tillett presided, and shaking his old comrade by the hand, said: 'Whatever you do and whatever you say, we love you, Tom Mann. It does not matter a damn about the intelligentsia or the economic basis. You have always fought for your class, and when you have fought for your class you have always fought for humanity. God bless you, Tom.'[25] Tom Mooney, an American trade-unionist whom Mann had tried to visit at San Quentin Gaol in San Francisco, sent a message from his prison cell. Percy Laidler of Melbourne, on behalf of Mann's Australian friends, sent a birthday gift of £50 and a resolution which said: 'You made in Australian Working Class history a mark which time has not and cannot erase.'[26] Burns, a notable absentee at the dinner, later wrote to him: 'I congratulate you on your recent 80th birthday and thank you most sincerely for your persistent devotion to the Common people. We both have done our best in many spheres of life and [you] in your case have worthily played the part of a devoted citizen.'[27]

The day after the birthday celebration, Tom sailed for Canada on board RMS *Duchess of Atholl*. He arrived in Montreal on 26 April and was received by a good many Party workers: 'knowing this to be a Reactionary City, French Canadians— I was much surprised to find so many District Party workers & organisers & of so good a type', he wrote to Harry Pollitt.[28] On May Day he addressed an audience of 9,000 at a meeting held in the Arena, Toronto. Just before he spoke, a cablegram had arrived to tell him that Mrs Mann had spoken at the May First Meeting held at Shoreditch. 'Good for you Mam,' wrote Tom, 'very glad you were there and took part. . . . The message was read by the chairman . . . and was cheered enthusiastically.' In London, Ben Tillett kept up his warm friendship for the Manns, evidently reawakened by the birthday celebration. 'Glad Ben has written,' wrote Mann to Elsie from Toronto, 'See him when convenient, he has worked very hard on the celebration & it is

[25] *News Chronicle* (16 Apr. 1936).
[26] Laidler to T. Mann, 5 May 1936, TMP.
[27] J. Burns to T. Mann, 19 Oct. 1936, TMP.
[28] T. Mann to H. Pollitt, 27 Apr. 1936, TMP.

largely due to him it went off so well.'[29] Ben invited Elsie to a
Lon Swales Dinner at the National Trade Union Club, his club,
as 'our Guest'. While in London, Ontario, Tom visited the
cemetery where George Loveless, the Tolpuddle martyr who
had emigrated to Canada, was buried. Reporting this to Ben,
Tom added: 'Tonight I am having a Banquet with a lot of the old
timers and moderns. The chief purpose is that I may have a
long talk on United Front, but it is good, Fellows who have
declined to be identified with the Lefts are coming along very
nicely, my youth makes it easier for them.'[30] While in Canada,
Tom became ill and had an operation in Toronto for some
internal trouble. Towards the end of May, after a few days'
rest, he left Montreal for home on board the same *Duchess of
Atholl*. 'The boat has been passing ice-bergs 45–50, some of
them standing out of water . . . new experience for me.'[31]

Back in London he had an X-ray examination at Manor
House Hospital, Hampstead. He was already on the move,
staying with Sid Elias, chairman of the NUWM, at his house at
Bradford, to attend a meeting there and also to have an interview with Fred Jowett, the veteran member of the ILP. He was
in Scotland in September, speaking at the Adam Smith Hall,
Kirkcaldy.[32] Then he travelled with Ben to Birmingham to
attend a dinner held on 17 October in his honour at the
'Cobden', attended by people from 'NCLC [National Council of
Labour Colleges] and T. Unions in majority, Co-op folk, C.P., &
nondescripts'. 'Complementary speeches to me . . . Ben made
short speech, & sung "Cockles", audience joined lustily in
chorus.'[33] This was four days before the reunion of the 1889
veterans.

Tom and Ben were now close to each other again as old friends.
They had a nice little arrangement by which they would meet
at the pubs' opening-time. Harry Pollitt recalled:

I acted as a kind of Secretary to Tom, and he always tipped me off
about these meetings so that perhaps I would at closing time keep an
appropriate eye on the two of them . . . To see them out of Henekeys in
the Strand, arm in arm winding their way to Charing Cross Station, and
giving some coppers to every flower girl, match seller and what have
you in the Strand was a sight for the gods. I never knew Tom Mann in

29 T. Mann to Elsie Mann, 2, 7 May 1936, TMP.
30 T. Mann to B. Tillett, 8 May 1936, TMP.
31 T. Mann to Elsie Mann, 31 May 1936. I owe this to Mr Charles Mann.
32 T. Mann to Elsie Mann, 16 Aug., 20 Sept. 1936, TMP.
33 T. Mann to Elsie Mann, 18 Oct. 1936, TMP.

any town I was with him refuse to give some money to any person he saw selling or begging in the street.[34]

Early in 1937 Mann was in Paris, assisting in a demonstration, and met many old friends including Charles Marck. Back in London he was again unwell. Willie Gallacher, who had been elected again at West Fife at the 1935 general election, wrote him from the House of Commons Library: 'I see by the Daily that you have been laid up for the time being. I hope it won't be for long. We need you now more than ever with the big drive for unity that is taking place.'[35] The cry for the 'United Front' was now spreading, and the Communists sought to secure a common front with the ILP and possibly with the Labour Party in their anti-Fascist crusade. Mann had been a crusader for unity all through, and proved to be a valuable asset 'more than ever' to the cause. It is interesting to note that Mann was elected for the first time to the Central Committee of the Communist Party at the party congress held at Battersea in May 1937.[36]

In November 1937 Tom paid his fourth visit to Russia with Ben Tillett and John Bell of the ETU. They sailed on board SS *Andrea Zhdanov* which picked up the crew of a sunken ship on the way. In Moscow they 'shared pretty well in the general celebration, meetings & concerts & plays &c.'. 'Each being in second childhood', wrote Mann, 'not wishful of a long trip & climbing factory stairs &c.', they decided to catch the boat that would sail home a week later.[37] Tillett was more enthusiastic and profuse in his praise of 'this wonderful city and the still more wonderful country's growth'. Compared with the Moscow he had seen thirteen years before with its unsurfaced streets and shabby-looking shops, he now saw 'architectural beauty'— buildings rising high to the sky, an underground railway 'surpassing anything in the world of electric traction', and the stations that 'are a veritable triumph of art'.[38]

Early in 1938 Tom played a prominent part in the boycott of the *Harunamaru*, a Japanese ship, as a protest against Japan's invasion of China. 'I have been more than ordinarily busy this week as on top of the usual I have had special meetings in the Dock area re boycott of the Jap. staff. Last night I was at a

---

[34] H. Pollitt to I. Mackay, 21 Jan. 1951, IMP.

[35] W. Gallacher to T. Mann, 10 Feb. 1937, TMP.

[36] Noreen Branson, *History of the Communist Party of Great Britain 1927-1941* (London, 1985), 341.

[37] T. Mann to Walter, 18 Nov. 1939, DTP.

[38] B. Tillett to Jack Gill, 16 Nov. 1937, IMP.

Spanish meeting at Sutton.'[39] He also paid serious attention to the decline of industry in the North. From Oldham he wrote:

It is very dark and raining heavily & I have to get off soon to Rochdale Open Air Meeting. ... Oldham is declining. Platts the celebrated Engineers now employ about 7000, as against their former 14,000. One textile factory near there formerly employing about 2500 workers now closed down & all the loom and spinning mules broken up. No longer wanted—Capitalism.[40]

On 4 July he flew from Croydon to Copenhagen via Amsterdam in four hours, a 'splendid flight', he said. He went to Denmark as the British delegate on the Danish Communist Party conference. In September he was on a visit to Sweden, where a Social Democratic government had held office almost continuously from the early 1930s. He visited Göteborg and Stockholm to assist municipal election campaigns on behalf of the Swedish Communist Party.[41] Back in England he took the chair at the annual conference of the Communist Party of Great Britain held in Birmingham also in July. On 7 December the surviving members of the British battalion—305 of them—who had fought hard and heroic battles against Franco and the forces of international Fascism in Spain at great cost to themselves returned to Victoria Station, and were welcomed by Attlee and Stafford Cripps, Gallacher and Mann, and Will Lawther of the Mine Workers' Federation, whose brother had been killed in Spain. Tom wrote a few days later to Sam Wild, a labourer from Manchester who had served in the Navy and had also served as commander of the British battalion in Spain, saying that he would be glad to appear at a *Daily Worker* bazaar for the veterans of the Spanish Civil War: 'Good luck to you old lad and to all the Boys who came with you.'[42]

Tom sent to Sam Wild a copy of his leaflet *Sixty Years of an Agitator's Life 1878–1938*, which was in fact a list of lectures he was prepared to give at meetings sponsored by Trades Councils, Trade Unions, Co-operatives, and others. Indeed, the subjects covered his whole life: 'The Fight for the Shorter Working Day' including 'Youthful Recollections'; 'Pioneers of Democracy and Socialism' which ended with Lenin, not with Kropotkin; '"Direct Action" and its Forms', dealing with the London Dock Strike of 1889 and the Broken Hill Strike of 1908

[39] T. Mann to Dona Torr, 5 Feb. 1938, DTP.
[40] T. Mann to Elsie Mann, 16 May 1938, TMP.
[41] T. Mann to Elsie Mann, Whit Sunday, 3 June, 5, 7, 8 Sept. 1938, TMP.
[42] T. Mann to Sam Wild, 13 Dec. 1938, Frow Collection, Salford.

as well as the Liverpool Transport Strike of 1911 and the General Strike of 1926; 'Development of the International Workers' Movement'; 'Plutocracy or Democracy—Which?'; and 'Russia—Old and New'.[43] In July 1939 Tom was preparing for a meeting to be held at Whitechapel to celebrate the centenary of the Chartist movement.[44]

By then 'peace with honour' supposedly obtained at Munich had wrecked itself. Events moved swiftly. Less than ten days after the conclusion of the Russo-German non-aggression pact, the German invasion of Poland began. The British Communists supported Britain's war against Hitler when it was declared on 3 September. With Soviet Russia maintaining her neutrality in the 'Imperialist' war, the party had to alter its attitude, despite resistance by Pollitt and Campbell and possibly by the more independent members of the Central Committee such as Tom Mann and Arthur Horner.[45] In the end the party had to toe the line provided by Moscow, and Pollitt and Campbell were deprived of their responsibilities at the party centre.

On 3 September Tillett was staying at the Station Hotel, Bridlington, where the TUC was to be held from the following day. Neville Chamberlain's apologetic voice was on the air, announcing the beginning of the war against Germany. 'Who wants peace with the devil?' murmured Ben. And he characteristically added: 'Why didn't they send me to Berchtesgarden? I'd have killed the ——, taken what was coming and the world would have been a cleaner place.'[46]

As the fateful year drew to its end, Tom again felt unwell. Pollitt wrote to Elsie, telling her that he had asked for 'some good Party Nurse' and would try to secure 'the best Specialist that can be got'.[47] On the New Year's Eve Tillett sent greetings to Tom:

The world is all bloody mad, including Stalin and U.S.S.R., with war on the brain, if brains there be, and Imperialism is stalking the world, but here are we—having fought for the brotherhood of man, and for world's peace, face to face with the whole 'cabudulum', rank, staring mad, in a frozen winter, and Xtians of Europe as silly as the Dictator of U.S.S.R.

[43] T. Mann, *Sixty Years of an Agitator's Life* (London, 1938).
[44] T. Mann to Tom Mann, Jun., 12 July 1939, TMP.
[45] Henry Pelling, *British Communist Party* (1958; London, 1975), 112.
[46] An unspecified typed MS, 74/6/2/50i, IMP.
[47] H. Pollitt to Elsie Mann, 11 Dec. 1939. I owe this to Mr Charles Mann.

Any Socialism is becoming frozen and paralyzed, and the mono-
polistic Capitalism being built in with further profiteering.

We two will get together again, and we can make the 'welkin' ring
again against the 'Powers that be'. I send you a Comrade's loving
wishes for the New Year of better health for you.[48]

R. Palme Dutt on behalf of the Political Bureau of the Communist Party sent him good wishes on his eighty-fourth birthday
and sympathy with his illness with the inevitable reference to
'the fight against the imperialist war' and 'unity with the
Socialist Soviet Union'.[49] It was a time when the Anglo-French
adventure in Scandinavia which smacked (in some quarters) of
an anti-Russian crusade, began to show signs of a blunder.
France was to collapse in June. The Battle of Britain, in which
the RAF fighters proved more than a match for the *Luftwaffe*,
was followed by the Blitz on London that caused great damage.
Tom Mann, who had been living for the last few years in a
house secured by his son Tom at Sidcup, Kent, now moved to
Moorside, Grassington, to be near his wife's relatives. Tom
Mann, Jun. and his wife Doris were living at North Ferriby near
Hull and offered help. Pollitt wrote him in December: 'I hear
you are still smiling even if you feel a little tired. . . . Things are
very, very quiet in the meeting and conference line.'[50] Pollitt
visited Mann several times at Grassington.

In March 1941 the old man took a turn for the worse; Pollitt
hastened to the Yorkshire dales and arrived in time to shake
his hand for the last time. Tom's last words Pollitt caught were
'Go on with the work. There will be set-backs, partial success
and final success.'[51] Tom Mann died on 13 March 1941 at the
age of eighty-four. The cause of his death was diagnosed as
cerebral thrombosis and intermittent auricular fibrillation.
Four days later his coffin, draped in the banner of the Communist Party, was carried to Lawnswood Crematorium in
Leeds, followed by many of his old friends and delegates from
workers' organizations. Pollitt helped with arrangements for
the funeral. When Ben Tillett arrived he 'explained the pro-
cedure to him. That he, Krishna Menon and I', wrote Pollitt,

would sit in the same pew, and that my job after Ben's oration would be
press the button and let the coffin go through. 'Kid', Ben said, 'I want to
sit next to you, and when I speak I shall get hold of your left wrist, and

[48] B. Tillett to Tom and Elsie Mann, 31 Dec. 1939, TMP.
[49] P. Dutt to T. Mann, 13 Apr. 1940, TMP.
[50] H. Pollitt to T. Mann, 2 Dec. 1940, TMP.
[51] H. Pollitt, *Tom Mann: A Tribute* (London, n.d.).

draw strength from your younger blood'. He did, and I could not use that wrist for days, but what an oration. It was the most beautiful wording and phrasing I have ever listened to. Not only generous tributes to Tom Mann but Ben painted the lily in regard to the kind of Socialism that Tom had fought for. I have always regretted that no one was there to take it down. It was unforgettable, and despite the sadness of the occasion, those present walked out of that Crematorium as if they were already living in the kind of land that William Morris wrote about.[52]

The *Labour Monthly* published what purported to be Ben's funeral oration in its issue of April 1941. This speech or article was copied almost word for word from a relevant section in Ben's own memoirs published in 1931. There he wrote:

I am vain enough to believe that the best of his work was with myself. ... I wish to the bottom of my heart, that he had held on to his plough in the Trade Union furrow, treading his way to the western sunset of life, until he met the golden rays of his declining day and had fallen face downwards over the handles of the plough he could so sturdily have guided.[53]

'He chose other paths' and became a propagandist for international communism though he devoted himself to the trade-union side of its work.

In his speech given at the funeral, Gallacher stressed Tom's work for the party: 'To the party he gave himself without reserve. No task was too humble, no task was too hard, no journey too onerous or exhausting. We never spared him. He never spared himself.'[54] Tom endured the vacillating tactics of international communism. He did so for the sake of the unity of revolutionary forces—'Three Cheers for Unity' he would call at his platform.[55] At the same time, as *The Times* obituary pointed out, Tom avowed himself a communist 'when Communism appeared as an independent organisation'.[56] He valued the indomitable, independent mind of the proud working-man like Tillett and even Burns, though they were never communist.

In the Second World War as in the First, Tillett's main concern was the dignity and welfare of his own class.[57] He himself,

[52] H. Pollitt to I. Mackay, 21 Jan. 1951, IMP.

[53] B. Tillett, *Memories and Reflections* (London, 1931), 94.

[54] *Labour Monthly* (Apr. 1941).

[55] John Mahon, *Harry Pollitt: A Biography* (London, 1976), 267.

[56] *The Times* (14 Mar. 1941).

[57] See B. Tillett to Hugh Chevins, *Daily Telegraph* (n.d. [early 1941]), IMP. Towards the very end of his life Tillett became interested in the Moral Rearma-

however, was not well, felt weak by the summer of 1942, and died of cancer of the stomach on 27 January 1943. Prayers at his funeral were followed by remembrance by the Right Honourable Ernest Bevin, Minister of Labour and National Service.[58] A pamphlet in commemoration of Tillett as 'Fighter and Pioneer' was published, in which was featured his speech made in 1913 at Ruskin College: he stressed 'Liberty of mind and body' for the working-class—'If Ruskin College does nothing better than teach you to live uprightly in the strength of a great manhood, loving others and helping others—if it does nothing better than that, it will do a great work.' This can be compared to Tom's farewell address to the members of the AEU already quoted. Ben's advocacy of 'a new vista of a greater, nobler citizenship' would perhaps place him closer to John Burns.

In 1939 Burns wrote about his past devoted work for the fiftieth anniversary not of the London Dock Strike but of the London County Council.[59] He, too, began to feel the strain of old age, and was practically bedridden for the last year or so of his life. For his eighty-fourth and last birthday (20 October 1942) a telegram of sympathy came from the Prime Minister, his old ministerial colleague Winston Churchill. He died of heart failure on 24 January 1943, three days before the death of Tillett. Among the mourners at his funeral there were William Gallacher and Harry Pollitt, perhaps representing his past connection with the revolutionary movement. Possibly his belief that a Russian pact would have avoided war had something to do with their interest in Burns.[60]

All through his life, Burns was a remarkable collector of books, and it was reported in *The Times* that he had left a valuable library of 12,000 volumes.[61] His wife 'Pattie', his sole legatee, had been dead since 1936. Just as his house, standing on one of Thomas More's lands, was converted into six flats and sold off, his library was disposed of by auction at Sotheby's. Apart from the volumes on labour and socialism that were saved by Yvonne Kapp, the AEU's research worker at the time, for her union (and eventually for the TUC)[62] and those on

ment Movement perhaps for the same reasons. See the anonymous *Ben Tillett: Fighter and Pioneer*, 12–13.

[58] Anon., *In Memoriam Benjamin Tillett* (London, n.d.). I owe this to Mr Charles Mann.   [59] *Star* (21 Mar. 1939).

[60] Kent, *John Burns*, 292, 295.   [61] *The Times* (3 Feb. 1943).

[62] Yvonne Kapp, *John Burns' Library* (Our History Pamphlet, 16; winter 1959), *passim*.

London bought by Viscount Southwood for the LCC, Burns's magnificent library including the invaluable Thomas More collection and Shakespeare folios melted away in the market. Its disappearance symbolized the rise and fall, or the success and frustration, of Citizen John Burns, though his voluminous papers entrusted to the British Library remain and are the major sources from which to reconstruct his life, which was at times so closely entangled with Tom's life and work, and indeed from which to portray all the major figures who were found in Tom Mann's circle.

Epilogue

TOM Mann was an outstanding educator of British labour at the turning-point in its history when it emerged as an independent political and social force: he was a 'political lecturer' almost by profession, wrote a number of pamphlets on labour, and edited a succession of labour journals. As an organizer and a strategist he was at once firm and flexible. His development as a labour leader dated from his agitation for the eight-hour day in the 1880s, but it was the London Dock Strike of 1889 that gave him an unshakeable belief in the efficacy of industrial action not only for improving conditions of work for each worker but also for preparing the ground for a future co-operative society. The strike was remarkable for its collective leadership. Of the three men who conducted the struggle of the unskilled workers on the London waterfront, Mann and Burns came from the advanced section of the labour aristocracy, being skilled engineers who devoted themselves to the propagation of the new gospel of socialism. Tillett the sailor and dock labourer supplied the ethos of hard, physical labour as well as an almost religious belief in the salvation of his own class. Mann was a bold strategist, while Burns was a cautious tactician. Out of these complementary elements was created the spirit of 1889 which permeated Tom's circle for many years.

When Tom rushed to the scene of the strike in the summer of 1889, Tillett explained the situation to him, and he at once grasped all the issues involved. From the strike and its aftermath he learned that the basic issue was control of labour, whether the dockers were to be hired outside the dock-gates or inside, who should decide their working conditions, who was to introduce a decasualization scheme. It was the same with the engineers. The problem of piece-work or time-work appeared secondary and even irrelevant before the central issue of who should control the work. With him, New Unionism was bound to develop into syndicalism.

Tom apparently kept in touch with J. Havelock Wilson in the 1890s when New Unionism stood on the defensive: indeed, Wilson embodied class struggle or class confrontation vis-à-vis the Shipping Federation, the common enemy for the Seamen and for the Dockers, and John Burns was cautious enough to warn Tom not to be too deeply involved in Wilson's tactics. We might suggest, with a certain reservation, that Tom's faith in direct action owed something to Wilson's feud with the Shipping Federation. His Australian experiences, on the other hand, were decisive in forging a fighter and a syndicalist out of him. The years of labour unrest, 1911–12, recaptured the scene as well as the spirit of 1889: the old heroes played the same old roles in a more articulate and intelligent fashion—Mann as an astute strategist, Tillett as a somewhat unruly battalion commander, Burns as a cautious negotiator (now from the government side) and Wilson, if we may add him to the list, perhaps an instigator of fresh confrontation. The First World War, however, put an end to Wilson's confrontation tactics and also to Tom's friendship with him.

Tom was perhaps at his best as the general secretary of the ASE–AEU, when he was able to go on preaching the gospel of syndicalism and advocating the tactic of trade-union amalgamation. Perhaps he was happier when he was helping the 'Bottom Dogs of Labour' in the East End of London, in the Black Country, and in Liverpool. He felt more at home when he worked with the rank-and-file trade-unionists and assisted their unofficial organizations such as the Shop Stewards' and Workers' Committees and various rank-and-file amalgamation committees. This plebeian characteristic of his work will explain why he assumed responsibility so willingly for the Minority Movement initiated by the Communist Party.

He remained a syndicalist at heart even when he appeared to be paying deference to the 'Class against Class' policy of the Comintern and the RILU. Harry McShane recalls Tom's visit to Mansfield where the Communist Party had a room in the local Labour Club. He came the night before the scheduled meeting, and that night he entertained about 200 people whom he found in the club:

he sang a Chinese song, a French drinking song, and he kissed all the women, and everyone was delighted with him. His meeting was in the Grand Theatre, where no communist meeting had ever been held before. He packed it. ... He gave the old type of syndicalist speech I had always heard him make in Glasgow. Although he was the great figurehead of the National Minority Movement and other activities led by the Communist Party, he was still a syndicalist at heart.[1]

---

[1] Harry McShane and Joan Smith, *Harry McShane* (London, 1978), 155.

Wal Hannington said, 'he was acutely aware of the power of the working-class, if properly organised, at the point of production'.[2] His was syndicalism in its best and simplest form. Such an academic definition of syndicalism as 'a version of unitary corporatism' of labour organizations[3] would not have interested Tom. It is true Tom thought of syndicalism as a working-class response to 'capitalist organisations' which 'have travelled much faster' and 'have syndicated their forces'.[4] His remark only reveals his awareness of the rise of monopoly capitalism which evidently strengthened his belief in the urgent need as well as the efficacy of workers' control of their working conditions.

In fact, syndicalism preached the gospel of work, and as such it even attracted Burns the puritan. Burns, however, was realistic enough to perceive the one-sidedness of direct action under the existing circumstances. He valued the workers' self-help more, an attitude which brought an outcry against him as a traitor to his class. 'Had he died in 1892 he would be remembered as the most impressive of the Socialist pioneers', wrote Eric Hobsbawm—a rather unkind comment.[5] He was ambitious enough, and his prime ambition was to form a trade-union labour party with himself as its leader. But a clever little political game he carried on against the ILP in the nineties, bore him away from the main current of the labour movement and landed him on the shore of Liberalism, and Burns consoled himself with what he took to be his contribution to the growth of the civic spirit among the working class. He was a complex figure, as his reasons for resignation from the Cabinet in August 1914 show, and he cut a tragic figure as well. In his declining years he wanted to see Tom Mann, but was too proud to go and visit him.

Relations between Mann and Tillett were on an entirely different plane: the two families were friends, and Mann's children called Mrs Tillett 'Ma-Two'.[6] We have had occasion to note Ben's pugnacious nature. 'Ben was a very protective father', wrote Terry McCarthy, the grand-son of Tom McCarthy, 'and woe betide anybody that took Jeanette [his daughter, born in 1890] home, not that this was without justification! Jeanette

---

[2] Wal Hannington, *Tom Mann, 1856–1941: A Short Biography* (London, 1947).
[3] Robert Currie, *Industrial Politics* (Oxford, 1979), 82.   [4] See Ch. 9.
[5] E. Hobsbawm, 'John Burns, 1858–1943', in Yvonne Kapp, *John Burns' Library* (Our History Pamphlet, 16; winter 1959), 2.
[6] An interview with Charles Mann, 10 Feb. 1982.

recalled the pearl-handled pistol that she herself was taught to use in their back garden, just off the Commercial Road.'[7]

Mann had prepared a will dated 20 July 1913, by which 'Elsie Harker of 18 Beech Range, Levenshulme' was appointed sole executrix and all his real and personal property were bequeathed to her. It is of some interest to note that Elsie Mann officially remained Elsie Harker till the last: on 2 October 1941 the administration of Mann's estate, the gross value of which amounted to £233 4s. 2d. was granted to Elsie Harker of 29 Norfold Crescent, Sidcup, Kent. Ellen Mann as well as Elsie survived Tom, but we can more or less safely assume that Tom had not been in touch with Ellen for the last thirty-five years or so of his life. Nevertheless, it is also natural to assume that he took an interest in his daughters by Ellen, or at least in some of them. Among the papers and photographs still left with Tom Mann's family today, there is his address book for 1934 which contains an item: 'Effie—c/o Mme Lazzari, Csalogàny Utca, 55 Budapest, Hungary'. This may well be Effie Mann, the music-hall singer about whom her father talked without inhibition to his sons.

Tom and Ben resumed their comradeship and strengthened it in the last few years of their life. They had been happy together ploughing the trade-union furrow with workers' control as their guide mark. Tom as a strategist had another grand scheme to deal with, the international dimensions of the class struggle, in which Tillett also took his full share. We have seen Tom's prophetic assertion on this issue. Under the circumstances of the inter-war period it is not surprising that his internationalist orientation should have taken the form of international communism.

The Comintern that embodied international communism, however, was in a moribund state by the time of Tom's death. It was doomed when the German army attacked the Soviet Union, and was formally dissolved in 1943. Now the Russian Communism of the dictatorship of the proletariat is liquidating itself, as it seems, in a vastly different world situation in which all the instruments of confrontational politics born of the Russian Revolution of 1917 (and of the Allied intervention that followed) and formalized in the Cold War structures and policies after the Second World War are revised and reorientated. Yet Tom's simple saying: 'We are part of the International Proletariat' still has a ringing resonance, relevant to

---

[7] *The Record* (July 1976).

the problems of today, since capital, as Tom would say, 'travelled' much faster than labour on the road to internationalization, involving the whole world, north and south, west and east.

Tom and his friends had seen heroic days of the class struggle which was fought in a more direct and tangible form than later generations would have to face. 'Perhaps more consistently than any other British trade unionist he adhered to the policy of the class war', read *The Times*'s obituary of Tom Mann.[8] He conducted various phases of that war without spite, bitterness, or arrogance, but with tact, courage, and understanding, and sometimes even with a witty, comic touch. At a time when London's Dockland is undergoing rapid and drastic change in its physical appearance as well as in social content, Tom Mann's strenuous life and the tradition of 1889, which was kept alive in various forms and in varying degrees of intensity among his circle, deserve a little monument at least to record the phases of that heroic struggle fought for the working class in the meridian days of British capitalism and industrialism.

When the relative decline of the British economy became apparent, it was some of the salient features of working-class culture such as the restrictive practices of trade unions that were blamed for the real or supposed evils. Tom Mann, like Robert Owen before him, welcomed the introduction of advanced technology and only sought to humanize the conditions of its introduction under workers' control. Working-class culture is not simply materialist as it has often been made out to be. The values and battle-cries brought out in the course of their struggles—solidarity, comradeship, manhood, or the recognition of each worker's dignity as a man, equal citizenship for all the working men—have relevance beyond the limits of one social class of one nation. Indeed, Tom Mann claimed with justice that working-class culture inherited the intellectual and moral values of Rousseau and Paine, Owen and Proudhon, Marx and Morris, Kropotkin and Lenin. In these days of manoeuvring with the peculiarities and relativities of cultural traditions and the form of economic development for ideological arguments and for academic exercises, Tom's life and work presents the positive and universal values of British working-class culture in the years of 'emancipatory' trade-unionism.

8 *The Times* (14 Mar. 1941).

Select Bibliography

MANUSCRIPT SOURCES

Dock Companies Joint Committee Documents, National Museum of Labour History, formerly at the Limehouse Town Hall, London.
Dona Torr Papers, Communist Party Library, London.
Glasier (J. Bruce) Diary, Liverpool University Library.
Ian Mackay Papers, Modern Records Centre, University of Warwick.
ILP Papers, British Library of Political and Economic Science.
International Transport Workers' Federation Archives, Modern Records Centre, University of Warwick.
John Burns Papers, British Library, Additional Manuscripts.
Passfield Papers, British Library of Political and Economic Science.
Tom Mann Papers, Coventry City Library.
Webb Trade Union Collection, British Library of Political and Economic Science.

WORKS BY TOM MANN

Books and Pamphlets (in chronological order)

What a Compulsory Eight Hour Working Day Means to the Workers (London, 1886).
The Eight Hours Movement (London, 1889).
The 'New' Trades Unionism: A Reply to Mr. George Shipton (London, 1890) [with Ben Tillett].
The Eight Hour Day: How to Get It by Trade and Local Option (London, 1891).
The Regulation of Working Hours: As Submitted to the Royal Commission on Labour (London, 1891).
The Duties of Co-operators in regard to the Hours and Conditions of Labour [Paper read at the twenty-fourth annual congress of the Co-operative Societies held at Rochdale, June 1892] (Manchester, 1892).
An Appeal to the Yorkshire Textile Workers (London, 1893).
'Preachers and Churches', in Andrew Reid (ed.), *Vox Clamantium: The Gospel of the People* (London, 1894), repr. as *A Socialist View of Religion and the Churches* (London, 1896).
The Socialists' Programme [a speech delivered at North Aberdeen, 25 Apr. 1896] (n.p., n.d.).
The Hamburg Dockers' Strike: Help Urgently Needed (n.p., 16 Dec. 1896), ITWFA.

The Position of Dockers and Sailors in 1897 (London, 1897).
The International Labour Movement (Socialist and Trade Unionist) (London, 1897).
The Labour Movement in Both Hemispheres (Melbourne, 1903).
The Labourer's Minimum Wage (Manchester, 1913).
From Single Tax to Syndicalism (London, 1913).
Debate between Tom Mann and Arthur M. Lewis [at the Garrick Theatre, Chicago, 16 Nov. 1913] (Chicago, 1914).
Required Now! One Big Union of Boiler Makers, Foundry Men, Engineers, and Steel Workers (London, 1920).
'Payment by Results': 'Piece Work and Time Work' (London, 1920).
Russia in 1921 [Report of Tom Mann as delegate to the Red Trade Union International at Moscow, July 1921] (London, 1921).
Tom Mann's Memoirs (London, 1923), repr. with preface by Ken Coates (London, 1967).
What I Saw in China (London, 1927).
Tom Mann and the I.L.P. (London, n.d.).
Sixty Years of an Agitator's Life (London, 1938).

Articles (in chronological order)

'Labour Organization in America', *Justice* (24 Apr. 1886).
'The Development of the Labour Movement', *Nineteenth Century* 27: 159 (May 1890).
'How I Became a Socialist', in *How I Became a Socialist: A Series of Biographical Sketches* (London, c.1894).
'A Socialist View of Co-Partnership', *Labour Co-Partnership* (Dec. 1895).
'Trade Unionism and Co-operation in the Future', in *Forecasts of the Coming Century by a Decade of Writers*, ed. Edward Carpenter (Manchester, 1897).
'A Co-operative Settlement in Australia', *Clarion* (21 Aug. 1903).
'Socialism in Australia', *Clarion* (14 Apr. 1905).
'A Liberal–Labour Alliance', *Clarion* (9 June 1905).
'Slavery in Queensland', *Clarion* (30 June 1905).
'Two Years' Work', *Socialist* (31 Aug. 1907).
'Prepare for Action', *Industrial Syndicalist* (July 1910).
'All Hail Solidarity', *Industrial Syndicalist* (Oct. 1910).
'Class War in Wales', *Justice* (10 Dec. 1910).
'Bravo Railwaymen', *Transport Worker* (Aug. 1911).
'Looking Backward and Forward', *Transport Worker* (Jan. 1912).
'The Eight Hour Day: Get Ready for the Fray', *Transport Worker* (Feb. 1912).
'The Uprising of the British Miners', *International Socialist Review* (May 1912).
'The Workers' Union', *Workers' Union Record* (Mar., Apr., and May 1916).
'Where Are We with the Wage System', ASE, *Monthly Journal and Report* (Feb. 1920).

'The Six-Hour Day', ASE, *Monthly Journal and Report* (Mar. 1920).
'The Trades Union Congress and Direct Action', ASE, *Monthly Journal and Report* (Apr. 1920).
'To the Young Members of the A.E.U.', AEU, *Monthly Journal and Report* (Jan. 1921).
'Men who have Changed the World's Thought', AEU, *Monthly Journal and Report* (Feb. 1921).
'Foreword' to Edgar T. Whitehead, *The Labour Abstentionist Party* (London, 1921).
'From Syndicalism to Communism', *Labour Monthly* (Oct. 1922).
'My Visit to China', *Labour Monthly* (Aug. 1927).
'Recollections of Morris', *Daily Worker* (24 Mar. 1934).
'The Dock Strike of 1889 and After', *Labour Monthly*, 20/9 (1938).

Periodicals edited by Tom Mann (in chronological order)

Trade Unionist (4 Apr.–22 Aug. 1891), continued as *Trade Unionist and Trades Council Record* (29 Aug. 1891–19 Mar. 1892).
Central Office of the International Federation of Ship, Dock, and River Workers, *Report Sheet* (Apr. and June 1897), ITWFA.
British Socialist News (27 Oct. 1899) [with Ben Tillett].
Socialist (Melbourne) (Apr.1906–Oct. 1908).
Industrial Syndicalist (July 1910–May 1911).
Transport Worker (Liverpool) (Aug. 1911–Mar. 1912).
Trade Unionist (Nov. 1915–Nov. 1916) [with W. F. Watson and E. L. Pratt].
ASE (later AEU), *Monthly Journal and Report* (Nov. 1919–Apr. 1921).
Militant Trade Unionist (1 May 1933–   ).

OTHER WORKS CONSULTED

Anon., *Ben Tillett: Fighter and Pioneer*, memorial vol. (London, n.d.).
Anon., *In Memoriam Benjamin Tillett* (n.p., n.d.).
ARNOT, R. PAGE, *South Wales Miners: A History of the South Wales Miners' Federation 1898–1914* (London, 1967).
—— *The Impact of the Russian Revolution in Britain* (London, 1967).
BELL, TOM, *Pioneering Days* (London, 1941).
BRANSON, NOREEN, *History of the Communist Party of Great Britain 1927–1941* (London, 1985).
BRAUNTHAL, JULIUS, *History of the International 1864–1914* (London, 1966).
—— *History of the International 1914–1943* (London, 1967).
British Labour and the Russian Revolution: The Leeds Convention, A Report from the Daily Herald, introd. by Ken Coates (Nottingham, n.d.).
British Parliamentary Papers, Select Committee on the Sweating System, 1888 (Industrial Relations, 14; Shannon, 1970).

—— Royal Commission on Labour, 1891–4 (Industrial Relations, 26, 43, 44; Shannon, 1970).

BROWDER, EARL, *Civil War in Nationalist China* (Chicago, 1927).

BROWN, KENNETH D., *John Burns* (London, 1977).

BRUNET, JEAN-PAUL, *Jacques Doriot: Du communisme au fascisme* (Paris, 1986).

BULLOCK, ALAN, *The Life and Times of Ernest Bevin*, i (London, 1960).

BURGESS, JOSEPH, *John Burns: The Rise and Progress of a Right Honourable* (Glasgow, 1911).

BURNS, J., *The Man with the Red Flag* (London, 1886).

—— *Trafalgar Square: Speech for Defence* (London, 1888).

—— 'The Paris International Congress', *Labour Elector* (3 Aug. 1889).

—— 'The Great Strike', *New Review* (Oct. 1889).

—— 'The Eight-Hours Day', *Daily Graphic* (3 May 1890).

—— *The Liverpool Congress* (London, 1890).

—— *Trades Unionism, Past, Present, and Future* (Rotherham, 1890).

CALHOUN, DANIEL, *The United Front: The TUC and the Russians* (Cambridge, 1976).

CARR, E. H., *The Twilight of Comintern* (London, 1982).

CHAMPION, H. H., *The Great Dock Strike in London* (London, 1890).

CITRINE, LORD, *Men and Work* (London, 1964).

CLARK, DAVID, *Colne Valley: Radicalism to Socialism* (London, 1981).

CLEGG, H. A., FOX, ALAN, and THOMPSON, A. F., *A History of British Trade Unionism since 1889*, i (Oxford, 1964).

CLIFF, TONY, and GLUCKSTEIN, DONNY, *Marxism and Trade Union Struggle: The General Strike of 1926* (London, 1986).

CLYNES, J. R., *Memoirs 1924–1937* (London, 1937).

COATES, KEN, and TOPHAM, TONY, *The New Unionism: The Case for Workers' Control* (Harmondsworth, 1972).

COLE, G. D. H., *John Burns* (Fabian Biographical Series 14; London, 1943).

Communist Party of Great Britain, *Tom Mann: His Life and Work: An Outline for Speakers* (London, n.d.).

CONNOLLY, JAMES, *The Workers' Republic: A Selection from the Writings of James Connolly*, ed. Desmond Ryan (Dublin, 1951).

CROUCHER, RICHARD, *We Refuse to Starve in Silence: A History of the National Unemployed Workers' Movement* (London, 1987).

CURRIE, ROBERT, *Industrial Politics* (Oxford, 1979).

DEGRAS, JANE (ed.), *The Communist International 1919–1943: Documents*, ii (Oxford, 1960).

Dock, Wharf, Riverside and General Labourers' Union, *General Secretary's Report to the Annual Delegate Meeting* (London, 1891).

—— *Tom Mann's Presidential Address* (London, 1891).

—— *Ben Tillett's Address on 'Man's Individual Responsibility'* (London, 1891).

DUFFY, A. E. P., 'The Eight-Hour Day Movement in Britain 1886–1893', *Manchester School of Economic and Social Studies*, 36 (1968).

ENGELS, FRIEDRICH, *Engels–Lafargue Correspondance*, ii (Paris, 1956).

GALENSON, WALTER (ed.), *Comparative Labor Movements* (New York, 1952).

GALLACHER, WILLIAM, *Revolt on the Clyde* (London, 1949).

GEORGES, BERNARD, and TINTANT, DENISE, *Léon Jouhaux*, i (Paris, 1962).

GOLLAN, ROBIN, *Radical and Working Class Politics: A Study of Eastern Australia 1850-1910* (Melbourne, 1960).

GOSLING, HARRY, *Up and Down Stream* (London, 1927).

GRUBB, ARTHUR PAGE, *From Candle Factory to British Cabinet: The Life Story of the Right Hon. John Burns* (London, 1908).

HANNINGTON, WAL, *Tom Mann, 1856-1941: A Short Biography* (London, 1947).

—— *Never on our Knees* (London, 1967).

—— *Unemployed Struggles 1919-1936* (London, 1979).

HARKER, BAILEY JOHN, *'The Buxton of Yorkshire': Being a Complete Guide to Grassington* (Manchester, 1890).

—— *Christianity and the New Social Demands: A Reply to the Rev. J. Dawson* (Manchester, 1892).

HAUPT, GEORGES, *Socialism and the Great War* (Oxford, 1972).

HAZLEHURST, CAMERON, *Politicians at War* (London, 1971).

HIKINS, H. R., 'The Liverpool General Transport Strike 1911', *Historical Society of Lancashire and Cheshire Transactions*, 113 (1961).

HOBSBAWM, ERIC, *Labouring Men* (London, 1964).

—— *World of Labour* (London, 1984).

HOLTON, BOB, *British Syndicalism 1900-1914* (London, 1976).

HORNER, ARTHUR, *Incorrigible Rebel* (London, 1960).

HOWELL, DAVID, *British Workers and the Independent Labour Party 1888-1906* (Manchester, 1983).

HYMAN, RICHARD, *The Workers' Union* (Oxford, 1971).

—— 'Introduction' to Tom Mann, *What a Compulsory Eight Hour Working Day Means to the Workers* (1886; London, 1972).

ILP, *Report of the First General Conference* (Bradford, 1893).

—— *Conference Report* (1895).

—— *Conference Report* (1898).

International Conference of Ship, Dock, and River Workers, *Minutes of Proceedings* (London, 1897), ITWFA.

International Federation of Ship, Dock, and River Workers, *What We Want, Why We Want It, and How We Mean to Get It* (London, 1896), ITWFA.

International Socialist Workers and Trades Union Congress, London, *Report* (London, 1896).

ISAACS, HAROLD R., *The Tragedy of the Chinese Revolution* (Stanford, 1951).

Japanese Institute for the Study of International Problems (Chinese Section) (ed.), *Sources of the History of the Chinese Communist Party*, iii (Tokyo, 1971) [in Japanese].

JEFFERYS, JAMES B., *The Story of the Engineers* (London, 1945).

JONES, GARETH STEDMAN, *Outcast London* (London, 1971).

KAPP, YVONNE, *John Burns' Library* (Our History Pamphlet, 16; winter 1959).

KENT, WILLIAM, *John Burns: Labour's Lost Leader* (London, 1950).

KINGSFORD, PETER, *The Hunger Marchers in Britain 1920–1940* (London, 1982).

KIPNIS, IRA, *The American Socialist Movement 1897–1912* (New York, 1952).

KLUGMANN, JAMES, *History of the Communist Party of Great Britain*, i (London, 1968), ii (London, 1969).

Labour Party, *Conference Report* (1919).

—— *Conference Report* (1920).

Labour Representation Committee, *Report of the Conference on Labour Representation* (London, 1900).

LEE, H. W., and ARCHBOLD, E., *Social-Democracy in Britain* (London, 1935).

LLOYD GEORGE, DAVID, *War Memoirs*, ii (London, 1936).

LOSOVSKY, ALEXANDER, *British and Russian Workers* (London, n.d. [1926]).

LOVELL, JOHN, *Stevedores and Dockers* (London, 1969).

MACINTYRE, STUART, *Little Moscows: Communism and Working-class Militancy in Inter-War Britain* (London, 1980).

MCSHANE, HARRY, and SMITH, JOAN, *Harry McShane* (London, 1978).

MARTIN, RODERICK, *Communism and the British Trade Unions 1924–1933: A Study of the National Minority Movement* (Oxford, 1969).

MORLEY, JOHN, *Memorandum on Resignation* (London, 1928).

MURPHY, J. T., *New Horizons* (London, 1941).

NMM, *International Unity of the World's Trade Union Movement* (London, n.d. [1924]).

—— *Fourth Annual Conference: Chairman's Address* (London, 1927).

—— *Report of the Fifth Annual Conference* (London, 1928).

—— *Another Year of Rationalisation: Report presented to the Sixth Annual Conference of the NMM, 24 and 25 Aug. 1929* (London, 1929).

National Sailors' and Firemen's Union, *Report of the Twenty-Seventh Annual General Meeting held at Caxton Hall, Westminster, 26 and 27 Jan. 1915* (London, 1915).

—— *Report of the Twenty-Eighth Annual General Meeting held at Caxton Hall, Westminster, 26 Sept. 1916* (London, 1916).

NTWF, *Report of the Sixth Annual General Council Meeting held in Glasgow, 8 and 9 June 1916* (London, 1916).

—— *Report of the Seventh Annual General Council Meeting held in Bristol, 14 and 15 June 1917* (London, 1917).

NEWTON, DOUGLAS, J., *British Labour, European Socialism and the Struggle for Peace 1888–1914* (Oxford, 1985).

NORTH, ROBERT C., and EUDIN, XENIA J., *M. N. Roy's Mission to China: The Communist Kuomintang Split of 1927* (Berkeley, Calif., 1963).

PEACOCK, W. A. (ed.), *Tom Mann: 80th Birthday Souvenir* (London, 1936).

PELLING, HENRY, 'H. H. Champion', *Cambridge Journal*, 6: 4 (Jan. 1953).
—— *The Origins of the Labour Party* (1954; London, 1965).
—— *The British Communist Party* (1958; London, 1975).
PHILLIPS, GORDON, and WHITESIDE, NOEL, *Casual Labour* (Oxford, 1985).
POLLITT, HARRY, *Tom Mann: A Tribute* (London, n.d.).
—— *Serving my Time* (London, 1950 edn.).
POSTGATE, RAYMOND, 'Cloth Cap and Red Flag', *Listener* (8 July 1948).
POTTER, BEATRICE, 'The Dock Life of East London', *Nineteenth Century*, 22: 128 (Oct. 1887).
PRIBICEVIC, BRANCO, *The Shop Stewards' Movement and Workers' Control* (Oxford, 1959).
PRICE, RICHARD, *An Imperialist War and the British Working-Class* (London, 1972).
RABINOVITCH, VICTOR, 'British Marxist Socialism and Trade Unionism: The Attitudes, Experiences and Activities of the Social-Democratic Federation 1884–1901', Ph.D. thesis (Sussex, 1977).
Rank and File Conference on Amalgamation, Report (Leeds, 11 and 12 Nov. 1916).
—— *Report* (Manchester, 9 and 10 June 1917).
RILU, *The Position of the Minority Movement and its Immediate Tasks: Resolution of the 8th Session of the Central Council of the RILU* (London, n.d.).
RUST, WILLIAM, *Britons in Spain* (London, 1939).
SANDERS, W. STEPHEN, *Early Socialist Days* (London, 1927).
SCHNEER, JONATHAN, *Ben Tillett: Portrait of a Labour Leader* (London, 1982).
SMITH, H. LLEWELLYN, and NASH, VAUGHAN, *The Story of the Dockers' Strike* (London, 1889).
SNELL, LORD, *Men, Movements, and Myself* (1936; London, 1938).
Special National Conference of Action, Report (London, 1926).
STAFFORD, DAVID, *From Anarchism to Reformism: A Study of the Political Activities of Paul Brousse* (London, 1971).
Strike Committee, London Dock Strike of 1889, *The Great Dock Labourers' Strike 1889: Manifesto and Statement* (London, 1889).
TAPLIN, ERIC, *The Dockers' Union: A Study of the National Union of Dock Labourers 1889–1922* (Leicester, 1985).
THORNE, WILL, *My Life's Battle* (London, 1925).
TILLETT, B., *A Dock Labourer's Bitter Cry* (London, 1887).
—— 'The Dockers' Story', *English Illustrated Magazine*, 3: 74 (Nov. 1889).
—— 'The World, the Church and the Agitator', *Trade Unionist* (11 July 1891).
—— 'The World's Will-O'-The-Wisp', *Labour Prophet* (Apr. 1892).
—— *Is the Parliamentary Labour Party a Failure?* (London, 1908).
—— *A Brief History of the Dockers' Union: Commemorating the 1889 Dockers' Strike* (London, 1910).
—— *History of the London Transport Workers' Strike* (London, 1911).
—— *Memories and Reflections* (London, 1931).

TORR, DONA, *Tom Mann* (London, 1936), ed. with an introd. by Harry Pollitt (London, 1944).
—— *Tom Mann and his Times* (London, 1956).
—— *Tom Mann and his Times 1890–1892* (Our History Pamphlet, 26–7; summer–autumn 1962), repr. in *The Luddites and Other Essays*, ed. M. Mumby (London, 1971).
[——] *Tom Mann in Australasia 1902–1909* (Our History Pamphlet, 38; summer 1965).
TUC, *Report* (1920).
—— *Report* (1921).
TSUZUKI, CHUSHICHI, *H. M. Hyndman and British Socialism* (Oxford, 1961).
—— *The Life of Eleanor Marx* (Oxford, 1967).
—— 'John Burns and the Great War', *Hitotsubashi Journal of Social Studies*, 21: 1 (1989).
VISHNYAKOVA-AKIMOVA, V. V., *Two Years in Revolutionary China 1925–1927* (Cambridge, Mass., 1971).
WEBB, BEATRICE, *The Diary of Beatrice Webb*, ed. Norman and Jean MacKenzie, i (London, 1982), ii (London, 1983).
WEBB, SIDNEY, and WEBB, BEATRICE, *History of Trade Unionism* (new edn., London, 1920).
WEEKES, B. C. M., 'The Amalgamated Society of Engineers 1880–1914', Ph.D. thesis (Warwick, 1970).
WILSON, J. HAVELOCK, *My Stormy Voyage through Life*, i (London, 1925).
WRIGLEY, CHRIS, 'Liberals and the Desire for Working-Class Representatives in Battersea', in Kenneth D. Brown (ed.), *Essays in Anti-Labour History* (London, 1974).

Index